Political Scandal, Corruption, and Legitimacy in the Age of Social Media

Kamil Demirhan
Bülent Ecevit University, Turkey

Derya Çakır-Demirhan
Bülent Ecevit University, Turkey

A volume in the Advances in Social Networking and Online Communities (ASNOC) Book Series

IGI Global
DISSEMINATOR OF KNOWLEDGE

www.igi-global.com

Published in the United States of America by
IGI Global
Information Science Reference (an imprint of IGI Global)
701 E. Chocolate Avenue
Hershey PA 17033
Tel: 717-533-8845
Fax: 717-533-8661
E-mail: cust@igi-global.com
Web site: http://www.igi-global.com

Library of Congress Cataloging-in-Publication Data

Names: Demirhan, Kamil, 1984- editor. | Cakir-Demirhan, Derya, 1987- editor.
Title: Political scandal, corruption, and legitimacy in the age of social media / Kamil Demirhan, Derya Cakir-Demirhan.
Description: Hershey, Pennsylvania : IGI Global, Disseminator of Knowledge [2017] | Series: Advances in social networking and online communities book series, ISSN 2328-1405 | Includes bibliographical references and index.
Identifiers: LCCN 2016052519| ISBN 1522520198 | ISBN 9781522520191 | ISBN 9781522520399 (eISBN)
Subjects: LCSH: Social media--Political aspects. | Political corruption.
Classification: LCC HM742 .P65 2017 | DDC 302.23/1--dc23 LC record available at https://lccn.loc.gov/2016052519

This book is published in the IGI Global book series Advances in Social Networking and Online Communities (ASNOC) (ISSN: 2328-1405; eISSN: 2328-1413)

British Cataloguing in Publication Data
A Cataloguing in Publication record for this book is available from the British Library.

All work contributed to this book is new, previously-unpublished material. The views expressed in this book are those of the authors, but not necessarily of the publisher.

Advances in Social Networking and Online Communities (ASNOC) Book Series

ISSN:2328-1405
EISSN:2328-1413

Mission

The advancements of internet technologies and the creation of various social networks provide a new channel of knowledge development processes that's dependent on social networking and online communities. This emerging concept of social innovation is comprised of ideas and strategies designed to improve society.

The **Advances in Social Networking and Online Communities** book series serves as a forum for scholars and practitioners to present comprehensive research on the social, cultural, organizational, and human issues related to the use of virtual communities and social networking. This series will provide an analytical approach to the holistic and newly emerging concepts of online knowledge communities and social networks.

Coverage

- Knowledge Chains
- Methodologies to Analyze, Design and Deploy Distributed Knowledge Management Solutions
- Performance Evaluation and Benchmarking of Deployed Systems
- Epistemology of Knowledge Society
- Information Policy Overview
- Communication of Knowledge in Organizations
- Knowledge Management System Architectures, Infrastructure, and Middleware
- Whole-Network Properties and Knowledge Communication
- Supporting Virtual Communities of Practice and Interest Networks
- Knowledge Communication and Impact of Network Structures

IGI Global is currently accepting manuscripts for publication within this series. To submit a proposal for a volume in this series, please contact our Acquisition Editors at Acquisitions@igi-global.com or visit: http://www.igi-global.com/publish/.

The Advances in Social Networking and Online Communities (ASNOC) Book Series (ISSN 2328-1405) is published by IGI Global, 701 E. Chocolate Avenue, Hershey, PA 17033-1240, USA, www.igi-global.com. This series is composed of titles available for purchase individually; each title is edited to be contextually exclusive from any other title within the series. For pricing and ordering information please visit http://www.igi-global.com/book-series/advances-social-networking-online-communities/37168. Postmaster: Send all address changes to above address.

Titles in this Series

For a list of additional titles in this series, please visit: www.igi-global.com

Power, Surveillance, and Culture in YouTube™'s Digital Sphere
Matthew Crick (William Paterson University, USA)
Information Science Reference • copyright 2016 • 317pp • H/C (ISBN: 9781466698550) • US $185.00 (our price)

Social Media and the Transformation of Interaction in Society
John P. Sahlin (The George Washington University, USA)
Information Science Reference • copyright 2015 • 300pp • H/C (ISBN: 9781466685567) • US $200.00 (our price)

Cases on Strategic Social Media Utilization in the Nonprofit Sector
Hugo Asencio (California State University – Dominguez Hills, USA) and Rui Sun (California State University – Dominguez Hills, USA)
Information Science Reference • copyright 2015 • 375pp • H/C (ISBN: 9781466681880) • US $195.00 (our price)

Handbook of Research on Interactive Information Quality in Expanding Social Network Communications
Francisco V. Cipolla-Ficarra (Latin Association of Human-Computer Interaction, Spain & International Association of Interactive Communication, Italy)
Information Science Reference • copyright 2015 • 449pp • H/C (ISBN: 9781466673779) • US $255.00 (our price)

Implications of Social Media Use in Personal and Professional Settings
Vladlena Benson (Kingston Business School, Kingston University, UK) and Stephanie Morgan (Kingston Business School, Kingston University, UK)
Information Science Reference • copyright 2015 • 362pp • H/C (ISBN: 9781466674011) • US $195.00 (our price)

Identity and Leadership in Virtual Communities Establishing Credibility and Influence
Dona J. Hickey (University of Richmond, USA) and Joe Essid (University of Richmond, USA)
Information Science Reference • copyright 2014 • 321pp • H/C (ISBN: 9781466651500) • US $205.00 (our price)

Harnessing the Power of Social Media and Web Analytics
Anteneh Ayanso (Brock University, Canada) and Kaveepan Lertwachara (California Polytechnic State University, USA)
Information Science Reference • copyright 2014 • 305pp • H/C (ISBN: 9781466651944) • US $215.00 (our price)

Editorial Advisory Board

Table of Contents

Detailed Table of Contents

The article analyses a political scandal that occurred in Finland in 2015, when an MP of the populist right-wing Finns Party, Olli Immonen, published a Facebook update in which he used the same kind of militant–nationalist rhetoric against multiculturalism that Norwegian mass-murderer Anders Behring Breivik had used a couple of years earlier. By analyzing the content published in both social and news media, the role of social media and the relationship between news reporting and social media are explored by analyzing the progress of the scandal. The analysis indicates the prominent role of social media as being a starting point for scandal and for keeping scandal in the public eye, serving as forums for supporters and opponents of the scandalized politician. The relationship between social and news media seems symbiotic in this case because both of them fed and inspired each other during the scandal. However, further research is needed to fully understand the role of social media in scandals linked to north and west European populist right-wing parties, as well as political scandals occurring in different political contexts and media environments.

This study focuses on scandal politics and political scandals in the era of digital interactive media. Scandals are the part of symbolic power struggles. Media is one of the main actors of these struggles. In fact, political scandals have a constructive function in democracies because they help releasing corruptions. After scandals, the

assessed the success or otherwise of the institutional counter-measures in checkmating the excesses of social media. Situated within the framework of reputation repair and social responsibility theories, the paper acknowledges that the conventional mass media has ties with the political and economic forces in the society, thus, are somewhat incapacitated in rising to the societal challenges. Consequently, the paper presents the social media as a veritable alternative, arguing that social media tools have what it takes to serve as a platform for citizen participation in governance.

In this chapter, the author aims to empirically examine the effect of social media use and e-government adoption on citizens' perceived corruption. It is hypothesized that the use of social media by citizens is positively related to their perceptions of corruption, while the use of government websites is negatively related to perceived corruption. The author draws on a recent national telephone survey of citizens in 36 major cities in China to empirically test the above hypotheses. The multilevel model estimates suggest that social media use is insignificantly related to corruption perceptions, but government website use is negatively associated with perceived corruptions. The findings of this study help understand the anti-corruption effects of social media and e-government, and also generate helpful implications for other countries and regions in utilizing digital applications for anti-corruption purposes.

This chapter is an attempt to show how the use of social media in one country, the Republic of the Philippines, has grown and has been used to encourage political awareness and participation among the Filipino masses. The country is ranked among the most technologically savvy in the world but ironically is also considered one of the most corrupt countries as well. The authors believe that, as a result of the showings Filipinos have made when called upon via social media to oust corrupt officials, there is a method whereby such knowledge can be harnessed for the good thus alleviating scandals and ultimately corruption in the country. This research points to the direction the country, and various other countries in the world in similar situations, may take in order to combat corruption through greater citizen participation.

Preface

Political scandals, corruptions and legitimacy crises are the substantial components of current politics at both national and international levels. The character of political scandals, corruptions and the problems of legitimacy in a country are the strong indicators of the nature of political culture, democratic development, socio-political and economic institutions. Social media as a new information and communication platform has a growing role in the control and in the manipulation of the public opinion during the times of scandals and crisis. Social media is widely believed to be a space for a more interactive public discussion, political propaganda and opinion formation. It is also possible to talk about a considerable amount of opponents seeing social media as the perpetuator of the conventional relations of power. Accordingly, there is a growing interest in the relationship between social media and politics. However, the impact of social media on political scandals, corruptions and legitimacy crises remains a less investigated topic.

Political Scandal, Corruption and Legitimacy in the Age of Social Media includes chapters mostly on popular political corruptions and political scandals from researchers all around the world. The authors of this book mostly stress the relationship between social media and corruptions. In some chapters of this book, social media is handled as a way to cope with corruption. However, there are some chapters in this book in which the relationship between corruptions, political scandals and social media is indicated as a double-sided issue. Various cases from various countries help to increase our understanding toward the nature of the political scandals and corruptions. This book is designed to be a useful work to evaluate the political scandals, corruptions and legitimacy in the age of social media.

The target audience includes, but is not limited to, researchers in political science and public administration, researchers in communication and media studies, political science professionals, media and communication professionals, political science students, media and communication students, politicians, politicians' advisors, public officials, journalists, computer scientists, technology and society specialists, members of civil society organizations, public relation professionals, government agents, and public policy actors.

In "Neo-Populist Scandal and Social Media: The Finnish Olli Immonen Affair" by Juha Herkman and Janne Matikainen, the authors researches Olli Immonen, an MP of the Finns Party. Regarding this scandal, the authors point out the social media and news media as the ones inspiring and feeding each other.

In "Scandal Politics and Political Scandals in the Era of Digital Interactive Media" by Kamil Demirhan, the author evaluates the maintaining role of traditional media in the era of digital media, and the features of scandal politics and political scandals in the era of digital interactive media to analyze the constructive functions of political scandals in democracies. In this respect, the author focuses on the cases of WikiLeaks and Ashley Madison affair.

In "Information Control, Transparency, and Social Media: Implications for Corruption" by Chandan Kumar Jha, the author points out social media as an important tool in fighting corruption. In this chapter, Jha supports freedom on Internet for the effects of social media on corruption are to be fully realized.

In "There Is an App for That Too: Citizen-centric Approach to Combating Corruption in the Digital Age through the Use of ICTs" by Lloyd G. Waller, the author researches the use of information and communication technologies (ICTs) by citizens. The author, in this chapter, has the aim to address the citizen-centric empowerment strategies to fight with corruption all around the world.

In "Hashtag Ideology: Practice and Politics of Alternative Ideology" by Smarak Samarjeet, the author searches for the power relations in social media and cross-media focusing on #HeForShe and #BringBackOurGirls campaigns. The author argues that hashtags have become a site for political and cultural appropriation.

In "The Role of Social Media in Enforcing Environmental Justice around the World" by Gayle M. Pohl, the author analyzes the role that social media plays enforcing environmental justice around the world and focusing on the cases from three different countries; India, Canada and Russia. The author concludes that social media is possible to be used to promote environmental justice globally.

In "Navigating the Nexus between Social Media, Political Scandal, and Good Governance in Nigeria: Its Ethical Implications" by Essien D. Essien, the author claims the social media as a platform for citizen participation in governance. Analyzing the Nigerian case, the author demonstrates the conventional mass media as incapacitated in societal challenges due to its ties with political and economic sources.

In "Government Website, Social Media, and Citizens' Perceptions of Corruption: Evidence from Chinese Cities" by Liang Ma, the author empirically examines the impacts of media channels on citizen perceptions of corruption. The author concludes that e-government plays a key role in anticorruption.

In "Social Media's Role in Alleviating Political Corruption and Scandals: The Philippines during and after the Marcos Regime" by Cecilia G. Manrique and Gabriel G. Manrique researches how the use of social media in the Republic of the

Philippines has been used to enhance political awareness and political participation. The authors support the idea that the use of social media can reduce corruptions.

In “Participation, Civil Society and the Facebook Use of NGOs in Turkey” by Kamil Demirhan, the author examines the use of Facebook by Non-Governmental Organizations (NGOs) in Turkey and searches social media’s potentiality for being a new channel to promote civic and political participation. The author emphasizes social media as the one promoting social and political life.

The researches and analyzes in these chapters help to develop a new perspective on the changing nature of media and politics. They help the reader see the different sides of the popular public events. Is a scandal just a scandal? The book helps the audience to see the winner/loser dichotomy in political scandals or corruptions. Technology has changed the nature of social life as well as the nature of politics. This book questions the relationship between social media and political scandals being a significant sample of a neglected literature.

Derya Çakır-Demirhan
Bülent Ecevit University, Turkey

Chapter 1
Neo-Populist Scandal and Social Media: The Finnish Olli Immonen Affair

Juha Herkman
University of Helsinki, Finland

Janne Matikainen
University of Helsinki, Finland

ABSTRACT

The article analyses a political scandal that occurred in Finland in 2015, when an MP of the populist right-wing Finns Party, Olli Immonen, published a Facebook update in which he used the same kind of militant–nationalist rhetoric against multiculturalism that Norwegian mass-murderer Anders Behring Breivik had used a couple of years earlier. By analyzing the content published in both social and news media, the role of social media and the relationship between news reporting and social media are explored by analyzing the progress of the scandal. The analysis indicates the prominent role of social media as being a starting point for scandal and for keeping scandal in the public eye, serving as forums for supporters and opponents of the scandalized politician. The relationship between social and news media seems symbiotic in this case because both of them fed and inspired each other during the scandal. However, further research is needed to fully understand the role of social media in scandals linked to north and west European populist right-wing parties, as well as political scandals occurring in different political contexts and media environments.

DOI: 10.4018/978-1-5225-2019-1.ch001

INTRODUCTION

As populist parties in Europe have gained increasing press coverage and political power, scandals linked to these parties have become increasingly common as well. However, although the relationship between populist movements and the media has been extensively analysed (e.g. Mazzoleni et al., 2003; Boomgaarden & Vliegenthart, 2007; Koopmans & Muis, 2009; Bos et al., 2010; Roodjuin, 2014), the type of scandals linked to these parties have rarely been studied. This is slightly surprising, since, as Mazzoleni (2008, pp. 55-57) has pointed out, playing the role of the underdog and being provocative, organising rallies and creating media sensations are common events in these movements and have even played significant roles in their communication strategies (also Wodak, 2015, pp. 19-20). Herkman (2016a) has studied scandals connected with radical, right-wing populist parties in the Nordic countries and identified a specific type of political scandal: the 'neo-populist scandal', in which the populist rhetoric of the radical right confronts and conflicts with the liberal ethos of journalistic news media.

Herkman's (2016a) study showed that one fifth of all major political scandals in Sweden, Finland and Denmark between 2005 and 2015 were linked to domestic neo-populist parties. The analysis reveals the significant role of social media, especially in launching the scandals, since neo-populist scandals often begin with derogatory comments, images or video-clips being made about a minority group by a neo-populist, which are then subsequently highlighted on social media. In addition, social media also comes to the fore during scandals, when supporters of the populist promote 'a counter-cycle' (Jenssen & Fladmoe, 2012) against the mainstream media. Nevertheless, the role of social media in neo-populist scandal has not been empirically proven. Thus, the aim of this article is to determine the role of social media during the different stages of neo-populist scandal. In this context, social media refers to Internet services that have their form and content mostly determined and produced by the users of the service. Therefore, social media may be regarded as an umbrella term that covers many kinds of user-based platforms, such as blogs, Facebook, Twitter, discussion forums, YouTube and Wikipedia (Lietsala & Sirkkunen, 2008, p. 161).

This article analyses the role of social media by producing a case study of an infamous neo-populist scandal that occurred in Finland, the 'Olli Immonen affair'. Consequently, further research will be needed to prove the link between social media and scandals connected to right-wing populist parties. However, we believe that by taking advantage of our analysis, some preliminary observations can be made on a general level about scandals generated by northern and western European radical right-wing parties that promote 'nativist' ideology and anti-immigrant policies (cf. Mudde, 2007).

The Olli Immonen scandal started in summer 2015 on Facebook. The furore around Immonen's Facebook post quickly escalated within Finnish social media when Finland's largest newspaper stated that Immonen, an MP of the populist Finns Party, had used similar militant rhetoric against multiculturalism to that of Anders Behring Breivik, the Norwegian terrorist and mass murderer. Supporters and opponents of Immonen soon occupied the social media forums and started to comment on the public treatment of the affair in the news media. Whereas the Finnish news media represents mostly liberal values, social media serves as a platform for both liberal and conservative camps. The tabloid media may, in general, promote a more positive attitude towards right-wing populist movements and their nationalist approach than the quality news media, but it does not usually support perspectives that are explicitly hostile against minorities (see Herkman, 2015). The Immonen affair therefore represents an interesting case, highlighting the complicated role of social media in today's political scandals and the increasingly pronounced relationship between the news media and social media. The precise research questions of the case study are:

RQ1: How was the dramaturgy of the scandal constructed by the news media and social media?

RQ2: What was the role of social media in the dramaturgy of the scandal?

a. In which phases of the scandal was social media most actively involved?

b. What kinds of platforms, actors and topics dominated the social media messages linked to the scandal?

RQ3: How did social media react to and regard the news media during the scandal?

NEO-POPULIST SCANDALS IN WESTERN EUROPE: HISTORICAL AND THEORETICAL CONSIDERATIONS

As widely agreed among 'scandalogists', there is always a transgression of norms, values or moral codes at stake in political scandal. Essentially, a transgression becomes significant for the general public when it becomes the recipient of media attention in the news media, making the political scandal a mediated event (Thompson, 2000; Allern & Pollack, 2012). Political scandals can be linked to public institutions, but most scandals have a public figure at the centre, e.g. a politician, public official or celebrity, who becomes the target of a media witch-hunt (Garrard, 2006, p. 18).

British sociologist John B. Thompson (2000, pp. 120-123) has defined the three most prominent types of political scandal: sexual, financial and power. These are indeed the categories into which most political scandals can be classified. However, Thompson's scandal types remain quite general classifications. Therefore, new scandal forms and amendments to the original categories have been made to the typology of scandal in recent years. Ekström and Johansson (2008, p. 62), for example, have emphasised the central role of mediatised talk 'for modern political scandals as well as their origins, dynamics and dramatization' and called such scandals 'talk scandals'. Allern et al. (2012, p. 36) have also made a more nuanced categorisation according to the type of norm transgression that occurs in a specific political scandal, including: 'offences in economic affairs', 'offences concerning other laws and regulation', 'the abuse of power', 'unacceptable talk', 'unacceptable personal behaviour' and 'other or mixed types'.

During this era of political scandals, populist movements have gained great success in Europe. The concept of populism is slippery and can mean different things (Canovan, 1999, p. 3; Taggart, 2000, p. 1). However, in modern democracies, populism generally refers to political movements and parties that use 'populist rhetoric' against political and economic elites or against groups other than the 'native inhabitants' of a nation state by appealing to 'the people' (Canovan, 1999; Mudde & Kaltwasser, 2012). Contemporary European populist movements have also been called neo-populist to distinguish them from previous forms of populism (Taggart, 2000; Mazzoleni et al., 2003). Many of these movements have been identified as right-wing radicals promoting a 'nativist' ideology that emphasises a favoured status for native inhabitants and sees immigrants as threats to a vaguely defined national homogeneity (see Mudde, 2007). Provocative words and action and the transgressions of norms are essential in neo-populist rhetoric. Nevertheless, populist, radical, right-wing movements have generally been able to positively exploit public scandals (Wodak, 2015).

In his recent study, Herkman (2016a) discovered that one fifth of all major political scandals were linked to the domestic populist parties in Finland, Sweden and Denmark between 2005 and 2015 – alongside several minor media sensations concerning these parties. The scandals connected to domestic populist parties help to explain the increase in scandal types regarding moral transgressions created by unacceptable talk or behaviour (cf. Allern & Pollack, 2016, pp. 154-155). The most prominent scandals were the 'Morten Messerschmidt affair' in Denmark, in which the Danish People's Party's MP Messerschmidt was accused of making Nazi salutes, singing Nazi songs and publicly insulting people in 2007; the 'iron bar scandal' in Sweden in 2012, when three key members of the Sweden Democrats Party were found to have taken iron bars from scaffolding and threatened several passers-by with them and insulted people with sexist and racist comments; and scandals in Finland caused by Jussi Halla-aho and Olli Immonen, Finns Party MPs, who used insulting and militant rhetoric against immigrants and multiculturalism in social media between 2008 and 2015.

Dozens of similar sensations caused by domestic right-wing populists have arisen in several European countries during the last two decades: the Dutch populist politician Geert Wilders compared the *Quran* to Hitler's *Mein Kampf*, the prohibition of minarets in Switzerland was promoted by the Swiss People's Party, burqa bans were demanded by France's National Front, Austrian Freedom Party leader, Jörg Heider (1950–2008), was often accused of Nazi sympathies and antisemitism, and insulting comments were made by Nigel Farage, former UKIP leader, against the Belgian-born president of the European Council, Herman Van Rompuy, in the European Parliament – just to mention a few incidents that received international attention. However, whether these affairs can be defined as neo-populist political scandals is unclear and depends on the particular volume and duration of news media attention, which is essential for all political scandals.

Herkman (2016a) defined a neo-populist scandal as a scandal that is linked to a radical, right-wing, populist movement and its nationalist or nativist ideology. The starting point of these scandals is usually an intentional moral transgression during which a member of the neo-populist movement makes an insulting comment about minorities being immigrants, uses Nazi gestures or symbols, or associates with extreme-right radicals. The journalistic media has then usually orchestrated 'a media witch-hunt', fuelling the scandal, leading to a backlash in which supporters of the target of the hunt then arrange a counter-cycle via social media, criticising the mainstream media and its methods of supporting a corrupt elite.

The consequences of the scandal depend on the life-cycle of the neo-populist movement and on the political status of the figure involved in the scandal (Herkman, 2015). Scandals may even be positive for the neo-populist movement or its representatives when the party is going through its 'insurgent phase' (cf. Stewart et al., 2003, pp. 219-224) and its supporters believe that the target is being 'witch-hunted' by political and cultural elites, thereby making it a brave proponent of 'the people' (cf. Wodak, 2015). However, if the movement has reached an 'established phase' and gained seats in parliament it has to gain support from a larger group of voters, become more mainstream and also balance its rhetoric. Consequently, such scandals can become rather negative for a representative, as has usually been the case in mediatised political scandals. Unlike 'talk scandals' (Ekström & Johansson, 2008), neo-populist scandals often lead to court cases, since demagogy and hate speech are criminalised in most liberal democracies. However, the political consequences of the court cases also vary depending on the life phase of the movement and on the political status of the accused.

The limitation in the definition of neo-populist scandal is that it is derived solely from right-wing populist movements in liberal, multi-party democracies representing 'Democratic Corporatist' countries in Hallin and Mancini's categorisation of politics and media systems (Hallin & Mancini, 2004). Thus, the questions arise: How well does the definition of neo-populist scandal fit with the different political and media systems of Nordic and Central European countries? Is the definition of a neo-populist scandal also appropriate for left-wing populist movements like Syriza or Podemos? What role does social media play in neo-populist scandals? The latter question is asked, because political scandals are played out in traditional news media but populist movements inherently use social media in the formation of their identity (cf. Hatakka, 2016). By studying the Nordic context, this chapter tries to shed light on the last question.

THE FINNS PARTY AND THE OLLI IMMONEN AFFAIR

The Finns Party is one of the oldest and most traditional populist movements in the Nordic and Central European region as its roots lie in the Finnish Rural Party (SMP), established in 1959. The SMP was a populist protest movement attacking 'corrupt elites' and mainstream parties in the name of the 'real people'. The party was established during a period of rapid industrialisation with urbanisation causing radical structural change in Finland's rural areas (Helander, 1971). SMP's heyday was in the 1970s and early 1980s, when it joined the governing cabinet, but it faded during the 1980s, becoming a minor player in the Finnish political field with only one or two MPs.

The Finns Party is a spin-off of SMP. It was established in 1995 and its current leader, Timo Soini, was the last SMP party secretary. For two decades, the Finns Party had no real effect on Finnish politics. However, voter discontent with the mainstream parties' *status quo* rose during the 2000s and the party increased in popularity, being quite successful in the local elections of 2008. Nevertheless, it was not until the 2011 general elections than the Finnish party system was unsettled by the Finns Party's gaining an astonishing 19.1 percent share of the vote (Borg, 2012). Similar 'big bang elections' have occurred during the twenty-first century in many Nordic and Central European multi-party democracies, where the party political systems had remained undisturbed for decades (see Arter, 2012). In the 2015 general elections, the Finns Party lost some votes but became the second largest party and joined a Finnish government for the first time.

According to some commentators, the populist parties have been successful especially in countries with a strong tradition of consensual multi-party politics, because a group of established parties that resemble each other in several ways can easily be criticised as an elitist cartel (Paloheimo, 2012, p. 329). However, the populist parties in the Nordic countries, for example, cannot be directly compared to the neo-populist movements of Southern and Eastern Europe, since, according to the European Social Survey (ESS), their supporters are quite different and rely on a democratic society (Mesežnikov et al., 2008; Paloheimo, 2012). Populism in the Nordic countries has not been as radical or offensive as in countries where politics in general has been more confrontational (Widfeldt, 2010, p. 179).

Nevertheless, the new success of the European populist parties has often been based on their nationalistic and anti-immigration rhetoric. This is true of the Nordic countries, whose domestic populist parties can be linked to Europe's radical, right-wing parties on this issue (see Jungar & Jupskåps, 2014). The Finns Party's success in the two last general elections lies partly in its criticism of immigration and its nationalist agenda, despite much of its popularity being based on public dissatisfaction with mainstream parties. A significant faction of the party has especially focused on criticising previous governments' immigration policies, and some members of the party have faced several major or minor scandals concerning their statements on multiculturalism, immigration, Islam and ethnic or other minorities after 2011 (Herkman, 2016b).

The most infamous scandal concerned Finns Party's MEP Jussi Halla-aho, who, in 2012 – after four years of court proceedings, was condemned by the High Court of Justice for demagogy and attacking freedom of worship in his blog writings. The latest major scandal linked to the Finns Party was the Olli Immonen scandal of summer 2015 when he wrote on Facebook that he is 'dreaming of a strong, brave nation that will defeat this nightmare called multiculturalism' and that he has a 'strong belief in his fellow fighters' who 'will fight until the end for their homeland and one true Finnish nation'. Immonen had already drawn attention to himself a couple of weeks earlier with a Facebook update in which he posed with convicted neo-Nazis at an event commemorating Eugen Schauman, a Finnish nationalist and anarchist who murdered Governor General Nikolai Bobrikov in 1904 during Tsarist rule.

There are some studies concerning the Finns Party and their relationship to social media, for instance, the rhetoric used by the Finns Party's members in social media has been analysed (e.g. Niemi, 2013; Sakki & Pettersson, 2015; Hatakka, 2016), additionally the role of social media in the general election of 2011, in which the Finns Party became the third largest party, has been studied (e.g. Khaldarova et al., 2012). However, the role of social media in scandals connected to the Finns Party has not been explored, even if some scandals connected to the party and its members have been analysed (Herkman, 2016a; Herkman, 2016b). In this chapter, the data gathered from social media, such as Twitter, Facebook and from some popular Finnish debate portals, will be compared to the dramaturgy of the Immonen affair – as promoted by the news media and analysed in Herkman's (2016a) previous studies.

MATERIALS AND METHODS

The material related to the Immonen affair were gathered from social media by a Finnish market research company (Futusome) using the company´s software. The company gathers open and public Finnish language data from social media: Twitter, Facebook (public sites), discussion forums, news forums and blogs. They have collected all data from Finnish social media since 2014, but have been collecting from limited data sources since 2001. However, the focus in this article is solely on the Immonen affair, as the authors have access to almost all the Finnish social media data connected to it.

The data was collected from the period from 1 June to 11 September 2015, a timeline containing the whole dramaturgy of the scandal (Herkman, 2016b). The search word 'Immonen' was used, after which the data was cleaned with the help of the key words 'Finns Party', 'multiculturalism', 'nation' and 'immigrants', guaranteeing that the subject was related to the case study. The total messages on the subject and published in Finnish social media amounted to 77,722. The data include almost all the relevant messages (although some may have been missed) as well as obviously irrelevant messages. Nevertheless, a random check of the messages revealed that almost every message was related to the Immonen affair.

In addition to social media data, materials from the news media was searched during the same timeline and using the same keywords than with social media. The focus in this study was on the Finland's leading daily *Helsingin Sanomat* and on the leading tabloid paper *Ilta-Sanomat*, since they were among the most prominent players in portraying the affair, and their press archives serve a well-designed basis for research purposes. The dramaturgy of the scandal could be reached eloquently through the analysis of these two papers.

The data was analysed in a mainly quantitative way. The amount of comments and the role of different social media platforms bring out the extent and main dramaturgy of the scandal. In addition to a quantitative analysis, some qualitative observations was made concerning the nature, atmosphere and polarisation of the social media conversations, because it is necessary to take into account the relationship between social media and the traditional news media in order to understand the dynamics of the neo-populist scandal as a whole. Thus, the comparison between the social media accounts of the story with those in the news media is proceeded.

SOCIAL MEDIA AND THE IMMONEN AFFAIR

The Immonen affair began in 24 July 2015, when Immonen posted the following message on Facebook late in the evening. Normally he writes in Finnish, but this update was in English:

I'm dreaming of a strong, brave nation that will defeat this nightmare called multiculturalism. This ugly bubble that our enemies live in, will soon enough burst into a million little pieces. Our lives are entwined in a very harsh times. These are the days, that will forever leave a mark on our nations future. I have strong belief in my fellow fighters. We will fight until the end for our homeland and one true Finnish nation. The victory will be ours.

The update soon had about 1,200 likes and 115 comments on Facebook, which is not outstanding. Many commentators supported Immonen, but there were some critical comments and questions too, for example, 'who are your enemies?', or 'you really should quit drinking'. The update was shared 570 times on Facebook. Interestingly, due to the use of English, the update was also shared by people other than native Finns.

In addition to Facebook, the update was quickly shared on other forms of social media too. Figure 1 shows the total number of social media messages on the subject during the scandal. The discussion exploded during weeks 30 and 31, and the most active phase lasted no more than two to three weeks. However, after a few weeks (in week 35) the number of messages increased again because of a press conference held by the Finns Party. Nevertheless, the debate faded a week after the press conference and the scandal burnt out on social media in one and half months.

Figure 1. Number of messages published on the Immonen affair in Finnish social media (n=77,722)

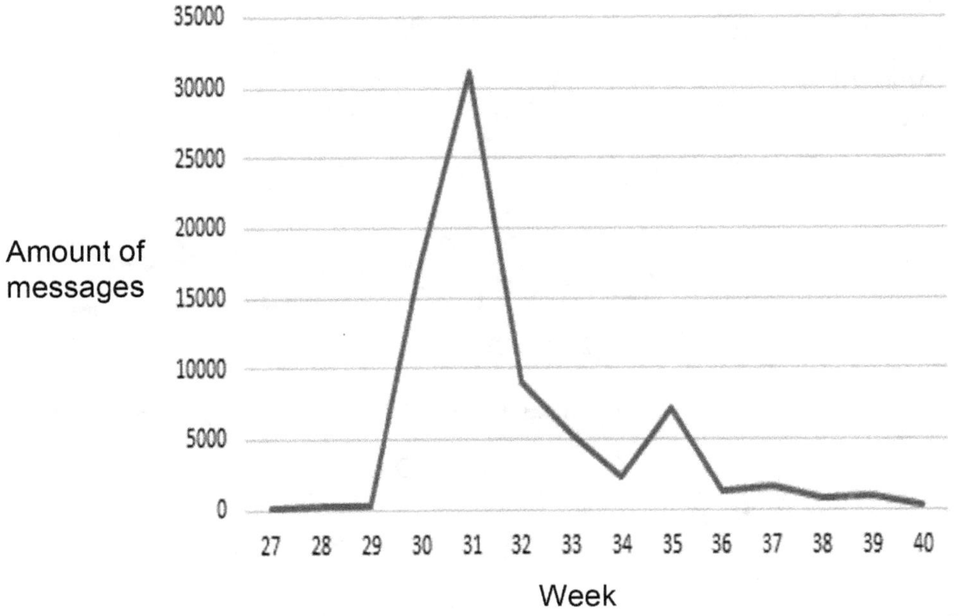

A more elaborate analysis of the first week shows that Twitter was the most popular and important forum for debate during the first four days of intense discussion at the beginning of the scandal (see Figure 2). Thus, even if the affair started on Facebook, the discussions spread to other social media and to the news media sites that are essential for generating the scandalising process. The result can be partly explained by the fact that only public Facebook sites could be included in the analysis. However, as indicated in several studies, the significance of Twitter is emphasised by its status as an information forum for societal elites, such as politicians, NGOs, journalists, business life and scholars – and it therefore plays a specific role in public debates (e.g. Engesser & Humprecht, 2015; Verweij, 2012).

Subsequently, discussion forums (forum posts) became more popular during the affair. Thus, it seems that Twitter serves as a means of quick communication and information sharing, but the actual debates were carried out in the discussion forums when the affair moved on. Obviously, discussion forums enable longer comments

Figure 2. Messages published on the various social media sites during the first week of the Immonen affair (n=46,448)

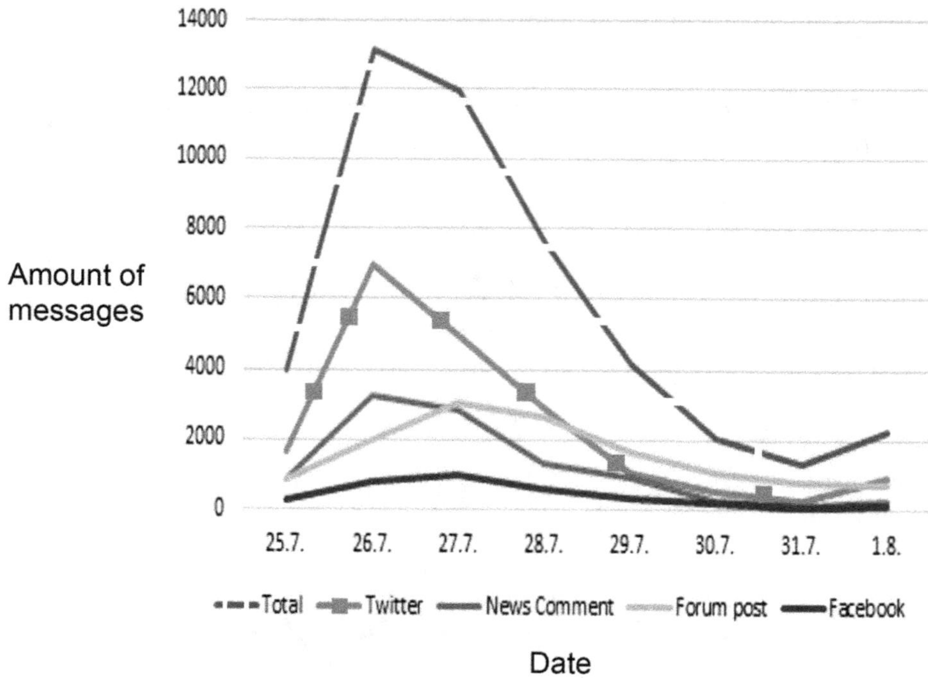

and deeper discussions than Twitter, enabling the more thorough argumentation of ideas and opinions. Naturally, it is possible that the messages spread from Twitter to the discussion forums, but also that the discussion activity might also depend on the attention given to the affair by the news media.

The total number of social media messages posted during the Immonen affair indicates the significance of Twitter, which was by far the most important channel for debate based on the sheer amount of messages (see Table 1). The next most popular site for messages was the discussion forum Suomi24, third place belonged to a portal of Finland's most popular tabloid paper, *Ilta-Sanomat*. Facebook was ranked just fourth in the number of messages. It is necessary to keep in mind the fact that the limited number of characters in tweets creates a different forum for debate than other social media, emphasising the speed and amount of messages at the cost of their scale and richness.

If we exclude clear social media services such as Twitter, Facebook and Reddit from the account, the news media sites contained about 24 per cent and the discussion forums about 21 per cent of all messages in the top 10 list. The portals of the tabloid papers dominated the news media sites, even if the *Helsingin Sanomat* (hs.fi) site – the largest and most prestigious daily in Finland – plus the sites of sig-

Table 1. Amount of messages on the top 10 Internet sites used for discussing the Immonen affair (n=68,444)

Name	Description	Number of Messages
twitter.com	social media	29674
keskustelu.suomi24.fi	discussion forum	7066
www.iltasanomat.fi	news media	6757
www.facebook.com	social media	6046
www.iltalehti.fi	news media	4370
www.vauva.fi	discussion forum	3269
www.kaleva.fi	news media	2340
hommaforum.org	discussion forum	1770
www.hs.fi	news media	1488
www.aamulehti.fi	news media	1345
www.tiede.fi	magazine	1283
www.reddit.com	social media	1061
keskustelu.jatkoaika.com	discussion forum	1037
murobbs.muropaketti.com	discussion forum	938

nificant regional newspapers like *Aamulehti* and *Kaleva* received many messages. Regarding discussion forums, Suomi24, the oldest and largest domestic discussion forum in Finland, containing all kinds of topics, was the most popular, but *Hommaforum*, the most prominent Finnish portal for combining blogs and discussions that are critical of immigration and multiculturalism, as well as vauva.fi, which is favoured by the mothers of young children, were remarkably popular discussion sites, too.

As expected, the social media public sphere was very diffused and fragmented in terms of people participating in discussions or distributing links during the Immonen affair. The most active and frequent actors within social media were 'visitors' (n=3,429) – a title that covers many kinds of social media users. About four per cent of the messages concerning the Immonen affair were sent by this user category, indicating the high variety of actors and the thousands of individual commentators during the scandal. Only two real names (Marko Hietikko and Valtteri Hellgren) are represented at the top of the user lists, both rather unknown in Finland's public sphere, although the former works as a journalist. However, almost all their messages were retweets, thus making them active content deliverers rather than producers (cf. Villi & Matikainen, 2015).

It can also be argued that the most active social media users were not the most significant. For example, the affair was launched with a tweet by a quite unknown Twitter user, whose message was quickly retweeted about 50 times. Several well-known politicians and public figures commented on Immonen's update in Twitter, thus making the original tweet very significant, even if its sender did not participate in the affair as an active commentator.

The themes and topics became highly polarised in social media. Twitter users mostly presented themselves as liberal and criticised Immonen's Facebook update. In practice, none of Immonen's supporters appeared on Twitter, indicating the 'elitist' status of Twitter within the sphere of public debate on Finnish politics – as indicated also by previous studies (e.g. Vainikka & Huhtamäki, 2015). Instead, the online discussion forums served as a platform for Immonen's supporters. In these forums, discussion revolved around four themes: 1) interpretations of Immonen's 'message'; 2) definitions of multiculturalism, nationalism and racism; 3) criticism of the news media; and 4) confrontation between conservative and liberal camps.

The first theme involved the different interpretations of Immonen's update, especially its 'true meaning' and its relationship to Breivik's terrorist attack in Norway. Many discussants defended Immonen and stated that references to Breivik were imagined by critics themselves: 'There's nothing like Breivik in Immonen's text.' Many commentators claimed that Immonen 'dared to tell the truth about multiculturalism'. However, some discussants reminded readers that Immonen's update was 'quite like Breivik's text'.

The second discussion theme was related to multiculturalism, nationalism and racism, especially their definitions. Supporters did not regard Immonen's update as racist, but his critics did: 'Just the extreme leftist idiots think that Immonen's writing is racist.' Due to Finland's rather mono-cultural history, racism is a relatively new discussion theme in the Finnish public sphere. Therefore, it seems that multiculturalism is a strange concept for the discussants and there were no unanimously accepted definitions of racism either.

The third theme related the scandal to the news media, which was mostly criticised. Supporters of the Finns Party have in general criticised the Finnish media as being too liberal and sympathetic to multiculturalism: 'Finnish media label even moderate opinions as racist.' Thus, it was not a surprise that the news media were criticised in this case too. Some comments by researchers were presented in the news media were particularly criticised: 'Researcher X [name removed] and others far too tolerant and prejudiced Professors speak just for themselves.' Therefore, this discussion theme verified the essential role of the news media in social media debates.

Fourth, the discussion forums served as a platform for an endless mutual dispute between the conservative and liberal blocs. The discussions on the forums were polarised, poorly argued and no conclusions or agreements were reached between the discussants: 'You Finns Party's copycats can't even read the news! Why don't you hang yourself? I can give you some practical advice…' This dimension is reminiscent of the results of computer-mediated communication research, indicating that computer-mediated communication is typically aggressive or 'flaming' in nature (e.g. Lea et al., 1992).

One can claim that – in a Habermasian (1989) sense – this kind of polarised dispute does not support the idea of social media serving as a public sphere for rational argumentation and deliberation. In addition, there is a wide variation between the many locations that different groups inhabit within the public sphere of the Internet (Dahlgren, 2005). Thus, our data indicates that the social media is quite fragmented within the public sphere. Nevertheless, no matter how ill-defined and fragmented the discussions were, one can also argue that the discussion forums served as an open space for the expression of different opinions and arguments, in contrast to Twitter, which appeared rather unanimous and dominated by hegemonic elites criticising Immonen.

THE IMMONEN AFFAIR AS PRESENTED IN THE NEWS MEDIA

The news media published several articles about the Immonen affair, mostly interviewing politicians from other parties condemning Immonen's statements and requiring explanations from Timo Soini, the leader of the Finns Party (Herkman, 2016b). In total, 134 articles about the 'Immonen affair' were published in Finland's leading daily newspaper *Helsingin Sanomat* and the leading tabloid paper *Ilta-Sanomat* during the scandal period (see Figure 3). *Helsingin Sanomat* (n=53) initiated the scandal with its news story, but the tabloid paper *Ilta-Sanomat* (n=81) dominated the scandal coverage and had more articles.

Most of the articles were published at the beginning of the scandal when the mainstream media eagerly scandalised Immonen's Facebook updates. The second peak in newspaper articles was seen just before the end of the scandal when Immonen resigned from the Finns Party's parliamentary group and Finns Party spokesperson Matti Putkonen commented on the scandal (see below).

According to the news media, the Prime Minster of Finland condemned Immonen's article via Twitter on 26 July. Within the Finns Party, their parliamentary group leader, Sampo Terho, mostly provided comments for the news media, emphasising that Immonen presented his own opinions, not those of the party. The

Figure 3. Number of articles published in the leading daily and tabloid paper during the Immonen affair (n=134)

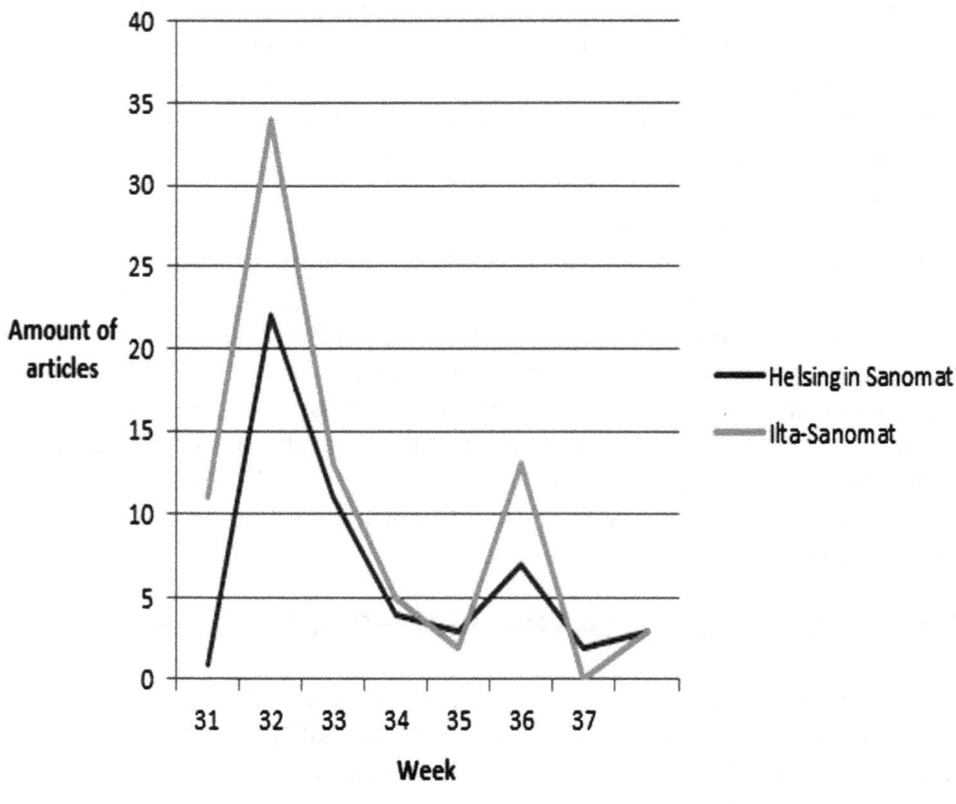

party leader, Soini, commented on the affair for first time in the tabloid paper *Ilta-Sanomat* on 27 July, stressing that the party's parliamentary group would handle the issue. Immonen himself did not comment on the affair in the mainstream media but continued his Facebook updates.

Most Finns Party's MPs interviewed by *Helsingin Sanomat* on 28 July did not agree with Immonen's ideas but neither did they completely condemn him. The next day, Immonen declared, via the party's own web magazine, *Suomen Uutiset*, that he opposed violence and only fought multi-culturalism politically. A week later, the police said that Immonen did not commit a crime with his updates because he did not name any groups and presented his ideas on a general level. However, Immonen did not join the party conference on 8–9 August, but announced that he was to resign from party's parliamentary group for two months on 26 August. In the news media, the scandal faded after a month. However, Putkonen's publishing (on 27 August) of 'a blacklist' of persons who had fuelled the media hunt against Immonen provided a slight return to the issue – an aftermath.

The scandal also resulted in civic protest – more than 10.000 people marched against racism in demonstrations in Helsinki and other Finnish cities at the end of July. However, on 1 August, the same neo-Nazis Immonen had posed with before the scandal (seen in his Facebook updates), protested violently against multi-culturalism in Jyväskylä, a medium-sized Finnish city in the Central region of the country. Both events were reported prominently by the Finnish news media. Nevertheless, they also demonstrate that the scandal was not solely a news media or social media event but had real life consequences, which, in turn, affected news media content and social media debates (cf. Ekström & Johansson, 2008).

DISCUSSION

Only one neo-populist scandal from Finland is analysed in detail here. Since all political scandals are different, it is not clear how well this case study represents the role of social media in neo-populist scandals in general. Even if there are many other examples in the Finnish political field of political scandal originating from the unacceptable talk or behaviour of Finns Party's members in social media (Herkman, 2016b), not all neo-populist scandals originate from social media updates. Contextual dimensions define all scandals significantly and might even have an effect on which affairs turn (and which do not turn) into public scandals (see Entman, 2012).

For example, the Immonen affair broke during the Finnish summer holiday season, meaning that the news media suffered from a lack of interesting domestic news and that people had more time to use social media. The holiday season does not explain the scandal, but it might have played a role in the spread and scale of the scandal. The status and popularity of different social media sites such as Twitter, Facebook, blogs and discussion forums can also vary between countries, producing different emphases for their role in scandals – not to mention the differences between the political systems and their relationships to the news media (e.g. Hallin & Mancini, 2004). Thus, historical, political, technological and cultural dimensions always make scandals particular to a specific time and place.

However, Herkman's (2016b) previous analysis indicates that in multi-party democracies similar to Finland, the dramaturgies and the role of social media do resemble the Immonen affair with regard to some neo-populist scandals. Social media especially function as the initial arenas for neo-populist scandals and, during the scandals, they serve as forums for supporters of the populist movement and their critics, fuelling the scandal for the news media. Several similar kinds of neo-populist scandals have occurred in Finland during the twenty-first century (Herkman, 2016b), and in Sweden some neo-populist scandals concerning the Sweden Democrats party are quite reminiscent of the Immonen affair – especially the 'Avpixlat-scandal' in which the tabloid paper *Expressen* revealed the previously anonymous racist social media writings of several Sweden Democrat members, resulting in them receiving much negative attention in 2013 (Herkman, 2016a). In Denmark, three minor political scandals linked to unacceptable updates on social media have appeared during the 2010s, two of them can be defined as neo-populist scandals concerning the populist right-wing Danish People's Party.

There is no much research on precise scandals concerning other contemporary neo-populist movements in Europe. However, it is presumed that radical, right-wing, populist parties in northern and central European multi-party democracies, like the Netherlands, Belgium, Austria and Switzerland, have faced similar scandals, because they all represent similar 'Democratic Corporatist' countries, in which the welfare state ideology has enjoyed large-scale support, the population is well-educated and eagerly follows news media, and where the autonomous and highly professionalised news media generally promotes liberal values (Hallin & Mancini, 2004). In this context, the conservative–nativist ideology favoured by populist right-wing radicals confronts the liberal ethos generally promoted by mainstream politicians and the news media, therefore social media serve as a platform for bypassing journalistic control (cf. Wodak, 2015).

However, it has to be emphasised that in today's converged media environment the border between news media and social media is blurring all the time (Jenkins, 2008). In general, social media appears not to compose – in the Habermasian sense – any political public sphere in which various rational arguments are deliberated for achieving a common public opinion (cf. Strandberg, 2008). Rather it seems to create differentiated segments or 'bubbles' in which factions of similar-minded individuals unite and then disagree with factions opposing their values and beliefs, leading to intractable online disputes (see Davis, 2010). Hence, the link between social media, societal segments and neo-populist scandals needs further exploration that go beyond our case study. It can also be argued that when neo-populist parties become more established in their party fields, the agendas they promote may be normalized and thus less eagerly scandalised by the news media (e.g. Herkman, 2015).

The bigger questions then are: What is the role of social media in neo-populist scandals in countries whose political and media systems differ from 'Democratic Corporatist' countries? Will we be able to find similar kinds of political scandals, concerning populist parties, in all countries? Has there been, for example, neo-populist scandals in the 'Polarised Pluralised' countries of the Mediterranean region in which politics have traditionally been more confrontational and the media less liberal than in northern European democracies? Or, is it also possible to find neo-populist scandals in the 'North Atlantic Liberal' countries, in which the media has been predominantly market-driven and politics has relied on individualism instead of corporative parties or organisations (cf. Hallin & Mancini, 2004)? Furthermore, what is the situation in former Eastern Bloc, post-communist countries, where populism has quite recently taken on a more authoritarian form than in Northern Europe?

CONCLUSION

Based on our case study, we can draw five conclusions. First, the dramaturgy of the Immonen affair nicely matches the life-cycle models used in political scandal studies (see Thompson 2000; Garrard, 2006; Jenssen & Fladmoe, 2012). 'A pre-phase' was played when Immonen, in June 2015, published a Facebook photo showing his participation at the event commemorating Eugen Schauman. Immonen posed for a photograph with convicted neo-Nazis. Sampo Terho then reprimanded Immonen. However, 'a full scandal' broke on 25 July after the leading daily of Finland *Helsingin Sanomat* published an article about Immonen's Facebook update from 24 July (see Herkman, 2016a; 2016b). 'The culmination phase' occurred when Immonen did not join the party conference on 8–9 August, and then announced that he was to resign from Finns Party's parliamentary group. 'The aftermath' was played out when Putkonen published his 'blacklist'.

Second, the news media plays a crucial role in neo-populist scandals as it does in all modern political scandals, which are accordingly described as mediated events (Thompson, 2000, pp. 60-61). It can be argued that no major political scandal can appear and be sustained without receiving massive media attention and in many cases the media operates actively as 'a scandalising machine' (Lull & Hinerman, 1997; Ekström & Johansson, 2008; Allern & Pollack, 2012; Entman, 2012). Furthermore, the Immonen affair only became a public scandal after the leading daily

Helsingin Sanomat had raised the issue. However, our analysis of the Immonen affair demonstrates the significant role of social media in contemporary political scandals. In today's media landscape both news media and social media participate in scandal construction, and in neo-populist scandals their relationship could be called symbiotic.

Third, platforms, actors and discussion themes were strongly polarised within social media. In the Immonen affair, social media sites became essential players since the whole scandal derived from Immonen's Facebook updates and, in addition, the affair was actively commented on and constructed via various social media sites. Social media has quickly become an essential part of neo-populist scandals, since much of the identity construction of neo-populist movements occurs through social media sites (cf. Sakki & Petterson, 2015).

Fourth, social media and the news media played an intermittent role in the scandal. Thus, both social media and news media feed and inspire each other during a scandal (cf. Rogstad, 2016). In our analysis, many of the most popular social media sites during the Immonen affair were forums run by traditional news media, where commentators debated the affair with reference to the online news articles they had been reading. The tabloid media seems an especially important source and platform for generating and sustaining neo-populist scandal, demonstrating the inherent link of addressing an audience receptive to populist views via the tabloid media (cf. Mazzoleni, 2003, p. 8).

The symbiosis between the news media and social media in the Immonen affair was also revealed by the amount of published content being similarly high and low during the same phases of the scandal (see Figure 1 and 3). Nonetheless, it seems that the social media was slightly quicker in its response and that news media followed half a day behind, but if we keep in mind the fact that many of the discussion forums categorised as social media were located in news media online portals, the difference is negligible. And, in some social media debates, e.g. commenting on researchers' observations, the news media content served as a vital starting point for the discussion.

Fifth, the most striking difference between the news media and social media was that the news media very clearly represented a liberal democratic view and criticised Immonen, whereas social media was divided into liberal and conservative blocks fighting each other. Immonen's supporters, anti-immigration views and even racism and xenophobia raised their voices in the social media, attacking mainstream news media and politics for being far too liberal and an elitist cartel – in their opinion. Within social media Twitter seemed to communicate liberal views, whereas discussion forums provided arenas for both liberal and conservative (nativist, neo-populist) voices.

In contrast to the Nordic countries, social media in authoritarian and totalitarian environments commonly serves to create public forums for liberal democratic opposition, which is otherwise excluded from the state-controlled media sphere. Thus, social media seems to provide a forum for 'counter-publics' (Fraser, 1992), even if they do not serve as a totalising public sphere in a Habermasian sense. However, counter-publics are always formed in the specific context of a media environment and political culture, meaning either a conservative emphasis within liberal democracies or a liberal emphasis in countries with authoritarian regimes. Therefore, the question about the role of social media in contextually very different neo-populist scandals remain open after our analysis. However, what is clear is that the role of social media in the formation of populist movements and in the scandals linked to them is increasing all the time.

REFERENCES

Allern, S., Kantola, A., Pollack, E., & Blach-Ørsten, M. (2012). Increased Scandalization. Nordic Political Scandals 1980–2010. In S. Allern & E. Pollack (Eds.), *Scandalous! The Mediated Construction of Political Scandals in Four Nordic Countries* (pp. 29–50). Gothenburg: Nordicom.

Allern, S., & Pollack, E. (2012). Mediated Scandals. In S. Allern & E. Pollack (Eds.), *Scandalous! The Mediated Construction of Political Scandals in Four Nordic Countries* (pp. 9–28). Gothenburg: Nordicom.

Allern, S., & Pollack, E. (2016). Nordic political scandals – Frequency, type and consequences. In M. Ludwig, T. Schierl, & C. Von Sikorski (Eds.), *Mediated Scandals* (pp. 146–163). Köln: Halem.

Arter, D. (2012). Big Bang Elections and Party System Change in Scandinavia: Farewell to the Enduring Party System? *Parliamentary Affairs*, *65*(4), 822–844. doi:10.1093/pa/gsr050

Boomgaarden, H. G., & Vliegenthart, R. (2007). Explaining the rise of anti-immigrant parties: The role of news media content. *Electoral Studies*, *26*(2), 404–417. doi:10.1016/j.electstud.2006.10.018

Borg, S. (2012). Perussuomalaiset. In S. Borg (Ed.), *Muutosvaalit 2011* (pp. 191–210). Helsinki: Oikeusministeriö.

Bos, L., Van Der Brug, W., & De Vreese, C. (2010). Media Coverage of Right-Wing Populist Leaders. *Communications*, *35*(2), 141–163. doi:10.1515/comm.2010.008

Canovan, M. (1999). Trust the People! Populism and the Two Faces of Democracy. *Political Studies*, *XLVII*(1), 2–16. doi:10.1111/1467-9248.00184

Dahlgren, P. (2005). The Internet, Public Spheres, and Political Communication: Dispersion and Deliberation. *Political Communication*, *22*(2), 147–162. doi:10.1080/10584600590933160

Davis, A. (2010). New media and fat democracy: The paradox of online participation. *New Media & Society*, *12*(5), 745–761. doi:10.1177/1461444809341435

Ekström, M., & Johansson, B. (2008). Talk scandals. *Media Culture & Society*, *30*(1), 61–79. doi:10.1177/0163443707084350

Engesser, S., & Humprecht, E. (2015). Frequency or Skillfulness. *Journalism Studies*, *16*(4), 513–529. doi:10.1080/1461670X.2014.939849

Entman, R. (2012). *Scandal and Silence: Media Responses to Presidential Misconduct*. Cambridge: Polity Press.

Fraser, N. (1992). Rethinking the Public Sphere: A Contribution to the Critique of Actually Existing Democracy. In G. Calhoun (Ed.), *Habermas and the Public Sphere* (pp. 109–142). Cambridge: The MIT Press.

Garrard, J. (2006). Scandals: an overview. In J. Garrard & J. L. Newell (Eds.), *Scandals in past and contemporary politics* (pp. 13–29). Manchester: Manchester University Press.

Habermas, J. (1989). *Structural Transformation of the Public Sphere*. Oxford: Polity Press.

Hallin, D., & Mancini, P. (2004). *Comparing Media Systems: Three Models of Media and Politics*. Cambridge: Cambridge University Press. doi:10.1017/CBO9780511790867

Hatakka, N. (2016). When logics of party politics and online activism collide: The populist Finns Partys identity under negotiation. *New Media & Society*. doi:10.1177/1461444816660728

Helander, V. (1971). *Vennamolaisuus populistisena joukkoliikkeenä*. Hämeenlinna: Karisto.

Herkman, J. (2015). The Life Cycle Model and Press Coverage of Nordic Populist Parties. *Journalism Studies*. doi:10.1080/1461670X.2015.1066231

Herkman, J. (2016a, April). *Neo-populist Scandal: The Nordic Case*. Paper presented at the first international conference of scandalogy in Bamberg, Germany.

Herkman, J. (2016b). Populistiskandaalit: Esimerkkeinä Halla-ahon ja Immosen tapaukset. *Sosiologia*, *53*(4), 238-256.

Jenkins, H. (2008). *Convergence Culture: Where the Old and New Media Collide*. New York: New York University Press.

Jenssen, A. T., & Fladmoe, A. (2012). Ten Commandments for the Scandalization of Political Opponents. In S. Allern & E. Pollack (Eds.), *Scandalous! The Mediated Construction of Political Scandals in Four Nordic Countries* (pp. 51–71). Gothenburg: Nordicom.

Jungar, A.-C., & Jupskås, A. R. (2014). Populist Radical Right Parties in the Nordic Region: A New and Distinct Party Family? *Scandinavian Political Studies*, *37*(3), 215–238. doi:10.1111/1467-9477.12024

Khaldarova, I., Laaksonen, S.-M., & Matikainen, J. (2012). *The use of social media in the Finnish Parliament Elections 2011*. Helsinki: Communication Research Centre, University of Helsinki.

Koopmans, R., & Muis, J. (2009). The Rise of Right-wing Populist Pim Fortuyn in the Netherlands: A Discursive Opportunity Approach. *European Journal of Political Research, 48*(5), 642–664. doi:10.1111/j.1475-6765.2009.00846.x

Lea, M., O'Shea, T., Fung, P., & Spears, R. (1992). 'Flamig' in computer-mediated communication. In M. Lea (Ed.), *Contexts of Computer-Mediated Communication* (pp. 89–112). New York: Harvester Wheatsheaf.

Lietsala, K., & Sirkkunen, E. (2008). Social Media. Introduction to the tools and processes of participatory economy. Tampere: University of Tampere.

Lull, J., & Hinerman, S. (1997). *Media Scandals: Morality and Desire in the Popular Culture Marketplace*. Cambridge: Polity Press.

Mazzoleni, G. (2003). The Media and the Growth of Neo-Populism in Contemporary Democracies. In G. Mazzoleni, J. Stewart, & B. Horsfield (Eds.), *The Media and Neo-Populism: A Contemporary Comparative Analysis* (pp. 1–20). Westport: Praeger.

Mazzoleni, G. (2008). Populism and the Media. In D. Albertazzi & D. McDonnell (Eds.), Twenty-First Century Populism: The Spectre of Western European Democracy (pp. 49-64). Hamphshire: Palgrave Macmillan. doi:10.1057/9780230592100_4

Mesežnikov, G., Gyárfášova, O., & Smilov, D. (2008). *Populist Politics and Liberal Democracy in Central and Eastern Europe*. Bratislava: Institute for Public Affairs.

Mudde, C. (2007). *Populist radical right parties in Europe*. Cambridge: Cambridge University Press. doi:10.1017/CBO9780511492037

Mudde, C., & Kaltwasser, C. R. (2012). Populism and (liberal) democracy: a framework for analysis. In C. Mudde & C. R. Kaltwasser (Eds.), *Populism in Europe and the Americas: Threat of Corrective for Democracy?* (pp. 1–26). Cambridge: Cambridge University Press. doi:10.1017/CBO9781139152365.002

Niemi, M. K. (2013). The True Finns Identity Politics and Populist Leadership on the Threshold of the Party's Electoral Triumph. *Javnost – The Public, 20*(3), 77–92.

Paloheimo, H. (2012). Populismi Puoluejärjestelmän vedenjakajana. In S. Borg (Ed.), *Muutosvaalit 2011* (pp. 324–344). Helsinki: Oikeusministeriö.

Rogstad, I. (2016). Is Twitter just rehashing? Intermedia agenda setting between Twitter and mainstream media. *Journal of Information Technology & Politics, 13*(2), 142–158. doi:10.1080/19331681.2016.1160263

Roodjuin, M. (2014). The Mesmerising Message: The Diffusion of Populism in Public Debates in Western European Media. *Political Studies, 62*(4), 726–744. doi:10.1111/1467-9248.12074

Sakki, I., & Pettersson, K. (2015). Discursive Construction of Otherness in Populist Radical Right Political Blogs. *European Journal of Social Psychology, 46*(2), 156–170. doi:10.1002/ejsp.2142

Stewart, J., Mazzoleni, G., & Horsfield, B. (2003). Conclusion: Power to the Media Managers. In G. Mazzoleni, J. Stewart, & B. Horsfield (Eds.), *The Media and Neo-Populism: A Contemporary Comparative Analysis* (pp. 217–236). Westport: Praeger.

Strandberg, K. (2008). Public Deliberation Goes On-line? An Analysis of Citizens' Political Discussions on the Internet Prior to the Finnish Parliamentary Elections in 2007. *Javnost – The Public, 15*(1), 71-90.

Taggart, P. (2000). *Populism*. Buckingham: Open University Press.

Thompson, J. B. (2000). *Political Scandal. Power and Visibility in the Media Age*. Cambridge: Polity Press.

Vainikka, E., & Huhtamäki, J. (2015). Tviittien politiikkaa – poliittisen viestinnän sisäpiirit Twitterissä. *Media & viestintä, 38*(3), 165-183.

Verweij, P. (2012). Twitter links between politicians and journalists. *Journalism Practice, 6*(5-6), 680–691. doi:10.1080/17512786.2012.667272

Villi, M., & Matikainen, J. (2015). Mobile UDC: Online media content distribution among Finnish mobile Internet users. *Mobile Media & Communication, 3*(2), 214–229. doi:10.1177/2050157914552156

Widfeldt, A. (2010). Högerpopulismen: ett växande politiskt fenomen. In J. Ekman & J. Linde (Eds.), *Politik, protest, populism – deltagande på nya villkor* (pp. 158–181). Malmö: Liber.

Wodak, R. (2015). *The Politics of Fear. What Right-Wing Populist Discourses Mean*. London: Sage. doi:10.4135/9781446270073

KEY TERMS AND DEFINITIONS

Democratic-Corporatist Model: A model of politics and media systems in which corporatist political structure and strong welfare state are combined with highly professionalized journalistic tradition and well-developed media markets. Common in Northern and Central European countries.

Finns Party: The Finnish populist party that combines both left-wing social demands and right-wing nationalist approach with immigration criticism. The second largest party in the parliamentary elections of 2015.

Multiparty Democracy: A form of democracy in which the political representation is divided between several parties unlike in, for example, dualistic party system of such countries as the UK and the US. Most Northern and Central European countries are multiparty democracies.

Political Populism: Political style, movement or logic that relies on antagonist confrontation between 'the real people' and 'corrupt elite' or other groups such as immigrants that are excluded from the idea of 'the real people'.

Political Scandal: A public event in which a serious norm or moral transgression of individual politician or political organization is revealed and widely debated in media gaining vast attention.

Public Sphere: An arena or space in which public deliberation is proceeded, various rational arguments expressed and thus a public opinion formed.

Social Media: An umbrella term that covers many kinds of user-based Internet platforms, such as blogs, Facebook, Twitter, discussion forums, YouTube and Wikipedia, in which the form and content are mostly determined and produced by the users of the service emphasizing interactive and community dimensions of communication technologies.

Chapter 2
Scandal Politics and Political Scandals in the Era of Digital Interactive Media

Kamil Demirhan
Bülent Ecevit University, Turkey

ABSTRACT

This study focuses on scandal politics and political scandals in the era of digital interactive media. Scandals are the part of symbolic power struggles. Media is one of the main actors of these struggles. In fact, political scandals have a constructive function in democracies because they help releasing corruptions. After scandals, the public get the opportunity to discuss on the legitimacy of political-legal institutions and political system. However, this discussion is not possible in the conditions of scandal politics. This study is interested in scandal politics and political scandals in the era of digital interactive media. It evaluates the maintaining role of traditional media in the era of digital media, and the potentials of digital interactive media to utilize the constructive functions of political scandals in democracies. The cases of WikiLeaks and Ashley Madison affair are used to evaluate the scandal politics and political scandals in the era of digital interactive media.

DOI: 10.4018/978-1-5225-2019-1.ch002

INTRODUCTION

This study aims at clarifying the relationship between scandals and media in the era of digital interactive media in terms of scandal politics and political scandals. This study explains the difference between scandal politics and political scandals in terms of the presence or the absence of critical public discussion. The presence of critical public discussion on the legitimacy of political system after the release of a corruption is considered as essential for making political scandals functional in democratic system. This study separates the media power on political scandals as before and after the use of digital interactive media. It has critical points about the optimistic views on the role of digital interactive media on political participation and its role as an alternative media to challenge the dominancy of scandal politics. This study examines authoritarian responses in democratic countries towards digital interactive media. However, this study does not deny the challenges in communication and information processes realized by the development of digital media. It tries to find these challenges and understand the main characteristic of political scandals and scandal politics in the age of digital interactive media.

Scandal politics is a concept related to the power of information in politics. Participative democracy supports the access to information by the public and the active participation of citizens to political processes by the way of public discussions. Scandal politics does not comply with the participative democracy consisting of critical public debate about public issues even if it is essential for the revision of political system. However, in scandal politics, scandals are the important parts of political power struggles. Media companies characterize scandal politics using scandals for both making profit and using these struggles as a part of reputation wars. Symbolic power is useful for manipulating people's opinion in order to get their vote in elections or eliminate political rivals. Media has an important role in this manipulation process. In terms of scandal politics, media holds the power of producing information and forming opinion. Moreover, media elites corporate with power elites in this process.

Scandal wars among politicians is a part of politics. Politicians search for information about the corruptions of their rivals useful to attack or counter-attack to them. Journalists and whistle-blowers are main information sources for mainstream media. Blackmailing is a part of political struggles in the conditions of scandal politics. These struggles cause to the loss of political importance of information promoting public debate. Thus, disinformation increases and trust to media dissolves. Details and stories about corruptions are used as profitable commodities by media. In this system, the link between scandals and the unethical character of corruptions disappears. Corruptions as sensational events take the attention of audiences temporarily instead of being a part of long term public discussion as a main problem of political systems.

With the development of information and communication technologies (ICTs), digital interactive media is regarded as an alternative space and channel to challenge the dominancy of scandal politics. People tend to use new and alternative media channels (Castells, 2009).There is a respectable literature on the role of Internet, social media and multimedia systems for the establishment of a new critical public sphere (Dahlberg, 2001; van Dijk, 2006; Halpern & Gibbs, 2013). It is claimed that Internet has various information sources, and transforms the rules of traditional media and traditional journalism. It promotes investigative and participative ways for releasing information. Corruptions are becoming more and more visible by means of Internet and social media such as blogs, microblogs, wikis, or interactive online forums. In the last decade, new digital interactive media channels are used during the protests against governments accused by corruption (Rahimi, 2011). These new communication technologies are thought as a new potential to develop participative politics including critical public discussion.

This study firstly explains interconnection among political scandals, scandal politics and media. This part underlines the importance of scandals as a catalyst for public discussion focusing on the legitimacy of political institutions. Secondly, it dwells on the main characteristic of traditional media in relation to political scandals. Thirdly, it explains the role of digital interactive media in scandals, and scandal politics in digital era. This last part tries to clarify following issues: the maintaining role of traditional media in the era of digital interactive media; obstacles for digital interactive media; and changes in the nature of scandals in this new media era. The arguments of this study are discussed in terms of the cases of WikiLeaks and Ashley Madison affair affected the character of scandals in the last decade.

POLITICAL SCANDALS, SCANDAL POLITICS AND MEDIA

The term of scandal is used “to describe a broader form of moral transgression” (Thompson, 2000). Scandals are related to releasing of the transgression of moral values or norms. Scandal is briefly explained as a released corruption (Lowi, 1988). Corruption is explained as illegal or unethical actions of public authorities or political elites including the use of official positions illegally ignoring public duties (Klitgaard, 1988).Corruption occurs with the breaking of a law or moral norm by public figures or political elites. Thompson (2000, p. 29) explains that “corruption can give rise to scandal, and some of the most important and consequential scandals have been based on charges of corruption.” When a corruption released, then it becomes a scandal. By the way of scandal, corruption gains a public character. Therefore, a political scandal can be called as a released corruption of public figures, politicians or officers.

Corruptions become public issues. Thus, scandals play a positive role in democratic countries informing the public about corruptions. In democratic countries, scandals help evaluating democratic system in terms of its stability, powerfulness and trustfulness. Tumber and Waisbord (2004a) explain that "scandals allow us to analyze and gauge the effectiveness of democratic process and procedure. In fact, scandals encapsulate the dynamics of accountability in liberal democracies." Even though scandals have this function in democracies, it needs to meet some conditions to operate successfully. For example, personalization of a scandal is one of the mistakes causes to decrease in the importance of the relationship between scandal and politics in a large extent. This relationship stands on the concept of legitimacy. Attitudes breaking political, social, economic or ethical norms have to be punished. However, this is not enough, the conditions of corruption have to be discussed by the public to make necessary challenges in political system. The discussion about the legitimacy of political system indicates the power of public opinion. In democratic systems, all political decisions and policies have to be debated by the public to gain legitimacy. Therefore, scandals should create an environment for realizing extensive and inclusive public discussion about the legitimacy of institutions and public figures. Legitimacy needs critical public discussion. The presence of a critical public deliberation, and freedom of press, expression and organization are essential requirements for the development of legitimacy.

Although scandals have important role in democracies making corruptions apparent for the public, the functions of scandals can only be useful in the presence of democratic conditions. Evidences about corruptions coming to light after scandals cannot be functional in dictatorships or authoritarian regimes. However, there are also obstacles in democracies to utilize the functions of scandals. The manipulation of public opinion and the commoditization of scandals by media limit the legitimacy discussion by the public. In this situation, political scandals become a part of political competition among politicians and media holds the control of politics in reputation wars. Therefore, discussion of legitimacy and the importance of released corruptions lost their importance as public issues in the conditions of scandal politics.

In terms of scandal politics, media has not the potential to be a catalyst for the development of critical public discussion. Instead, it is one of the actors in scandal wars. Media holds the power of the control of information and communication channels. It can manipulate public opinion and lead informational processes during scandals. In this position, media is a part of symbolic power struggles. It is also not an independent actor. There are political and financial control on media. Thus, media losses its critical role and scandals start to determine the political system instead of political reason. Scandal hunters, sensationalizing and tabloidization of scandals by media, damage to the potential of public debate on corruptions. Therefore, the term of scandal politics insists on the loss of critical role of media in public issues. And it indicates the increase of the importance of political appearance on media. Thus, corruptions stay behind the presentation of corruption on media.

Media has important role in the disclosure process of corruptions and the breaking out of scandals. Thompson (2000) uses the term of “mediated scandal.” Scandals are mediated events so media organizations hold the power of leading people opinion about scandals. In fact, media has the responsibility of informing people about public issues in democracies (Habermas, 1991; Bennett & Entman, 2001). With regard to this responsibility, news about scandals should not be perceived as commodities by media companies for making profit. Events should be seriously mediated in appropriate to the principles of trustfulness and the independency of media. However, when the power of media industry is considered, media companies regard political scandals as marketable products. And they write interesting stories about scandals for taking audiences’ attention. These stories become more important than the principles. The next section explains to the background of the challenge on the role of media in politics.

TRADITIONAL MEDIA: THE FALL OF INVESTIGATIVE JOURNALISM AND THE RISE OF SENSATION AND SURVEILLANCE

The development of scandal politics is related to the industrialization of media. Media has lost its public role when it became an industrial power (Habermas, 1991). Media productions focus on consumption. Thus, political communication turns to an activity of political marketing and political advertising. Media conglomerations aim at maximizing their profits. Media contents are under the control of advertisers and media bosses. In this situation, media contents focus on producing enjoyable times for audiences instead of motivating them for public debates. Conglomeration and monopolization in media industry cause to the standardization of media contents (Croteu & Hoynes, 2003, p. 47). This situation damages to the plurality in media environment.

The loss of the productive role of media in public issues has a historical background. It is seen that there is a rise and fall in the public role of journalism in history. The importance of investigative journalism in scandals raised in 1960s and 70s. Investigative journalism consists of bringing truth into open. The press was responsible to inform the public to develop civic culture and political life. However, in 1980s, the importance of investigative journalism started to fall due to the high costs, the gap between costs and profits, and the problems with legal, political and financial authorities. These factors encouraged to sensational journalism instead of investigative one (Tumber & Waisbord, 2004b).

Ekström and Johansson (2008) insist that broadcasting a scandal is an activity more than bringing information into open. As mentioned before, scandals are mediated events. In terms of consumption, the role of media is not only transforming information but also dramatizing it for taking public attention. It uses story telling technics and makes news more interesting for audiences. In terms of scandal politics, sensationalizing is very important. Media uses the strategies of dramatization, sensationalizing, and shocking for attracting audiences. This situation shows that a corruption is not enough to cause to break out a scandal. As Castells (2006) claimed with the terms of scandal politics, media manages scandals and gets power in politics. Its power as an actor in the political struggles is not limited to the sensationalizing of scandals for making profit. Media power in politics causes to new relationships between media and political elites based on mutual interests. Politicians utilize media to increase their symbolic power during political campaigns. Some of politicians are also media bosses, and they use their media power to increase their political interests. For example, in 2001, Michael Bloomberg, used his media power to become New York governor. At the same year, Silvio Berlusconi, another famous politician and media boss, used his media power in political competition (Croteu & Hoynes, 2003).

The power of media is not only owned by politicians. Public authorities also hold the media power in hand and use its power. Governments have power to control information and communication process. Also, they try to get their own media or cooperate with established private media organizations (Croteu & Hoynes, 2003). With regards to this relationship between media and politics, scandals are open to manipulation of financial and political actors due to their commercial interests or political deals with media bosses, or the control of governments. Therefore, media is not an independent or neutral actor in politics. Its contribution to public sphere and critical public debates about scandals is weak. Thus, questioning the legitimacy of public figures seems not possible. The democratic responsibility of media disappears in the conditions of scandal politics.

The position of audiences in scandal politics is insufficient to recognize them as a part of critical public debate and discussants of the legitimacy of political system. Media provides a huge amount of commodity for audiences. It provides enjoyable times, so people regards media commodities as means for enjoyment. People do not trust to media due to its commercial concerns and its close relation with politicians. Furthermore, people are aware of the government control on media. Therefore, they are unresponsive to media contents. People watch programs instead of considering the public role of media. Medium is considered as a means for passing time. The claim of McLuhan (2001), “medium is the message”, is important to evaluate this situation. Content is less important for people than the medium. They are mostly interested in medium and having fun watching programs rather than thinking on messages, so they do not have real demands from media. Therefore, a scandal mediated by mainstream media with sensationalizing and dramatization cannot get enough potential to develop a public debate, and contribute to the discussion of legitimacy about political system due to the problems of value, trustfulness and perception.

Scandals mediated by mainstream media are not seen as reality by the public (Castells, 2009). Highly charged debates about scandals broadcasted on TV do not have special meaning for audiences more than TV series or talk shows. These broadcasts may mobilize some feelings for a short time but they do not continue when TV turned off. Therefore, it is hard to separate their effects from fictional entertainments. Audiences watch the conflict between prospective bride and groom on a marriage program; competition in a floor show, and a talk show about a political scandal on same screen. People watch or read news about sensationalized scandals among countless violence news. In programs about scandals, the sides of a scandal (political elites, journalists, media producers) are making highly charged discussions, they threaten each other. These are similar to competitors in show programs who always accuse each other. The main point of scandal, corruption or transgression of a moral or legal norm disappears in the noise pollution on media. The media environment does not have the capacity to develop a critical public debate and to solve the problems of political system (causing corruptions) around a legitimacy discussion.

Scandals create several public reactions limited to unorganized and discrete events. Some people follow discussions and talk about them but these reactions have not a real aim and consistency. Thompson (2000) explains that "scandals have been described as frenetic events, media and political frenzies that initially capture a great deal of attention and later, gradually or suddenly, disappear." Tumber and Waisbord (2004a) insisted that media is failed to create public reaction. This reaction is essential for critical public discussion to reinstate the legitimacy of political-legal system. In this context, legitimacy crises have no more connection to the public because of the influence of symbolic power struggles in political wars and their presentation on traditional media provides high ratings.

DIGITAL INTERACTIVE MEDIA, SCANDALS AND LEGITIMACY

Social media as an alternative media having potential to pass over the dominancy of scandal politics (Castells, 2009). It has a role in the process of diffusion of information and ideas. Lee and Lio (2016) insists that Internet helps the processes of information production and dissemination. It improves the freedom of expression and plurality in communication. These are important components of critical public discussion. A high level of public access to information improves accountability and supports the struggle against corruptions.

Williams and Delli-Carpini (2004) claims that mainstream media cannot maintain its power as a gatekeeper in the era of digital interactive media. Any actors has no central position in communication process in this new era. Williams and Delli-Carpini (2004) explains that there are so much information on Internet ready to progress. People do not only consume the contents of media but they also produce information on Internet. Consumers have more impact than before, the interaction between producers and consumers is stronger in this new media era than traditional media. Users are not only audiences on digital interactive media but they are also producers so they are called as prosumers. Prosumers produce contents besides consuming them (Dunn, 2013). For example, teacher violence against students in class can be recorded by students using mobile phones, and records can rapidly flow through users' online social networks. Bribery can be recorded and uncovered on social media. New actors (amateurs) engage in the production and dissemination process of information and communication. The users of digital interactive media have power to investigate corruptions as well as journalists, public investigators or political advisors. Also, so many people have capacity to mediate corruptions sharing information with people in their social networks. Williams and Delli-Carpini (2004) claim that the gatekeeping and issue-framing roles of mainstream media are challenged by the development of digital interactive media.

The number of scandals have been increased seriously by the use of information and communication technologies (ICTs). Since, Internet provides more accessible and interactive spaces than mainstream media. Information and news are cycling through social networks. New mobile multimedia systems (van Dijk) record videos and voices which are useful to get proofs about corruptions. The multimedia systems and social networks help releasing corruptions. The files as voices, videos or texts can be used in a combination by means of digital interactive media (Dunn, 2013). The types of the presentation of proofs as visual, audible and written forms with a combination make scandals more impressive for audiences. Also, access to these technologies is easier than to access the mainstream media channels.

Mainstream media manipulates public opinion in the conditions of scandal politics. However, new digital interactive media may increase the awareness of public about the role of scandals. People share information and news about corruptions, and they talk about scandals on Internet. Lee and Lio (2016, p.128) imply that Internet users create pressure on governments. This is important to overcome corruptions in governmental level. Reporting has become easier by means of Internet. It improves the auditing potential of people on public officers. Tumber and Waisbord (2004b) insist that digital interactive media reduces the power of official media under the control of state. Thus, corruptions in governmental level become more visible for the public. For this reason, digital interactive media is seen as an important part of democratization process especially in "authoritarian regimes" and "weak democracies". Dunn (2013) stresses that ICTs are used considerably to release concealed corruptions in the last decade. Therefore, digital interactive media technologies are seen as necessary for increasing public interests and civic culture.

Although new digital interactive media has strengths for accountability, transparency and participation, it is not totally characterized as a critical and alterative media. It also improves conditions for scandal politics. Tumber (2004b) claims that new digital media provides additional spaces to rumor and talk about scandals. There are new actors who are desired to mention scandals and many blogs and websites make profit by this way. This new era is open to tabloidization, too. There is many information supplier and a huge amount of information on Internet. Scandals cycle on social media by means of online talk forums, rapidly, consistently, and without huge costs. For example, the sites like Drudge Report has role as a forum for spreading rumor and sensationalizing scandals. Tumber and Waisbord (2004b) insist that "by validating claims and providing the illusion of immediacy to acts of wrongdoing, video and sound tapes are important ammunition for actors involved in scandal politics."

However, scandal politics on digital interactive media is different from traditional media. Miltner and Baym (2015) imply that the control power of stories about scandals is challenged by the development of digital technologies. There are different mechanisms and actors in scandalizing process. Investigation of scandals and distribution of them are easier on digital interactive media rather than traditional media because the processes of investigation, storytelling and broadcasting are not only realized by professionals. There are many various actors having role in the investigation of scandals and in the process of information dissemination after scandals. There is not only special investigators, but also whistle-blowers or political advisors hunting scandals. All people can be a potential whistle-blower having a mobile phone and an account on social media platforms. The necessity of professionality in the processes of investigation and broadcasting are challenged by the digital interactive media. The subjects of scandals are also changed in this era. Usually, scandals mediated by traditional media are related to public figures, officers or political elites. On social media, scandals can be related to ordinary people.

The dominancy of scandal politics on digital interactive media is a contradictory issue. Literature on the role of social media in politics presents that social media is not a powerful channel to develop a public discussion challenging the current political environment (Morozov, 2009). However, events in the last decade show that people have had power using social media during protests after political scandals. Especially, in the countries called as "weak democracies" in terms of their political system, scandals caused to social and political reactions and political changes.

Nevertheless, these movements have not a real effort to challenge the problems of democratic system around a discussion on legitimacy regarding the problems on the basis of scandals. Therefore, it is not certain whether these political movements are a part of public discussion or temporal reactions open to manipulation by the actors of scandal politics.

The availability of information on Internet about scandals, the rapid flow of information on social media and mentions cannot directly prevent corruptions. Accountability and transparency can only be realized in the presence of political control of the public, the presence of discussion about the legitimacy of public institutions and public figures, and the presence of sharing some common social or moral values. Scandals can only be constructive if they promote to public discussion, legitimacy crises and the revision of political-legal system. Digital interactive media cannot challenge scandal politics although it has potential. From this point, it seems that factors due to financial, political and governmental control on traditional media are important problems against political change in the era of digital interactive media, too. Moreover, there is political control on social media in liberal democracies as well as "authoritarian regimes" or "weak democracies." The control prevents the freedom of expression and damages the main conditions of public discussion. Therefore, the limits of public discussion and legitimacy debate in the era of digital interactive media makes the situation similar to the one of traditional media.

The opportunities of digital interactive media for social and political movements promise hope for people to develop critical public discussion. People may cause to change in the position of traditional media because they are reacted to its reckless and unresponsive position. Digital interactive media channels have become alternative media in these protests. However, communication on digital media is not totally independent from traditional media. Traditional media becomes a part of communication process a short time after the beginning of social movements. It leads the information flow and takes public attention. The role of taking public attention is a powerful function of mainstream media in the new media era. Digital interactive media is investigative, and information on digital media needs to some editorial assistance by media professionals. Therefore, digital interactive media actors corporate with traditional media companies, and they carry on business. Thus, they find places on the era of digital interactive media supplying their products and continue to use their strategies like storytelling and sensationalizing.

The opportunities increase with taped telephone conversations, the records of videos or secret talks are obtained by and accessible on digital interactive media. These materials are seen as the proofs of corruptions. It is claimed that communication on social media creating pressure on public figures, and it has the role to prevent corruptions. However, it is not sure whether the huge number of proofs have a real impact to overcome corruptions. Discussions on social media are similar to traditional media focusing on the subjects of scandals. However, the main issue is not public figures or politicians as subjects. The issue should be the reasons of corruptions. Scandals sometimes cause to resignation of public figures or punishment. However, scandals do not create debates on the legitimacy of political-legal system. The main reason of this situation is the absence of critical public discussion.

In terms of scandal politics, the huge number of scandals on social media cause to decrease in the importance of scandals. People consider scandals as media events in the abundance of scandals. There are many scandals on social media but they do not cause to public discussion and not resulted with decrease in the number of corruptions. Also, ordinary people becomes a potential subject of scandals in digital interactive media era. Sometimes, people share their unmoral or illegal attitudes on social media and cause to scandals about themselves in their social networks. It seems like self-whistleblowing behavior. Moreover, they become parts of unmoral activities which are accessible as well as information on the era of digital interactive media. Thus, the popularization of scandals causes to decrease in the importance of their political character. It also has impact on scandal politics. If somebody is already a subject of scandal what does a scandal about public figure mean for this person? Popularization, increase in the number of scandals, their inefficiency in political area make scandals meaningless media events for people. This situation also makes the boundaries between private and public blurred.

WIKILEAKS AND ASHLEY MADISON AFFAIR

This part evaluates the arguments of this study by means of WikiLeaks and Ashley Madison affair, famous websites related to popular scandals in the era of digital interactive media. WikiLeaks is a digital interactive media platform played an important role releasing corruptions related to the public authorities of countries in the world. The case of WikiLeaks is useful to understand the role of new digital technologies in political scandals, and it clarifies change in the role of traditional media. WikiLeaks uses digital technologies and has new methods for investigating and broadcasting corruptions. Anonymous information networks, using hacking attacks for investigation, and the online publication of documents are some of the methods used by WikiLeaks.

In the last decade, WikiLeaks has played an important role to disclosure many political scandals. It is crucial to understand scandal politics in the age of digital interactive media. Since, WikiLeaks is scandalized by traditional media by means of allegations about Julian Assange. The case of WikiLeaks clarifies the changes in scandal politics and political scandals in the era of digital interactive media in terms of the processes of investigating and broadcasting corruptions, the role of traditional media in digital era, and surveillance in modern democratic countries.

Another digital interactive media platform is the website Ashley Madison. The website was scandalized with the disclosure of users' identities after a hacking attack. In this case, scandals were about ordinary people rather than important public figures. It seems that although this case includes unmoral relationships of many number of public officers, it cannot be seen as a classical political scandal. In fact, it has political character if its political and social consequences are regarded. The scandal was not only about the disclosure of users' identities, but also Ashley Madison website has a potential to be a scandal with regards to its service "arranging extramarital relationships." After this affair, the number of registration to website has increased surprisingly.

The cases of WikiLeaks and Ashley Madison are useful examples to understand scandal politics and political scandals in the era of digital interactive media. The main point about these digital interactive platforms is finding out the challenges of scandal politics and the change of political scandals. In this context, this study discusses the possibility of critical public discussion about the legitimacy of political-legal system after political scandals in the era of digital interactive media. Political scandals are defined as functional events in democratic systems if they can contribute to the revision of political system. In other way, corruptions can be apparent in authoritarian regimes but if it is not discussed by the public, scandals cannot realize their function in political system.

WikiLeaks

The case of WikiLeaks is evaluated in terms of the following issues: i. the maintaining role of traditional media as storyteller and gatekeeper; ii. the role of traditional media due to the weakness of investigative journalism, tabloidization and sensationalizing on social media; iii. surveillance on social media; iv. the challenge of scandal politics.

WikiLeaks (WikiLeaks, 2016) is explained as "a multi-national media organization and associated library." It was founded in 2006 by Julian Assange. It publishes "censored datasets or otherwise restricted official materials involving war, spying and corruption." WikiLeaks published more than 10 million documents and associated analyses (WikiLeaks, 2016). It is called as "a whistle-blowing organization and website that publishes materials provided by anonymous sources" (Beyer, 2014, p. 143). Volunteers in anonymous networks are important in the process of obtaining secret information about governments or corporations, and sharing documents on digital interactive era.

WikiLeaks aims at contributing to the establishment of a networked public sphere (Benkler, 2013). It is regarded as a powerful source for a real democracy. In democracies, people have the right to access true and reliable information about the policies of governments. Also, people have to be a part of policy making process in appropriate to participatory culture (Jenkins, 2009; Dunn, 2013). People in anonymous networks all around the world provide information and proofs about corruptions using digital interactive channels (Dunn, 2013). These features of WikiLeaks are compatible with the claims about the advantages of digital interactive media for revitalizing democracy.

WikiLeaks has important role in scandals releasing corruptions in international level. It became popular in 2010, after the publication of U.S. secret documents. These documents claim that U.S. army and U.S. government broke the official principle of secrecy. WikiLeaks' documents caused a couple of scandals called as Collateral Murder, The Iraq War Logs, The Afghan War Diary, and Cablegate. The Collateral Murder is an important one of these scandals about U.S. air strike in the July, 2007 that killed Iraqi journalists working for Reuters (Brevini et al., 2013). Investigation efforts failed and a copy of the video requested by Reuters as an evidence was not launched. However, WikiLeaks obtained and launched this video, and made it available to the international public (The video on YouTube is viewed by 15.547.171 user by the June, 2016.). It clarifies the power of WikiLeaks releasing scandals. The popularity of WikiLeaks increased rapidly after the broadcasting of this video.

The Maintaining Role of Traditional Media as Storyteller and Gatekeeper

WikiLeaks uses investigative methods such as whistle-blowing and hacking activities. And it has various publication methods. It publishes secret documents on its website and/or makes contract with mainstream media for the publication of these documents. Its self-publication activity is different from traditional standards of journalism. It does not use editing procedures or arrangements like storytelling, or dramatization of news. Therefore, the form of documents in the website are regarded as investigative data rather than news. These data do not make sense for the public because they seem as raw material and need to gain a frame. Therefore, traditional media and new media collaborate. WikiLeaks has contractual relationships with more than 100 major traditional media organizations (Wikileaks, 2016). New York Times, the Guardian, Le Monde, El Cezire TV and Der Spiegel have published the documents provided by WikiLeaks. These traditional channels are functional for the dissemination of information, attracting public attention to corruptions, and providing financial support to WikiLeaks. As Rogers (2011) stressed that WikiLeaks helps journalists to obtain information, classify and analyze data, and present information to the public. Making news using data is the work of data journalists. It could be seen as intervene on the raw material (investigative documents) by traditional media.

Getting information from an organized partners instead of unknown personal sources is also an advantage for established news organizations. It is insisted that WikiLeaks has been challenged the relationship between journalists and whistle-blowers (Thorsen et al., 2013). Organizations such as Al Jazeera and New York Times get information from organizations like WikiLeaks, and collaborate them in the status of partnership to obtain leaks and to secure this process. This new collaboration challenges the sources of leaks. Organizations like WikiLeaks are more responsible and reliable than personal sources (Benkler, 2013).

The Role of Traditional Media Due to the Weakness of Investigative Journalism, Tabloidization of Social Media and Sensationalization

Traditional media helps WikiLeaks for publication and increases public attention about corruptions (Dunn, 2013). It means that even if sources are investigative documents obtained by WikiLeaks, these documents reach to the public by the stories of traditional media. The methods of the publication of documents used by mainstream media are different from WikiLeaks. Mainstream media companies need to analyze data and provide story about investigations.

Although traditional and new digital media have a cooperation, there are some contradictories. WikiLeaks is different from traditional media in terms of its non-profit nature. The main aim of WikiLeaks is revitalizing critical public debate about governments and politics lightening corruptions with documentary evidences obtained by a volunteer global information networks (Benkler, 2013). On the contrary, mainstream media aims at making more profit. Moreover, the collaboration between WikiLeaks and mainstream media has risks for both of them. Media players faced with economic and political risks due to the collaboration with WikiLeaks producing scandal including government agents. Media companies also strive for preserving their authenticity. It is also complicated for WikiLeaks because it aims at creating an opponent public and challenging hegemony. It is a counter-hegemonic project against both traditional media and political elites.

This collaboration has also ideological and methodological risks. Storytelling and sensation, and regarding news as commodity are not appropriate to the strategies of WikiLeaks. Another problem is the main components of the nature of traditional media that are tabloidization and sensationalization. WikiLeaks and its symbol name Assange are also marked as sensational news by mainstream media. While many corruptions in international level were scandalized by WikiLeaks, mainstream media scandalized Assange due to the allegations about sexual misconducts. Dunn (2013) stresses that there was a tension occurred between traditional media when collaborators, Guardian and New York Times, reported the allegations of sexual misconduct by Assange, denied by him. This scandal caused to the decrease in the meaning of WikiLeaks, and it caused to the tabloidization of WikiLeaks.

Surveillance on Social Media

Digital interactive media is considered as a space providing the freedom of information for people. In Arab spring, western countries claimed that Internet is a channel to challenge authoritarian regimes. However, it is seen that this declaration is not trustworthy. The power of Internet is considered as a part of struggle for freedom against authoritarian countries. However, modern democratic countries apply surveillance and control on the platforms of digital interactive media like WikiLeaks as well as authoritarian regimes (Hintz, 2013).

WikiLeaks is seen as a symbol of the freedom of information (Beyer, 2014). McCarthy (2015, p. 439) explains that groups like Anonymous and WikiLeaks are "a part of information movement against practices of information asymmetry." WikiLeaks is an example of "the use of liberation technology and experiences of individuals and movements in advancing free expression, transparency and social transformation" (Hintz, 2013, p.147). Beyer (2014), suggests that "the cross-national online norm of freedom of information" has troubles with domestic legal practices. According to Beyer (2014) this conflict is clearly seen in the U.S. government's effort to get rid of WikiLeaks from the Internet. After the scandals of Collateral Murder, The Iraq War Logs, The Afghan War Diary, Cablegate, U.S. government started to censor on web servers providing services to WikiLeaks (Assange, 2012). After this censorship, WikiLeaks supporters started to mass-mirroring to continue broadcast the website (Enriquedans, 2010).

Also, there are financial, political and legal control on digital interactive media. In this context, digital media is similar to traditional media. This control is explained as control on infrastructure, control on financial support provided by the supporters of radical online disclosure, and control on analytical labor interpreting raw material (Brevini & Murdock, 2013). Political, financial and legal control on digital media causes to the limitation of freedoms. Internet provides advantages for companies. Some of huge companies control the digital media market. Google, Facebook, YouTube hold the large part of information and communication economy. Web-sites use web services provided by these powerful companies. Service providers establish control on digital interactive media (Brevini & Murdock, 2013).

After the disclosure of U.S. embassy diplomatic cables, WikiLeaks is declared as a threat for homeland security by government. The service providers cut off their services to WikiLeaks due to the reaction of U.S. government. In terms of financial control, an unofficial pressure was applied on the banks to prevent the transfers of donations via banking service or credit cards (Brevini & Murdock, 2013). Financial control also affected the analytic labor which needs high prices to work (Brevini & Murdock, 2013). If an Internet platform cannot pay these costs, it could not be publicly visible.

Control on digital media in democratic countries is similar to authoritarian regimes filtering the web contents and blocking access to websites during social-political movements. Governments have control on web service providers, search engines, and infrastructure. Political power collaborates with corporations in this process. Surveillance is applied on the contents of communication like emails. User's data (activist or supporters) are collected from social media sites (Hintz, 2013; Winseck, 2013) as proof for accusations. These controls were applied in the case of WikiLeaks. Moreover, Assange accused of spying; surveillance was applied on supporters, on publications of WikiLeaks and the use of WikiLeaks' documents by mainstream media, public officials or academicians (Beyer, 2014; Hintz, 2013).

Scandal Politics and Digital Interactive Media

Scandal politics consists of the manipulation of public opinion by media and political elites. However, public opinion established through public debate is very important to use scandals for democracy. In terms of WikiLeaks, Beyer (2014) explains that surveys present that the majority of U.S. citizens did not support WikiLeaks. Chaiken (2014) writes that Washington Post-ABC News poll finds that "most of those polled (68%) say the WikiLeaks' exposure of government documents about the State Department and U.S. diplomacy harms the public interest. Nearly as many (59%) say the U.S. government should arrest Assange and charge him with a crime for releasing the diplomatic cables." However, Beyer (2014) stresses that an age considering survey shows that especially young people supported both Assange and their information freedom. Also, Beyer (2014) claims that the new movement for freedom of information presents evidence for the power of Internet and political participation, especially for the participation of young people.[1]Dunn (2013) suggests that the scandals broken out by WikiLeaks contributed to public discussions. For example, politically conservative Newspaper group The Gleaner's publication in Jamaica took partner with WikiLeaks and publicized information about the U.S. Embassy cables was very important for Jamaican civic life. The Gleaner's publication of U.S. Diplomacy Cables developed public debate and deliberation in Jamaica. Dunn (2013) claims that this publication has contribution to the development of organized, connected and broadened civic culture.

The relationship between WikiLeaks and Arab Spring is important for the development of public debate and legitimacy crises in authoritarian countries. The documents of Cablegate provided many information about corruptions in administration level in MENA countries. Saleh (2013) summarizes the cables about Arab

Spring released by WikiLeaks in terms of three issues. The first one is the cables related to "the diplomatic positions of Arab leaders towards Iran and Israel; the second one is related to "the US backing of dictators in the region"; the third one is "focused heavily on abuses of civil liberties particularly in Egypt" (Saleh, 2013, p. 237). These are important allegations about the political authorities in the world.

In terms of WikiLeaks' impact on Arab Spring, Saleh (2013) takes attention to the low level of information literacy, and Internet access gap in MENA countries. Saleh, also stresses the prohibition of access to social media sites, and the gap between Internet users and politically active young population. In this situation, Saleh insisted that there was an interaction between online and offline political participation in Arab Spring. WikiLeaks' cables had an important role promoting public debate and anger against political authorities. It contributed to the development of democratic politics in Arab countries providing information about corrupt relations among governments (Saleh, 2013).

York (2013) claims that in the Arab world, demands for transparency are encouraged after the cables released by WikiLeaks, and by traditional media. For example, Al Jazeera released more than 1,600 documents about Israeli-Palestinian peace process, Palestine Papers (Aljazeera, 2016). Corruptions about the president of Tunis were released by the WikiLeaks two weeks before the protests (Bachrach, 2011). WikiLeaks partnered with Nawaat.org - an activist media site- published cables on a site called as TuniLeaks. Cables related to Morocco also released by means of similar version of TuniLeaks called as MoroLeaks (York, 2013). However, it is not certain that WikiLeaks is directly related to uprisings in Arab world. In terms of the demands for transparency, WikiLeaks can be regarded as a catalyst for the uprisings rather than as a reason.

After the releases of corruptions, demonstrations aimed at defending both the freedom of information and democracy. It shows that information freedom was a part of these movements. The problem about freedom is also one of the problems of liberal democracies because surveillance and control on digital interactive media maintain in democratic countries. The development of public debate using digital interactive media is closely related to the freedom of expression and freedom of information. This is the reason of the claim that scandals have a function in democratic countries. However, surveillance on digital interactive media like WikiLeaks is an important obstacle to characterize interactive platforms on Internet as alternative channels for disclosure (Brevini & Murdock, 2013). Although WikiLeaks documents about corruptions motivate struggles for democracy and public debate, debates on corruptions cannot cause to a real change in political system. They could create a powerful doubt about the public figures, elites and institutions resulting with the revision of political system. However, it is not certain that WikiLeaks and Assange have strong support from the global public opinion.

Ashley Madison Website

The Ashley Madison affair explains how scandals in digital interactive media are socialized events. Many ordinary people become the parts of scandals in the age of digital interactive media by this event. Interaction spaces on digital era open to act transgressing social norms. People have access to online services providing unmoral experiences. These services are mostly conflicting with social norms and public values. However, the privacy of users are not safe in digital interactive media. Hackers' attacks, leaks in companies' privacy systems, and personal information sharing for profit among companies cause to scandals. In fact, the services of companies providing unmoral relations or damaging social values are already scandalous. However; the release of personnel information makes scandals more apparent for the public. In the age of digital interactive media, political figures are no longer the single actors of political scandals. All the people have a potential to be a part of scandals. Socialization of scandals affects the political scandals including the members of the public, the main source of critical public discussion.

Ashley Madison is a digital interactive media platform the center of which is in Canada established in 2002. The running company of this website is Avid Life Media (ALM) (Mansfield-Devine, 2015). Ashley Madison is a social networking site aiming at providing extramarital relationships to its users from all around the world and its motto is "Life is short. Have an affair." (Mansfield-Devine, 2015). A group of hackers who called themselves as the Impact Team hacked this website in July, 2015. Hackers threatened ALM to uncover the identities of users. However, Ashley Madison continued its service. In August, hackers started to explain the identities of the users.

There are 39 million registration in this site from 53 countries (Mansfield-Devine, 2015). According to analysis, 34% of accounts are fake. With regard to this information the number of valid accounts is founded about 25 million (Mansfield-Devine, 2015). The broadcasting of a huge number of users' identities caused the Ashley Madison affair. This case is not seem as directly political at the first glance. However, it is related to the transgression of a modern ethical norm (faith among family members) by a huge number of people from many countries. After the hackers attack and the disclosure of personal information, many people have become a part of social scandal all around the world. The scandal become a public event including public figures politicians, priests, military members, civil servants, celebrities (Lamont, 2016).

In general, extramarital relationship is accepted as unmoral behavior in many societies. However, this digital interactive media company provides extramarital relationship to its users. It has about 25 million users. This situation means that an unmoral service is not directly create a scandal. The scandal was broken out after the release of users' identities. The company stayed calm and continued to provide its services without any restriction (Mansfield-Devine, 2015). This attack was declared by the company as a criminal attack rather than hacktivism, and it was insisted that "The criminal, or criminals, involved in this act have appointed themselves as the moral judge, juror and executioner, seeing fit to impose a personal notion of virtue on all of society" (cf. Mansfield-Devine, 2015, p.12).

This scandal affected the social status of people and their careers. However, its impact was wider than any other media scandal about popular public figures. Because many ordinary people were affected by this scandal. For example, nearly 15.000 official email addresses related to U.S. military and government (.mil and .gov) used during registration to website are released. There are many email addresses related to public institutions and private companies. People are punished according to institutional procedures. However, the effects are not only about the careers of people. Couples were divorced, families were damaged, people lost their social status, and the affair was mentioned in relation to suicides (Mansfield-Devine, 2015, p.13). This attack is considered as a crime and unmoral attack to people life (Mansfield-Devine, 2015, p.13).

In order to understand the relationship between Ashley Madison affair and political scandals in the era of digital interactive media, evaluating this service and the aim of people for using this service are necessary. According to the research of Pelucio (2015, p.45) man registered on Ashley Madison website enjoy due to the risks of using this service. They think that the service supports their masculinity. Users are taking risks like controlling information about them, they use nick names, and the risk of disclosure of personal photos. However, users claim that they have abilities to manage risks and these risks mean for them having control, power and autonomy contributing their masculinity. Any problem in the process of risk management is shown as fun, and they regard this situation as "risk adventure" rather than a trouble (Pelucio, 2015, p.45).

There is a relationship between providing an unmoral service and its use by people, and public reaction to political scandals. People are the parts of public who are responsible for the evaluation of the attitudes of public figures or political elites in public issues, and the evaluation of the transgression of socio-political norms organizing the societies. In this situation, the scandal of Ashley Madison is related to degeneration of social norms and public values. By the way of this scandal, ordinary people became the subject of a scandal besides public figures related to scandals. The subjects of Ashley Madison affair are the part of the public as the subjects of critical deliberation.

In the era of social media, many people become a part of scandals, and scandals become ordinary events. This situation causes to fall of the importance of public discussion and legitimacy debates about corruptions. The concepts of risk management and risk adventure used in terms of the risks about the extramarital relationship have connection with people's perception about public figures involved in scandals. In this situation, people cannot ask ethical questions, and they do not discuss about the reasons of corruptions. Thus, they do not try to find the ways of change. On the contrary, people consider scandals as the failures of public figures and political elites in the process of risk management.

Scandals should create public discussion about the legitimacy of political institutions, and they should cause to the revision of political-legal system. Therefore, the meaning of scandal for public is important to talk about the political character of scandals. When corruption is not considered as media event, or most people become a part of scandals, scandals loss their political meaning. If people conceive scandals as unsuccessful corruption attempts, scandals will be seen as a personal fails of the subjects. If corrupt persons can manage their corruption successfully, they can continue their social and political position. If they fail to manage this crisis, the person has to be leave his/her position. The consideration of scandals between the scale of success and fail, causes to the fall of discussion about legitimacy, and the process cannot be completed with the revision of political-legal system.

CONCLUSION

This study focused on scandal politics and political scandals in the era of digital interactive media. It supports that scandal politics is still affecting the politics in the era of digital interactive media. Although the power of traditional media is challenged by the innovations in ICTs, it has important function in the same era. The challenges mainly consist of changes in the investigation and broadcasting process. The investigation of scandals and broadcasting process include many actors different from traditional media organizations and professional journalists. The gatekeeping role of mainstream media is challenged, too. Recently, many people are a part of the whistle-blowing process. Nevertheless, traditional media has some functions in digital interactive media era. The financial cooperation and taking public attention are the maintaining roles of traditional media. The rules of scandal politics are also valid in this era. Scandalization, tabloidization, and surveillance are important problems preventing the realization of critical public discussion. These are also causes to the loss of the importance of investigative information.

The case of WikiLeaks presents that traditional media is not any more the single actor in the process of investigation and the publication of news. Governments' control on information and communication process is decreased by the way of hacking activities and anonymous networks. The communication process is not central in social media and media elite is no single power in the process of scandalizing. However, political, financial and technological control still maintain on digital era.

Ashley Madison affair presents the change in the nature of scandals. Digital interactive platforms provide new spaces open to the transgression of social-moral norms. Inclusion of a variety of subjects in scandals besides public figures causes to the popularization of scandals. Scandal politics are not only about the public figures in political area but also it is about the figures of social area. It affects the families' lives, careers and relationships between ordinary people. Digital media caused to the increase of the number of scandals. The spectrum of scandal is widened. Hacktivism and leaks, or information leaks from services ignoring their users' privacy are an important part of the releases of scandals. Even, accessible profiles on social media are useful to break out scandals about people because they share their own unmoral or illegal activities there. Although, there is an important increase in the number of scandals, there are not affective public discussions about the legitimacy of system. Because scandals are popularizing day to day. When everybody being a part of a scandal, scandals may lose their importance in politics.

REFERENCES

Aljazeera (2016). Palestine papers. Retrieved from http://www.aljazeera.com/palestinepapers/

Assange, J., Appelbaum, J., & Muller-Maguhn, A. (2012). *Cypherpunks: Freedom and the Future of the Internet*. USA: OR Books.

Bachrach, J. (2011). WikiHistory: Did the Leaks Inspire the Arab Spring? *World Affairs Journal*. Retrieved from http://www.worldaffairsjournal.org/article/wikihistory-did-leaks-inspire-arab-spring

Benkler, Y. (2013). Following the Money: WikiLeaks and the Political Economy of Disclosure. In B. Brevini, A. Hintz, & P. McCurdy (Eds.), *Beyond WikiLeaks: Implications for the Future of Communications, Journalism and Society* (pp. 11–34). UK: Palgrave Macmillan. doi:10.1057/9781137275745_2

Bennett, W. L., & Entman, R. M. (2001). Mediated Politics: An Introduction. In W. L. Bennett & R. M. Entman (Eds.), *Mediated Politics* (pp. 1–33). New York: Cambridge University Press.

Beyer, J. L. (2014). The Emergence of a Freedom of Information Movement: Anonymous, WikiLeaks, the Pirate Party, and Iceland. *Journal of Computer-Mediated Communication, 19*(2), 141–154. doi:10.1111/jcc4.12050

Brevini, B., Hintz, A., & McCurdy, P. (2013). Introduction. In B. Brevini, A. Hintz, & P. McCurdy (Eds.), *Beyond WikiLeaks: Implications for the Future of Communications, Journalism and Society* (pp. 1–10). UK: Palgrave Macmillan. doi:10.1057/9781137275745_1

Brevini, B., & Murdock, G. (2013). Following the Money: WikiLeaks and the Political Economy of Disclosure. In B. Brevini, A. Hintz, & P. McCurdy (Eds.), *Beyond WikiLeaks: Implications for the Future of Communications, Journalism and Society* (pp. 35–55). UK: Palgrave Macmillan. doi:10.1057/9781137275745_3

Castells, M. (2009). *The Rise of the Network Society, The Information Age: Economy, Society and Culture* (Vol. I). Malden, MA; Oxford, UK: Blackwell. doi:10.1002/9781444319514

Chaiken, M. (2014). Poll: Americans say WikiLeaks harmed public interest; most want Assange arrested. Retrieved from http://www.washingtonpost.com/wp-dyn/content/article/2010/12/14/AR2010121401650.html

Croteu, D., & Hoynes, W. (2003). *Media/Society: Industries, Images and Audiences*. London: Sage.

Dahlberg, L. (2001). The Internet and Democratic Discourse: Exploring the prospects of online deliberative forums extending the public sphere. *Information Communication and Society*, *4*(4), 615–633. doi:10.1080/13691180110097030

Dunn, H. S. (2013). Something Old, Something New… "WikiLeaks and the Collaborating Newspapers –Exploring the Limits of Conjoint Approaches to Political Exposure. In B. Brevini, A. Hintz, & P. McCurdy (Eds.), *Beyond WikiLeaks: Implications for the Future of Communications, Journalism and Society* (pp. 85–100). UK: Palgrave Macmillan. doi:10.1057/9781137275745_6

Ekström, M., & Johansson, B. (2008). Talk Scandals. *Media Culture & Society*, *30*(61), 61–79. doi:10.1177/0163443707084350

Enriquedans (2010). WikiLeaks Mass Mirroring. Retrieved from https://www.enriquedans.com/wp-content/uploads/2010/12/WikiLeaks-Mass-Mirroring-our-website.pdf

Habermas, J. (1991). *The Structural Transformation of the Public Sphere*. USA: MIT Press.

Halpern, D., & Gibbs, J. L. (2013). Social media as a catalyst for online deliberation? Exploring the affordances of Facebook and YouTube for political expression. *Computers in Human Behavior*, *29*(3), 1159–1168. doi:10.1016/j.chb.2012.10.008

Hintz, A. (2013). Dimensions of Modern Freedom of Expression: WikiLeaks, Policy Hacking, and Digital Freedoms. In B. Brevini, A. Hintz, & P. McCurdy (Eds.), *Beyond WikiLeaks: Implications for the Future of Communications, Journalism and Society* (pp. 146–165). UK: Palgrave Macmillan. doi:10.1057/9781137275745_9

Jenkins, H. (2009). *Confronting the Challenges of Participatory Culture Media Education for the 21st Century*. Cambridge: The MIT Press.

Klitgaard, R. (1988). *Controlling Corruption*. Berkeley: University of California Press.

Lamont, T. (2016). Life after the Ashley Madison affair. Retrieved from https://www.theguardian.com/technology/2016/feb/28/what-happened-after-ashley-madison-was-hacked

Lee, M. H., & Lio, M. C. (2016). The impact of information and communication technology on public governance and corruption in China. *Information Development*, *32*(2), 127–141. doi:10.1177/0266666914529293

Lowi, T. (1988). Foreword. In A. S. Markovits & M. Silverstein (Eds.), *The Politics of Scandal: Power and Process in Liberal Democracies* (pp. vii–xii). New York: Holmes & Meier.

Mansfield-Devine, S. (2015, September). The Ashley Madison Affair. *Network Security*, *2015*(9), 8–15. doi:10.1016/S1353-4858(15)30080-5

McCarthy, M. T. (2015). Toward a Free Information Movement. *Sociological Forum*, *30*(2), 439–458. doi:10.1111/socf.12170

Mcluhan, M. (2001). *Understanding Media*. New York: Routledge.

Miltner, K. M., & Baym, N. K. (2015). The Selfie of the Year of the Selfie: Reflections on a Media Scandal. *International Journal of Communication*, *9*, 1701–1715.

Morozov, E. (2009). Iran: Downside to the Twitter Revolution. DISSENT Retrieved from http://www.evgenymorozov.com/morozov_twitter_dissent.pdf

Pelucio, L. (2015). Unfaithful narratives: methodological and affective notes about experiences of masculinity in a dating website for married people. *Cadernos Pagu, 44,* 31-60. doi.10.1590/1809-4449201500440031

Rahimi, B. (2011). The Agonistic Social Media: Cyberspace in the Formation of Dissent and Consolidation of State Power in Postelection Iran. *Communication Review*, *14*(3), 158–178. doi:10.1080/10714421.2011.597240

Rogers, S. (2011). WikiLeaks data journalism. *The Guardian*. Retrieved from http://www.theguardian.com/news/datablog/2011/jan/31/wikileaks-data-journalism

Saleh, I. (2013). WikiLeaks and the Arab Spring: The Twists and Turns of Media, Culture, and Power. In B. Brevini, A. Hintz, & P. McCurdy (Eds.), *Beyond WikiLeaks: Implications for the Future of Communications, Journalism and Society* (pp. 166–177). UK: Palgrave Macmillan. doi:10.1057/9781137275745_15

Thompson, J. B. (2000). *Political Scandal Power and Visibility in the Media Age*. UK: Polity Press.

Thorsen, E., Sreedharan, C., & Allan, S. (2013). WikiLeaks and Whistle-blowing: The Framing of Bradley Manning. In B. Brevini, A. Hintz, & P. McCurdy (Eds.), *Beyond WikiLeaks: Implications for the Future of Communications, Journalism and Society* (pp. 101–122). UK: Palgrave Macmillan. doi:10.1057/9781137275745_7

Tumber, H., & Waisbord, S. R. (2004a). Political Scandals and Media across Democracies (Vol. I). *The American Behavioral Scientist*, *47*(8), 1031–1039. doi:10.1177/0002764203262275

Tumber, H., & Waisbord, S. R. (2004b). Political Scandals and Media across Democracies (Vol. II). *The American Behavioral Scientist, 47*(9), 1143–1152. doi:10.1177/0002764203262340

van Dijk, J. (2006). *The Network Society: Social Aspects of New Media*. London: Sage.

WikiLeaks. (2016). What is WikiLeaks? Retrieved from https://wikileaks.org/What-is-Wikileaks.html

Williams, B. A., & Delli-Carpini, M. X. (2004). Monica and Bill All the Time and Everywhere: The Collapse of Gatekeeping and Agenda Setting in the New Media Environment. *The American Behavioral Scientist, 47*(9), 1208–1230. doi:10.1177/0002764203262344

Winseck, D. (2013). Weak Links and WikiLeaks: How Control of Critical Internet Resources and Social Media Companies' Business Models Undermine the Networked free Press. In B. Brevini, A. Hintz, & P. McCurdy (Eds.), *Beyond WikiLeaks: Implications for the Future of Communications, Journalism and Society* (pp. 166–177). UK: Palgrave Macmillan. doi:10.1057/9781137275745_10

York, J. C. (2013). The Internet and Transparency beyond WikiLeaks. In B. Brevini, A. Hintz, & P. McCurdy (Eds.), *Beyond WikiLeaks: Implications for the Future of Communications, Journalism and Society* (pp. 229–235). UK: Palgrave Macmillan. doi:10.1057/9781137275745_14

KEY TERMS AND DEFINITIONS

Ashley Madison: A digital interactive media platform services extramarital relationships to its users.

Corruption: The actions of public authorities or political elites including transgression of the social and political norms of society.

Political Scandal: Political scandal means a scandal breaking out after the releases of corruptions related to public figures and political elites.

Critical Public Discussion: The base of public opinion in participative politics having potential to challenge scandal politics.

Scandal Politics: It means the use of scandals as a component of political struggles in symbolic power wars. Media is a powerful actor in politics as holding the means of information and communication channels.

Social Media: All digital technologies and platforms provide opportunities to users for interaction. Video recording mobile phones with social media applications, social media platforms like Twitter, Facebook, YouTube, Instagram, blogs, wikis, forums and interactive website like WikiLeaks.

WikiLeaks: A digital interactive media organization aims at releasing corruptions all around the world. It investigates information about corruptions and publish on the website. Its aims at increasing public awareness and contribute to the transparency of governments.

ENDNOTES

1 http://www.ifla.org/publications/what-is-the-effect-of-wikileaks-for-freedom-of-information

2 http://www.support-julian-assange.com/tag/impact-of-wikileaks/

3 https://prezi.com/sohsmg8jpszt/the-negative-impact-of-wikileaks-in-todays-society/

4 https://read.amazon.com/?asin=B00C2RDZEC

Chapter 3
Information Control, Transparency, and Social Media:
Implications for Corruption

Chandan Kumar Jha
Madden School of Business, Le Moyne College, USA

ABSTRACT

Although the research linking social media and corruption is still in infancy, it provides important insights. It has been shown that social media can prove to be an important tool in fighting corruption. At the same time, freedom on the net is under threat in many parts of the world with governments using a variety of methods, including designing vague and flexible security laws as well as employing technological means, to censor the content that can be shared and accessed by net users. This chapter discusses the implications that government control over information can have for the effects of social media on corruption. It suggests that freedom on the net and the anonymity of net users must be protected if the effects of social media on corruption are to be fully realized.

DOI: 10.4018/978-1-5225-2019-1.ch003

INTRODUCTION

One of the greatest advantages of the Internet is to disseminate information, and social media has played an instrumental role in facilitating the spread of information. The reason is simple: social media platforms cannot only be used to disseminate new, user-generated information but can also be used to spread the information that originally appeared elsewhere. A significant amount of the content shared on social media platforms originates elsewhere on the Internet and even off-Internet. People routinely share links to online news articles, blog posts, pictures, and audio and video clips from radios, televisions, and several Internet source as well as photos and audio and video clips recorded by themselves using mobile phones or other electronic devices, and even pages from printed books, leaflets, and newspapers. Social media, thus, enables individuals to share information in a quick and cheap manner that was never possible before, to an audience that was never so big and diverse, and in a way that no one could have imagined a decade or so ago!

Since the primary objective of social media is to facilitate the communication and interaction between users and allowing them to edit and share content, social media platforms are designed to facilitate the exchange of information, even when users are geographically separated (Tepper, 2003; Porter, 2008). Social media platforms are, thus, intended to be dialogue platforms as opposed to traditional media such as newspapers, radio, and television, which serves as a broadcast platform (Porter, 2008). The new information and communication technologies (ICTs), such as computer, Internet, mobile phones, social media platforms such as Facebook, Google Plus, and Twitter, and numerous applications that are used for communication have an important advantage over radio and television: While radio and television can be used for only one-way communication, the new ICTs allow for a two-way and even multi-way communication (Diamond, 2010). Many Internet users rely on social media platforms to communicate– sharing photos and videos, links to news and other stories, sharing their status updates–with their friends, family members, and a growing network of contacts (Madden, 2010). The popularity of and the reliance of Internet users on social media for communication have been increasing rapidly over time as reflected by the impressive growth in the number of social media users in recent years among both teens and adults in the United States (Madden, 2010; Lenhart, 2015). Worldwide, the number of Facebook users has increased massively in the last decade – from 1 million in 2004 to 1230 million by the end of 2013 (The Guardian, 2014). According to Statista, one of the world's leading statistics database, the total number of social media users increased by more than 230 percent in past 5 years – from under 1 billion in 2010 to 2.34 billion in 2015 (Statista, 2016). It is then not surprising that the exponential growth of social media users, not only in developed but also in developing and underdeveloped world, has drawn the attention of the academics. As a result, a significant body of research that evaluates whether social media (a form of the new ICT) can have causal effects on democratic, economic, and political outcomes[1] has emerged.

There are obvious advantages of such technologies that can facilitate and quicken the exchange of information. By allowing people to anonymously share their ideas and beliefs on multiple online platforms such as webpages, chat rooms, bulletin boards, blogs (Salbu, 2001), and, more recently social media websites, the ICTs augment the freedom of speech and the freedom of expression. The new ICTs enable the "citizens to report news, expose wrongdoing, express opinions, mobilize protest, monitor elections, scrutinize government, deepen participation, and expand the horizons of freedom" (Diamond, 2010). Therefore, in many cases, the governments, especially (but not only) autocratic regimes, may feel the need for controlling certain types of information such as those related to political and bureaucratic corruption, police brutality, and judicial failures. Countries such as China, Malaysia, and Iran have been censoring information related to corruption, human rights violations, and policy brutality by controlling or even owning the print and broadcast media (Freedom House, 2009a). For example, in Malaysia, the government had a clear dominance over print and broadcast media through direct ownership and monopoly practices (Freedom House, 2009b). The 2009 Freedom of the Press Report documents that all of the 11 dominant national daily newspapers were owned by either the ruling coalition or individuals closely associated with the government. The report further points out that the state-owned Radio Television Malaysia operated a large number of radio stations along with two television channels (providing the government substantial control over the diffusion of information).

Indeed, the new ICTs have been recognized to be playing an instrumental role in promoting transparency and accountability and acting as deterrents for human rights violations and the abuses of democratic rights of the citizens (Diamond, 2010). The advent of the Internet and, more recently, social media has expanded the audience to which information can be shared and therefore has made controlling the diffusion of information much more difficult (Jha & Sarangi, 2014). The Internet and social media not only make it possible for the information to flow very quickly to a large number of people but also enable grassroots organizing (Diamond, 2010). Consequently, the cases of human rights violations and corruption in many of these countries have started to come out to the public through blogs and social media sites, which often find places in international media (Freedom House, 2009a). The online media thus challenges the monopoly of the government over information. In several countries, *e.g.,* Malaysia, with a greater share of the population gaining access to the Internet and the use of online media has provided the public with the alternative sources of information and has resulted in the loss of government control over information (Freedom House, 2009b). Furthermore, social media, by allowing the transmission of messages through social networks increases the "shared awareness" where each member of a group understands the situation at hand and knows that everyone else is aware of the situation too (Shirky, 2011). Thus, social media plays a key role in facilitating the coordination among public with common agendas such as movements against corruption, human rights violations, and police brutality. Therefore, it has become even more important for autocratic (and democratic) regimes to censor the content that can threaten the power held by the rulers. Expectedly, then, not only autocratic but even democratic countries have placed restrictions on the exchange of information over the Internet directly or indirectly (Freedom House, 2015).

This chapter briefly reviews the literature on the effects of information technologies, with a focus on social media, on democratic and political outcomes, with an emphasis on corruption. The chapter goes on to discuss the recent attempts made by the governments around the world targeted to curtail the freedom on the net and discusses the implications that the government control over information can have on the effects of social media on corruption. Finally, based on the existing evidence, some policy conclusions are drawn and the avenues for further research are identified and discussed.

INFORMATION ACCESS, TRANSPARENCY, AND CORRUPTION

The availability and transparency of information can play an important role in reducing corruption for a variety of reasons. The first and foremost reason is the obvious fact that free and easy availability of information increases transparency making it more likely that any financial irregularities will be caught and, hence, increases the likelihood that both the bribe-taker and the bribe-giver will be caught (Salbu, 2001). As a result, the cost of committing corrupt practices rises discouraging the corrupt activities. The end result is a decline in corruption. The transparency of laws has long been recognized as one of the most important tools in the fight against corruption (Tanzi, 1998). It has also been argued that the lack of transparency acts as a deterrent for the honest and efficient people to be selected as public employees and undermines social norms and reduces trust (Kolstad & Wiig, 2009). While it is easy to imagine that with dishonest people entering government jobs, corruption is likely to rise; it has been found that corruption thrives in the presence of mistrust (Uslaner, 2005).

Furthermore, it has been suggested by the previous studies that a greater competition adversely affects corruption. Ades and Di Tella (1999), for instance, contend that a greater competition implies that firms enjoy little rents and hence smaller is the bribe that can be extracted from them by bureaucrats and politicians. Consistent with their argument, the authors find that corruption levels are higher in countries where firms extract larger rents. An easy access to information will reduce the scope of bribing by the firms in the same way: An easy access to and the transparency of information is likely to boost competition by increasing the applications for tenders for public contracts, which, in turn, will increase the bidding for these projects, leaving little room for bribing.

An enhanced access to information and a greater transparency through the use of online portals can also be utilized by the governments to raise awareness regarding different public projects and welfare schemes, which will reduce the scope of misappropriation by government officials. An online system that facilitates public's access to government programs and services reduces the discretion of public officials, increases the likelihood of exposure of wrongdoing and, therefore, makes the demand of bribes less likely (Bhatnagar, 2003; Lio, 2011). In addition to that, political corruption is likely to be adversely affected if the public has an easy and unhindered access to information regarding the corrupt activities of politicians. In democratic countries, the politicians are under pressure not to get involved in corrupt practices in order to ensure their re-election. There are instances when corruption has been an important issue in elections. In the 2014 Indian General Election, for example, corruption was the main election issue raised by the Bharatiya Janta Party-led National Democratic Alliance (NDA) that culminated in the historic defeat of the Indian National Congress-led United Progressive Alliance (UPA). It has widely been argued that the Indian population, fed up with the stories of all the financial scams involving the ministers of the incumbent UPA government, decided to vote against the incumbent government, which ultimately led to the grand defeat of the UPA and resulted in the lowest ever parliamentary seats secured by the INC since independence (Chakrabarty & Hazra, 2016). Corruption has also been an issue in the ongoing U.S. presidential elections 2016 (Zurcher, 2016). On the other hand, in autocratic regimes, the dictators would want to keep the frustrations of the public under the threshold such that the demand for democracy does not take the form of a revolution that succeeds in overthrowing the government as it happened in several middle-east countries such as Tunisia and Egypt. A greater access to information thus forces the ruling party to keep corruption in check not only by the bureaucrats but also by their own members. In China, for example, the famous crackdown on corruption by the president Xi Jinping convicted several leaders from his own communist party (The Atlantic, 2015)

Figure 1 shows the relationship between access to information (proxied by the Internet penetration, defined as the proportion of the population with Internet access) and the Control of Corruption Index (henceforth, CCI) across countries. The CCI is an index published by the World Bank that measures the extent of corruption across countries and is designed to capture the "perceptions of the extent to which public power is exercised for private gain, including both petty and grand forms of corruption, as well as "capture" of the state by elites and private interests" (Kaufmann et al., 2010)[2]. Note that the CCI takes values in the range of -2.5 to 2.5, with greater values indicating lower corruption. I have adjusted the scale of the CCI such that higher values of the index imply greater corruption. A strong, negative correlation is clearly visible in Figure 1, suggesting that corruption levels are lower in countries with greater access to information.

Quite possibly, however, the access to and the transparency of information alone may not be sufficient to have desirable effects on corruption. Consider, for example, that the government in a country provides information on the net and/or through newspapers or television regarding a welfare scheme that the poor are entitled to. In many developing countries, literacy rates are very low among the poor and they may not have the ability to access and process that information to understand and claim their rights. In several developing countries, such a situation may give rise to a group of individuals that demands a share of the benefits provided by the government. Usually, government officials encourage such groups and form a nexus in order to share part of the benefits. In countries like India, such nexuses are widespread in rural areas. The beneficiaries of several government schemes receive a

Figure 1. Internet penetration and corruption in 2012

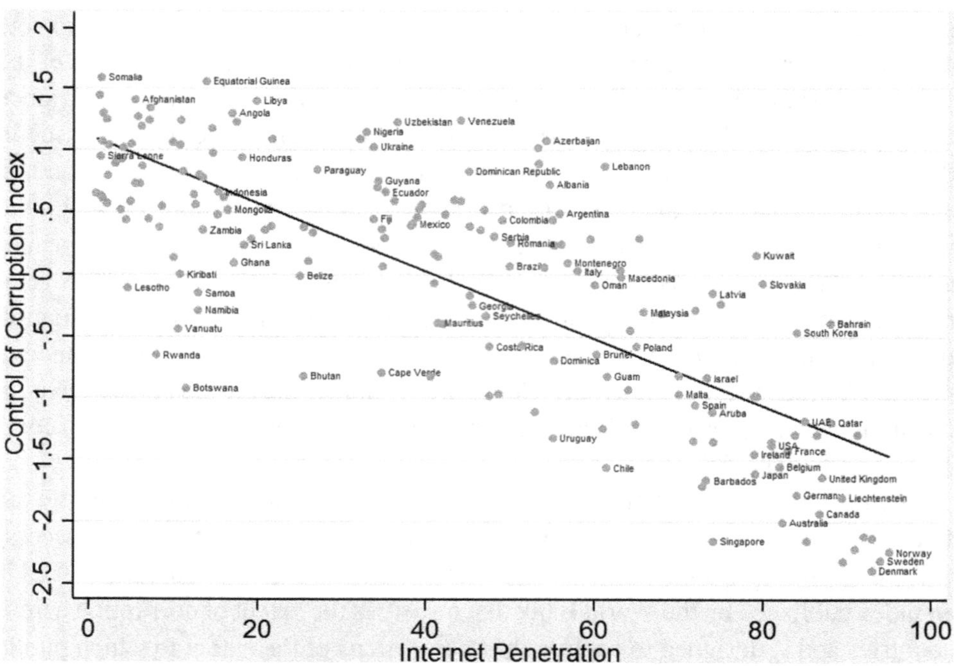

mere fraction of the benefits that they are entitled to, yet these recipients are forced to sign acknowledging that they received the full amount. For example, the Public Distribution System (PDS) in India that is targeted to provide subsidized food products to the poor is deeply mired in corruption. The complex procedures, even for simple tasks, are conducive to the flourishing of the middlemen and touts. The beneficiaries of the PDS, besides having to pay bribes for even getting a ration card, often do not get the quantity that they are entitled to (Kumari & Kumari, 2016). An increased access to information in such situations may even lead to an increase in corruption by increasing the number of beneficiaries.

Recently, some authors have raised this important issue contending that the transparency of information is not a sufficient condition for tackling government and bureaucratic corruption and have noted that the new ICTs have failed to show desirable effects on corruption in some countries for various reasons. These studies, *e.g.*, Bertot et al. (2010), have argued that the success of the ICTs depends on factors such as effective implementation, education, and the culture concerning the acceptance of the ICTs among the public. Furthermore, Kolstad and Wiig (2009) argue that transparency will have desirable effects on corruption only if the agents, whose access to information has been enhanced, have both the ability to process the information and the incentives to act on that information such that they can benefit from the newly available information. It is obvious from the above discussion that, along with providing the infrastructure that eases the access to information, implementing policies that raise awareness by increasing literacy rates (and other measures) is essential to realize the full potential of an increased access to and enhanced transparency of information on corruption.

TRADITIONAL MEDIA VS. ICT AND CORRUPTION

Although the traditional – print and broadcast – media has been serving the purpose of information dissemination, the advent of the modern ICTs has revolutionized the information industry. The modern ICTs are much more inclusive than the traditional media and have provided access to information to the marginalized sections of the society that previously faced many obstacles in the access to information and was deprived of consuming and acting on many relevant information and projects that were targeted towards their betterment. Thus, besides promoting transparency and accountability of governments and businesses, social media has played a crucial role in the inclusive social and economic development (United Nations, 2014).

One of the earliest studies investigating the link between access to information and corruption, DiRienzo et al. (2007), found that a greater access to information is associated with lower levels of corruption across countries. Authors use the digital access index (DAI) as a proxy for information access. The DAI is constructed on the basis of the number of users of fixed telephone, mobile phones, and the Internet, affordability of Internet access, knowledge to use these technologies as measured by literacy and school enrolment levels, and the quality of information and communication technology services. Since then there have been a number of studies that have investigated the impact of the ICTs, especially Internet penetration, on corruption. The impact of Internet penetration (defined as the proportion of the population with access to the Internet) on corruption has been explored more extensively than any other form of the ICT (Lio et al., 2011; Andersen et al., 2011; Elbahnasawy, 2014; Jha & Sarangi, 2014). It has been argued that the Internet can impact corruption by facilitating the exchange of information and promoting transparency. Note that these studies use various empirical techniques, including instrumental variables analysis (Jha & Sarangi, 2014; Andersen et al., 2011) and dynamic panel estimation (Lio et al., 2011; Elbahnasawy, 2014), to ascertain whether the relationship between Internet penetration and corruption is causal. Furthermore, these studies have controlled for a number of economic, political, institutional, and cultural factors that may potentially be correlated with Internet penetration and/or corruption to address the concerns that their results may be confounded due to the omission of factors that are potentially correlated with Internet penetration and/or corruption. Most of these studies, for example, control for the political rights enjoyed by the citizens of the country to ensure that the results are not driven by the omission of the institutional quality (see, for example, Jha & Sarangi, 2014, Elbahnasawy, 2014). In order to ensure that the results are not driven by the omission of cultural factors, studies often include the proportions of the population belonging to different religions in the empirical specification (Jha & Sarangi, 2014). Furthermore, almost all the studies control for per capita income in order to rule out the possibility that the results may be driven by economic disparities across countries. Finally, studies have also controlled for several other variables (such as education, press freedom, inflation, telecom infrastructure, urbanization) to account for heterogeneity across countries (Elbahnasawy, 2014; Jha & Sarangi, 2014; Lio et al., 2011).

One of the primary ways in which the Internet can be used to combat corruption is through the use of electronic-government (in short, e-government) services. E-government services can be used to provide public services online that eliminate or diminish the need for a direct interaction between public officials and the applicants and, hence, make the exchange of bribes more difficult or even impossible in certain cases. Furthermore, since online system is based on standardized rules and procedures, it reduces the discretion of civil servants and increases transparency (Lio et al., 2011; Bhatnagar, 2003). Bhatnagar (2003) discusses several case studies that underscore the importance of e-government for transparency and corruption. For instance, the Online Procedures Enhancement for Civil Applications (known as OPEN), adopted by Seoul Municipality in South Korea, allows for online checking of individual applications for municipal licenses. In a survey, it was found that OPEN has resulted in greater transparency and lower corruption. In India, the computerization of land records, under the *Bhoomi* (meaning land) project, was very effective in combating corruption because it reduced the discretion of public officials significantly. Elbahnasawy (2014) studies the effect of e-government on corruption using a dynamic panel data model. His results suggest that e-government has a causal, negative effect on corruption. Moreover, Banerjee et al. (2014) find evidence from a field experiment that e-governance reduces leakages of public funds.

Furthermore, the ICTs have been used by the governments and non-government organizations to design websites that allow people to share their bribery experiences anonymously. Sometimes, the statistics collected from such websites are used to gauge the extent of corruption in a region, which are then used to pressurize policymakers to take actions to constrain corruption. For instance, in India, "I Paid a Bribe" encourages people to report the details (nature, location, frequency, values) of any bribes they were forced to pay and uses the information "to argue for improving governance systems and procedures, tightening law enforcement and regulation and thereby reduce the scope for corruption in obtaining services from the government" ("I Paid a Bribe" 2016). As of September 23, 2016, 100,412 cases of bribes amounting 2873.19 crores Indian rupees (about USD 430.67 million) were reported in 1,071 cities across India. Following the success of this portal, similar websites now exist for many countries around the world and are underway for several others. Even the governments have used online portals to allow anonymous reporting of bribes. One such initiative has been taken by the Anti-Corruption Commission of the Kingdom of Bhutan in the form of a web-page that can be used to report corruption anonymously.[3]

SOCIAL MEDIA, DEMOCRACY, AND CORRUPTION: SOME RECENT CASES

On December 17, 2010, a young vegetable merchant set himself ablaze in front of a municipal building in Tunisia to protest against the corrupt system and the government. The fire that he set upon himself would not only burn him but in months and years to come it would result in the entire Tunisia and most part of the Arab world burning. Since then an extensive body of research has emerged trying to explain the factors that made large-scale protests seeking democracy in Tunisia possible, which would spread over other Arab countries. And, the most important factor that undoubtedly emerges is the presence and an extensive use of social media.

So how did the self-immolation of a street vendor turn into the large-scale protests across Tunisia that paved the way for democracy in the country? There were restrictions on the Internet in Tunisia, including on YouTube, at the time of the incident. However, Facebook was not under close watch by the authorities at the time allowing a blogger to share a video recorded using a mobile phone that captured the protest held by the public in front of Sidi Bouzid's city hall against the way vendors were treated.[4] Within days the video was posted on Facebook, protesters across the country took to the street demanding the prosecution of the corrupt officials. Howard et al. (2011) have analyzed the data collected from Facebook, Twitter, and YouTube. Their analysis underscores the importance of social media in overthrowing the dictator in Tunisia. The tech-savvy young population (median age in Tunisia is 30 years) was able to effectively use social media. Social media also facilitated the participation of women in political debates –41 percent of Facebook and 30 percent of Twitter users in Tunisia were women. The protesters used social media extensively for political conversation and to share ideas in favor of democracy. Social media thus played an important role in shaping the political debate regarding democracy and helped the protestors pressurize the government. Furthermore, social media was also used to connect with the outside world not only the foreign news channels were provided with the information regarding what was happening in the country but the protesters also attracted followers and got support from people around the world. The role of the Internet and social media in the Tunisian revolution is further confirmed in a study by (Bruer et al., 2015). The authors find that the digital elites used the Internet and social media to bypass the barriers that prevented the transmission of information and aggregated and shared the stories of government abuses and oppressions to the masses.

In the same year on June 8, another revolution began on Facebook, a popular social media website, when a Google marketing executive named Wael Ghonim came across the photo of a bloodied and disfigured face while browsing Facebook. The disfigured face belonged to a 28-year-old Khaled Said, who was killed by the Egyptian police. Ghonim created a Facebook page titled "Kullena Khaled Said" (translated as "We are all Khaled Said") that was joined by more than 250,000 people in the next three months (The New York Times, 2012). Ghonim also used Twitter to spread the information to English-speaking audience abroad. On January 25, 2011, thousands of protesters gathered on Tahrir Square demanding the President Hosni Mubarak to step down. Social media was again recognized to be playing a key role in the success of the revolution that culminated in the overthrow of the Egyptian president (Howard et al., 2011). Like Tunisia, Egypt also has a young, tech-savvy population and women actively participated in the democracy debate – the median age is 24, and 36 percent of the Facebook users and 33 percent of actively tweeting Egyptian were females (Howard et al., 2011). An Egyptian protester's statement further sheds light on the importance of social media in the revolution: "We use Facebook to schedule the protests, Twitter to coordinate, and YouTube to tell the world." (The Guardian, 2016).

Next year, in 2011, the anti-corruption movement in India was placed among the top 10 news stories of the year by Time (2011) magazine. The movement gained huge support from the masses that was frustrated by reading the cases of corruption in newspapers every day. The protesters took advantage of the extensive use of social media, especially by the youth of the country, to mobilize support for the anti-corruption movement. A Facebook page titled "India Against Corruption" was created that provided a platform to the protesters to share their activities. The page was liked by more than 1.37 million people as of September 24, 2016. Social media has been recognized to be the most important factor that facilitated the largest anti-corruption movement possible and led to the huge crowds appearing to demand the passage of anti-corruption bill famously known as "Jan Lokpal Bill" (Bong et al., 2012; Jha, 2014).

Social media was said to have played a role in overthrowing the Communist Party in Moldova in 2009. Social media sites such as Facebook and Twitter provided means that facilitated coordination among the people against the fraudulent elections and resulted in the massive protests in the country (Shirky, 2011). Some scholars (*e.g.,*Hale, 2013) have, however, argued that the role of social media was much-hyped and overestimated in the 2009 Moldovan political upheaval and the social media played a secondary role at best. There have been other instances when the dissents were not successful, even though social media was employed to disseminate information and organize demonstrations. For instance, the Green Movement in Iran, where activists used technological means to coordinate against the miscount of votes for Mir Hossein Mousavi, failed in June 2009 due to the violent crackdown (Shirky, 2011). Another notable failure was the "Red Shirt" protest that erupted in Thailand in March 2010, where tech-savvy protesters used social media platforms such as Facebook and Twitter to share the information regarding protests and demonstrations throughout the country (Newley, 2011). A military crackdown on the protesters resulted in at least 90 deaths and more than 2,000 injuries. Yet, the charges against the Prime Minister Abhisit Vejjajiva, along with his deputy Suthep Thaugsuban and former army chief General Anupong Paojinda were dropped by the National Anti-Corruption Commission (NACC) on December 29, 2015, which was recognized as "a serious setback for accountability in the country" by Humans Rights Watch (hrw.org, 2016). These instances emphasize that while social media has the potential to affect political and democratic outcomes, political accountability and the strength of civil society is important for this potential to be realized. In Shirky (2011)'s words "the potential of social media lies mainly in their support of civil society and the public sphere."

INFORMATION CONTROL, SOCIAL MEDIA, AND CORRUPTION

Traditional media such as newspapers and television can easily be controlled and, hence, curbed or manipulated or both by corrupt and authoritarian governments. Authoritarian regimes in many countries have filtered public's access to information by controlling and even owning the media channels (Freedom House, 2009a). On the other hand, it is often very difficult, though not impossible, to control the information that is available on the Internet and can be shared through social media websites, blogs, and other ways. Furthermore, studies have argued that the ICTs can have significant impacts on democratic outcomes even under strict government controls and even when the activities on the net are under close watch (Sunstein, 2009).

Moreover, the ICTs allow for multi-way communication as opposed to only one-way communication facilitated by the traditional media. It has the potential to strengthen democracy by empowering individuals, facilitating the exchange of information and mobilization for a given cause (Diamond, 2010). Individuals can not only share corruption stories that were published in major newspapers but they can also share their own personal experience related to corruption (Jha & Sarangi, 2014). Social media thus enables individuals to share their experiences regarding petty corruption, which was not possible through traditional media. Besides the spread of information, social media also enables people to organize and protest against corrupt activities. For instance, Facebook can be used to create pages for a cause such as corruption, which can be shared by the creators to their friends and others. Those who are interested in anti-corruption movement can become members of the page and invite others to join. The platform, then, can be used to share corruption related stories to create awareness and organize protests against corruption. The page allows people to communicate about the location where anti-corruption activists can gather to protest against corruption in large numbers, which the policymakers may find difficult to ignore. Other social media sites such as Twitter and Google+ can be used to circulate the information about the upcoming events to the public. And, finally, YouTube and other video sharing sites can be used to share the videos of the events that may include any police brutality on activists. In recent years, multiple cases of police violence against citizens have been evidenced by activists using videos even in democratic countries such as the United States[5]. As discussed earlier, the Facebook page "India Against Corruption" was heavily used for communicating and organizing protests by the activists of the anti-corruption movement in India. Social media has another important advantage over traditional media. It enables individuals to share their personal experiences with friends and family and even strangers who have been in similar situations and therefore can empathize with the victims of corruption (Jha & Sarangi, 2014).

Qin et al. (2016) find social media to be an effective surveillance tool and provide further evidence on the role of social media in spreading the information regarding corrupt stories and organizing protests. They find that millions of posts published on Sina Weibo – the most widely used microblogging platform in China – explicitly discussed the cases of corruption. They further find that a greater use of Sina Weibo is positively associated with the likelihood of the occurrence of protest and large-scale conflicts.

Based on these characteristics of social media, some studies have recently linked social media with corruption. Figure 2 shows that there is a strong, negative correlation between Facebook penetration (data obtained from Jha & Sarangi, 2014) defined as the percentage of the population using Facebook and corruption. Though research on social media and corruption is still in infancy, the available evidence indicates that social media can be used as a powerful weapon against corruption.

The obvious reason behind the lack of studies exploring the relationship between social media and corruption is the presence of endogeneity – it is possible that not only social media affects corruption, but corrupt countries are also more likely to

Figure 2. Facebook penetration and corruption in 2012

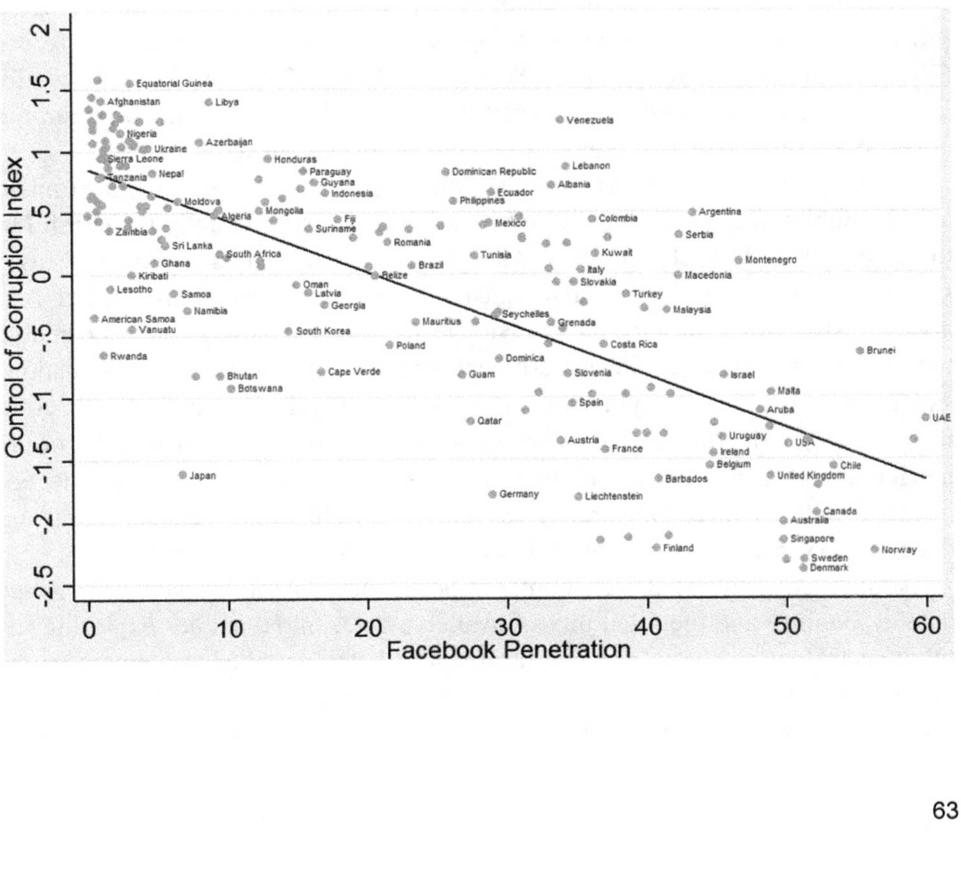

curb information dissemination, and hence, social media usage. In fact, even the democratic governments have recently placed restrictions on the information and the content that can be published and shared online. While some countries such as China, Belarus, and Iran have developed technologies that are used to filter and control the content that can be shared on the Internet, others have enacted vague laws that can be used to stifle the freedom of speech on the Internet (Freedom House, 2009a; Diamond, 2010).

Recently, some of the democratic countries that are considered to be the pioneers of the freedom of speech such as the United States and the United Kingdom have been subject to criticism for attacking freedom on the net by spying on users' activities online. One of the biggest stories of 2013 was the information leaked by Edward Snowden (the former National Security Agency contractor) who revealed that the National Security Agency (NSA) of the United States was running several surveillance programs that violated the privacy of Internet users. Government Communications Headquarters (GCHQ) of the United Kingdom has also been engaged in activities that compromise the privacy of the users and violates the promise that their private data would be inaccessible to criminals or the government. Both the NSA and the GCHQ have been accused of working on developing technologies that undermine the efficacy of Internet anonymizing tools and can be used to access encrypted traffic (Freedom House, 2015)[6]. Many Internet users may resort to self-censorship if they are afraid of being watched. For example, Freedom House (2015) documents that in the United States, one of the freest countries in the world, Internet users have resorted to stricter self-censorship after the information regarding government surveillance of online communications was leaked.

In many countries, there is a constant ongoing battle between the government and the public to control access to information that can potentially be harmful to the government. In such countries, while the government tries to conceal/censor specific information through technological means, social activists are quick to find a way to share relevant information. Bloggers and social activists have been able to share information regarding government corruption and human rights violations stealthily, sometimes anonymously and using virtual private networks (VPN). In many cases, by the time the government is able to take the information out of the net, it is already accessed by millions of the people and the harm is already done. For instance, millions of people already viewed "Under the Dome", an environmental documentary, before it was censored in China (Washington Post, 2015).

Additionally, studies also encounter important identification issues such as the data availability and the reliability of available data. Initial studies exploring the relationship between social media and corruption have attempted to overcome some of these issues to the extent possible and, despite their limitations, have provided important insights into the link between social media and corruption. For instance,

Jha and Sarangi (2014) use Facebook penetration across countries as a proxy for social media since the data on the latter was not available. In order to address endogeneity concerns, the study employs the adoption of communication technology in 1500 AD as an instrument for today's Internet penetration. Their identification assumption is that Internet penetration is responsible for the endogeneity in exploring the relationship between social media and corruption. The authors' argument behind this assumption is that while the exclusion of Internet penetration leads to omitted variables bias, its inclusion introduces endogeneity in the model. The authors show that social media has statistically and economically significant negative impact on corruption. The authors show that this relationship is robust across different samples of countries, including and excluding those which have placed severe restrictions on information dissemination, in general, and on Facebook or social media usage, in particular.

In another notable study, Enikolopov et al. (2016) show that anti-corruption blog posts negatively impacted the market returns of state-controlled companies in Russia. The authors go on to conclude that social media has the potential to negatively impact corruption even in countries where political competition is very limited and mass media is heavily controlled.

INTERNET FREEDOM, SOCIAL MEDIA, AND CORRUPTION

It is obvious from the above discussion that freedom on the net is critical for having desirable effects on corruption. In countries where people do not enjoy the freedom to share their opinion and views, the spread of anti-corruption ideas would be limited even if the number of Internet and social media users is substantial.

Freedom House collects information on the freedom that net users enjoy in different countries and assigns numerical scores on the basis of three broad categories. The first category, obstacles to access, evaluates the barriers to access to information created by infrastructural and economic limitations, legal and ownership controls as well as the freedom enjoyed by regulatory institutions. The second category, limits on content, measures the freedom to share contents on the net and analyzes the legal restrictions and technological means that are used to control the contents that can be published or shared, whether certain websites are blocked, as well as takes into account the diversity of online news media and the extent to which the use of digital technology is used to mobilize citizens. The final category, violations of user rights, deals with the "surveillance, privacy, and repercussions for online speech and activities, such as imprisonment, extralegal harassment, or cyberattacks" ("Freedom House Report" 2016). The score ranges from 0 (most free) to 100 (not free). Note that the index, besides freedom on the net, also includes the access to and the freedom that users enjoy in using technologies such as mobile phones and text messaging services that can be used to exchange information.

Figure 3 plots the relationship between Internet freedom using the index from Freedom House and corruption. In the figure, I have adjusted the scale of the index such that a higher value implies greater freedom on the net. Expectedly, we can see that there is a strong and negative correlation between freedom on the net and corruption across countries. The observed correlation in the figure indicates the need for further research to ascertain whether the observed correlation between Internet freedom and corruption is causal.

As argued earlier, although social media has undermined the government's ability to control the dissemination of information, governments around the world still censor the content that can be shared on the net using technological means and vague security laws (Freedom House, 2009a; Freedom House, 2015). Some countries, such as China (where the Chinese Communist Party exercises tight control over the traditional media), have actively launched crackdown on social media activism to eliminate the threat imposed by social media (Fortune, 2013). Hence, one should expect that in countries with greater Internet freedom, social media should have a

Figure 3. Freedom on the net and corruption in 2014

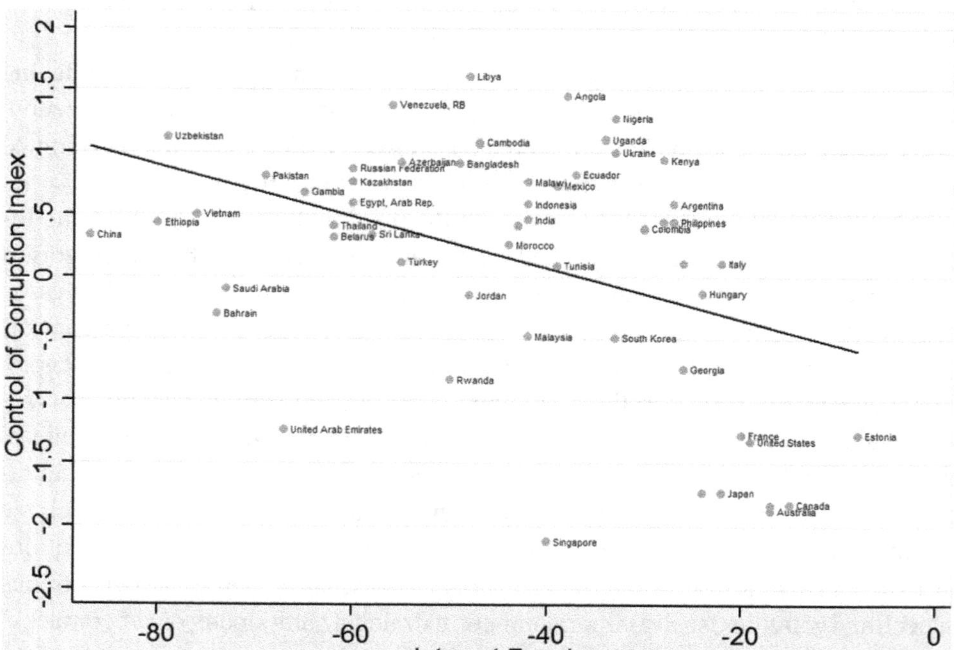

stronger effect on corruption because in such countries bloggers and journalists can share news exposing corrupt practices without fear. On the other hand, countries where the government has near monopoly over information or where there is a threat to those who share articles and news exposing the corrupt practices of the government officials, cases involving political and bureaucratic corruption are unlikely to come out to the public and hence the effects of social media on corruption might be very limited. Future research should investigate the implications that the government's control over information can have for the effects of social media on corruption.

It is also noteworthy here that studies have found the evidence that a free press can have significant negative impacts on corruption (Brunetti & Weder, 2003). Arguably, free press reduces the cost of fighting corruption and acts as an external control of corruption. In many countries, journalists and bloggers are under threat of legal actions and being imprisoned (Freedom House, 2015). Although sharing information on the net provides more anonymity than newspaper and TV journalism, it is not entirely anonymous given recent developments in technology that are used by governments to attack the anonymity of net users. Under these circumstances, it is plausible that an increased anonymity and greater freedom on the net will result in a much greater effect of social media on corruption than the effect that we observe now.

DISCUSSION AND CONCLUSION

The Internet freedom is in danger across the world. According to Freedom House's "Freedom on the Net 2015" report, freedom on the net has been declining over time around the world for last 5 consecutive years. Out of 65 countries, more than 40 have some restrictions in place relating to political, religious, and social issues that can be shared on the web. Many countries have imprisoned people for sharing information related to such issues. Not only the authoritarian regimes but also democracies have been criticized for spying on the activities of net users and violating their privacy.

The role of the new ICTs in augmenting the individual freedom has been so significant that Diamond (2010) goes as far as terming them the "liberation technology" – defined as "any form of information and communication technology (ICT) that can expand political, social, and economic freedom." In recent years, social media has played a profound role in promoting democracy around the world and therefore has been subject to restrictions. The activities of net users have been scrutinized and spied upon. A greater control over what can be shared will discourage people to use the Internet and join social media platforms. In many countries, the governments have attempted to stifle the freedom of speech on social media sites and blogs using legal means and by designing vague laws. Such laws are likely to prevent people from becoming members of social media sites and hence limit the exchange of information. The privacy settings of social media can play an important role in alleviating these concerns. Recently, many social media sites and short messaging services have developed and adopted technology to preserve the anonymity of individuals, which may partially address some of these concerns. For instance, Whatsapp, a leading short messaging services provider, has enabled end-to-end encryption that ensures that the conversation between two people cannot be ready by anyone else, not even Whatsapp ("Whats App FAQ" 2016). End-to-end encryption is now also offered by other communication platforms such as Facebook messenger and Viber (Wired, 2016). The civil society must fight to preserve the freedom of speech and the freedom to share ideas, and the degree of anonymity enjoyed by net users is significant in this regard. As Diamond (2010) states, technological progress alone will not decide the winner in the race of democrats versus autocrats. Rather, the role of political organizations and economic forces will be significant in determining the outcome and it is people, organization, and governments that will decide who wins. The democratic governments around the world must support the freedom on the net not only in their own countries but also in other countries. Towards this end, Hillary Clinton, secretary of state of the United States, declared in her famous speech delivered on January 21, 2010: "We stand for a single Internet where all of humanity has equal access to knowledge and ideas" (Foreign Policy, 2010).

Corruption is an important concern for both the policymakers and the citizens around the globe because of its undesirable effects on outcomes such as economic growth, poverty, and inequality (Mauro, 1985; Gupta et al., 2002). A number of factors such as the quality of institutions, economic development, democratic and cultural factors, and openness among others (see Treisman (2000) for a review) and, more recently, the ICTs have been identified to be the determinants of corruption. Social media is amongst the newest factors that have been shown by researchers to negatively impact corruption.

At the same time, freedom on the net is under threat in many parts of the world. Freedom on the net is critical for the effects of social media on corruption to be fully realized. With countries around the world trying to control the way information is being shared, the effects of social media on corruption is likely to be undermined. It is also important to note that some authoritarian regimes may allow some independent reporting simply because it may actually help them by unearthing any upcoming threat, information regarding which can be used to pacify discontented citizens by improving local level governance. For example, the Chinese Communist Party leaders in China use media as a watchdog to monitor the activities of subordinate officials so the problems can be identified and solved before they turn into popular public unrest. The media is, however, prevented from reporting the wrongdoings of higher levels of government (Shirk, 2011). Recent studies have developed models to help explain such censorship practices. For instance, Lorentzen (2014), using a formal model, shows that an authoritarian regime may benefit from allowing the media to report the misconducts of low-level officials, while, at the same time, controlling the amount of information such that citizens do not have enough information to determine whether a revolt will be successful. Regarding social media, Qin et al. (2016) find evidence that the Chinese government regulates social media to ensure that there is no threat to the stability of the regime. It is important for the civil society to recognize and act against such censorship practices.

There is a need for further research that explores the complementarity between Internet freedom and social media usage in the context of their effects on corruption. It will also be an important exercise to investigate the implications of the interaction between institutional quality and social media on corruption. Furthermore, while there is ample evidence that the Internet is being used by the governments around the world to promote transparency, the use of social media by governments in promoting e-participation is still in infancy (Bonsón et al., 2012). The use of the ICTs and social media is not ubiquitous and there is a room for many countries to improve infrastructural quality that enhances public's access to the ICTs (Dutta et al., 2015). Since many of these countries are mired in corruption, it would be advisable for the governments in these countries to implement policies that enhance the access to the ICTs and use them to promote transparency and accountability.

REFERENCES

Ades, A., & Di Tella, R. (1999). Rents, Competition, and Corruption. *The American Economic Review*, *89*(4), 982–993. doi:10.1257/aer.89.4.982

Andersen, T. B., Bentzen, J., Dalgaard, C. J., & Selaya, P. (2011). Does the Internet Reduce Corruption? Evidence from US States and across Countries. *The World Bank Economic Review*, *25*(3), 387–417. doi:10.1093/wber/lhr025

Banerjee, A., Duflo, E., Imbert, C., Mathew, S., & Pande, R. (2014). Can E-Governance Reduce Capture of Public Programs? *Poverty Action Lab*. Retrieved from https://www.povertyactionlab.org/evaluation/enhancing-local-public-service-delivery-through-financial-reform-india%E2%80%99s-employment

Bertot, J. C., Jaeger, P. T., & Grimes, J. M. (2010). Using ICTs to Create a Culture of Transparency: E-government and Social Media as Openness and Anti-corruption Tools for Societies. *Government Information Quarterly*, *27*(3), 264–271. doi:10.1016/j.giq.2010.03.001

Bhatnagar, S. (2003). E-government and Access to Information. *Global Corruption Report*, *2003*, 24–32.

Bong, S., Chung, K., Parkinson, K., Peppard, A., Rabbach, J., & Thiher, N. (2012). *Analyzing Social Media Momentum*. Workshop in International Public Affairs.

Bonsón, E., Torres, L., Royo, S., & Flores, F. (2012). Local E-government 2.0: Social Media and Corporate Transparency in Municipalities. *Government Information Quarterly*, *29*(2), 123–132. doi:10.1016/j.giq.2011.10.001

Bruer, A., Landman, T., & Farquhar, D. (2015). Social Media and Protest Mobilization: Evidence from the Tunisian Revolution. *Democratization*, *22*(4), 764–792. doi:10.1080/13510347.2014.885505

Brunetti, A., & Weder, B. (2003). A Free Press is Bad News for Corruption. *Journal of Public Economics*, *87*(7), 1801–1824. doi:10.1016/S0047-2727(01)00186-4

Caselli, F., & Coleman, W. J. II. (2001). Cross-Country Technology Diffusion: The Case of Computers. *The American Economic Review*, *91*(2), 328–335. doi:10.1257/aer.91.2.328

Chakrabarty, B., & Hazra, S. (2016). *Winning the Mandate: The Indian Experience*. India: SAGE Publications.

Diamond, L. (2010). Liberation Technology. *Journal of Democracy*, *21*(3), 69–83. doi:10.1353/jod.0.0190

DiRienzo, C. E., Das, J., Cort, K. T., & Burbridge, J. Jr. (2007). Corruption and the Role of Information. *Journal of International Business Studies, 38*(2), 320–332. doi:10.1057/palgrave.jibs.8400262

Dutta, S., López-Claros, A., & Mia, I. (Eds.). (2015). *The Global Information Technology Report: ICTs for Inclusive Growth.* World Economic Forum.

Elbahnasawy, N. G. (2014). E-government, Internet Adoption, and Corruption: An Empirical Investigation. *World Development, 57*, 114–126. doi:10.1016/j.worlddev.2013.12.005

Enikolopov, R., Petrova, M., & Sonin, K. (2016). Social Media and Corruption. *CEPR Discussion Paper No. DP11263.* Retrieved from http://ssrn.com/abstract=2777570

Foreignpolicy.com. (2010). Internet freedom. Retrieved from http://foreignpolicy.com/2010/01/21/internet-freedom/

Fortune (2013). Social media activism. Retrieved from http://fortune.com/2013/09/12/chinas-tragic-crackdown-on-social-media-activism/

Freedom House (2009a). Freedom on the Net: A Global Assessment of Internet and Digital Media.

Freedom House (2009b). Freedom of the Press 2009.

Freedom House (2015). Freedom on the Net 2015.

Greenberg, A. (2016). 'Secret conversations:' end-to-end encryption comes to Facebook messenger. *Wired.* Retrieved from https://www.wired.com/2016/07/secret-conversations-end-end-encryption-facebook-messenger-arrived/

Gupta, S., Davoodi, H., & Alonso-Terme, R. (2002). Does Corruption Affect Income Inequality and Poverty? *Economics of Governance, 3*(1), 23–45. doi:10.1007/s101010100039

Hale, H. E. (2013). Did the Internet Break the Political Machine? Moldova's 2009 "Twitter Revolution that Wasn't". *Demokratizatsiya (Washington, D.C.), 21*(4), 481–505.

Howard, P. N., Duffy, A., Freelon, D., Hussain, M. M., Mari, W., & Maziad, M. (2011). Opening Closed Regimes: What was the Role of Social Media during the Arab Spring? Retrieved from http://ssrn.com/abstract=2595096

Hrw.org. (2016). *Thailand: New whitewash of 2010 political violence.* Retrieved from https://www.hrw.org/news/2016/01/07/thailand-new-whitewash-2010-political-violence

I Paid a Bribe (2016). *I Paid a Bribe*. Retrieved from http://www.ipaidabribe.com/#gsc.tab=0F

Jha, C. K. (2014). Can Social Media and Internet Help Reduce Corruption? *Ideas for India*. Retrieved from http://ideasforindia.in/article.aspx?article_id=353

Jha, C. K., & Sarangi, S. (2014). Social Media, Internet and Corruption. Retrieved from http://ssrn.com/abstract=2391904

Jorgenson, D. W. (2001). Information Technology and the US Economy. *The American Economic Review*, *91*(1), 1–32. doi:10.1257/aer.91.1.1

Kaufmann, D., Kraay, A., & Mastruzzi, M. (2010). *The Worldwide Governance Indicators: A Summary of Methodology, Data and Analytical Issues*. World Bank Policy Research Working Paper.

Keliher, M., & Wu, H. (2015). How to discipline 90 million people. *The Atlantic*. Retrieved from http://www.theatlantic.com/international/archive/2015/04/xi-jinping-china-corruption-political-culture/389787/

Kolstad, I., & Wiig, A. (2009). Is transparency the key to reducing corruption in resource-rich countries? *World Development*, *37*(3), 521–532. doi:10.1016/j.worlddev.2008.07.002

Kumari, D. L., & Kumari, K. S. (2016). Public Distribution System in India: An Overview. *Indian Journal of Applied Research*, *5*(5).

Lenhart, A. (2015). *Teens, Social Media & Technology Overview 2015*. Washington, DC: Pew Research Center.

Lio, M.-C., Liu, M.-C., & Ou, Y.-P. (2011). Can the Internet Reduce Corruption? A Cross-country Study based on Dynamic Panel Data Models. *Government Information Quarterly*, *28*(1), 47–53. doi:10.1016/j.giq.2010.01.005

Lorentzen, P. (2014). China's Strategic Censorship. *American Journal of Political Science*, *58*(2), 402–414. doi:10.1111/ajps.12065

Madden, M. (2010). *Older Adults and Social Media*. Washington, DC: Pew Research Center.

Mauro, P. (1995). Corruption and Growth. *The Quarterly Journal of Economics*, *110*(3), 681–712. doi:10.2307/2946696

Mufson, S. (2015). This documentary went viral in China. Then it was censored. It won't be forgotten. *Washington Post.* Retrieved from https://www.washingtonpost.com/news/energy-environment/wp/2015/03/16/this-documentary-went-viral-in-china-then-it-was-censored-it-wont-be-forgotten/?utm_term=.fdbb8ae67fb4

Newley. (2011). *Social media and Thailand's red shirt protests.* Retrieved from http://newley.com/2011/01/25/social-media-and-thailand%E2%80%99s-red-shirt-protests/

Oliner, S. D., & Sichel, D. E. (2000). The Resurgence of Growth in the Late 1990s: Is Information Technology the Story? *The Journal of Economic Perspectives*, *14*(4), 3–22. doi:10.1257/jep.14.4.3

Porter, J. (2008). *Designing for the Social Web.* New Riders Press.

Qin, B., Strömberg, D., & Wu, Y. (2016). The Political Economy of Social Media in China.

Salbu, S. R. (2001). Information Technology in the War against International Bribery and Corruption: The Next Frontier of Institutional Reform. *Harvard Journal on Legislation*, *38*(1), 67–102.

Shirk, S. (2011). Changing Media, Changing China. In S. Shirk (Ed.), Changing Media, Changing China, 1–37. New York: Oxford University Press.

Shirky, C. (2011). The Political Power of Social Media: Technology, the Public Sphere, and Political Change. In *Foreign Affairs* (pp. 28–41).

Statista (2016). Number of worldwide social network users. Retrieved from https://www.statista.com/statistics/278414/number-of-worldwide-social-network-users/

Sunstein, C. R. (2009). *Republic.com 2.0.* Princeton University Press.

Tanzi, V. (1998). Corruption Around the World: Causes, Consequences, Scope, and Cures. *IMF Staff Papers*, *45*(4), 559–594. doi:10.2307/3867585

Tepper, M. (2003). The Rise of Social Software. *netWorker*, *7*(3), 18–23. doi:10.1145/940830.940831

Sedghi, A. (2014). Facebook: 10 years of social networking, in numbers. *The Guardian.* Retrieved from https://www.theguardian.com/news/datablog/2014/feb/04/facebook-in-numbers-statistics

Shearlaw, M. (2016). Egypt five years on: was it ever a 'social media revolution'? *The Guardian.* Retrieved from https://www.theguardian.com/world/2016/jan/25/egypt-5-years-on-was-it-ever-a-social-media-revolution

Vargas, J.A. (2012). Spring Awakening: How an Egyptian revolution began on Facebook. The New York Times. Retrieved from http://www.nytimes.com/2012/02/19/books/review/how-an-egyptian-revolution-began-on-facebook.html

Time (2011). The Top 10 Everything of 2011. Retrieved from http://content.time.com/time/specials/packages/article/0,28804,2101344_2101368_2101650,00.html

Treisman, D. (2000). The Causes of Corruption: A Cross-National Study. *Journal of Public Economics*, *76*(3), 399–457. doi:10.1016/S0047-2727(99)00092-4

United Nations. (2014). Information and Communications Technologies for Inclusive Social and Economic Development. Geneva: UN.

Uslaner, E. M. (2005). Trust and Corruption. In J. G. Lambsdorff, M. Taube & M. Schramm (Eds.) The New Institutional Economics of Corruption (pp. 76-92). USA: Routledge.

WhatsApp. (2016). End-to-end Encryption. Retrieved from: https://www.whatsapp.com/faq/en/general/28030015

Zurcher, A. (2016). US election: Why is Clinton's foundation so controversial? *BBC*. Retrieved from http://www.bbc.com/news/election-us-2016-37168505

KEY TERMS AND DEFINITIONS

Corruption: The misuse of entrusted power by government officials or elected political leaders for illegitimate personal gains.

Facebook: A popular social media website.

Information and Communication Technology: The forms of technology that allow people to transmit information and communicate with one another and/or a broad general audience.

Information Control: Restrictions placed by the government authorities on the content, the audience, or the way the information can be shared on the Internet, social media, traditional media, and elsewhere.

Internet Freedom: The ability of Internet users to express their opinions and share ideas and content freely and without restrictions using social media websites, news portals, blogs, and other means using the Internet.

Multi-Way Communication: A form of communication in which more than one (often several) involved parties can exchange information with one another.

Social Media: A form of the information and communication technologies that enables users to access, create, and share information with the members from both within and outside their network.

Traditional Media: The form of media such as the print and broadcast media that has traditionally (before recent developments in information and communication technologies) been used to transmit information and can be used for only one-way communication.

ENDNOTES

1 This chapter focuses on the effects of the ICTs, in general, and social media—in particular—on democratic and political outcomes, with an emphasis on corruption. The effects of the ICTs on economic outcomes, such as economic growth, productivity, human capital and manufacturing trade openness, are well documented in the literature (Oliner & Sichel, 2000; Jorgenson, 2001; Caselli & Coleman, 2001). Readers interested in the effects of the ICTs on economic outcomes may refer to these studies.

2 Visit http://info.worldbank.org/governance/wgi/index.aspx#home for details regarding the construction of the CCI.

3 http://www.anti-corruption.org.bt/?q=node/295

4 See the link for details about the protest: https://www.washingtonpost.com/world/in-tunisia-act-of-one-fruit-vendor-sparks-wave-of-revolution-through-arab-world/2011/03/16/AFjfsueB_story.html (Retrieved August 8, 2016)

5 One such example can be found at: http://www.npr.org/2016/07/07/485138688/activists-use-video-to-document-police-violence

6 Also see https://www.theguardian.com/world/2013/sep/05/nsa-gchq-encryption-codes-security?CMP=share_btn_tw

Chapter 4
There Is an App for That Too: Citizen-Centric Approach to Combating Corruption in the Digital Age through the Use of ICTs

Lloyd G. Waller
University of the West Indies (Mona), Jamaica

ABSTRACT

Combating corruption is critical to the economic and social development of a country. Recent discussions surrounding strategies to combat corruption now include the role of information and communication technologies (ICTs). Currently, there is a growing body of research on the role of ICTs to combat corruption, however scholarly research on the use of these technologies by citizens in this regard is wholly lacking. The objective of this study is to address this gap in the literature as well as to popularize citizen-centric empowerment strategies to combat corruption around the world.

DOI: 10.4018/978-1-5225-2019-1.ch004

INTRODUCTION

The insurmountable complex web of interrelated causes, consequences, and measures regarding the problem of corruption has for years been a critical area of research and policy interest globally (McMullan, 1961; Leff, 1964; Nye, 1967; Rose-Ackerman, 1978, 1999, 2008; Svensson, 2005; Akçay, 2006; Donchev & Ujhelyi, 2009; Ata & Arvas, 2011). Recent discussions regarding solutions to the problem of corruption now include the role of information and communication technologies (ICTs). Scholarly research related to the use of ICTs to combat corruption has largely been located within the electronic governance for development conceptual framework (Heeks, 2001). Such a framework, articulates how and in what ways ICTs can be used to enhance good governance and development. Within the context of combating corruption, this framework has typically focused on either:

1. The use of ICTs by the state to create an open government to facilitate transparency and accountability with the use of websites that allow citizens to access information about government related actors, issues and events (e-government related issues); or
2. The use of ICTs by the state to monitor and control government activities through the automation of state internal operations (e-administration related issues).

There exists a paucity of scholarly research on the use of ICTs by citizens to combat corruption. This I refer to as a citizen-centric approach to the use of ICTs to combat corruption. The present paper seeks to address this gap by making a unique contribution to the emerging scholarly literature on the use of ICTs to combat corruption. The following research question was used to guide this study (1) How and in what ways have citizens used ICTs to combat corruption?

BACKGROUND AND CONTEXT

In the last five decades or so, there has been considerable interest in efforts to combat corruption (whether political[1], bureaucratic[2], or economic[3]). Various disciplines and professions from all over the world have been committed to this project (Nye, 1967; Huntington, 1968; Akçay, 2006; Ata & Arvas, 2011; Donchev & Ujhelyi, 2009; Leff, 1964; Macrae, 1982; Mauro, 1995; McMullan, 1961; Myrdal, 1970; Nye, 1967; Rose-Ackerman, 1978, 1999, 2008; Andvig et al., 2000; Coolidge & Rose-Ackerman, 2000; Ades & Di Tella, 1999). Two main objectives of this project have been to address both developmental failures and democratic shortfalls associated with corruption (See also McGee & Gaventa, 2010). Since the mid-1990s, research on transparency and accountability has made a case for the link between corruption and development (Mauro, 1995; Akçay, 2006; Habib & Zurawicki, 2002; Wei, 2000; Alam, 1995; Husted, 1999; Lee et al., 2005; Campos, Lien, & Pradhan, 1999). Indeed, enhancing accountability and transparency have emerged as two critical ways to address these problems (Kuriyan, et al., 2011; McGee & Gaventa, 2010; Galtung & Pope, 1999). According to Kuriyan et al. (2011), activities to enhance transparency and accountability help to improve the quality of governance and support democratic outcomes (See also Fox, 2007).

Generally speaking, research on corruption has typically been guided by various theoretical and conceptual frameworks, which vary from the principal-agent model and psychoanalyst approach (Spotnitz, 1952; Ormont, 1995; Cohen, Nelson & Walsh, 2002; Lear, 1998) to several economic growth models (including Coase, 1960; Cheung, 1982, 1983; Williamson, 1975, 1985; North, 1990, 2005; Hirschman, 1967, 1970). Such frameworks have been instrumental in exploring and understanding the determinants of corruption and in so doing have built a platform for formulating strategies for combating corruption. To date, however, many strategies formulated from such frameworks have been unsuccessful as evidenced by the static or slow movement of countries along Transparency International's Corruption Perception Index (CPI). Since 2001, we have seen the emergence of techno-centric and technological deterministic frameworks that have sought to explore, understand, and explain various aspects of combating corruption (Heeks, 2001; Bertot, Jaeger, & Grimes, 2010). Such an approach has focussed on Information and Communication Technologies (ICTs). The present study locates itself with this framework.

INFORMATION AND COMMUNICATION TECHNOLOGIES FOR GOOD GOVERNANCE AND DEVELOPMENT

Information and communication technologies are a range of tools that are used to gather, communicate, store, retrieve, exchange, process, analyse, and share information. ICTs generally include: computers and wireless devices, peripherals and storage instruments; software applications; network infrastructures, and the technical protocols they require such as SMTP, TCP/IP, FTP; particularly significant are security (SSL) and privacy (P2K) protocols for e-commerce and commercial surveillance (cookies etc.) as well as legal and regulatory frameworks such as patents, copyright etc. (i.e., these are not contextual to ICT: they are integral). Research on the use of ICTs to fight corruption is generally located within the emerging and promising electronic governance conceptual framework (Heeks, 2001). Shailendra, Palvia and Sharma (2007) defined electronic governance (e-governance) as the use of ICTs at various levels of the government and the public sector and beyond, for the purpose of enhancing good governance (p. 2) and, which has wider implications for development (Neumayer, 2003). According to Sheridan and Riley (2006), electronic governance is a broad term that encompasses several constructs. These include e-government or e-services, e-administration, and e-society.

Electronic Government

Electronic government (e-government or in some circles e-services) is the use of information and communication technologies (ICTs) to provide government services to the public. This can include government to citizen interactions (G2C) such as paying taxes online (e-taxes), government to business (G2B) and government to government interactions (G2G), for example, government's procurement of goods and services from the private sector, between government agencies or between government agencies and other non-government bodies (e-procurement), government to employee interactions (G2E) such as the provision of online services for employees in a government agency (e-services). It can also include government to donor interactions (G2D) such as the provision of information about government spending of donor funds.

With e-government, ICTs are used by the state to create an open government thereby providing easy access to information about government related actors, issues and events. Based on the literature reviewed e-government projects and programmes have helped to promote transparency and accountability in several countries around the world; and, there is an emerging body of work in this area of e-governance (Bhatnagar, 2003, 2004; Relly & Sabharwal, 2009; Bertot, Jaeger, & Grimes, 2010; World Bank, 2004; Andersen, 2009; Vinod, 1999; Soper, 2007; Bertot et al., 2012).

E-Administration

Governments around the world are currently employing ICTs to automate their internal operations and business processes with the aim of making them more efficient, effective, productive, as well as to enhance accountability and transparency. This is referred to as electronic administration or e-administration. With e-administration, ICTs have been used to monitor and to some extent control employee behaviour. The existing literature suggests that this has led to greater government accountability and transparency, and has been determined as an effective means of combating corruption (Devanathan, 2003; Bertot, Jaeger, & Grimes, 2010). Bertot et al. (2010), in an article on the role of ICTs in enhancing transparency and reducing corruption provided a veritable menu of empirical research which demonstrates the legitimate value of e-administration. From Bhatngar's (2003) work on economic land reform systems in Karnataka, India and follow-up research undertaken by the World Bank (2004) to research on the tax system in Pakistan and the Philippines (Andersen, 2009); Shim and Ecom's (2008) work on electronic procurement in Chile as well as Kim and Cho's (2005) and Lee's (2005) cutting edge research on the Seoul Metropolitan Government's Online Procurement Enhancement for civil application (OPEN) system; it is clear that ICTs do indeed provide the means by which to combat corruption within government agencies.

E-Society

Not much scholarly or policy research has been undertaken to explore the use of ICTs by citizens, business, civil society and communities to combat corruption. Such issues are usually located within the very sparse scholarly space of 'e-society'. Electronic society (e-society), part of the general e-governance framework, is concerned with how and in what ways citizens, civil society, businesses and communities are empowered through the use of ICTs to achieve a common interest or goal such as e-governance, e-democracy, e-learning, e-business, or e-health (Heeks, 2001). E-Society is based on information, knowledge, access, use and availability of ICTs to citizens (Ibid). Electronic Society is a relatively unchartered but critical area within the ICT for development literature generally and, the e-governance literature specifically. The literature on e-society remains in an inchoate stage of development. E-society offers researchers a conceptual framework to explore the use of ICTs as an empowerment tool to achieve good governance and democracy. This e-society conceptual framework guides this study, which explores a citizen-centric empowerment approach to combat corruption through the use of ICTs.

Bekri, et al. (2011) has observed that this is indeed a grey area in the corruption literature. According to Bekri, et al. (2011) more needs to be done to move beyond the existing government-centric approach to combat corruption and, there is a need to explore and popularize the nuances surrounding how and in what ways citizens can take action against corruption themselves (p. 2). Bekri, et al. (2011) further observed that ICT's are effective tools for civic engagement that may address any resource constraints of governments around the world [as well as citizens] in combating corruption given that these technologies "greatly reduce the physical and logistical costs associated with the social organisation of combating corruption (p. 7). ICTs, they further articulate, can help citizens to:

...enhance the rate and scope of investigation once provided by professional journalists. These platforms, enabled by online networks, technologies and social media are engaging Internet and mobile phone users to demand transparency and making corrupt behaviour risky for public and private sector actors alike. Social media

will undoubtedly play a central role in combating corruption in the twenty-first century. Such technologies have enabled booms in the quantity, quality and speed of communication, as their widespread use has granted political voice to millions, motivating masses and reinvigorating efforts to fight corruption. The influence of well-known and emerging social media platforms is expanding. Political activists, campaigners and civil society organisations are in an unprecedented position to leverage their impact. (Bekri, et al., 2011, p. 3)

Similar sentiments were echoed by Gronlund et al, (2010) who, in an edited text published by the The Swedish Program for ICT in Developing Regions (SPIDER), highlighted and drew attention to the notion that an empowered citizenry is the best way to fight corruption. The 2010 publication started a discussion which sought to research, document, disseminate and popularize how and in what ways ICTs can be used by citizens to combat corruption. Since the SPIDER publication, there have been several working papers, technical reports and other non-scholarly documents that have emerged surrounding the use of ICTs by citizens to combat corruption. None have, however, made the leap to the scholarly space. This chapter now continues that work and also addresses that gap.

Indeed, this chapter is significant in that it is expected further help researchers, policy makers and more importantly citizens to: understand the landscape of corruption and available ICT related mitigating tools; identify, understand, and; present lessons as well as best practices for others to follow in the use of ICTs by citizens to combat corruption. Such a holistic approach to fight corruption can help to extend the range of options currently available, particularly for citizens, many of whom would want to participate in this critical fight for good governance and development. This research is believed to serve to extend the avenues available to governments in their attempts to combat corruption. In other words, significance of this research, therefore, is to fill the aforementioned intellectual gap while at the same time create a repository of policy and practical knowledge for those interested in this aspect of combating corruption. Finally, it is expected that this chapter will also serve to start a conversation in the academic space regarding e-society and in so doing, expand the current conceptual framework established by Heeks (2001).

RESEARCH DESIGN

Not much is known about the use of ICTs by citizens to combat corruption. Concepts are neither conceptualized nor operationalized and patterns are not established or organised in any specific way. Thus there is a need to provide insights and understanding about this phenomenon. Therefore, for the purpose of this study, the exploratory research design was used to explore this phenomenon. Exploratory research designs often rely on secondary data such as reviewing available literature. For this reason, one of the more popular textual analysis methodologies available in qualitative research – document analysis, was employed.

Methodology, Sampling and Methods

The document analysis methodology is a systematic procedure for reviewing or evaluating documents-both printed and electronic. Like other analytical methods in qualitative research, document analysis requires that data be examined and interpreted in order to elicit meaning, gain understanding, and insights as well as develop empirical knowledge about a particular object, subject, process, event or phenomenon (Bowen, 2009, p. 27).

The sample for this study consisted of 22 books, 42 journal articles, 21 reports, 54 websites, 18 Facebook pages, 31 YouTube videos, 28 online news portals and 48 blogposts. The selection of sample was based on the purposive sampling technique. The literature was surveyed to determine the overall approach for the use of ICTs to combat corruption within the last two decades with a particular interest in e-society related activities. The documents that were analysed for this study underwent a process of data reduction - examining the material, and interpreting the texts through an iterative process which combines elements of the content analysis, thematic analysis and the constant comparative analysis of grounded theory. Through this process, various themes and sub-themes were identified. These are presented in the section below.

COMBATING CORRUPTION WITH ICTS: EMPOWERMENT SOLUTIONS FOR CITIZENS

Though not a panacea nor a black box, ICTs such as mobile communications and the Internet driven by software application (apps), can enable and empower citizens with the tools to participate more directly in the democratic space in counties around the world (Hoque, 2005; Pathak & Prasad, 2005; Pathak, Singh, Belwal, & Smith, 2007; Pathak, Singh, Belwal, Naz, & Smith, 2008; Bertot, Jaeger, & Grimes, 2010; Backus, 2001; Andersen et al., 2010; Bertot et al., 2010; Shim & Eom, 2009; Waller & Taylor, 2013; Forestier, Grace, & Kenny, 2002; Gascó-Hernández, Equiza-Lopez & Acevedo-Ruiz, 2007; Soper, 2007; Opoku-Mensah, 2000; Rahman, 2007). More specifically and, as it relates to combating corruption, from the data analysed, it was observed that ICTs can be used as a public education tool that can empower citizens with the tools to raise awareness about the importance of transparency, accountability and controlling corruption for development (Oye, 2013; Avila, Feigenblatt, & Heacock, 2010; Sanford & Rose, 2007; Kuriyan, et al., 2011). ICTs can also empower citizens with the means to monitor the activities of elected officials, government agencies, and agents of the state; mobilisation against corrupt officials as well as report on acts of corruption. In the next section, we will explore these and other experiences in the use of ICTs to enhance transparency and accountability as well as combating corruption by citizens.

Citizen-Centric Apps for Combat Corruption through Public Education

The use of software applications for public awareness about corruption was one of the major themes that emerged from the data that was analysed for this study. It is well established that transparency and accountability are key goals of good governance (Woods, 2000; Santiso, 2001; Ndou, 2004). Several studies have revealed that in countries where this practice is present, there exists a healthy democracy and a substantive pathway to development (Rivera-Batiz, 2002; Shim & Eom, 2008; Sen, 2014). In many countries around the word, such practices are not regularly observed leading to corruption, which undermines the development process of that country. A lack of awareness about the importance of transparency, accountability and strategies to combat corruption can sometimes be blamed for the absence of these practices themselves. According to Asiimwe et al. (2013):

Transparency and accountability are known to reduce corruption by making procedures more open and forcing governments to assume more responsibility for improving and controlling service delivery to citizens and companies and to reduce the opportunities to abuse positions of power for private gains. (Asiimwe et al., 2013, p. 39)

In many societies, particularly developing societies, a lack of transparency and accountability in government and corrupt practices among agents of the state are recognised as the norm largely as the result of:

1. The lip-service paid to these corrupt acts by agents of the state, many of whom benefit from corruption;
2. The absence of any information dissemination or awareness/sensitization activities across the agents of socialization - the home, school, groups or the media - particularly in depressed and rural communities (low-resource communities);

3. The education/reasoning or understanding level of large portions of the population; and/or
4. The negative cultural milieu associated with reporting corruption in many of these societies.

It has, however, been observed that as the awareness of corruption increases, so does the understanding of its negative effects on political, economic and social reforms and this understanding can change the behaviour and attitudes of citizens (Oye, 2013).

In instances where government intervention is weak or wholly lacking as it relates to combating corruption in some countries around the world, many international organization and civil society organisations operating in these countries have taken up the responsibility of making citizen aware about the importance of transparency, accountability and controlling corruption for development (See for example National Integrity Action, 2013). More recently it has been observed that public education campaigns using ICTs such as the television, radio, Internet, mobile phones images, sounds, videos and texts such as photo-stories, or animations podcasts and YouTube video, to name a few, have been successful in raising awareness and enhancing peoples' knowledge-base about transparency, accountability and combating corruption (Cecchini & Scott, 2003). More specifically and, based on the data analyzed, ICTs have been successfully used to raise awareness about the importance and impact of accountability and transparency initiatives on poor peoples' "well-being" in many countries around the world (Kuriyan et al., 2011, p. 7). ICTs such as the mobile phone for example, offer an inexpensive, uncomplicated and multi-platform to disseminate information about critical corruption related issues, over a vast space, in a relatively short period of time.

Several African, Caribbean, Indian and Latin American countries, have and are utilizing ICTs as a means of sharing information between and among citizens, civil society organisations, groups, individuals, the media, and other development stakeholders about corrupt practices. One example of this is the Website http://voices-against-corruption.ning.com/ which operates in many of these countries. Voices against Corruption is an initiative of the Global Youth Anti-Corruption (GYAC), which is "a global network of young leaders, journalists, artists and ICT experts from civil society who work to improve transparency and social accountability for better governance" (GYAC, 2011, p. 1). This website provides its members with a space "to share knowledge and experience", develop their capacity and knowledge-base "in various governance areas" using ICTs. This in turn has provided youth in several developing countries around the world with the tools to "drive the reform processes and contribute to positive results in their respective countries and regions" (GYAC, 2011, p. 1). The website also helps in connecting youth all around the world to combat corruption, raise awareness about corrupt activities, as well as facilitate the "sharing of knowledge, experiences, ideas, and collaborating on anti-corruption initiatives from a distance through its web platform and social media outlets, and via face-to-face conferences" (GYAC, 2011, p. 1).

Other examples include:

1. **uReport:** A free SMS- based system used by UNICEF in Uganda to enable communities to share common issues and work together with community leaders. These issues also include raising awareness about accountability and transparency (see for example http://ureport.ug/, 2014);
2. **TRAC-FM:** A governance and accountability tool which uses SMS technology to collect and disseminate information and help citizens to make informed decisions and to hold leaders accountable (See for example www.tracfm.org/);
3. **FrontlineSMS:** Is a two-way SMS messaging system that enables direct communication between large groups and a central database (See for example www.frontlinesms.com, 2016); and
4. **SeeClickFix:** Which is an application which allows citizens to report issues in their neighbourhoods and which can facilitate social accountability.

These apps are easily accessible for citizens, easy to use and inexpensive making them an ideal citizen-centric tool for fighting corruption. Despite this, raising awareness using such a techno-centric approach can sometimes be challenging for many citizens in several developing countries as not all citizens have access to ICTs, not all know how to use these technologies and some still suffer from simple literacy issues (reading and writing). This problem of access and/or use of ICTs because of socio-economic factors, geographic location or levels of education is a well-established problem in the ICT for development literature that has undermined many e-commerce and e-governance projects world-wide (Lau, et. al., 2003). This is referred to as the digital divide. The digital divide is a term used to refer to a state of unequal access to digital technology within or between countries. It is the gap between those who have access to ICTs, the availability of ICTs and the ability to actually use these ICTs. Of particular concern here are the poor and the most vulnerable - those most impacted by corruption. Individuals are, however, not the only persons affected by this divide: organisations are affected too. Technologically savvy civil-society organisations, community based organisations and non-governmental organisations are better able to take advantages of the informational revolution. They are better able to harness the power of ICTs such as the Internet or mobile phones to reach a wider audience through emails, tweeting, YouTube videos, blogs or text messages to communicate with persons particularly the young tech savvy emerging e-citizen.

Additionally, in some instances access is inhibited by control systems. According to Berki et al. (2011), in countries with repressive regimes, authorities sometimes prevent citizens from accessing information using ICTs or control what information is available (and sometimes even mislead citizens). This constrains transparency and accountability efforts, therefore making it challenging to combat corruption. This type of divide is a form of control divide whereby those who control the technology also determines who is allowed to access.

Monitoring, Mobilising and Reporting Corruption using Software Application

The use of software applications by citizens to simultaneously monitor corruption (citizen monitoring), mobilise against corruption (citizen mobilisation) as well as to report acts of corruption (citizen reporting) were also major inter-related themes which emerged from the data analysed. Citizen monitoring is defined here as any monitoring activity that relies in whole or in part on the participation of non-paid actors in a state. In the offline world, this includes volunteers, members of a community, or a crowd to observe or check or record state owned enterprises, state actors, procurement practices, elections, the selection of state actors, as well as how governments spend their budget (Avila, Feigenblatt, & Heacock, 2010). Citizen mobilising is defined here as preparing, organising and/or assembling people for an event or action, which normally occur. In the offline world, this is done through dialogue, conversations, letters or meetings or sometimes protests or petitions. Finally, citizen reporting means to give an account of an event or occurrences. In the offline world, it is usually reporting via the print media, conversations, letters, and filing reports to name a few.

The literature on citizen monitoring, mobilising and reporting of corruption currently focuses on offline activities such as site visits, face-to-face dialogue with state actors or witnesses, review of documents such as budgets, mobilising through meetings, petitions and other fora as well as reporting acts of corruption through the print media, letters and face-to-face interactions (Fung & Wright, 2003; Acharya, Lavalle, & Houtzager, 2004; Cabannes, 2004; Fjeldstad, 2004; Dehn, 2002; Ghonkrokta & Lather, 2007; Joshi, 2013). Examples of these activities, processes and apparatuses include participatory budgeting (PB) (Fung & Wright, 2003; Acharya, Lavalle, & Houtzager, 2004; Cabannes, 2004), independent budget analysis (IBA) (Robinson, 2006) and public expenditure tracking surveys (PETS) (Bjorkman and Madestam, 2003; Fjeldstad, 2004; Dehn, 2002). It also involves social auditing tools such as community score cards, citizen report cards, public procurement monitoring, social audits and other citizen feedback mechanisms. (Ghonkrokta & Lather, 2007; Joshi

& Houtzager, 2012). In the next section I will highlight online activates associated with citizen monitoring, mobilising and reporting of corruption. This includes the use of apps to facilitate crowdsourcing and citizen journalism to combat corruption.

Combating Corruption with Crowdsourcing

ICTs such as the mobile phone (specifically smartphones), PCs, laptops as well as slates (and the apps which drive these technologies) facilitate the monitoring, mobilising and reporting corruption by citizens. One way in which this is done is through a process referred to as 'crowdsourcing'. Crowdsourcing, is defined as the practice of leveraging the collective intelligence of the online community by outsourcing the gathering of information, ideas, or content by soliciting contributions from a large group of people using various ICTs with the aim of producing participatory and collaborative content to which anyone can contribute (Howe, 2009; Bekri et al., 2011; Estellés-Arolas & González Ladrón-de-Guevara, 2012). It is a means of harnessing the creative solution of multiple dispersed networks of talented citizens. With crowdsourcing, citizens use web-based applications such as multimedia sharing sites like YouTube and Instagram, social network sites such as Facebook, Twitter, and Wikis as well as blogs to share information globally and in real time about these inconsistencies, and to take action through the monitoring of mobilising against and reporting corrupt practices. More specifically, through crowdsourcing, e-citizens have been able to observe the activities of elected officials, government agencies and agents of the state, in order to mobilise and collectively take action in the form of public campaigns to report as well as address corrupt activities through curative measures.

One example of this phenomenon is the website ipaidabribe.com. Ipaidabribe.com is [a] unique initiative to tackle corruption by harnessing the collective energy of online citizens (ipaidabribe.com, 2016, p. 1). The website allows citizens to monitor, mobilise and report acts of corruption. E-citizens can report on the nature, number, pattern, types, location, frequency and values of actual corrupt acts on this website (ipaidabribe.com/about-us). Furthermore, e-citizens have access to reports of other e-citizens about their experiences with corrupt practices, which can be shared online through social networking sites such as Facebook and Twitter. And, from these social networking sites e-citizens can engage in dialogue about mobilising against corruption using online or electronic petition (e-petitions) facilities of these or other sites. Other examples of monitoring, mobilising against and reporting of corruption include 'Excelèncias a Brazilian' website which monitors the spending of parliamentarians; 'Cuidemos el vote', a Mexican initiative whereby citizens can send SMS messages, emails or Twitter posts about electoral fraud; 'Guatemala visible', a Guatemalan website, with links to a YouTube channel and Facebook page which monitors transparency and accountability in the appointment of government officials (http://guatemalavisible.net/).

It is important to note also the literature on the challenges to crowdsourcing. Bekri et al. (2011), for example, noted "real-time data collected via crowd-sourcing cannot always be verified and poses threats to emergency response efforts and the accuracy of published information" (p. 13). Similar sentiments were raised in Chris Sherman's 2002 Book, 'Web of Deception: Misinformation on the Internet'. The text 'Web of Deception' essentially highlighted how and in what way information on the Internet can sometimes be, among other things, inaccurate, misleading, or erroneous. In other words and to use Mark Twain's famous aphorism, "don't always believe everything you read." This raises the issue of trust. How much trust can we have in the information provided by citizens?

Combating Corruption through Citizen Journalism

In addition to the use of crowdsourcing as means of citizen monitoring, mobilising and reporting, another way in which citizens have used ICTs to combat corruption is through 'Citizen Journalism'. Citizen journalism involves ordinary citizens "playing an active role in the process of collecting, reporting, analysing, and disseminating news and information" (Bowman, & Willis, 2003). Citizen journalism many argue is a response to the many shortcomings in the professional journalistic field (Radsch, 2013). Citizen journalists rely on ICTs such as new media technologies (social networking websites such as Facebook and Twitter and media sharing websites such as Instagram and YouTube) to collect and disseminate information. One good example of how citizen journalism has been used to combat corruption is the site CNN-IBN Citizen Journalist show on the Citizen Journalist website. Through this website, and particularly the Citizen Journalist show, which is aired on the website, citizens are able to share, monitor, mobilise and report corrupt practices. Another very well-known example of the importance of citizen journalism is WikiLeaks, which according to salon.com (an award winning credible news site which has been operating since the emergence of the digital era), has exposed the "breadth of the corruption, deceit, brutality and criminality on the part of the world's most powerful factions" (p. 1).

WikiLeaks and CNN-IBN are just two of many citizen journalism websites that exist. There are indeed hundreds of these websites currently operating in virtually every country in the world. In some instances, these websites are interconnected through portals that allow them to share information globally thereby giving them a world-wide presence. In the last five years or so, we have witnessed the power and world-wide reach of these online tools; from taking photographs of criminal and corrupt acts in Egypt, uploading and sharing this information globally via CNN and starting an online and/or an offline conversation which eventually leads to government officials from other countries or/watchdog organisations taking action against the corrupt act in Egypt. Citizen journalism demonstrated that it is indeed an effective means of combating corruption.

Though citizen journalism can be seen as a substantive activity in the fight against corruption, there is a caveat of note. There have been some concerns about the quality (accuracy, legitimacy and ethics) of this form of 'journalism' (Papandrea, 2007). Professional journalists argue that citizen journalists are not trained media professional. Many tend to be agenda based, overgeneralised, base their arguments on selective observations, make inaccurate observations, provide premature closure, sensationalise the news and do not follow reporting protocol. Conversely, citizen journalists would claim that mainstream journalists are themselves guilty of these actions and that these actions have themselves given rise to citizen journalism. Whichever the case, it is indeed evident that citizen journalists armed with the power of ICTs have proven to be an effective means of combating corruption today.

CONCLUSION

The objective of this chapter was to illustrate the tools (ICTs) that can be used by citizens to combat corruption and the processes surrounding the use of these tools (how these tools are used). Whereas past research has focussed on the conceptual characteristics of the use of ICTs in government and by governments to combat corruption, this paper provides a specific analysis of the use of ICTs by citizens in combating corruption. The study highlights the use of ICTs by citizens to combat corruption. The study recognizes the contributive value of ICTs as it relates to the fact that many of these technologies are easily accessible for most citizens, easy to use and relatively inexpensive. However, the study also recognizes that there are, however, several challenges, which can undermine the use of ICTs by some citizens to combat corruption. They include: the digital divide (the inability of some groups to access ICTs because of a lack of availability of these technologies due to cost or a lack of capacities on the part of these citizens to understand how to use these technologies); lack of adequate infrastructure (the absence of modern ICT platforms and networks in a country); as well as trust and privacy (how far citizens can and should go when monitoring public officials).

Though not perfect, in today's world, ICTs can be viewed as an ideal and convenient tool for citizens to hold public officials, organizations and even a government accountable. ICTs can therefore be seen as a substantive tool to combat corruption. Indeed, the study draws attention to and helps to validate the utility of e-society as a conceptual framework for exploring citizen-centric issues regarding achieving good governance. Certainly, as more citizens become connected and informed and online becomes the norm; and the need for transparency and accountability become a demand then citizens, civil society and communities can act as a formidable force in combating corruption world-wide. Not only will they have the ability to monitor corruption and inform others about corruption but they will also be able to contribute to and influence policy, decision-making about corruption through public discourse and communicative action (Habermas, 1994).

REFERENCES

Acharya, A., Lavalle, A. G., & Houtzager, P. (2004). Civil Society Representation in the Participatory Budget and Deliberative Councils of São Paulo, Brazil. IDS Bulletin, 35(2), 40-48.

Ades, A., & Di Tella, R. (1999). Rents, Competition, and Corruption. *The American Economic Review*, *89*(4), 982–993. doi:10.1257/aer.89.4.982

Akçay, S. (2006). Corruption and Human Development. *The Cato Journal*, *26*(1), 29–48.

Alam, M. S. (1995). A Theory of Limits on Corruption and some Applications. *Kyklos*, *48*(3), 419–435. doi:10.1111/j.1467-6435.1995.tb02323.x

Andersen, K. N., Henriksen, H. Z., Medaglia, R., Danziger, J. N., Sannarnes, M. K., & Enemærke, M. (2010). Fads and facts of E-government: A review of impacts of E-government (2003–2009). *International Journal of Public Administration*, *33*(11), 564–579. doi:10.1080/01900692.2010.517724

Andersen, T. B. (2009). E-government as an anti-corruption strategy. *Information Economics and Policy*, *21*(3), 201–210. doi:10.1016/j.infoecopol.2008.11.003

Andvig, J. C., Fjelstad, O., Amundsen, I., & Soreide, T. (2000). *Research on Corruption: A policy oriented survey*. Norwegian Agency for Development Co-operation.

Asiimwe, E. N., Ake, G., & Wakabi, W. (2013). Using Technology for Enhancing Transparency and Accountability in Low Resource Communities: Experiences from Uganda. In K. Sarajeva (Ed.), *ICT for Anti-Corruption, Democracy and Education in East Africa*. Stockholm: Spider.

Ata, A. Y., & Arvas, M. A. (2011). Determinants of Economic Corruption: A Cross-Country Data Analysis. *International Journal of Business and Social Science*, *2*(13), 161–169.

Avila, R., Feigenblatt, H., Heacock, R., & Heller, N. (2010). *Global mapping of technology for transparency and accountability: New Technologies*. London: Open Society Foundation.

Backus, M. (2001). E-governance and developing countries: Introduction and examples. International Institute for Communication and Development.

Bekri, D., Dunn, B., Oguzertem, I., Su, Y., & Upreti, S. (2011). *Harnessing Social Media Tools to Fight Corruption*. London.

Bertot, J. C., Jaeger, P. T., & Grimes, J. M. (2010). Using ICTs to create a culture of transparency: E-government and social media as openness and anti-corruption tools for societies. *Government Information Quarterly*, *27*(3), 264–271. doi:10.1016/j.giq.2010.03.001

Bertot, J. C., Jaeger, P. T., & Grimes, J. M. (2012). Promoting transparency and accountability through ICTs, social media, and collaborative e-government. *Transforming Government: People. Process and Policy*, *6*(1), 78–91.

Bhatnagar, S. (2003). *E-government and access to information: Global Corruption Report*. Washington, D.C.: Transparency International.

Bjorkman, M., & Madestam, A. (2003). *Public Expenditure Tracking Survey (PETS): Primary School Pilot*. Stockholm: The World Bank.

Bowen, G. A. (2009). Document Analysis as a Qualitative Research Method. *Qualitative Research Journal*, *9*(2), 27–40. doi:10.3316/QRJ0902027

Bowman, S., & Willis, C. (2003). *We Media: How audiences are shaping the future of news and information*. Reston: The Media Center.

Cabannes, Y. (2004). Participatory budgeting: A significant contribution to participatory democracy. *Environment and Urbanization*, *16*(1), 27–46. doi:10.1177/095624780401600104

Campos, E. J., Lien, D., & Pradhan, S. (1999). The Impact of Corruption on Investment: Predictability Matters. *World Development*, *27*(6), 1059–1067. doi:10.1016/S0305-750X(99)00040-6

Cecchini, S., & Scott, C. (2003). Can information and communications technology applications contribute to poverty reduction? Lessons from rural India. *Information Technology for Development*, *10*(2), 73–84. doi:10.1002/itdj.1590100203

Cheung, S. N. S. (1982). Will China Go 'Capitalist'? Institute of Economic Affairs.

Cheung, S. N. S. (1983). The Contractual Nature of the Firm. *The Journal of Law & Economics*, *26*(1), 1–21. doi:10.1086/467023

Chang.org. (2014). CNN-IBN Citizen Journalist Show, Retrieved from https://www.change.org/en-IN/organisations/ibncj

Coase, R. H. (1960). The Problem of Social Cost. *The Journal of Law & Economics, 26*, 1–21. doi:10.1086/466560

Cohen, W. M., Nelson, R. R., & Walsh, J. P. (2002). Links and impacts: The influence of public research on industrial R&D. *Management Science, 48*(1), 1–23. doi:10.1287/mnsc.48.1.1.14273

Coolidge, J., & Rose-Ackerman, S. (1999). Kleptocracy and Reform in African Regimes: Theory and Cases. In K. R. Hope (Ed.), *Corruption and Development in Africa: Lessons from Country Case Studies*. London: Macmillan Press.

Dehn, J., Reinikka, R., & Svensson, J. (2002). *Survey Tools for Assessing Service Delivery*: World Bank/ Development Research Group.

Devanathan, G. (2009). e-Administration an e-Platform for e-Governance to introduce Transparency and Accountability in Governments and Organisations. *Paper presented at the Annual Meeting of the Southern Political Science Association.* Retrieved from http://citation.allacademic.com/meta/p281478_index.html

Donchev, D., & Ujhelyi, G. (2009). What Do Corruption Indices Measure? *University of Houston Economics Department Working Paper.*

Estellés-Arolas, E., & González Ladrón-de-Guevara, F. (2012). Towards an integrated crowdsourcing definition. *Journal of Information Science, 38*(2), 189–200. doi:10.1177/0165551512437638

Fjeldstad, O. H. (2004). *Trust in Public Finance: Citizens Views on Taxation by Local Authorities in Tanzania. Chr. Michelsen Institute*. CMI.

Forestier, E., Grace, J., & Kenny, C. (2002). Can information and communication technologies be pro-poor? *Telecommunications Policy, 26*(11), 623–646. doi:10.1016/S0308-5961(02)00061-7

Fox, J. (2007). Government transparency and policymaking. *Public Choice, 131*(1-2), 23–44. doi:10.1007/s11127-006-9103-3

Fung, A., & Wright, E. O. (2003). *Deepening democracy: institutional innovations in empowered participatory governance*. London: Verso.

Galtung, F., & Pope, J. (1999). The Global coalition against corruption: evaluating Transparency International. In A. Schedler, L. Diamond, & M. F. Plattner (Eds.), *The Self-Restraining State: Power and Accountability in New Democracies*. Boulder: Lynne Rienner Publishers.

Gascó-Hernández, M., Equiza-López, F., & Acevedo-Ruiz, M. (2007). *Information communication technologies and human development: Opportunities and challenges*. Hershey, PA, USA: IGI Global. doi:10.4018/978-1-59904-057-8

Ghonkrokta, S. S., & Lather, A. S. (2007). Identification of Role of Social Audit by Stakeholders as Accountability Tool in Good Governance. *Journal of Management Research*, *7*(1), 18–26.

Global Youth Anti-Corruption Network (GYAC). (2011). Global Youth Anti-Corruption Network (GYAC). Retrieved from https://www.facebook.com/GYACNetwork/

Gronlund, A., Heacock, R., Sasaki, D., Hellstrom, J., & Al-Saqaf, W. (2010). *Increasing Transparency and Fighting: Corruption through ICT Empowering People and Communities*. Stockholm: Swedish Program for ICT in Developing Regions.

Habermas, J. (1994). *The Theory of Communicative Action*. Boston: Beacon Press.

Habib, M., & Zurawicki, L. (2002). Corruption Differentials and Foreign Direct Investment. *Journal of International Business Studies*, *33*(2), 291–308. doi:10.1057/palgrave.jibs.8491017

Heeks, R. B. (2001). Building e-Governance for Development. Retrieved from http://www.man.ac.uk/idpm/idpm_dp.htm#ig

Hirschman, A. O. (1967). *Development Economics Observed*. Washington, DC: Brookings Institution.

Hirschman, A. O. (1970). *Exit, Voice and Loyalty: Responses to Decline in Firms, Organizations and States*. Cambridge: Harvard University Press.

Hoque, S. M. S. (2005). E-governance in Bangladesh: A scrutiny from the citizens' perspective. In R. Ahmad (Ed.), *The role of public administration in building a harmonious society*. Beijing: Asian Development Bank.

Howe, J. (2009). *Crowdsourcing: Why the Power of the Crowd Is Driving the Future of Business*. London: Random House Business.

Huntington, S. (1968). *Political Order in Changing Societies*. New Haven: Yale University Press.

Husted, B. W. (1999). Wealth, Culture and Corruption. *Journal of International Business Studies*, *30*(2), 339–359. doi:10.1057/palgrave.jibs.8490073 ipaidabribe.com. (2016). About I Paid a Bribe. Retrieved from http://www.ipaidabribe.or.ug/about-i-paid-bribe

Jaeger, P. T., & Bertot, J. C. (2010). Transparency and technological change: Ensuring equal and sustained public access to government information. *Government Information Quarterly*, *27*(4), 371–376. doi:10.1016/j.giq.2010.05.003

Joshi, A., & Houtzager, P. P. (2012). Widgets or watchdogs? Conceptual explorations in social accountability. *Public Management Review*, *14*(2), 145–162. doi:10.1080/14719037.2012.657837

Kim, P. S., Halligan, J., Cho, N., Oh, C. H., & Eikenberry, A. M. (2005). Toward Participatory and Transparent Governance: Report on the Sixth Global Forum on Reinventing Government. *Public Administration Review*, *65*(6), 646–654. doi:10.1111/j.1540-6210.2005.00494.x

Kuriyan, R., Bailur, S., Gigler, S., & Park, K. (2011). *Technologies for transparency and accountability: Implications for ICT policy and implementation*. Washington, DC: World Bank.

Lau, B. T., & Sim, C. H. (2003). Exploring the extent of ICT adoption among secondary school Teachers in Malaysia. *International Journal of Computing and ICT Research*, *2*(2), 19–36.

Lear, J. (1998). *Open Minded*. Cambridge: Harvard University Press.

Lee, H., Oh, S., & Shim, Y. (2005). Do we need broadband? Impacts of broadband in Korea. *Info*, *7*(4), 47–56. doi:10.1108/14636690510607295

Leff, N. H. (1964). Economic Development through Bureaucratic Corruption. *The American Behavioral Scientist*, *8*(3), 8–14. doi:10.1177/000276426400800303

Macrae, J. (1982). Underdevelopment and the Economics of Corruption: A Game Theory Approach. *World Development*, *10*(8), 677–687. doi:10.1016/0305-750X(82)90093-6

Mauro, P. (1995). Corruption and Growth. *The Quarterly Journal of Economics*, *110*(3), 681–711. doi:10.2307/2946696

McGee, R., & Gaventa, J. (2010). *Review of Impact and Effectiveness of Accountability and Transparency Initiatives: Synthesis Report*. London: Department for International Development.

McMullan, M. (1961). A Theory of Corruption Based on a Consideration of Corruption in the Public Services and Governments of British Colonies and ex-Colonies in West Africa. *The Sociological Review*, *9*(2), 181–201. doi:10.1111/j.1467-954X.1961.tb01093.x

Myrdal, G. (1970). *The challenge of world poverty: a world anti-poverty program in outline*. New York: Pantheon Books.

National Integrity Action. (2013). Building Integrity…A Work in Progress. Retrieved from https://www.niajamaica.org/publications/NIA%202nd%20Year%20Gleaner%20Supplement.pdf

Ndou, V. (2004). E-government for developing countries: Opportunities and challenges. *The Electronic Journal of Information Systems in Developing Countries*, *18*(1), 1–24.

Neumayer, E. (2003). *The pattern of aid giving: The impact of good governance on development assistance*. London: Routledge. doi:10.4324/9780203986837

North, D. C. (1990). *Institutions, Institutional Change, and Economic Performance*. Cambridge: Cambridge University Press. doi:10.1017/CBO9780511808678

North, D. C. (2005). *Understanding the Process of Economic Change*. Princeton: Princeton University Press. doi:10.1515/9781400829484

Nye, J. S. (1967). Corruption and Political Development: A Cost-Benefit Analysis. *The American Political Science Review*, *61*(2), 417–427. doi:10.2307/1953254

Opoku-Mensah, A. (2000). ICTs as tools of democratization: African women speak out. In E. M. Rathgeber & E. O. Adera (Eds.), *Gender and the information revolution in Africa*. Ottawa: International Development Research Centre.

Ormont, L. (1995). A View of the Rise of Modern Group Analysis. *Modern Psychoanalysis*, *21*, 31–42.

Oye, N. D. (2013). Reducing Corruption in African Developing Countries: The Relevance of E-Governance. *Greener Journal of Social Sciences*, *3*(1), 6–13. doi:10.15580/GJSS.2013.1.103112183

Papandrea, M. R. (2007). Citizen Journalism and the Reporter's Privilege. *Minnesota Law Review*, *91*, 515–591.

Pathak, R. D., & Prasad, R. S. (2005). Role of e-governance in tackling corruption: The Indian experience. In R. Ahmad (Ed.), *The role of public administration in building a harmonious society*. Beijing: Asian Development Bank.

Pathak, R. D., Singh, G., Belwal, R., Naz, R., & Smith, R. F. I. (2008). E-governance, corruption and public service delivery: A comparative study of Fiji and Ethiopia. *Journal of Administration & Governance*, *3*(1), 65–79.

Pathak, R. D., Singh, G., Belwal, R., & Smith, R. F. I. (2007). E-governance and corruption-development issues in Ethiopia. *Public Organization Review*, *7*(3), 195–208. doi:10.1007/s11115-007-0031-6

Radsch, C. (2013). The Revolutions will be Blogged: Cyberactivism and the 4th Estate in Egypt [Unpublished Doctoral Dissertation]. American University.

Rahman, H. (2007). *Information and communication technologies for economic and regional developments*. Hershey, PA, USA: IGI Global. doi:10.4018/978-1-59904-186-5

Relly, J. E., & Sabharwal, M. (2009). Perceptions of transparency of government policymaking: A cross-national study. *Government Information Quarterly*, *26*(1), 148–157. doi:10.1016/j.giq.2008.04.002

Rios, J., Rios Insua, D., Fernandez, D., & Rivero, J. A. (2005, March 2-4). Participatory Budget Formation through the Web. In M. Bohlen, Gamper, J., Polasek, W., & Wimmer, M. A. (Ed.), *E-Government: Towards Electronic Democracy: Proceedings of theInternational Conference, TCGOV 2005*, Bolzano, Italy (pp. 268-276). Zurich: Springer.

Rivera-Batiz, F. L. (2002). Democracy, governance, and economic growth: Theory and evidence. *Review of Development Economics*, *6*(2), 225–247. doi:10.1111/1467-9361.00151

Robinson, M. (2006). *Budget Analysis and Policy Advocacy: The Role of Nongovernmental Public Action* (Working Paper No. IDS Working Paper 279). Brighton: Institute of Development Studies

Rose-Ackerman, S. (1978). *Corruption: a study in political economy*. New York: Academic Press.

Rose-Ackerman, S. (1999). *Corruption and government: causes, consequences, and reform*. New York: Cambridge Press. doi:10.1017/CBO9781139175098

Rose-Ackerman, S. (2008). Corruption and government. *International Peacekeeping*, *15*(3), 328–343. doi:10.1080/13533310802058802

Sanford, C., & Rose, J. (2007). Characterizing eParticipation. *International Journal of Information Management*, *27*(6), 406–421. doi:10.1016/j.ijinfomgt.2007.08.002

Santiso, C. (2001). World Bank and good governance: good governance and aid effectiveness: the World Bank and conditionality. *Geo. Public Pol'y Rev., 7*, 1-137.

Sen, K. (2014). Governance and Development Outcomes in Asia. *Asian Development Bank Economics Working Paper Series*

Shailendra, C., Palvia, J., & Sharma, S. S. (2007). E-Government and E-Governance: Definitions/Domain Framework and Status around the World Retrieved from http://www.iceg.net/2007/books/1/1_369.pdf

Sheridan, W., & Riley, T. B. (2006). Comparing e-government vs. e-governance. Commonwealth Center for e-Governance. *Commonwealth Center for e-Governance*. Retrieved from http://www.egovmonitor.com/node/655

Shim, D. C., & Eom, T. H. (2008). E-government and anti-corruption: Empirical analysis of International data. *International Journal of Public Administration*, *31*(3), 298–316. doi:10.1080/01900690701590553

Shim, D. C., & Eom, T. H. (2009). Anticorruption effects of information communication and technology (ICT) and social capital. *International Review of Administrative Sciences*, *75*(1), 99–116. doi:10.1177/0020852308099508

Soper, D. S. (2007). ICT Investment Impacts on Future Levels of Democracy, Corruption, and E-Government Acceptance in Emerging Countries. *Paper presented at theAmericas Conference on Information Systems*, Keystone Colorado.

Spotnitz, H. (1952). Group Therapy as a Specialized Psychotherapeutic Technique. In G. Bychovsky, & Despart. J.L. (Ed.), Specialized Techniques in Psychotherapy. New York: Basic Books.

Svensson, J. (2005). Eight Questions about Corruption. *The Journal of Economic Perspectives*, *19*(3), 19–42. doi:10.1257/089533005774357860

Trac.Fm. (2014). What is Trac FM? Retrieved from http://www.tracfm.org

Ureport. (2014). Uganda Voice Matters. Retrieved from http://ureport.ug/

Vinod, H. D. (1999). Statistical analysis of corruption data and using the Internet to reduce corruption. *Journal of Asian Economics*, *10*(4), 591–603. doi:10.1016/S1049-0078(00)00034-8

Waller, L., & Taylor, C. A. (2013). A Case Study of Citizen—to—Government Mobile. In Z. Mahmood (Ed.), *E-Government Implementation and Practice in Developing Countries*. Hershey: IGI Global. doi:10.4018/978-1-4666-4090-0.ch008

Wei, S. (2000). How Taxing is Corruption on International Investors. *The Review of Economics and Statistics*, *82*(1), 1–11. doi:10.1162/003465300558533

Williamson, O. (1975). *Markets and Hierarchies: Analysis and Antitrust Implications*. New York: Free Press.

Williamson, O. (1985). *The Economic Institution of Capitalism: Firms, Markets, Relational Contracting*. London: Collier Macmillan.

Woods, N. (2000). The challenge of good governance for the IMF and the World Bank Themselves. *World Development*, *28*(5), 823–841. doi:10.1016/S0305-750X(99)00156-4

World Development Report: Making Services Work for Poor People. (2004). Washington, DC: The World Bank and Oxford University Press.

KEY TERMS AND DEFINITIONS

Citizen-Centric: Where the citizen is at the centre of government policies and service delivery.

Citizen Journalism: The collection, analysis and reporting of news by the general public by electronic means.

Crowdsourcing: Obtaining information, ideas, services, tasks or content from a crowd of online users.

Corruption: The use of power entrusted by the people for personal gain.

E-Society: How and in what ways citizens, civil society, businesses and communities use Information and Communication Technologies to achieve a common interest or goal.

Good Governance: The act of facilitating participation, the rule of law, accountability, transparency, efficient and effective government, fostering value consensus and equity.

Information and Communication-Technologies: A range of tools that are used to gather, communicate, store, retrieve, exchange, process, analyse, and share information.

ENDNOTES

1 The use of public office or power for personal gain.

2 The corrupt behaviour in the administration of public policy.

3 The exchange of tangible goods in a market-like situation such as bribes or rent-seeking.

Chapter 5
Hashtag Ideology:
Practice and Politics of Alternative Ideology

Smarak Samarjeet
Indian Institute of Management Kashipur, India

ABSTRACT

Hashtag is powerful in nature and gains undivided attention of the social media users. The dialectical phenomenon existing around these hashtags portrays collective consciousness spread across continents. Moreover, the discourse specific political engagements have one thing in common – fuelling global sentiment, perhaps, that is more homogenous and speculative. But the real question is how powerful as this hashtag phenomenon has become? Is it a disruptive culture that has become part of our everyday life? Consequently, the aim of this chapter is to deal with the recent hashtag phenomenon, engaging users in personal and social level. Hashtags such as #BringBackOurGirls and #HeForShe are used in this chapter as a case study to understand the power relations they exercise in the social media space and across cross-media platforms. The aim of this chapter is to contribute to the growing literature of social media activism and the hashtag ideology.

DOI: 10.4018/978-1-5225-2019-1.ch005

INTRODUCTION

Hashtags are metadata tags used to organize contents. It serves as a unique window to a large number of content, especially social media data, organized for the users to easily go through or interact. Small (2011) considers hashtag as a keyword that aids in searching. "Hashtags are keywords or strings of text prefixed with a hash symbol (#) that can be clicked as a link to a global search of tweets using that same keyword" (Bastos, Raimundo, & Travitzki, 2013, p. 264). Increasingly, these hashtags are serving non-linear content interaction points.

Using hashtags in different forms of social media posts might sound natural these days, but in a carefully constructed online social and political discourse, these strings of text carry the expressive character. The hash sign reflects the social consensus for organized activity and collective discourse. Its regular and conscious use defines the contemporary culture and the media practices. The attempt to document expressive contents and facilitate easy access by providing universal hashtags is a part of the activism culture or protest related content diffusion mechanism. "As digital artifacts, hashtags locate cultures across time and space. No matter the context—that is, grassroots, institutional, or corporate—hashtags compel us to act" (Conley, 2014, p.1111).

As we know, in a networked society, cyber-activism is a rational choice to sustain the cyber-democracy, as democracy in its simplest form is contested. When people wish to develop a dialogue, there is a desire to build consensus. As there is a risk to the common interest of the larger social group, activism of any form strives for democratic rights (Ganesh & Zoller, 2012; Kim & Sriramesh, 2009).

Be it in fragmented or a full force activism, the existence of technology and interface supports the rhetoric. One can witness immense political possibilities embedded in hypertexts. Furthermore, the change in protest related choreography has now assumed a larger social space and networked individuals. The democratic right to dissent and hope for a change is practiced like a religion. What we witness is the redesigned protest landscape with multiple source points. And, with the arrival of the 'shout out' culture, we also experience diversity in view points and their complex yet subtle unison under the effect of politicized techno-subcultures (Kahn & Kellner, 2005).

However, the technology itself is ideological as it restricts and defines our viewpoints. We are given what we like the most, not the opposing views that would build a rational argument. The views posted on social media networks are heavily influenced by the kind of personalized search tools we use. As an activist, people do not get to decide what gets through their filter. It's the technology that determines our visuality (Green, 2011).

It is also important to note that evolution of expressive and interactive interfaces has remodeled the power structure in the society. We are living in a time where 'participation' is the real freedom – from passive participation to active action or activism. The path is determined by historical character of the action, flexibility in registering an opinion, and a reward system. Participation provides a sense of ownership. Talking about Web 2.0, Blank and Reisdorf (2012) says, "It opens opportunities for participation by ordinary users; they can become producers of content in a way that is impossible without the Internet" (p. 537). It's a complete process determined by the technology that facilitates a space for democracy to be a shared experience.

Moreover, the positioning of the hashtag as a hybrid gateway creates a network that is participatory intensive. There is a scope for seamless integration of cross media territories and transnational participation. The possibility of a parallel action and establishing hashtag as a common frame of reference serves the ideological objective of such media platforms. According to Anduiza, Cantijoch and Gallego (2009), "The impact on the levels of participation will depend on the extent to which the new channels are used: if use is marginal, it is unlikely to produce a more participative society" (p.862). The nature of such hashtags is to create interest in an event and traverse to become a viral content. When people tweet, retweet and share in different platforms, the hashtag is shaped by a multiplicity of user generated contents. Social activists, political activists, celebrities, fans and the government etc. have their own agenda which leads into construction of hashtags of different character. And, one finds multiplicity of contents curated under these hashtags. Though one can't see the plethora of contents, the related hashtag organizes contents for easy accessibility and commercial opportunity. When the hashtag is designed, it ensures redirecting requests to different third party sites, allowing content to have visibility.

Recently, hashtags have been used in excess by political activists, house representatives, and protest groups to design and proliferate their ideologue. Hashtags such as #AzadiFromCongress (Independence from Congress Government in India), #brexit, #NeverTrump are examples of politics and activism of different quality and taste. As anyone can create hashtags, and can allow automatic content curation, it is important to understand the network politics and the vulnerability loop that it creates. It's no more an option for the users; rather it is a compulsion to push their opinion within their networks using hashtags. Protest legitimacy is a question that needs answering.

The objective of this chapter is to understand the hashtag engagements in the process of political activism, understand the ideology behind the construction of such hashtags, understand the idea of shared space and hashtag interlinking, understand the nature of global narrative that used those hashtags and contribute to the growing literature on hashtag activism. The author has considered #BringBackOurGirls and

#HeForShe hashtags to understand the phenomenon. At first, the author provides a background, especially the evolution of such hashtags. Then, major issues related hashtag culture is enumerated. The author locates the politics of hashtag within the narrative of #BringBackOurGirls and #HeForShe.

BACKGROUND

This chapter considers two important hashtags and the discourse around them. These hashtags have managed to grab the attention of politicians, celebrities and world leaders. Hashtags were used as an appeal to the mass to come forward and take action.

While new communication technologies have triggered a participatory culture, it has also helped individuals transcend physical and geographical barriers, especially a leaderless movement to surface and grow. The dynamics of shared space, where political intent and ideology is amalgamated to foster movements such as 'Occupy Wall Street' and 'Gaza under Attack', is an indicator of expressive political participation. While people considered Occupy movement as rhetorical performance (Kim, 2015), Gaza movement was an online narrative experience of people, their sufferings and struggle (Siapera, Hunt, & Lynn, 2015).

Similarly, the Femen protest, with their glaringly objectified movement, generated an 'activist imaginary', nonetheless an attempt to spread an ideology of global kind – affective activism culture (Reestorff, 2014). As networking opportunity is the part and parcel any activism, the flow of alternative information sans the mainstream media is an interesting development. It is an activism driven resource mobilization process that affects the collective identity and action. "As a medium, the Internet seems to correspond very well with the alternative organizations' network-like structures, and possibly even encourages further organizational development along networking lines" (Olsson, 2008, p.672). Hashtag activism such as #BoardTheBus, #StopStreetHarrassment, and #EverydaySexism has the characteristic of sparking larger social conversations (Eagle, 2015). Whether it's a mediated political campaign driven by the social media elite (Chakravartyy & Roy, 2015), or the systematized, multistage activism concerning 'Occupy Central' movement in Hong Kong (Lee & Chan, 2016), the entire social media affair is deliberate. The content produced has immense rhetorical power to initiate participatory behavior.

However, using tools to reflect a false sense of democratic participation which could neither translate the key objectives nor accommodate a game changing revolution is ideologically stylized. Give people the hashtag, they will share it with anyone and anywhere. The content produced, thus, is insensitive to the real cause of the activism. Moreover, the social media template has the ability of hijacking the true purpose of activism, irrespective of user generated contents (Ogunlesi, 2014).

Hashtag Ideology

Irrespective of the nature of such social activism, the orientation remains pre-defined – an approach for political symbolism. Crafting of political communication is more of spectacle driven. There lies a provoking moment that shapes the collective action. Whether it's 'Occupy Movement' or 'Israel-Hamas Conflict', 'Save Donbass People' or 'Intolerance' debate, the propaganda is to interact and influence global publics; initiate a campaign.

The important aspect of any activism, therefore, is the visually arresting propaganda. Bernays (1930) said "Propaganda will never die out. Intelligent men must realize that propaganda is the modern instrument by which they can fight for productive ends and help to bring order out of chaos" (p.86). Though 'productive ends' is always a contested term, considering how it is achieved and what is achieved, it is pertinent to look at the hegemonic imagery and understand the design of the message, how images establish a reciprocal relationship between collective intent and agency driven ideology. Kim (2015) argues that the visual messages in terms of profile pictures on Facebook have a pre-defined orientation. Seo (2014) has the opinion that in the networked information age, visual propaganda bears themes and frames, furthering diplomacy and strategic communication spirits. The question is who drives the collective intent? And, who decides what the 'collective intent' must strive for? To answer these questions, we must examine two most important social media activism: '#BringBackOurGirls' and '#HeForShe'. These are two different actions that furthers the cause of feminism and brings together stakeholders to react and act. "#BringBackOurGirls showed how digital activists could use their voice to support or encourage real-world change" (Olson, 2016, p.4).

There is also an attempt to pitch a legitimate voice that could choreograph the protests across the nations. Though a lot of information related to #BringBackOurGirls movement was shared first on platforms like Twitter, Murthy (2011) questions the legitimacy of Twitter as an information source. The growing trend among people who prefer Twitter as a platform to report 'snippet' type news is also an interesting phenomenon to observe. One can question the legitimacy of the 'perspective' used to influence or create an opinion. Polarization of views, especially when politicians use social media to increase a favorable public opinion (Hong, 2013), determines the magnitude of effect cast by using tweets and self-made hashtags.

The campaign motivation is directed towards sensitizing publics. One single narrative that can fuel an action. According to Khoja-Moolji (2015), "The explosion of tweets in the aftermath of the kidnapping of approximately three hundred schoolgirls in Chibok, Nigeria, in April 2014 with the hashtag #BringBackOurGirls is a clear example of a feminist campaign that relied on rallying support via social media and using it to pressure the United States and Nigerian governments to take action" (p.348). Nonetheless, it also prepared a ground for imperialist claims to amplify (Loken, 2014).

#BringBackOurGirls

#BringBackOurGirls is not a campaign but a strong appeal that made the whole world unite and raise their voice against the abduction of 276 girls by an extremist group called 'Boko Haram' in Nigeria. The hashtag was originally advocated by ObyEzekwesili, the Vice President of the World Bank for Africa, who urged the government of Nigeria to intervene in this matter and 'bring back the girls' (Gibson, 2014). Since that day, the phrase achieved its true purpose and became one of the strongest and powerful hashtags to invoke wide public sentiments. In order to materialize the public outcry and give it a proper shape, numerous physical protests were organized. The hashtag managed to catch the attention of world leaders across the globe; a flurry of social media activity kick-started, especially on twitter and other social media platforms.

While the 'celebrated' remained immersed in feeding the rhetoric, they were also challenged by others for hijacking the campaign. Questions have been raised about the inception of the idea – bringbackourgirls. Arit John (2014) wrote in The Wired magazine about the American filmmaker Ramaa Mosley who claimed #BringBackOurGirls hashtag as her own intellectual creation. Whereas, The Wall Street Journal reported that a Nigerian Muslim Man was behind the hashtag. There have been numerous incidents of fake content sharing such as doctored images and falsifying facts. Loken (2014) argues that there is a sign of imperialistic connotation in the statements released by the western leaders, especially the phrase 'Our Girl'. "She becomes our girl, contextually indistinguishable and thus deserving protection from her communal struggle-in-kind" (p.1101). Locating 'our girl' is easy and it helps underscore global solidarity.

The activism gathered huge support from people around the world. The social media coverage of the activism was viral in nature and touched many platforms. The hashtag was created to tell the story to the world, especially how young school girls are suffering and how the world must unite to bring them back home. However, Gibson (2014) concerns about the social media and its usefulness: can spreadable contents realize the true objective of such campaign? Is the western world and its powerful rhetoric are as strong as the conviction of Boko Haram (Western Education is Sinful) (Gibson, 2014). We observe a distracted world dwelling in a utopian timeline in which neither it can fully achieve what it propagates nor it can really save the girls.

Two years have gone by and the hashtag activism is ready to enter its saturation point. Furthermore, "International efforts to recover the girls failed, including several rounds of negotiations to exchange the girls for Boko Haram fighters held in Nigerian jails" (Sam, 2015, para 4). Above all, it's a well-conceived narrative that defines power and revisits the first world glory.

#HeForShe

The second hashtag #HeForShe is considered a game changer activism for gender equality. Powered by a celebrity persona, it unlocked the potential male feminists from the stereotype framework of the society. "We are struggling for a uniting world but the good news is we have a uniting movement. It is called HeForShe. I am inviting you to step forward, to be seen to speak up, to be the 'he' for 'she'. And to ask yourself if not me, who? If not now, when?" (Emma Watson's Speech delivered at a special event, United Nations Headquarters, 2014).

The moment was historic as many celebrities (male) came forward and expressed their solidarity by tweeting the hashtag. The most important of all was the images of celebrities, holding a piece of paper depicting #HeForShe, uploaded on the twitter. The power of the images coupled with persuasive 140 characters was construed significant, considering the spirited campaign ever to be created. Emma Watson became the iconic feminist.

On October 8, 2014, she tweeted that "Between 20th Sep & 2nd Oct there were 1.1 million #HeForShe tweets from 750K different users, reaching 1.2 BILLION unique Twitter users" (Watson, 2014). The tweet was retweeted by 5761 users and was liked by 15,272 users.

However, the issue of equality and empowerment is glossy. People have raised concern about how naively Emma Watson posits gender binary and leaves out others. Chandrachud (2014) comments:

Perhaps the most noticeable issue missing from Watson's speech though, is her persistent reinforcement of the gender binary. She does mention that "gender exists on a spectrum" but shies away from directly involving trans and genderqueer people into her feminist conversation -- a noticeable trend in the mainstream feminist movement that only further marginalizes these groups. (Chandrachud, 2014, para 14).

When anything can be hashtag(able), the mediated society appears homogenous and political. A hashtag was made to define feminism and gender equality, whereas the practice fails to empower women in real life. The negotiated action recognizes only a piece of history while there are so many other aspects remain unacknowledged.

The Activism Conundrum

If the power of the tweet has to be determined, then one must determine the syntagmatic arrangement; the selection of words, case, numerals and the hashtag provides a glimpse of the persuasive quality of the message. Again, the use of hashtag and its wide political connotation is also contested. "There is a difference between simply talking about gender issues and making permanent changes that furthers the goals of feminist advocacy. It is important to raise awareness, but, in this case, the hashtag cannot stand in for taking action toward political and social changes" (Stache, 2015, p. 163). The mindless use of hashtag to increase visibility doesn't serve the true purpose of activism.

'Bring Back Our Girls' and 'He for She' exist on one basic tenet – raising voice for 'she'. Its propagators have requested the world to come together and have sought immediate action. The idea is to collaborate, grow the activism and take it to the streets. The attitude is to spark a revolution on social media and fuel the street protests. May be to convince the world to come forward and intervene. Whether it is Michelle Obama or Emma Watson, the calculated propaganda to facilitate an uber style leadership is misplaced. Specifically, the feminist activism is more of a fashionable symbolism, an idea to position the networked individuals and create a high spirited spectacle. According to Maxfield (2015), "Bring Back Our Girls and similar contemporary campaigns occur in a context in which the digital and the real are fundamentally imbricated". The fundamental question is what exactly is overlapping? Whether it is the perception among people both on and off screen or the invisible ideological attachment? While a lot of question have been raised regarding the effectiveness of such forms of activism (Khoja-Moolji, 2015; Loken, 2014; Maxfield, 2015; Olson, 2016), especially the nature of participation and its outcome, it remains to be observed whether a collective global narrative is effective enough to bring the change.

The conversation quality in/of social media is rich. Moreover, the participatory nature debunks the myth of isolated individuals. Everyone is an active participant and activist. "The Internet and other information and communication technologies affect nearly all aspects of our lives, from mundane activities such as shopping to more meaningful actions such as forming communities and engaging in political activism" (Eaton, 2010, p.174). The democratic right to participate and express views has embraced the hashtag (#) phenomenon; one reaches a wider audience. It doesn't matter if the target audience has a twitter account or not. "One does not have to be a Twitter user to follow the conversation because hashtags are visible to anyone" (Small, 2011, p.874).

There is also a major concern that the tagged tweets or any other social media posts with an attached hashtag are claiming our shared space and adding a sophisticated layer to the activism process. Though, the diffusion of a new techno-culture disrupts the existing power relations and empowers individuals (Anduiza, Cantijoch, & Gallego, 2009; Blank & Reisdorf, 2012; Eaton, 2010), the much talked about empowerment and activism has a fleeting characteristic. It begins with a celebrity action and then, dies out on its own. The society might have evolved in terms of technological access and quality interaction, but the pre-existing dominant power relations determine the collective social media mood. An activism turns out to be a visibility practice for the celebrity, not a game changing strategy. It will not bring back our girls and it won't influence every 'He' to stand for 'She'. It only creates commercial opportunity by incorporating 'resistance' ideology (Fiske, 2011).

HASHTAG(ING) IDEOLOGY

With the change in technology and development of rich content, activism on the web has gone to a different level. There evolves a culture in which the social media activism is positioned as a divine way to attend salvation. As Baudrillard (1998) says, "...salvation by grace is unattainable" (p.61), the collective intent defines the nature of activism culture and state of its operation. The networked individuals are motivated by the reward system embedded in the social media: followings, new connections and peer appraisals. Barassi (2015) while discussing about self-centered structure of social media says:

... it is the individual that is asked to communicate, share interests, and construct a profile on social media networks. Although this can lead to many positive and empowering situations at the individual level, in the context of social movements, the problem of positive understandings of networked individualism and creative autonomy is precisely that they prioritize individual agency over the political and ideological context. (Barassi 2015, p.68)

The individualistic sentiments fuel participatory behavior. As identity matters, people recognize and associate themselves with the performance driven activism. One must perform to draw attention and create an environment for collaborative practice. The associated discourse contains rhetorical elements, biased framing, and a structure that reinforces a hegemonic imagery. According to Manuel Castells (2010), identity is developed by the dominant institutions. And, the social actors create a definite meaning by internalizing such forms of identity. Identity can be a binary division between collective and individualistic. However, the persistent attempt to construct a global identity is influenced by the dominant apparatus and its rhetoric.

Furthermore, people recognize anything that is a part of the techno-social environment. Apart from the actor-centric propositions, the deliberations on social media platform and its syntagmatic structure creates a far-reaching impact. And, hashtag symbolism is an expressive participatory phenomenon that has recently empowered individuals to interact with their immediate social sphere.

Small (2011) defines hashtag as a keyword with a hash symbol that aids in searching the relevant content. However, it has more than the functional character.

Rambukkana (2015) considers hashtags as techno-social events. Hashtag allows space for negotiation of politics and identity (Vats, 2015). Moreover, hashtag is an enabler. It allows expressive contents to be organized and easily curated. And, when a networked society leverages on it to proliferate ideas, it becomes a mediated tool. Its function is ideological. "On a continuum with a derided notion of 'hashtag activism' at one pole and an inflated notion of the power of 'hashtag uprisings' at the other are all political hashtags and all the publics they subtend" (Rambukkana, 2015, p.4).

Hashtags are considered dedicated labels for social movements, and are powerful in nature in terms of raising collective participation. It's not necessary to stick to one particular set of hashtags; one can easily tweak and add one's imagination, and sometimes provide a hybrid character to the content. In a networked society, each individual influences and get influenced by each other. While articulating the activism instinct, each one prefers uniqueness. Jenkins, Ford, & Green (2013) while giving an example of Comic-Con, argues about the simultaneous and exclusivity factor of hashtag contents:

In more recent years, a push for exclusivity has given rise to a push for publicity, with panelists sharing their Twitter handles, publicists setting up their own hashtags to sustain the discussion, and videos released to blogs — such as Gawker's i09 — which target niche audiences more or less simultaneously with the real-time happenings in San Diego. (Jenkins, et. al., p.145)

Furthermore, it's not only a single hashtag that represents a particular content or a movement. Fragmented, and incoherent hashtags are clubbed together to categorize related content and allow "hashtag jumping" (Christensen, 2013). For example, #Obama, #Obamacare, #Romney and #debate can be clubbed together. Though individually they represent different set of contents but the syntagmatic arrangement posits an exclusive ideological character. "Hashtags, as a form of digital intimacy, are a way that things in the world touch other things in the world and form networks with them; they are multiple, open-ended, and contingent phenomena" (Rambukkana, 2015, p.5).

#BringBackOurGirls
@BBOG_Nigeria
#ChibokGirlsAmbassadors#365DaysOn#NeverToBeForgotten All they want is for the world to unite to #BringBackOurGirls (BBOG Nigeria, 2015)

The Bring Back Our Girls Nigeria official twitter account used multiple and inter-thematic hashtags to convey the urgency of the situation. These set of hashtags were placed to remind people that 365 days have passed but girls didn't come back to their home. While Barassi (2015) considers immediacy (the speed at which hashtags are arranged and bundled together with the content and shared at an instant) as motivation towards an weaker political discourse driven by emotional practice sans in-depth and reflective ideas, the temporal development of the social media contents based on activism has its own ideological character – to form a strong trigger event online community consisting of high affinity individuals. These are the individuals who would share anything without a second thought. "The participatory logic of spreadability leads to audiences using content in unanticipated ways as they retrofit material to the contours of their particular community. Such activities are difficult for creators to control and even more difficult to quantify" (Jenkins, Ford, & Green, 2013, p.6). Therefore, the individual ideas have their own way of interacting with each other under the larger theme of activism.

Hashtag, Imagery and Ideology

Visual propaganda has an ability to affect the cognitive capability of individuals. Nations across the world are spending huge amount of money crafting visual communication strategies to connect with the global publics. Whether the images of the Israel Palestine conflict or the famous picture of the ballerina dancing on the Wall Street bull during the Occupy movement, the fact is framing adds exclusivity. "The development of digital communication technologies and consequent changes in information consumption make visual propaganda more relevant" (Seo, 2014, p.52). The propaganda statements are kind of an art. Kohn (2015) considers hashtags as artistic statements. While discussing propaganda strategy of Israeli Defense Forces Website, Kohn argues that the use of hashtags in any propaganda statement has the ability to invoke emotion. The hashtag becomes ideological.

Moreover, it would be naïve to undermine the power of images, especially images that are part of collaborative activism and are shared with the contextual hashtags. Both image and hashtag develop an interaction. In the case of #BringBackOurGirls and #HeforShe, the images used to create awareness and raise collective conscience are basically character based. The characters are celebrities. They push forward an imagery – 'I am doing it. You should'. It's an easy and economical way to be part of the global narrative that prefers slacktivism over real and raw activism. While certain lives are at stake, some celebrity(ism) is cherished, not the real cause.

When Emma Watson stepped in for the real cause of Feminism, the world came together and appreciated her idea and vision. She was no more a beloved Harry Potter Movie Character, rather she was a global citizen pitching for women rights. Furthermore, it's the media that extensively portrayed her charismatic persona. She was trending on social media and still she continues to do so. "The first 24 hours were a barrage of YouTube clips of the speech paired with exciting phrases like 'feminism at the forefront!' and 'courageous!' and 'game changing!'" (Chandrachud, 2014, para 2).

And speaking of#Feminism, @EmWatson is doing a great project called #HeForShe. Go check it out http://t.co/vSrNTdFY3Q (Gordon-Levitt, 2014).

On the other hand, #BringBackOurGirls campaign was not initially a favorite subject for the news media until social media activism managed to get attention of the world by simply introducing a hashtag. It became a top trending hashtag when celebrities pitched in to support for the cause. Michelle Obama, the first lady, made her Mother's Day Speech:

In these girls, Barack and I see our own daughters…she could be someone's daughter, sister, friend or mother… We are committed to giving them the opportunities they deserve to fulfill every last bit of their God-given potential… So education is truly a girl's best chance for a bright future, not just for herself, but for her family and her nation…And that's true right here in the U.S. as well…so I hope the story of these Nigerian girls will serve as an inspiration for every girl – and boy – in this country. (The White House Press Release, 2014).

On a similar note, Malala Yousafzai claims Nigerian Girls to be her sisters, thus, allowing the global appropriation of local in a subtle manner. Malala Fund used its own innovative hashtag to sustain the momentum.

#LISTEN: Malala Reads Her Letter to the Abducted Chibok Schoolgirls bit.ly/1DWMVyj#BBOG#NeverToBeForgottenhttp://pbs.twimg.com/media/CCefQOmU-MAAPk6z.png (Malala Fund, 2015)

"Engaging people across multiple online platforms is a great way of connecting with them through a familiar format. But it can just as easily allow for a misguided sense of self-satisfaction without having really done anything" (Chandrachud, 2014, para 11). Using hashtag, retweeting the tweets and using social mentions: all these are self-satisfying activities. There is no reflection on reality: what Nigeria has suffered and what those Chibok girls are going through.

It always happens to be a binary division of issues and context while pushing forward an ideology. While Global appropriation of Nigerian Girls disregards local sentiments, HeForShe is a carefully constructed rhetoric that does not even speak about third gender. There was no attempt to accommodate such viewpoints on a global scale. The hashtag #HeForShe became ideological, as it only talked about gender binary; it's convenient and mainstream.

Furthermore, the culture industry leverages on such forms of activism by relying on its deputies: the intellectuals and the celebrated. Promoting for a cause or being part of it, one way or the other, the sign of reified activism. People consider such activities having a great value which eventually increases the brand value of such personalities who actively participate. As Gramsci (1992, p.12) says, "The intellectuals are the dominant group's 'deputies' exercising the subaltern functions of social hegemony and political government", the positioning of the celebrity in the society and aligning his or her identity with the cause of any given activism is a value creation exercise. Emma Watson is no exception to that.

Hashtag and Activism Agenda

Development of hashtag and its acceptance as part of daily social media discourse is interesting. Its inventor Chris Messina believed hashtag could really organize information online. It could enable piles of information to be clubbed under any given hashtag. But there has been a remarkable use of hashtags in terms of protest related sentiments, for example, the right to shout out. Activism has become new and sophisticated. Though, "Hashtag activism gained mainstream appeal in 2011, when Occupy Wall Street began using #OWS" (Vats, 2015, p. 210), one would consider such actions as enabler and empowering as activists were invoked offline and online. The social media congregation of protestors with different levels of activism surfaced. A consciousness was raised.

The creation of hashtags and their easy permeability within any given social media space positions the whole activism process as an agenda setting process. Within the social sphere, there are individuals or actors who have their own agenda set before themselves. They must confirm to the common identity shared by others so that they are in the loop and continue to be part of it. The agenda can be political imaginations, cultural reservations, social dilemmas etc. And, the hashtags dwell on social and cultural material produced elsewhere, which can be spread with own personal will. Hashtags act as connecting portal to different sphere of activism without any ending (Rambukkana, 2015).

In a networked society, digital democracy is much sought after. From one source decision making to multi source opinion making, things have radically changed. The time and space characteristic of social media allows divergent opinions to aggregate at its own pace. Socialization of opinions in a networked society is, thus, the fashionable outcome. According to Vandijk (2012), under the participatory democracy, "the emphasis lies on the broadest possible opinion formation about political affairs and on a particular combination of direct and representative democracy" (p.107).

The kind of democracy in which active participation leads to active citizenship, thus, building an active political character and ideology.

Hashtag, as a culture, has developed an identity which is globally known as tool for activist publics. The culture is essentially material that exhibits hope, outrage, judgment, and some hidden agenda. It has a hidden character of hailing (Althusser, 2006). "As digital artifacts, hashtags locate cultures across time and space. No matter the context—that is, grassroots, institutional, or corporate—hashtags compel us to act" (Conley, 2014, p.1111). Hashtags such as #MuslismsAreNotTerrorists, #Icebucketchallenge, #ihavedream etc., help locate an agenda which is specific for certain target audience, whereas hashtags such as #BringBackOurGirls and #HeForShe deliberate a universal appeal.

The characteristic of any given hashtag is its immediate acceptance and communicability. It can spread irrespective of the demography because it's designed to accommodate amplification value. However, when it's a hashtag, it just has to touch upon the deep anguish or celebrated moments, depending on the context the society is going through. Occupy Wall Street movement was a carefully orchestrated activism which initially used social media in a low profile manner and gradually relied on it to sustain the movement and connect with different ground actions. Its flagship hashtag #OccupyWallStreet created a deep impact worldwide. Several other activism carefully replicated the similar idea. Hashtags such as #OccupyBallroom, #OccupyUGC #Occupy etc, irrespective of their longevity, created a sense of ownership among the social media users.

On a similar note, #BringBackOurGirls and #HeForShe are two major efforts that were made to allow activism at a global scale. The selection of words and its syntagmatic arrangement created a powerful rhetoric. It's the power of hashtag that developed an attitude for activism. According to Khoja-Moolji (2015), the hashtag connects individuals who have an impression of the history and how history has affected the society; how it still affects. And, in the case of Nigerian girls, "...through the practices of hashtagging and (re)tweeting, the participants become part of a collectivity that seems to have certainty about the lives of girls in the global south as well as its own role in alleviating their suffering"(p.348).

SOLUTIONS AND RECOMMENDATIONS

It's a challenge for women to fight for their rights to live and function as an individual. This form of activism or movement that talks about the issues affecting women is collective in nature. Because women around the world are rising to claim what has long been denied to them. They are claiming spaces where previously there were no footprints of them. They are equally present in social media and building a strong online community. Apart from using hashtags to dissent, online communities are being formed to sustain the activism loyalty.

The "HeforShe" and "BringBackOurGirls" campaigns are a reminder to the world that we still need to go a long way. As there is a global outcry for gender equality, it is pertinent that the rhetoric of equality must include social media campaigns, offline protest related choreography and extensive celebrity endorsements. However, the collective activism has a misplaced orientation. Though there has been sincere attempts to incorporate legitimate voice to the activism sphere, the process has only managed to curate random thoughts under different hashtags. Breindel (2013) suggests that creating legitimacy has been recognized as an important aspect for interest groups. As discussed above in the discussion section, #BringBackOurGirls and #HeForShe has incorporated authenticity by bringing in the celebrities like Emma Watson, Michelle Obama, and Malala Yousafzai, and creating a strong agenda before the mass. Nevertheless, except embedding hashtags in social media posts, nothing concrete has been achieved so far. 'Social Actor' representation has become ideological.

Consequently, it is also important to understand the nature of authorship and how the content is developing an interactive field around it. Basically, the nature of interactivity must drive an action. It must create an impact on people who actually can intervene or have the power to bring a change. While we offer solidarity and hope to people in distress, we must understand that mere spectacle won't help. Besides, hashtags do not educate people about the real cause. There is a rise in fashionable use of such hashtags. There are instances of semantic error happening across social media. Hashtags such as #NotBuyingIt has been widely misrepresented (Stache, 2015). As digital activism can be of any shape, the protest must accommodate organic opinions, not just homogenous identity. A celebrity driven identity might have a pull effect, but it shouldn't undermine authorial character of individuals and their expressions. While physical protests are important aspect of any activism, private protests must find a space to evolve.

Gibson (2014) argues that #BringBackOurGirls hashtag has shed light on the problems in Nigeria, and it has also created a sympathetic community worldwide. The retweeting capabilities of the hashtags in general are powerful. Therefore, it must recognize the action effect of community resources. Moreover, the collective effort must connect with the true purpose of the activism. It should not produce mere spectacle.

In the case of #BringBackOurGirls and #HeforShe, the hashtags may enable women to share their own experiences and validate testimonies of other women (Eagle, 2015). However, the real life public spaces should be more interactive and it should add more competence, activity, authority and attitude for an effective activism. The crowd-sourcing efforts must not deviate from the real agenda and fall prey to a celebrity spectacled activism. Amid the growing practice of 'clicktivism' or 'desktop activism', collective sentiment must acknowledge solidarity by doing tangible things that really can create an impact on people who have the ability to intervene and score a change.

FUTURE RESEARCH DIRECTIONS

The recent development in the protest landscape has called for an in depth understanding of hashtags, their role and value beyond twitter. The radical changes, it has brought to the way social media functions is intriguing. The amalgamation of private and public spaces has given rise to new information and democracy order.

The future research must focus on the protest related discourse and the evolving ecology. There should be an attempt to explore the epistemological existence of the crowd sourced contents and its rhetorical capabilities. It is also necessary to understand the news value of hashtags and how they create an agenda in the society. Amid the global rhetoric of the girl power, education, and empowerment, there needs to be a study on how public conversations are mobilized and shaped into a public agenda. As social actors play a great role raising collective consciousness, future research may look into the aspect of intellectual labor and locate the existence of surplus value in social media discourse. Researchers may look into the relation between the activist performance and the activist interpersonal relationship on and off the screen. A diachronic study of the protest discourse may help in understanding the dynamics of the user contents.

CONCLUSION

#BringBackOurGirls and #HeForShe, both have created a social agenda that underscore the importance of women rights and equality. The evolving activist culture has given both these campaigns a great platform to disseminate persuasive contents. Moreover, digital activism nurtures the participatory instinct among users. In the case of the #BringBackOurGirls and #HeForShe campaign, sharing hashtags is self-explanatory. Hashtagging the protest sentiments and connecting different communities can sustain the social media discourse. Hashtags have become a part of daily life and they guide social dialogues, whether an introduction of a new product or asking people to register their view.

Furthermore, the collective intent is shaped by the agency, social actors and the ideology itself. "The #BringBackOurGirls movement coalesced a digital community into an in-person movement, which in turn produced political change for the people of Nigeria" (Olson 2016, p.13). As nowadays protest mobilization depends on the tools such as hashtag for political action, the motivated campaigns become people driven and assume the real-time characteristic i.e. current and mainstream sentiments. During Nigerian General Election, there was a huge pressure on President Goodluck Jonathan as he faced the politically charged hashtag #NigeriaDecides. The Boko Haram insurgency was the major issue that was raised before the government.

While #HeForshe and #BringBackOurGirls campaigns created a strong hashtag activism, there was also an opportunity for authorial expansion and imitation. It carried a decentralized authorship where the primary objective was repackaged and disseminated in a hybrid form, along with images, memes, sound bite and videos. For example, 'real men don't buy girls' is a message that came on social media along with #BringBackOurGirls.

Similarly, #HeForShe was a record breaking feminism call out. A hashtag was created and promoted by using a celebrity who enjoys a strong fan following globally, especially the young. Message was simple. The 'He' must stand for 'She'. The 'He' must act for gender equity. The most important thing about the campaign is its constant reminder to the world about the number of men who have signed for this. Using powerful infographics to persuade young people and channelize the activism rhetoric was dominant. It did not end there. Celebrity driven engagements were visible in other cross platforms. For Example, Emma Watson created a feminist Book Club on Goodreads to spread the awareness and further the cause of feminism.

It must be understood that the hashtags such as #BringBackOurGirls and #HeForShe gradually became a celebrity driven campaign. The new media environment which has the element of interactivity, convergence culture and participatory interface, allows celebrities to spread their star texts (Keller, 2014). Marwick and Boyd (2011) pointed out that the celebrity gossip, celebrity image, and institutional endorsements shape the new media narrative. "Celebrity is by necessity a co-performance that requires fan deference and mutual recognition of unequal status to succeed – otherwise, the practitioner is famous only in his or her own mind" (p.155). The performance value has an immediate effect and by default it achieves amplification. And, this gives hashtags a unique identity as they appear in cross-media platforms. Hashtags have become site for political and cultural appropriation.

REFERENCES

Althusser, L. (2006). *Lenin and Philosophy and Other Essays*. New Delhi: Aakar.

Anduiza, E., Cantijoch, M., & Gallego, A. (2009). Political Participation and the Internet. *Information Communication and Society*, *12*(6), 860–878. doi:10.1080/13691180802282720

Barassi, V. (2015). *Activism on the Web: Everyday Struggle against Digital Capitalism*. New York, NY: Routledge.

Bastos, M. T., Raimundo, R. L. G., & Travitzki, R. (2013). Gatekeeping Twitter: Message Diffusion in Political Hashtags. *Media Culture & Society*, *35*(2), 260–270. doi:10.1177/0163443712467594

Baudrillard, J. (1998). *The Consumer Society: Myths and Structures*. London: Sage.

BBOG Nigeria [BBOGNigeria] (2015, April 14). @BBOG_Nigeria#ChibokGirlsAmbassadors#365DaysOn#NeverToBeForgotten All they want is for the world to unite to #BringBackOurGirls [Tweet]. Retrieved from https://twitter.com/BBOG_Nigeria/status/587927237355302912

Bernays, E. L. (2004). *Propaganda*. Brooklyn: IG Publishing.

Blank, G., & Reisdorf, B. C. (2012). The Participatory Web. *Information Communication and Society*, *15*(4), 537–554. doi:10.1080/1369118X.2012.665935

Breindel, Y. (2013). Assessing success in internet campaigning. *Information Communication and Society*, *16*(9), 1419–1440. doi:10.1080/1369118X.2012.707673

Castells, M. (2010). *The Power of Identity* (2nd ed.). Oxford: Wiley Blackwell, Chakravartty, P., & Roy, S. (2015). Mr. Modi goes to Delhi: Mediated Populism and the 2014 Indian Elections. *Television & New Media*, *16*(4), 311–322. doi:10.1177/1527476415573957

Chandrachud, N. (2014). *We should be Critical, But Not Dismissive of Emma Watson's UN Campaign*. Retrieved from http://www.huffingtonpost.ca/neha-chandrachud/emma-watson-un-campaign_b_5883200.html

Christensen, C. (2013). Wave-riding and Hashtag-jumping. *Information Communication and Society*, *16*(5), 646–666. doi:10.1080/1369118X.2013.783609

Conley, T. L. (2014). From #RenishaMcBride to #RememberRenisha: Locating Our Stories and Finding Justice. *Feminist Media Studies*, *14*(6), 1111–1113. doi:10.1080/14680777.2014.975474

Eagle, R. B. (2015). Loitering, Lingering, Hashtagging: Women Reclaiming Public Space Via #BoardtheBus, #StopStreetHarassment, and the #EverydaySexism Project. *Feminist Media Studies*, *15*(2), 350–353. doi:10.1080/14680777.2015.1008748

Eaton, M. (2010). Manufacturing community in an online activist organization. *Information Communication and Society*, *13*(2), 174–192. doi:10.1080/13691180902890125

Emma Watson. Gender Equality is your issue too. (2014). Retrieved from http://www.unwomen.org/en/news/stories/2014/9/emma-watson-gender-equality-is-your-issue-too

Fiske, J. (2011). Introduction to Communication Studies (3rd ed.). New York, NY: Routledge.

Ganesh, S., & Zoller, H. M. (2012). Dialogue, Activism, and Democratic Social Change. *Communication Theory*, *22*(1), 66–91. doi:10.1111/j.1468-2885.2011.01396.x

Gerbaudo, P. (2012). *Tweets and the Streets: Social Media and Contemporary Activism*. London: Pluto Press.

Gibson, M. (2014). *Can A Social Media Campaign Really #BringBackOurGirls.* Retrieved from http://time.com/90693/bringbackourgirls-nigeria-boko-haram/

Gramsci, A. (1992). *Selection from the Prison Notebooks of Antonio Gramsci* (Q. Hoare & G. N. Smith, Eds.). New York, NY: International Publishers.

Green, H. (2011). Breaking Out of Your Internet Filter Bubble. Retrieved from http://www.forbes.com/sites/work-in-progress/2011/08/29/breaking-out-of-your-internet-filter-bubble/#51d199e5e90a

Hong, S. (2013). Who benefits from Twitter? Social media and political competition in the U.S. House of Representatives. *Government Information Quarterly*, *30*(4), 464–472. doi:10.1016/j.giq.2013.05.009

Jenkins, H., Ford, S., & Green, J. (2013). *Spreadable Media: Creating Value and Meaning in a Networked Culture*. New York, NY: New York University Press.

John, A. (2014). *What's Wrong With Our Well-Intentioned Boko Haram Coverage.* Retrieved from http://www.thewire.com/politics/2014/05/whats-wrong-with-our-well-intentioned-boko-haram-coverage/361993/

Keller, J. M. (2014). Fiercely Real? Tyra Banks and the making of new media celebrity. *Feminist Media Studies*, *14*(1), 147–164. doi:10.1080/14680777.2012.740490

Khoja-Moolji, S. (2015). Becoming an Intimate Publics: Exploring the Affective Intensities of Hashtag Feminism. *Feminist Media Studies*, *15*(2), 347–350. doi:10.1080/14680777.2015.1008747

Kim, J. N., & Sriramesh, K. (2009). A descriptive model of activism in global public relations research and practice. In K. Sriramesh & D. Vercic (Eds.), *The global public relations Handbook* (Rev. ed., pp. 79–97). New York: Routledge.

Kim, T. (2015). Defining the Occupy Movement: Visual Analysis of Facebook Profile Images Posted by Local Occupy Movement Groups. *Visual Communication Quarterly*, *22*(3), 174–186. doi:10.1080/15551393.2015.1069192

Kohn, A. (2015). Instagram as a naturalized propaganda tool: The Israel Defense Forces Web site and the phenomenon of shared values. *Convergence (London)*, *1*(18), 1–17. doi:10.1177/1354856515592505

Lee, F. L. F., & Chan, J. M. (2016). Digital media activities and mode of participation in a protest campaign: A study of the Umbrella Movement. *Information Communication and Society*, *19*(1), 4–22. doi:10.1080/1369118X.2015.1093530

Loken, M. (2014). #BringBackOurGirls and the Invisibility of Imperialism. *Feminist Media Studies*, *14*(6), 1100–1101. doi:10.1080/14680777.2014.975442

Malala Fund [MalalFund], (2015, April 13). #LISTEN: Malala Reads Her Letter to the Abducted Chibok Schoolgirls.

Marwick, A., & Boyd, D. (2011). To see and be seen: Celebrity Practice on Twitter. *Convergence*, *17*(2), 139–158. doi:10.1177/1354856510394539

Maxfield, M. (2015). History retweeting itself: Imperial feminist appropriations of "Bring Back Our Girls". *Feminist Media Studies*. doi:10.1080/14680777.2015.1116018

Murthy, D. (2011). Twitter: Microphone for the Masses. *Media Culture & Society*, *33*(5), 779–789. doi:10.1177/0163443711404744

Ogunlesi, T. (2014). *Hijacking Nigeria's #BringBackOurGirls campaign: Why does the West assume a tweet can fix Africa's problems*. Retrieved from http://www.aljazeera.com/indepth/opinion/2014/10/hijacking-nigeria-bringback-our-20141022135491484 65.html

Olson, C. C. (2016). #BringBackOurGirls: Digital communities supporting real-world change and influencing mainstream media agendas. *Feminist Media Studies*. doi:10.1080/14680777.2016.1154887

Olsson, T. (2008). The Practices of Internet Networking – A Resource for Alternative Political Movements. *Information Communication and Society*, *11*(5), 659–674. doi:10.1080/13691180802126760

Rambukkana, N. (2015). *Hashtag Publics: The Power and Politics of Discursive Networks*. New York, NY: Peter Lang. doi:10.3726/978-1-4539-1672-8

Reestorff, C. M. (2014). Mediatised Affective Activism: The Activist Imaginary and the Topless Body in the Femen Movement. *Convergence*, *20*(4), 478–495. doi:10.1177/1354856514541358

Sam, O. K. (2015). *Abducted Nigerian girls still missing, a distracted world must remember*. Retrieved from http://www.latimes.com/opinion/op-ed/la-oe-sam-bring-back-our-girls-20150108-story.html

Seo, H. (2014). Visual Propaganda in the Age of Social Media: An Empirical Analysis of Twitter Images during the 2012 Israeli–Hamas Conflict. *Visual Communication Quarterly*, *21*(3), 150–161. doi:10.1080/15551393.2014.955501

Siapera, E., Hunt, G., & Lynn, T. (2015). #GazaUnderAttack: Twitter, Palestine and Diffused War. *Information Communication and Society*, *18*(11), 1297–1319. doi:10.1080/1369118X.2015.1070188

Small, T. A. (2011). What the Hashtag. *Information Communication and Society*, *14*(6), 872–895. doi:10.1080/1369118X.2011.554572

Stache, L. C. (2015). Advocacy and Political Potential at the Convergence of Hashtag Activism and Commerce. *Feminist Media Studies*, *15*(1), 162–164. doi:10.1080/14680777.2015.987429

The White House, Office of the Press Secretary. (2014). *Weekly Address: The First Lady Marks Mother's Day and Speaks Out on the Tragic Kidnapping in Nigeria* [Press Release]. Retrieved from https://www.whitehouse.gov/the-press-office/2014/05/10/weekly-address-first-lady-marks-mother-s-day-and-speaks-out-tragic-kidnap

Vandijk, J. (2012). The Networked Society (3rded.). London: Sage.

Varnali, K., & Gorgulu, V. (2015). A social influence perspective on expressive political participation in Twitter: The case of #OccupyGezi. *Information Communication and Society*, *18*(1), 1–16. doi:10.1080/1369118X.2014.923480

Vats, A. (2015). Cooking Up Hashtag Activism: #PaulasBestDishes and Counter narratives of Southern Food. *Communication and Critical. Cultural Studies*, *12*(2), 209–213. doi:10.1080/14791420.2015.1014184

Watson, E. [EmmaWatson]. (2014, October 8). Between 20th Sep & 2nd Oct there were 1.1 million #HeForShe tweets from 750K different users, reaching 1.2 BILLION unique Twitter users [Tweet]. Retrieved from https://twitter.com/EmWatson/status/519844138716762113

KEY TERMS AND DEFINITIONS

Cross Media Narrative: Creating a narrative and adapting it to various media. The format varies from one media to another.

Cyberactivism: Otherwise known as Internet activism. It involves taking up an action or creating a movement online. Activist become part of online groups or forums and express their viewpoints.

Cyber-Democracy: Appropriation of democratic rights by exercising online activities. Basically, it is about how Internet facilitates interactivity and right to register opinion.

Hashtag: A hashtag is a sign (#) that is used before any word or character to organize any information. It was first used on twitter. Gradually, it's being used in every social media platform.

Hypertexts: Hypertexts are texts which has nonlinear characteristic. Hypertexts contain links to other sources. When a user clicks on it, the link redirects to another source.

Propaganda: Art of manipulating people by any means to avail personal gain. People spread information—true or false—to defend or offend any viewpoints.

Semiotics: It is the study of sign systems which includes the sign itself, the code system and the culture within which these signs operate.

Chapter 6
The Role of Social Media in Enforcing Environmental Justice around the World

Gayle M. Pohl
University of Northern Iowa, USA

ABSTRACT

This chapter is a critical analysis of the role that social media plays enforcing environmental justice around the world. It particularly examines how social media has been used internationally to foster Greenpeace International's actions to enforce environmental justice and compliance in three selected countries, namely India, Canada and Russia. The cases examined are a.) the Essar Ltd.'s coal mine project in the Mahan Forests in India; b.) Prirazlomnaya Oil Company's offshore drilling in the Artic Sea, and c.) Resolute Forests Products' mining in the Boreal Forest in Canada. The paper concludes that social media can be used to promote and foster environmental justice globally.

DOI: 10.4018/978-1-5225-2019-1.ch006

INTRODUCTION

This chapter is a critical analysis of the role that social media plays enforcing environmental justice around the world. Social media reaches millions of viewers and listeners. However; social media must be used wisely, because it takes many work hours to design messages and monitor them so, in essence, posting to social mediums are not free. Organizations need hundreds of followers before marketing is beneficial to the ROI (return on investment). Organic use of the social mediums restricts the geographic reach of your audience, but you will be able to probe deeply into behaviors and patterns of interaction of your targeted audience. Adapting the specific messages and mediums to the specific audiences is exhausting, but it is well worth the effort because of the resulting responses and actions.

Social capital is used as the theoretical framework for this study. In each of the three cases discussed, the organization uses its social capital in a corrupt, bureaucratic way whereas Greenpeace uses its social capital in a trusting, investment method to assist the poor and indigent population. The chapter also examines how social media has been used internationally to foster Greenpeace International's actions to enforce environmental justice and compliance in three selected countries, namely India, Canada and Russia. The cases examined are: a) the Essar Ltd.'s coal mine project in the Mahan Forests in India; b) Prirazlomnaya Oil Company's offshore drilling in the Artic Sea; and c) Resolute Forests Products' mining in the Boreal Forest in Canada. Through the use of case study research methodology this study concludes that social media can be used to promote and foster environmental justice globally.

SOCIAL CAPITAL THEORY AS THEORETICAL FRAMEWORK

The concept of organizations and community activists' groups interacting with one another is not a new factuality. Gaining and/or exchanging social capital through professional networking is a common business practice today. Therefore, when Greenpeace, an internationally well-known environmental organization received a whiff of perceived wrong-doing by an international corporate entity they were sure to play on their social capital and shout to their supporters across the globe that evil was being perpetrated. The corporate entities, who were supported by customers and other businesses (their social capital) cried they were following the letter of the law. So, what is social capital, how did this "fight" come about and who did this fight engage?

Social capital defined by Hanifan (1916, p.130) is:

Those tangible substances [that] count for most in the daily lives of people: namely good will, fellowship, sympathy, and social intercourse among the individuals and families who make up a social unit. . . . If [an individual comes] into contact with his neighbor, and they with other neighbors, there will be an accumulation of social capital, which may immediately satisfy his social needs and which may bear a social potentiality sufficient to the substantial improvement of living conditions in the whole community. (Hanifan, 1916, p.130)

Today, communication researchers believe that social capital is positive as long as it has a constructive effect on people's lives (Woolcook & Narayan, 2000). The idea of social capital is one of the important assets that can be used during a crisis, used for one's enjoyment or leveraged for one's gain. That is why people may volunteer for community groups, help disadvantaged children knowing that they need more than motivation, participating in church groups or assisting in fundraising for special causes. People in this type of community have more social capital and are in a stronger place to combat exposures from organizations and other invading forces.

Social relations and political ties lead to the first type of social capital that organizations and activists' groups rely heavily upon, the networks view. Granovetter (1973), "recognizes that strong intracommunity ties give families and communities a sense of identity and common purpose" (Astone et al., 1999). On the other hand, "...without weak intercommunity ties, such as those that cross various social divides based on religion, class, ethnicity, gender, and socioeconomic status, strong horizontal ties can become a basis for the pursuit of narrow sectarian interests" (Woolcock & Narayan, 2000).

The networks view of social capital can only be seen as two-headed. Valuable services for the community can result, but costs and negative outcomes can be a consequence in the form of claims on a person's sense of obligation and loyalty, along with economic repercussions. Group loyalties may be so strong that people may be isolated from information or opportunities or an atmosphere of ridicule or bullying may develop. The contexts of social capital need to be differentiated from one another. The rewards need to be discerned from the consequences. Woolcock and Narayan (2000, p. 231) say "Imputing only desirable outcomes to social capital, or equating them with it, ignores the possibility that these outcomes may be attained at another group's expense, that given outcomes may be suboptimal, or that desirable outcomes attained today come at the price of significant costs tomorrow."

Woolcock and Narayan (2000, p. 234) state that "the particular strength of the networks view is its willingness to engage in detailed policy discussions on the basis of compelling empirical evidence and detailed assessments of the veracity of competing explanations. The networks perspective recognizes that weak laws and overt discrimination can undermine efforts by poor minorities to act in their collective interest." This is a good case for organizations with strong social capital such as Greenpeace to come in and help the poor.

Another social capital perspective is the institutional perspective which posits that community networks and civil society reside as the result of political, legal and institutional environments, which gives rise to both good and bad outcomes (Woolcock & Narayan, 2000, p. 234). North (1990) argues "that the very capacity of social groups to act in their collective interest depends on the quality of the formal institutions under which they reside. He also stresses that the performance of states and firms themselves depends on their own internal coherence, credibility, and competence and on their external accountability to civil society."

In a study conducted by Knack and Keefer (1995; 1997) results showed that social capital paralleled with generalized trust, rules of law, civil liberties, and bureaucratic excellence are positively correlated with financial strength and growth. Woolcock and Naryan (2000, p. 235) believe "rampant corruption, frustrating bureaucratic delays, suppressed civil liberties, vast inequality, divisive ethnic tensions, and failure to safeguard property rights (to the extent that they exist at all) are major impediments to prosperity. In countries where these conditions prevail, there is little to show for well-intentioned efforts to build schools, hospitals, roads, and communications infrastructure or to encourage foreign investment…Investments in civic and government social capital are thus highly complementary to investments in more orthodox forms of capital accumulation." Profit organizations such as Essar, Gazprom and Resolute Forest Products use their social capital with foreign governments creating major impediments for the poor and indigent in the country. Greenpeace uses their social capital to advocate for the poor and indigent.

To measure social capital, we have to look at the membership in informal and formal associations and networks. In developing and rural countries measures are those that obtain the informal give and take of information and connections made through traditional networking. Narayan and Pritchett (1999) "developed an index of social capital at the household and community levels that included density and characteristics of informal and formal groups and networks. The dimensions of this index included group functioning, financial and in-kind contributions to groups, participation in decision-making, and heterogeneity of membership. A series of measures was also constructed on interpersonal trust and changes over time. These measures demonstrated that social capital was indeed both social and capital, generating returns that exceeded those to human capital" (Woolcock & Naryan, 2000, p. 240). Knack and Keefer (1997) added that trust and investment in a country are also factors in social capital measurement. Greenpeace's credibility with members garnered a larger bank of social capital and investment whereas a new organization such as Essar or Resolute Forest Product coming in and stripping the land or destroying the livelihoods of indigenous cultures diminished any thoughts of trust. The amount of social capital each organization brought to the table was announced loudly to the public through various social media platforms.

CASE STUDY RESEARCH

A case study is the study of the elements and peculiarities of a single or series of single cases, in an attempt to understand its complexities in a specified set of circumstances. This chapter focuses on three separate but similar cases. Since we are interested in the case itself we will be conducting intrinsic case study research. In case study research the cases are chosen for particularization and generalization. The emphasis is on interpretation of the events (Stake, 1995). Context of the cases are more salient than the method used for data analysis. Direct interpretation is used for intrinsic case study approaches (Yin, 2013).

The cases were chosen for their association with Greenpeace (a well-known international activists' group), their use of social media, and amount of information readily available for the case study. The primary sources of data gathering were articles from the Internet and videos and discussions from a variety of social media platforms. The similarities of the cases include: 1) an indigenous population is in jeopardy as a result of corporate action; 2) some wildlife species is threatened or endangered; and 3) an ecosystem is disrupted. Each case discusses how a corporate entity ignored established policy for perceived financial gain and how Greenpeace rallied activists internationally. The main goal was to determine if social media is to promote and foster environmental justice globally.

SOCIAL MEDIA MANAGEMENT

Online media allows people to interact, engage and collaborate easily and often. Due to a voluminous number of social media platforms available to us today, conversations happen spontaneously. Organizations and activists' groups such as the one we study in this chapter must carefully track conversations and monitor the discussions that occur within the context of their specific cases. Incoming, coming and outgoing interactions along with other activities can be monitored in a resourceful manner if social media management tools are used. These tools streamline how the organization listens to and participates in relevant social media conversations such as blogs, Tweets, Facebook comments and other web and private communities. They check to see what people are saying about the organization's situation, campaigns and events.

Social media is word of mouth at the speed of light. It is essential to know and understand what your communities are thinking and saying about your company. The strategy is to build credibility and a positive reputation with your targeted publics. It is also critical to mitigate damage should any negative comments and/or movements begin to shape into being. A company or group can alleviate negative situations by creating positive content in various social media platforms such as Facebook, Twitter, Instagram, or YouTube. No one venue will stop the damage but a combination will certainly stymie the concern. You will need to consistently promote goodwill on all fronts.

Of all Internet users, 74% use social media sites. Of those users, 71% use Facebook, 23% Twitter and 81% YouTube. Facebook users love to see photos or videos, want to know how to learn or help others, keep up with current events, receive support from others and be entertained (Pewresearchcenter.org, 2013).

YouTube has one billion users. Generation Z (14-17 year olds) comprise 81.9% of that group while millennial include 81%, Generation X 58% and Boomers 43%. There are 4 billion YouTube views per day, which translates into 300 hours of viewing per minute or 323 videos viewed per minute. 57% of Canadians find YouTube videos more engaging than television (YouTube Statistics, 2014).

One general rule of thumb is to increase the number of likes or impressions on your social media. These likes/impressions mean that the message is being read, which equates to validation and attention to the cause, organization and the people (Wallace, 2014). On the social media that have likes, it often turns into a competition to see who can obtain the most likes. The number of original tweets someone receives gives a true indication of the number of people reading the tweet and engaged it the topic (Guneluis, 2014). Once again, this is an example of attention and validation for the content and cause. Each of the cases discussed uses various social media platforms extensively.

THE CASE STUDIES

Greenpeace vs. Resolute Forest Products

The first contender is the Boreal Forest. Canada's boreal forest area comprises 60% of the country's land mass. It occupies all regions between Alaska and the Yukon.

It is the world's largest ecosystem, including wetlands, grasslands, tundra, and rivers. A third-party forest product industry company, Resolute Forest Products, specializing in pulp, tissue, and paper, decided to log into Canada's boreal forest. Resolute entered into an agreement with the Canadian Boreal Forest, creating the largest partnership of its kind. The partnership brought in nine environmental groups and 21 forest product businesses to guarantee the sustainability of the forest. The agreement stated that all land disturbed would be replanted, protected space would be sculpted and preserved, animal preservations would be created and some areas would be saved from logging.

The Cree Nation occupies part of the land near Quebec as their ancestral lands. The Cree Nation is the most densely inhabited aboriginal people in Canada. Self-government and economic development are goals of the Cree people. The Cree Nation has negotiated with development corporations and governments across Canada for their share of natural gas and energy revenues. In 2002 the Paix de Braves Agreement was signed between the government of Quebec and the Grand Council of Cree. This agreement stated that the Cree peoples would share in the revenues stemming from mining, hydroelectric development and forestry carried out on the lands of the Cree People (GCC, 2016).

The Cree Nation lives on ancestral lands with their friends the caribou. These creatures are also called reindeer. They have large hooves that they use to support their bulk in the snow and to paddle through water. The underside of the hoof is hollowed out like a scoop and is used for digging as they search for food. Both the male and female caribou have antlers. Caribou are very important to indigenous northern people. The boreal forest land is rich in fertile soil and food for people and animal alike (National Geographic, 2016).

Resolute Forest Products owns over 40 pulp, paper, tissue and wood companies in the United States, Canada, and South Korea. It markets its products in over 80 countries throughout the world. For many decades Resolute Forest Products has worked with and for communities and governments world-wide to protect and preserve wildlife, breeding ground and culturally important ecosystems in boreal forest systems. It is the mission of the Resolute Forest Products to return the forest to its original condition as much as possible after the logging has taken place. Resolute Forest Products believe their company benefits from operating in a highly regulated environment with active federal and local government involvement.

Greenpeace's states its mission as: the leading independent campaigning organization that uses peaceful protest and creative communication to expose global environmental problems and to promote solutions that are essential to a green and peaceful future (Greenpeace.org, 2016). In the Resolute Forest case study, Greenpeace is dedicated to the preservation of the indigenous communities, the caribou habitat and the protection of the boreal forest itself from destruction, harm and extinction. Greenpeace claims that plants and animals play a vital role in global climate change. The boreal forest is also a source of culture for Indigenous communities, which are now being threatened by logging. Various social media were used to call upon environmental activists to rise up in solidarity with Greenpeace to protest the destruction of the forest, the peoples and the animals.

The Problem

According to Greenpeace, there is cause for alarm because Resolute Forest Products are logging in woodland areas and destroying the caribou habitat. Logging has occurred in areas of Ontario and Quebec where the caribou are being destroyed. Quebec's Chief Forester reported that the caribou herds are at risk of extinction. To date, over 92% of the herd has been destroyed and if logging continues no caribou will be seen for a large span of time (Greenpeace.org, 2016) in the boreal region. According to Woolcock and Naryan (2000, p. 235), this is rampant corruption and suppressed civil liberties. Woodland areas were destroyed and wildlife are at risk of extinction.

The Cree Nation holds ancestral land in the boreal forest that has not been logged or fragmented. Since Resolute Forest Products has come into the area to log over 40 million cubic meters of wood has been extracted. The remaining 10% is pristine woodland and the Cree Nation wants to maintain that land as is. The Cree Nation, with the help of Greenpeace, has sounded the alarm internationally to tell the world what will happen to the land if Resolute Forest Products is allowed to degrade their land. The Cree Nation proudly display large banner on the shores of the Quenonisca Lake near the Broadback Valley (Mainville, 2015). It reads "*Save the Broadback*" (Mainville, 2015). The Cree Nation's civil liberties' were trampled upon due to the abuse of Resolute's social capital.

An intact forest area that has not been logged or fragmented by roads or other human infrastructures is vital to the sustainability of natural life cycles of the ecosystems. Natural forest states provide more stable climates that can recover from insect outbreaks and forest fires. The natural state of a forest provides for better coverage and protection for trees, plants and animals from sudden changes in the climate, absorbs carbon dioxide and stores it in the trees and offers homes to threatened and endangered animal species, like caribou (Greenpeace.org, 2014b). Intact woodlands and forests are endangered themselves. Only 8% of intact woodlands and forests worldwide are protected. This is another large reason to protect the Boreal Forest region (Greenpeace.org, 2014b).

The Resolute Forest Products believe mining in the Boreal Forest area produces the benefits of conservation activities, protected-area development and collaborative forest management strategies as well as profit-sharing between the involved businesses. Greenpeace identified the Boreal forest as one of five of the valuable intact wildernesses left in Canada's commercial forest area. Resolute Forest Products is logging in this area and destroying land and caribou habitats, according to Greenpeace. Resolute, though, is suing Greenpeace for $7 million on the basis of defamation. Greenpeace says it will not be silenced. It will stand up for the forest.

Greenpeace saw the degradation of the Boreal Forest as unacceptable when the Cree Nation began losing their ancestral grounds and the caribou were becoming extinct, so the organization started to look at the buyers of Resolute Forest Products' merchandise. Greenpeace's social capital was seen by the Cree Nation as building rust and investment.

Nigel Sizer, Director of the Forest Program for the World Resources Institute stated, "These intact forest landscapes are some of the most important landscapes on Earth…Canada is the country with the largest share of intact forest degradation in the world. It is No. 1 on the list" (greenpeace.org, 2014a). The Forest's Product Association of Canada (FPA), an association dedicated to maintaining strong environmental standards in Canada, estimates that the wood industry exports $28.5 billion worth of paper and pulp products from the boreal forest annually. This means that a carbon footprint has been left on over 180 million acres of the forest to date.

Consequently, Greenpeace decided to assess the sustainability policies of companies who purchased paper and paper supplies mined by the Resolute Forest Products Company. To effectively assess the sustainability policies of other companies, Greenpeace first established minimum criteria for a sustainable policy. Greenpeace laid out:

For a forest product originating in the Boreal to be mined using a sustained method, it must include the following: 1) traceability of all products to the forest of origin; 2) clear definition of forests that require protection to retain their ecological integrity, including high conservation value or endangered forests and intact forest landscapes; 3) protection of woodland caribou and/or endangered species; 4) commitment to respecting indigenous rights; 5) commitment to increase use of recycled fiber with milestones and timelines; 6) implementation of mechanisms, including investigating supply chains for unwanted sources; 7) communicate clear expectations to suppliers and recognize sustainable performance with increased business relationships; and 8) transparently and regularly meet with stakeholders, i.e., like environmental organizations (greenpeace.org, 2014a). After an extensive assessment of business that purchased paper, pulp and paper-supplies from the Resolute Forest Products,

Greenpeace found that the leaders in sustainability practices were Kimberly-Clark and Hewlett Packard, followed by Office Depot/Office Max. The worst business in sustainability practice was Best Buy (Sustainablebrands.com, 2014). Greenpeace then issued the following statement in an advertisement:

Canada's globally important Boreal Forest faces mounting pressure as governments and industry grapple to balance economic development with long term conservation(borealscience.org, 2014). Major buyers of wood and paper products originating from the Boreal Forest have a responsibility to support healthy forests and communities with purchasing decisions. However, not all companies are demonstrating a commitment to responsible buying. A Greenpeace investigation has revealed that electronics giant Best Buy may be sourcing over 100 million pounds of paper annually from just one supplier, much of which originates in Canada's Boreal (According to Greenpeace research, roughly 1,000 tons of paper are delivered weekly to Best Buy in the US alone. These products originate from Resolute Forest Products. 52 weeks multiplied by 1,000 tons is 52,000 tons. There are 2204 pounds in a ton. 52,000 multiplied by 2204 is 114,608,000 pounds.) and is used to produce junk mail and flyers which are quickly thrown away. Trees in the Canadian Boreal can take over ninety years to mature. According to Greenpeace research Best Buy sources these materials from the controversial logging company Resolute Forest Products (Resolute). Resolute is an outlier in the Canadian forest sector responsible for significant degradation of the Boreal, destruction of endangered species habitat and disputes with Indigenous communities. Best Buy's paper purchasing, in contrast to more responsible consumer companies, is therefore actively contributing to the degradation of the Boreal forest. (YouTube Statistics, 2014)

This type of messaging is typical of Greenpeace. It is straightforward and identifies all offending parties and their behavior. It also clearly indicates the desirable behavior for "responsible consumer companies." After receiving hundreds of negative comments on blogs and over 3K Facebook posts, Best Buy ultimately switched its paper sourcing company and created a sustainable buying policy. Best Buy could have seen the use of Greenpeace's social capital as both a threat and reward. We see Best Buy engaging in decision-making in regard to this policy, but they did not initially do the research. They agreed with the rampant corruption for profit. When that profit could potentially dry up due to Greenpeace's actions, Best Buy decided to change their sustainability purchasing policy, proving their social capital lies strictly on the lines of economic profitability and environmental justice.

Social Media

Greenpeace uses social media to disseminate information about the Resolute Forest Products and the Boreal Forest. Facebook, YouTube, Twitter and various Websites are flooded with information about the activities of Resolute in the Boreal forest. Greenpeace also broadcasted hundreds of podcasts that engage thousands of followers who then chat on various social mediums, building a sustainable environmental community.

Greenpeace produced a YouTube video about Canada's Boreal Forest, explaining the uniqueness of the forest and all the social, economic and ecological importance of the forest's life cycle. This one video has 25,859 views. Another video discusses the importance of the flora and fauna found in this forest. This video has 83,544 views. A third video discusses the canoeing in the Boreal. It has 38,090 views. A fourth video, with 19,376 views, discusses boreal as a sustainable forest. Overall, Greenpeace produced more than 87 YouTube videos, with more than 23 million views. This is broad message dissemination. To contrast, Resolute Forest Products produced approximately 24 YouTube videos with fewer than 6,000 total views.

Facebook is used by 71% of all Internet users. Greenpeace shows photos of animals, uses emotional appeals about the ancestral land, the caribou habitats, and the Cree Nation. They strongly urge all people to action in every Facebook post and ad. Their Facebook followers have reached 3.5K views. Resolute does not use persuasive message appeals. Instead they discuss and highlight the sponsor dollars they have given to various causes, emphasizing they are the "good guys" because they contributed dollars. In one Facebook post, comments indicated that Greenpeace lied saying caribou had died when in reality it was jobs that had died. This article was actually about jobs in a Resolute plant in Alabama not in Canada. The post did show a photo of caribou, but it only received 85 views. Resolute does not push a persuasive message like Greenpeace nor does it use emotionally charged photos.

Twitter is a medium that attracts Millennials and some Boomers, but at a lower rate. Effective articles, tweets and retweets produce followers. Resolute Forest Products tweet about financial and hiring practices, but they have not taken their sustainability policies to the community where Greenpeace has taken their message directly to the international communities. Resolute has one tweet with no followers and Greenpeace has 35.5K with 1.54M followers. Their battle cry is that they will fight for the forest.

Greenpeace also made use of blogs written by environmentalists or sustainability scientists. They generated approximately 220 blogs on this issue with innumerable responses. Podcasts, which can solicit social media interaction, were also used by Greenpeace to disseminate their message of Resolute degrading the Boreal Forest. Resolute did not produce either blogs or podcasts.

Greenpeace's message is consistent throughout each social medium: Resolute Forest Products are degrading the land itself and the ancestral grounds of the Cree Nation and destroying the caribou habitat, perhaps to the point of extinction. They use persuasive language, photos, and authoritative voices to reinforce their consistent message that Resolute is harming the land and the wildlife. Greenpeace is flooding Facebook, Twitter, and YouTube with messages, and supplementing it with podcasts and blogs. Resolute Forest Products is not responding to the same cause. The videos are about the company and their corporate social responsibility program. They did, though, answer Greenpeace with a $7 million lawsuit for defamation, saying Greenpeace had not shown that the land mined had been harmed. Instead, Resolute, counters, the land was preserved. However, Resolute offered no visual evidence. Greenpeace, on the other hand, has offered research evidence in word, photo and audio formats via the most popular social media sites.

Greenpeace vs. Essar Power

Essar Power acquired commercial coal operations of the 1200 mega-watt plant Mahan power plant. "Essar Power MP Ltd, the operator of the 1200 MW power plant, located in Madhya Pradesh, has secured 3 lakhs (i.e., 30,000) tons of coal through a special Government-conducted … e-auction" in April of 2011 (Coalpost, 2016).

Essar Power MP won a captive coal mine in Tokisud in Jharkhand state in the recent coal auction. Essar has invested over 10,000 crore (rupees) in the 1200 MW (megawatts) Mahan plant which requires an estimated 5.5 metric tons per year (MTPA) of domestic coal per year and the Tokisud captive coal mine. The decline in coal prices and captive mines will enable Essar Power to fulfill its commitment to supply affordable power to the nation. The company has long-term power purchase agreements and is in the process of securing more such commitments. (Coalpost, 2016)

Essar was counting on the Mahan Block to provide a low-cost fuel source for the power plant, making it the lowest cost generator in India Essar Power commissions 600MW Mahan I power project (essar.com, 2012). Essar's sustainability policy is integrated with its economic, social and environmental objectives and aligned with the company's vision to "be a respected global entrepreneur, through the power of positive action" (Sustainability, n.d.). The company's sustainability policy goes on to say:

Essar Energy is committed to minimizing pollution, reducing its environmental footprint and optimizing resource consumption by planning and carrying out operations through environmentally responsible processes and practices. (The company) continually assess(es) environmental risks in (their) operations through risk and impact assessments and audits. All of (their) operations have environmental management plans which are specific to each site. As a responsible global energy Company, Essar Energy recognizes its obligations with regard to climate change mitigation and adaptation. Our approach continues to aim at providing clean solutions to our customers and reducing our carbon footprint by adopting the latest technology and energy conservation measures. (Essarenergy.com, 2016)

Coal

Mining for coal requires vast amounts of water, siphoning off water needed by farmers. Indian farmers have been suffering from a severe water crisis for years. Debt, crop failure, bad monsoons, carbon pollution and forest fires have devastated the lives of many Indian farmers. In 2013, farmers experienced the worst drought in the country since 1972 (Greenpeace.org/india, 2016a). The Indian government, though, has sold the farmers' rights to water to thermal power plants running on coal.

Coal ash is a dangerous by-product of burning coal for electricity. Coal ash is toxic, so it has dangerous effects on humans and wildlife across the globe. Coal companies have been able to dump this toxic waste into unlined ponds and landfills, that eventually run into rivers, streams and whole communities. (Accounting for the Costs of Coal, 2016, www.nwf.org/What-we-do/energy-and-climate/drilling-and-mining/getting-off-oal.aspx)

Greenpeace's View

Greenpeace points out that the indigenous community, Madhya Pradesh, is in fear of extinction due to the toxicity of the coal ash.

(The) Mahan, Madhya Pradesh (community) is facing the threat of extinction. "Over 14,190 lives and livelihoods are dependent on the Mahan forests, Madhya Pradesh. Their culture, community and lives are intertwined with the forests that (Essar Power has) threaten to destroy. Displacement from their natural habitat is going to be devastating for the indigenous community". (Greenpeace.org/india, 2016b)

Greenpeace claims that the coal mine would mean felling more than five million trees. That number of mined trees would affect as many as 50,000 people with at least two communities being leveled. Queries about the effects of mining on the leopards, sloth bears, peacocks, tigers and elephants are being investigated (Chamberlain, 2014; Barry, 2014). Almost 35% of the 1700 wild tigers in India reside in Central India where the Mahan Forest lies. The tiger, a national symbol of India, is now suffering the threat of endangerment because of coal mining.

Mahan is one of the oldest forests in Asia, spreading across 3,953.7 acres, housing over 54 villages and over 50,000 indigenous people and many endangering wildlife species. The lives of these people and animals have been threatened. A way of life will cease to exist if Greenpeace is not successful in its fight to save the Mahan forest. Thousands of animals will be placed either on a vulnerable or endangered animal list.

To seek support to stop the destruction of forests through coal mining, Greenpeace India created the imaginary 'Republic of Junglistan' in November of 2011. To enlist supporters and pass out "virtual citizenship papers and passports," the mascots, Bhaalu (bear) and Sheru (tiger) were created. (Thehindu.com, 2011). They go on to report:

Shiva Sharma, public engagement campaigner, Greenpeace India, said: "Coal India Limited already has 2 lakhs (20,000) hectares of land with them, of which 55,000 hectares is forest land. Hence, their contention that forest clearances are hampering power generation is misleading. The Coal Ministry's insistence on more land for mining is nothing short of a land grab. We are inviting people to join Junglistan as a show of support to our forests." The protestors noted that there are alternative sources of energy that are cleaner and sustainable and the country would have to make that choice if it wants energy security as well as a safe environment. (Thehindu.com, 2011)

Greenpeace again recognizes the bureaucratic failings and the needs of the population. Essar focuses on the ROI. Greenpeace's social capital with the people allows the organization to begin and continue an activist movement.

The Problem

In a newspaper article it was reported that under Indian law the people are entitled to vote on a referendum to allow coal development or not (Chamberlain, 2014). The Mahan community says this right has been by-passed because Essar Energy was granted permission to mine for coal in the Mahan forest of Madhya Pradesh after a lobbying campaign was presented to the top government officials. Essar Energy sent letters to the Indian Prime Minister and Finance Minster articulating coal mining was vital to fuel a power station that was essential for India's financial-viability since some economic boosts may result from the mining (Chamberlain, 2014). The article goes on to state the ministers did not consider the lives of thousands of people who rely on the forest for their livelihoods and the sustainability environmentalists, including Greenpeace, when considering this coal mining, so a course of conflict was set (Chamberlain, 2014). Indigenous Mayan people complained that Essar forced them to sign a petition granting their permission for coal mining on their land in the Mahan forest of Madhya Pradesh. There were even reports of forged signatures.

Kripanath of the Amelia village in the Singrauli district of Madhya Pradesh said, "On the evening of the Gram Sabha, the tehsildar (tax inspector) along with local policemen went around the village forcing villagers to sign the resolution. Later several signatures were forged. After obtaining a copy of the resolution, I was shocked to see that my signature was forged as well" (Greenpeace.org/india, 2016b). Radhakali of Mahan Sangharsh Samiti said, "Companies scare us and threaten us. They tell us that if we don't leave the forests, they will have us thrown behind bars" (Greenpeace.org/india, 2016b).

In the words of the Mayan people, this fight is important because:

We have been dependent on the Mahan forests for generations, collecting a variety of forest produce, which is a very significant source of our livelihood. Now the company says that these forests belong to them and we have no RIGHT on it" Bechanlal, member of Mahan Sangarsh Samiti and a resident of Amelia village. (Greenpeace.org/india, 2016b)

Greenpeace India's social media started a petition to save the forests. The revolution to overturn the e-auction began by gathering close to 300,000 signatures. The villagers told the Prime Minister that they wanted electricity from renewable sources such as rice husks instead of coal. They wanted to preserve their forests. Ensuing battles occurred. Greenpeace International funds were blocked in a move to stop a campaign against coal mining. Greenpeace senior coal campaigner Priya Pillai was called "anti-national" and was prevented from leaving India to travel to the UK to speak to a group of British MPs about the violations of a London-registered company Essar, because it could lead to negative effects against the India government, including sanctions. The Intelligence Bureau accused Greenpeace India of acting against "national interests" for opposing the coal mining in the Mahan forest of Madhya Pradesh (Roy, 2015).

The Mayan people say this fight is about their rights. They claim the laws have been bypassed. Due to the notoriety of the case, the Indian government reviewed the environmental laws. Under the Forest Rights Act community forest rights must be recognized before any consent for mining is granted. In the Essar case no community forest rights were recognized before the e-auction was granted. Freedom of speech was violated when Priya Pillai was called an anti-national and denied the privilege to travel to the UK, and the right to access organizational funding was denied to Greenpeace India. Therefore, the Mahan forest of Madhya Pradesh was declared off limits to coal mining. Pillai said:

Even as we celebrate this win for thousands of Indians, we are painfully aware that Mahan is just one of hundreds of coal mines planned in forested India. The ministry's current criteria for determining forests closed to mining is clearly inadequate, only serving the interests of mining corporations, ignoring the needs of the communities and wildlife that depend on our forests. (Roy, 2015)

Social Media

According to the Social Media Examiner (McGrath, 2013) there are seven approaches to using social media effectively. The first is to establish your social medium as a place where you can have conversations about your issue and/or brand. The Essar group used Facebook as a medium to post positive messages about their companies. The following is an example of one of their only Facebook posts about the Mahan project:

It is with immense pride that we announce that the 600-megawatt (MW) unit 1 of our 1,200MW Mahan I power project has commenced generation. This is Essar Power's eighth operational power plant, taking its total generating capacity to 3,910MW. (http://bit.ly/V6HjGv)

The following Facebook post shows the Mahan project (Figure 1).

This Essar post received 65 likes. Greenpeace India posted specific and direct messages about the wrongs being done to their previous forest: Below is just one example of their thousands of Facebook messages.

The crackdown on forest rights activists continues in India. Yesterday, two Greenpeace campaigners were arrested and their communication equipment was seized (http://grnpc.org/Ig047).

Figure 1. The Mahan project
ESSAR.COM (Essar Power Facebook Post), January 3, 2013 "Essar Power commissions 600MW Mahan I power project"

Indian coal company, Essar, wants to build a mine that would destroy 1,000 hectares of the Mahan forest, which the local communities rely on for their livelihood. Nothing strengthens authority so much as silence. NOW is the moment to raise your voice: demand that Jual Oram, the Tribal Affairs Minister, ensures that a free and fair community vote (Gram Sabha) is held: http://grnpc.org/Ig047. (Greenpeace India Facebook post, July 31, 2014)

This Facebook post was accompanied by the photo shown in Figure 2.

Conversations are spurred by emotional words and well placed photos that show action and passion. This post alone has 2.1 thousand likes. Overall, Greenpeace India garnered 34.7 thousand likes whereas Essar only received approximately 200 likes on its posts about the Mahan project. Greenpeace India had previously established a relationship with its constituents as an organization that was there to help save their forests and preserve their livelihoods and wildlife. Essar is imaged as the big corporate giant that wanted to look for their own economic gain.

The Social Media Examiner (McGrath, 2013) states that the second approach to a successful social media usage is to build credibility by establishing the brand/issue as a thought, service leader in a geographic or professional area. You can do this by

Figure 2.

sharing press releases, media briefs, media kits, etc. Both Essar and Greenpeace do this equally well. Their tweets were followed up with press releases. They both post news and media releases as they are issued. Essar issued 8,321 tweets, 197 following with 35.9 thousand followers. Greenpeace, on the other hand, issued 9,773 tweets, 1,072 following with 24.5 thousand followers.

The third and fourth approaches to strategically enhance social media are to invite conversations and share blog content (McGrath, 2013). Greenpeace India has 194 blogs discussing the Mahan project and the Essar Company has no blogs. Both organizations have Instagram sites followed by conversations. Essar has 122 posts with children talking about various projects throughout the world. They did not discuss the Mahan Project. The Greenpeace project had 11 posts and they focused on the degradation of the Mahan forest, the destruction of the land, and the threat to the animals and children. Greenpeace of India also created a Flickr site with posts of the Mahan forest of Madhya Pradesh. They have 95 followers. All of these social media activities prompt conversations among the concerned parties.

The last three social media approaches are ones both companies have excelled at using, but have they:

1. Directed them at the correct audiences;
2. Been an on-going source of relevant information in the appropriate area of expertise;
3. Integrated current events into the relevant social media; and
4. Made direct calls to action? These are the strategic approaches that the Social Media Examiner recommend.

Essar is a leading excavation company, but it does mining by threatening the preservation of forests, wildlife habitats and indigenous communities. Essar's YouTube highlights the methods they use and the sponsorships they give to various communities. The organization has produced 20 videos with 22,000 views. Greenpeace India features the Mahan forest of Madhya Pradesh on YouTube with 103 videos with 400,000 views. Discussion follows each of the videos. Did Essar Power choose the correct audience as its targeted public for this project?

Greenpeace UK vs. Gazprom's Prirazlomnaya

Gazprom is a global energy company focused on the extraction, processing and sale of oil, natural gas and fuel. They are the "world's largest natural gas reserves. The Company's share in the global and Russian gas reserves amounts to 17 and 72 per cent respectively. Gazprom accounts for 12 and 69 per cent of the global and national gas output correspondingly. At present, the Company is actively implementing large-scale gas development projects in the Yamal Peninsula, the Arctic shelf, Eastern Siberia and the Russian Far East, as well as a number of hydrocarbon exploration and production projects abroad" (Gazprom.com, 2016).

Gazprom is a reliable supplier of gas to Russian and foreign consumers. The Company owns the world's largest gas transmission system with a total length of 170.7 thousand kilometers. Gazprom sells more than half of its gas to Russian consumers and exports gas to more than 30 countries within and beyond the former Soviet Union. Gazprom is among Russia's top four oil producers. The Company also owns major power-generating assets accounting for some 17 percent of the total installed capacity of the national energy system. In addition, Gazprom ranks number one in the world in terms of thermal energy generation. (Gazprom.com, 2016)

The company's sustainability stance is to be the global energy leader by moving into new markets, diversifying its activities and sales regions, offering trustworthy supplies, improving operating competencies and consistently improving it scientific and technical abilities (Sustainability Report, 2008). Crude oil makes natural oil. It is a combination of liquid, gas and sticky, tar-like substances. Oil and natural gas are cleaner fuels than coals, but they have disadvantages. These fossil fuels produce large amounts of carbon. The plants and other bio-matter on the seafloor emit these carbons. Hydrocarbons, including methane gas, are trapped in the rocks on the sea-floor. These petroleum sources contain pockets of trapped gas within rock layers underneath the seafloor. "Extracted crude oil is refined and used to manufacture gasoline (used in transportation) and petrochemicals (used in the production of plastics, pharmaceuticals, and cleaning products)" (Spooner, 2012, p.1).

The environmental impact of drilling for oil can be deleterious. Companies pump liquid oil out of the water by using drilling rigs. The oil fills rock layers like a sponge, spreading throughout the open spaces. After the area containing the oil is empty they move the rig. Oil rigs are placed on platforms in the ocean. Some of the most toxic effects of this process include:

- Refining petroleum creates air pollution: Transforming crude oil into petro-chemicals releases toxins into the atmosphere that are dangerous for human and ecosystem health.
- Burning gasoline releases CO2: Although oil doesn't produce the same amount of CO2 that coal burning does, it still contributes greenhouse gases to the atmosphere and increases global warming.
- Oil spills cause great environmental damage: Large oil spills some-times occur during drilling, transport, and use, which of course affect the surrounding environment. But these spills aren't the only risk (Spooner, 2012, p. 2).

In 2011 Greenpeace, World Wildlife Fund, and Bellona (an international, environmental sustainability NGO located in Oslo, Netherlands) requested that Gazprom delay it oil manufacturing plans, dreading it had not equipped its oil field appropriately or proved that it had all the required technology needed in case of an oil spill under the thick coat of Arctic ice.

Greenpeace released a report in 2012 entitled "Russian Arctic Offshore Hydrocarbon Exploration: Investment Risks," which clearly outlined all the risks of that Spooner (2012) discussed about offshore fossil fuel ex-traction, including the decrease in Arctic mammal and bird populations as well as creating abnormalities in fish. Greenpeace went on to discuss the injurious effects on the livelihoods of the indigenous populations and the failure to support those communities (Platform.reprisk.com, 2013).

One reason to object to Gazprom's oil plans is Prirazlomnaya is the first platform to start commercial oil pumping under the Arctic ice covered waters. This platform was built with decommissioned pieces of North Sea rigs that were rusting in a Murmansk shipyard. The Prirazlomnaya is built with used parts, operates in a remote area of the Arctic where ice is present 8 months of the year and where temperatures can be as low as 50 below centigrade. Logic concludes the Prirazlomnaya platform is a safety hazard in the conditions in which it will operate.

Furthermore, Gazprom will not reveal their oil spill crisis plan to the public. The Arctic Council (An intergovernmental forum for Arctic governments and residents) demand that all oil spill plans be made public. Gazprom has revealed only a short summary of their spill plan and it is evident the company can only handle a spill the size of a 73,000-barrel spill. Greenpeace says that the summary clearly shows that they are unable to deal with a crisis in the far north, which may discharge around 5 million barrels of oil.

Oil spills happen frequently and are, virtually, inevitable. The chance of a spill is even higher in icy waters with icebergs and extreme waters. This makes cleanup close too impossible. The Pew Environment Group "examined oil spill response plans for operations in the Arctic and warned that the oil industry is not prepared for the Arctic, the spill plans are thoroughly inadequate, adding that Arctic spill plans underestimate the probability and consequence of catastrophic blowouts (Ayliffe, 2013, p. 2). The World Wildlife Fund said Gazprom's spill plans were "Imagineering and not Engineering" (Ayliffe, 2013, p. 2).

Since the Prirazlomnaya sits next to national parks and wildlife sanctuaries (that house Atlantic walruses and bird habitats) oil spills will endanger these species. The livelihood of the Indigenous people on the Pechora Sea will be damaged as they fish and hunt daily. Whole regions in Russia are being harmed by oil spills. Over 5 million tons of oil spills have leaked into the Arctic Ocean. The Arctic region is fragile. The Arctic is 30% below its last calculation in ice coverage. The climate is changing as the ice thins. Oil must be left in the ground and under the water if the world is to remain inhabitable. The International Energy Agency recommends that 60% of known reserves remain in the ground or under the sea in order for the ground to stay 2 degrees Celsius of warming. This means that pumping oil of the sea is incompatible with global actions to limit climate change (Ayliffe, 2013, p. 3).

In September 2013, thirty Greenpeace activists boarded a ship called the 'Arctic Sunrise' and set sail from Norway for the Prirazlomnaya platform in Russia. Their mission was to stop the rig from drilling for oil in the Arctic Ocean. They were in international waters where the Russians could not, technically, arrest them. The Russians radioed the 'Arctic Sunrise' and said that the ship was not to approach the Prirazlomnaya. The activists sailed onward. The Coastguard fired five shots across the bow of the 'Arctic Sunrise.' As the activists reach the platform, two activists tried to scale the side of the Prirazlomnaya. A nearby Russian coast guard ship with agents who were masked responded by ramming and slashing the inflatable boats of the Greenpeace activists. They sprayed the activists with water cannons, fired warning shots and arrested the two who scaled the side of the platform (Goodman & Gonzalez, 2013).

The next day they descended on the 'Arctic Sunrise' with ropes and helicopters and held the remaining activists at gunpoint. President Putin said it would had better if Greenpeace had setup a meeting to discuss the issues and it was obvious that these people had violated international law. They charged all of the activists with piracy. If found guilty, the Greenpeace activists could face up to 15 years in prison (Goodman & Gonzalez, 2013).

Since the activists were from different countries, people from all over the globe formed protest groups to support the detained Greenpeace protestors, claiming there was no legal basis for the seizure. More than 50 environmental groups call for the release of the activists. On September 23, 2013, "Douglas Guilfoyle, Reader in Law, University College London, International law, Law of the Sea, Piracy Profile tweets: @Patagorda@Greenpeace. In my view, only protest which is violent and directed at another ship could be piracy" (Guilfoyle, 2013). On September 26, 2013, a preliminary hearing is held to determine if the piracy investigation should continue. The Russian authorities decided the activists should be detained for an additional 2 months pending a piracy investigation. In October 2013, the activists were charged with piracy. After the announcement of the charges the Dutch government initiated arbitration procedures against Russia under the UN Convention of the Law of the Sea to secure the release of the activists. Greenpeace International sent a public message applauding the decision of the Dutch government, to right a wrong (Greenpeace.org/international, 2016).

On October 18, 2013 more than 100 events across the globe were held, involving more than 10,000 people to demand the release of these imprisoned activists. On October 23, 2013 the Russian Foreign Ministry denied the Netherlands appeal for an international arbitration process. It also denied the request to attend a hearing at the International Tribunal for the Law of the Sea. The Russian authorities said they will drop the piracy charges and replaced with charges of hooliganism. These charges are seen as threats to freedom of expression and demonstration and democracy and carries a maximum prison sentence up to 7 years.

In response Greenpeace International released the following statement:

The (activists) are innocent of all charges. There can be no justification for locking them up in a cell in Murmansk (Russia). This was an entirely peaceful protest in international waters to shine a light on Gazprom's reckless Arctic oil drilling plans. Eleven warning shots were fired across the Arctic Sunrise, bullets were fired into the water next to the protesters, they were threatened with guns and knives and detained on trumped up charges to defend Gazprom's oil interests. Who are the real hooligans here? (Greenpeace.org/international, 2016)

Rampant corruption is evident with the use of social capital by the government authorities. Repeal of charges and new charges filed destroyed any level of trust the people may have held. Greenpeace International created a video calling for global support and then rounded up a legal team for the 30 jailed activists. On October 31, 2013 when Gazprom representatives were giving a presentation, 4 Danish activists unrolled a floor to ceiling banner to show their support of those incarcerated in Russia.

The court hearing for the activists continued on November 6, 2013 with the International Tribunal for the Law of the Sea. A full transcript was made available to the public. On November 11, 2013 the activists were relocated to a detention center in St. Petersburg. On November 15, 2013 the Russian Investigative team applied to the court for an additional 3-month detention extension for the activists. The next day thousands of social activists world-wide protested peacefully in 263 countries to show their solidarity. The St. Petersburg court, however, denied all

Figure 3. Banner showing support for those incarcerated in Russia

requests for bail. On December 18, 2013 the Russian parliament granted amnesty to all the imprisoned activists. It was not until June 6, 2014 that the ship, the Arctic Sunrise, was released to Greenpeace to return home (Greenpeace.org/international, 2016). Hundreds of blogs, news articles, videos, peaceful protests, letters, and tweets were sent to end the travesty in the Arctic Sea on Gazprom's Prirazlomnaya Platform.

Social Media

Social media is the most popular online activity in use today. The Web and all other social media platforms have become tools of information gathering, data collection and mass persuasion. Online communities form and accomplish tasks. James Caverlee, a Texas A&M computer scientist, states that an online gathering can be fueled by natural disasters or common goals such as the incarceration of the 30 Greenpeace activists in the Arctic Sea, where thousands of people begin sending messages, videos, and photos of support. It becomes a type of crowdsourcing. "When disaster strikes, (the) human impulse is for people on-site to use Facebook and Twitter to post photos and videos of the damage, status updates, and the locations. Once these online crowds have formed in response to this particular emergency are detected out of the hundreds of millions of other online activities, the challenge then becomes connecting the crowds to emergency responders" (Kriewald, 2012). One of the functions of social media is to assign tasks to supporters; a call of action. This increases support and investment and reduces decision-making and response time if people can just act.

Measures of quality of the social medium is page rank, the number of clicks on a page, the links around a page or site and the number of visits to a site. The higher the numbers and the more frequent the use, the more reputable the article, blog, paper and/or site. Infrequent usage may indicate spam. To evaluate quality, look for consistent numbers, especially when the topic is at its peak saliency (Kriewald, 2012).

In the case of the Gazprom and Prirazlomnaya and the Greenpeace activists' social media was not used by Gazprom or Russia. Gazprom has 21 Facebook posts, but none of them are related to the Prirazlomnaya platform. There are 3 tweets with zero followers, no YouTube videos, no Blogs and no photos on Instagram that relate to Prirazlomnaya. Positive photos, videos and discussions would have shown the global community the good work that the Gazprom Company claimed it was doing.

Greenpeace UK and Greenpeace International, on the other hand, used social media extensively. With over 24 relevant Facebook posts, Greenpeace International had 207K viewers and followers. The typical post denounced oil drilling in the Arctic and supported the actions of the 30 Greenpeace activists (referred to as the

Arctic 30) who tried to board the Prirazlomnaya Platform. Many of the Facebook posts criticized the actions of Gazprom asked that the activists be freed. One such Facebook post is shown below ("Greenpeace Free the Artic" 2016).

Greenpeace International October 22, 2013Take a stand for the Arctic 30!

28 activists and two journalists were in the Arctic to highlight the risks companies like Gazprom and Shell pose to this fragile environment and its wildlife.

9.9 thousand Greenpeace-facebook.com comments

The message in the post focuses on the activists and the risks to the wildlife and environment while the photo hones in on the ice and wildlife. The emotional appeal is ever present with the polar bears depicted on the ice with the message "The Arctic is Worth Saving" in the top left corner. The photo is then symmetrically balanced with the logos for the Arctic 30 and Save the Arctic in the bottom right corner. The

Figure 4. Save the Artic

pertinent messages in this case scream at the viewer from every angle in this post. It is an effective Facebook post that receives 2.1 thousand views and 114 comments.

With approximately 32 YouTube videos about Grazprom, Prirzalomnaya platform and the capture and detainment of the 30 activists, Greenpeace had over 872,336 viewers. Each of the videos go into depth about the situation and issue a call to action. Some videos show two of the activists trying to board the platform and shots being fired at them. Others show Greenpeace planning the peaceful protest. Each video received approximately 350 comments supporting Greenpeace's activities. The remaining activities chronicle the events of the case as they occurred and each received the same viewer interest and support.

The relevant tweets posted were not as numerous as the Facebook or YouTube posts, but the followers and following were higher. There were 16 tweets, but those tweets have 1,182,686 views, with 37,410 following and 3,825,060 followers. Comments from the followers were higher than from the other social mediums. Support from Twitter followers drove them to the other social mediums, particularly to YouTube to see what Grazprom was doing and how Greenpeace was helping the cause.

There were 45 blogs with 20,000 readers. The blogs were then posted on the web and linked to Facebook and Twitter. Information flowed about this case through these blogs. Supporters were informed of any new development the moment it occurred. Flickr posted 1695 photos. These photos included activists in prison, breaks in the arctic ice, polar bears, people holding signs saying "Save the Arctic 30," and other emotionally charged signs.

Greenpeace successfully used a variety of social media outlets to garner global support for the imprisoned Artic activists. Not only were the activists released, the oil drilling in the Artic Sea by Gazprom was stopped. Table 1 lays out the similarities and differences between the three companies that Greenpeace protested against.

CONCLUSION

In the three cases of Greenpeace versus Resolute Forest Products, Essar Power and Gazprom, the use of the various social media venues has propelled Greenpeace's messages to the forefront of environmental activists' minds and they came running. The supporters of the Indigenous communities in the Canadian Boreal Forest are flooding blogs with comments saying the Cree Nation and the caribou must be saved from logging by the Resolute Forest Products Company. YouTube videos, Facebook posts, and Twitter are inundated with posts, tweets, and responses screaming with

Table 1. Similarities and differences between the three companies Greenpeace protested against

Case	Similarities	Differences
Resolute	Greenpeace Opposition Social media used Wildlife displacement Woodland and forests endangered Endangered lives of indigenous community Protest groups formed	Logging Best buy sustainability purchasing Policy challenged Broadbeck River threatened
Essar	Greenpeace Opposition Displacement of Wildlife Social media used Endangered lives of Indian farmers Protest groups formed	Coal mining
Gazprom	Greenpeace Opposition Social media used Livelihoods endangered Protest groups formed	Oil drilling Located in Artic ice covered waters Prirazolmnaya platform charged with piracy Charges of privacy dropped replaced with charges of hooliganism 7 months later the activists were released from prison and all charges were dropped

"Save Our Forest" and "Save the Broadback." Corporations such as Best Buy have stopped purchasing paper and pulp supplies from Resolute Forest Products because of their lack of purposive, sustainable, environmental-friendly processes.

The power of social media in the case of the Mayan Forest in India stopped the coal mining. It took Facebook, YouTube, Twitter, Flickr, and Blogs and millions of responses to garner the support, but it was well worth it because the e-auction permission for the mining was rescinded.

The Gazprom versus Greenpeace case was unique in that the world was watching as the 30 activists were arrested and detained for nearly a year in Russian prisons. It was as political case as Russian President Putin said the artic activists did violate international law by traversing international waters and attempting to board the Priraloymnaya platform, but they were not guilty of piracy. The 30 activists were charged and convicted of piracy. Activists globally came to their aid through all the different social media, Facebook, Twitter, Instagram, Flickr, YouTube, Web, and Blogs, and shouted "Release the Arctic 30." The piracy charge was changed to hooliganism, which carried a 7-year prison charge. All 30 were convicted. The cry for release went up again. Social media usage increased and the activists were released after 8 months of constant protests.

Social media reaches millions of people globally, but it is only effective if it is adapted to the cause and the demographics of the targeted audiences. Social media messages must also be graphically enhanced (if allowed by the medium) and the message must be crafted for the targeted audience. Finally, each medium must be closely monitored, especially during a crisis. If these guidelines are followed these organizations can be just as effective as Greenpeace and the cases discussed in this chapter.

REFERENCES

Astone, N. M., Nathanson, C., Schoen, R., & Kim, Y. (1999). Family Demography, Social Theory, and Investment in Social Capital. *Population and Development Review*, *25*(1), 1–31. doi:10.1111/j.1728-4457.1999.00001.x

Ayliffe, B. (2013, September 23). *10 reasons to take action to stop Gazprom's Prirazlomnaya oil platform.* Retrieved from http://www.greenpeace.org/international/en/news/Blogs/makingwaves/10-reasons-to-take-action-to-stop-gazproms-pr/blog/46766/?expandid=b99864&entryid=46766

Barry, G. (2014, August 29). *Democracy and India Protect Mahan Forest and Global Climate from Coal.* Retrieved from www.ecointernet.org

Resolute Forest Products. (2016). Boreal Forest Facts. Retrieved from http://borealforestfacts.com

Badiou, P., Baldwin, R., Carlson, M., Darveau, M., Drapeau, P., Gaston, K., … Wells, J. (2014). Best Buy's Role in the Degradation of the Boreal Forest. *Borealscience.org*. Retrieved from http://borealscience.org/wp-content/uploads/2013/07/conserving-last-great-forests1.pdf

Chamberlain, G. (2014, June 28). Indian forest villagers' rise up to halt UK firm's bid to clear land for mining. *The Guardian*. Retrieved from http://www.theguardian.com/world/2014/jun/28/india-controversial-forest-coalmine-essar-energy

Coalpost.in. (2016, May 3). *Essar Mahan plant's 600 MW unit resumes power generation.* Retrieved from http://www.coalpost.in/essar-mahan-plants-600-mw-unit-resumes-power-generation/

Essar.com. (2012, December 26). Essar Power commissions 600MW Mahan I power project [Press release]. Retrieved from http://www.essar.com/article.aspx?cont_id=ln2dNPT66RM=

Essarenergy.com. (2016). CSR. Retrieved from http://www.essarenergy.com/sustainability/csr.aspx

Forest Products Association of Canada. (2015). *Environmental Credentials*. Retrieved from http://www.fpac.ca/sustainable-forestry/

Gazprom.com. (2016). *About Gazprom*. Retrieved from http://www.gazprom.com/about/

GCC. (2016). *The Grand Council of Cree*. Retrieved from http://www.gcc.ca/issues/paixdesbraves.php

Goodman, A., & Gonzalez, J. (2013, September 26). *Protest or Piracy? Greenpeace Activists remain jailed in Russia after boarding Arctic oil rig*. Retrieved from http://www.alternet.org/activism/protest-or-piracy-greenpeace-activists-remain-jailed-russia-after-boarding-arctic-oil-rig

Granovetter, M. (1973). The Strength of Weak Ties. *American Journal of Sociology*, *78*(6), 1360–1380. doi:10.1086/225469

Greenpeace Activists and Arctic. (2015). Retrieved from twitter.com

Greenpeace and Mahan Forest. (2015) Retrieved from facebook.com

Greenpeace and Mahan Forest. (2015) Retrieved from flickr.com

Greenpeace and Mahan Forest. (2015) Retrieved from twitter.com

Greenpeace and Mahan Forest. (2015) Retrieved from youtube.com

Greenpeace Free the Artic. (2016). Retrieved from: www.greenpeace.org/freethearctic30/?fbgpi22oct2

Greenpeace international. (2016, August 1). Updates from the Arctic Sunrise activists. Retrieved from http://www.greenpeace.org/international/en/news/features/From-peaceful-action-to-dramatic-seizure-a-timeline-of-events-since-the-Arctic-Sunrise-took-action-September-18-CET/

Greenpeace Mission. (2015) Retrieved from http://www.greenpeace.org/usa/about/

Greenpeace versus Grazprom. (2015). Retrieved from facebook.com

Greenpeace versus Grazprom. (2015). Retrieved from www.flickr.com

Greenpeace versus Grazprom. (2015). Retrieved from www.youtube.com

Greenpeace versus Resolute Forest Products. (2015). Retrieved from www.facebook.com

Greenpeace versus Resolute Forest Products. (2015). Retrieved from www.flickr.com

Greenpeace versus Resolute Forest Products. (2015). Retrieved from www.twitter.com

Greenpeace versus Resolute Forest Products. (2015). Retrieved from www.youtube.com

Greenpeace.org. (2014a, November 26). *Better Buying in the Boreal Forest.* Retrieved from www.greenpeace.org

Greenpeace.org. (2014b, March 24). *The Importance of Intact Forest Areas.* Retrieved from greenpeace.org

Greenpeace.org. (2016). *Resolute Forest Product Can Save Forests and Jobs and Respect Indigenous Rights.* Retrieved February 19, 2016, from greenpeace.org

Greenpeace.org/india. (2016a, April 28). Greenpeace: Coal Industry Is Deepening Water Crisis in Maharashtra. Retrieved from http://www.greenpeace.org/india/en/Press/Greenpeace-Coal-Industry-Is-Deepening-Water-Crisis-in-Maharashtra/

Greenpeace.org/india (2016b, May 20). Save Mahan, Our Forest, Our Rights. Retrieved from http://www.greenpeace.org/india/en/What-We-Do/Quit-Coal/save-mahan/

Guilfoyle, D. (2013, June 17). *Political Motivation and Piracy: What History Doesn't Teach Us About Law*. Retrieved from http://www.ejiltalk.org/political-motivation-and-piracy-what-history-doesnt-teach-us-about-law/

Guneluis, S. (2014). *10 Blog Metrics Bloggers Should Track Through Web Analytics Tools*. Retrieved from http://weblogs.about.com/od/addonsandplugins/tp/10-Blog-Metrics-Bloggers-Should-Track-Through-Web-Analytics-Tools.htm

Hanifan, L. J. (1916). The Rural School Community Center. *The Annals of the American Academy of Political and Social Science*, *67*(1), 130–138. doi:10.1177/000271621606700118

Knack, S., & Keefer, P. (1995). Institutions and Economic Performance: Cross-Country Tests Using Alternative Institutional Measures. *Economics and Politics*, *7*(3), 207–227. doi:10.1111/j.1468-0343.1995.tb00111.x

Knack, S., & Keefer, P. (1997). Does Social Capital Have an Economic Payoff? A Cross-Country Investigation. *The Quarterly Journal of Economics*, *112*(4), 1251–1288. doi:10.1162/003355300555475

Kriewald, L. (2012). *The Power of Social Media.* Retrieved from http://engineering.tamu.edu/research/2012/the-power-of-social-media

Mainville, N. (2015, November 15). *Boreal forest: Cree struggle to save the Broadback goes global.* Retrieved from greenpeace.org

McGrath, B. (2013). 7 Ways to improve your social media engagement. *Social Media Examiner*. Retrieved from http://www.socialmediaexaminer.com/7-ways-to-improve-your-social-media-engagement/

Narayan, D., & Pritchett, L. (1999). Cents and Sociability: Household Income and Social Capital in Rural Tanzania. *Economic Development and Cultural Change*, *47*(4), 871–897. doi:10.1086/452436

National Geographic (2016). *Caribou*. Retrieved from http://animals.nationalgeographic.com/animals/mammals/caribou/

National Wildlife Federation. (2016). *Accounting for the Costs of Coal*. Retrieved from https://www.nwf.org/What-We-Do/Energy-and-Climate/Climate-and-Energy/Reduce-Fossil-Fuel-Reliance/Accounting-for-Coal

North, D. C. (1990). *Institutions, Institutional Change, and Economic Performance*. New York: Cambridge University Press. doi:10.1017/CBO9780511808678

Pew Research. (2014, February 3). Six New Facts about Facebook Retrieved from http://www.pewresearch.org/fact-tank/2014/02/03/6-new-facts-about-facebook/

Pewresearchcenter.org (2013, December 27). Social Networking Fact Sheet. Retrieved from pewresearchcenter.org

Platform.reprisk.com. (2013). Special Report: Arctic Drilling. Retrieved from https://platform.reprisk.com/downloads/specialreports/32/Arctic Drilling Special Report.pdf

Roy, A. (2015, April 24). *Coal Mining in India's Mahan Forest: Campaigners Claim Victory*. Retrieved from www.climatechangenews.com/coal-mining-banned-in-indias-mahan-forest/

Roy, A. (2015, April 4). *Coal Mining Banned in India's Mahan Forest*. Retrieved from www.countercurrents.org/aroy050415.htm

Stake, R. (1995). *The art of case study research*. Thousand Oaks, New Jersey: Sage Publications.

Stein, K. (2014, December 16). *7 Tips to Improve Your Social Media Posts*. Retrieved from http://www.socialmediaexaminer.com/improve-your-social-media-posts/

Sustainability (n. d.). Retrieved from http://www.essar.com/section_level1.aspx?cont_id=cBd pT8Ha/0=

Gaxprom.com. (2008). Sustainability Report 2008-2009. Retrieved from http://www.gazprom.com/f/posts/71/879403/gazprom_sr_2008-2009_eng.pdf

Sustainablebrands.com. (2014, November 27). *New Greenpeace Report Calls Out Best Buy for Destroying Ancient Forest.* Retrieved from sustainablebrands.com

Thehindu.com. (2011, November 24). Republic is imaginary, social cause is real. Retrieved from thehindu.com

Wallace, K. (2014). *Teen like and FOMO Anxiety.* Digital Life. Retrieved from http://www.cnn.com/2014/10/16/living/teens-on-social-media-like-and-fomo-anxiety-digital-life/index.html

Woolcook, M., & Deepa, N. (2000). Social Capital: Implications for development theory, research, and policy. *The World Bank Research Observer, 15*(2), 225–249. doi:10.1093/wbro/15.2.225

Yin, Y. (2013). *Case Study Research: Design and Methods.* Thousand Oaks, New Jersey: Sage Publications.

Expandedramblings.com. (2014, April 23). YouTube Statistics: 120 Amazing YouTube Statistics. Retrieved from http://expandedramblings.com/index.php/youtube-statistics/

KEY TERMS AND DEFINITIONS

Boreal Forest: A forest located in Canada between Alaska and the Yukon. It is the world's largest ecosystem, including wetlands, grasslands, tundra and rivers.

Cree Nation: The most populous and distributed aboriginal people in Canada. As of 2015, the registered population of the First Cree Nation was more than 317,000.

Essar Power: One of India's largest private power generation companies. Subsidiaries include Essar Energy, Essar Steam and Essar Oil.

Gazprom: A global energy company that extracts, processes and sells oil, natural gas and fuel. They gather refine and sell the world's largest natural gas reserves.

Mahan Forest: One of the oldest forests of Asia. Essar Power wants the coal reserves below the surface of this forest that house the indigenous people of Mahan Sangarsh Samiti.

Madhya Pradesh: Known as the heart of India, it is a state located in the center of the country.

Prirazlomnaya: This is Gazprom's first oil platform used to start commercial oil pumping under the Arctic ice covered waters. This platform was built with pieces of old used rigs that were rusting in a shipyard.

Resolute Forest Products: A forest industry company specializing in pulp, tissue, and paper.

Social Capital: These are tangible goods or elements that people place high value on, such as personal reputation, social needs, social power, social relations or sympathy.

Chapter 7
Navigating the Nexus between Social Media, Political Scandal, and Good Governance in Nigeria:
Its Ethical Implications

Essien D. Essien
University of Uyo, Nigeria

ABSTRACT

The advent of the social media revolution in contemporary time has had a phenomenal impact in almost every area of human endeavor in many societies. However, social media has some credibility burden that could hinder its effective use and also produce unintended consequences such as political propaganda, and other unwholesome activities as it affects politics and governance. This study sought to assess the nexus between social media, political scandal and good governance in Nigeria. It also assessed the success or otherwise of the institutional counter-measures in checkmating the excesses of social media. Situated within the framework of reputation repair and social responsibility theories, the paper acknowledges that the conventional mass media has ties with the political and economic forces in the society, thus, are somewhat incapacitated in rising to the societal challenges. Consequently, the paper presents the social media as a veritable alternative, arguing that social media tools have what it takes to serve as a platform for citizen participation in governance.

DOI: 10.4018/978-1-5225-2019-1.ch007

INTRODUCTION

The media continue to be a fundamental component of scandal politics in many countries of the world with the situation in Nigeria reaching a crescendo in contemporary times. Today, the media is no longer simply conveyors of political scandal but they are active participants in scandal politics (Baran, 2010). This however is simply because there is a changing media environment which has recorded important implications for the rise of scandal politics. The rapid and pervasive growth of social media technologies and their relative ease of use and availability have made social media a popular form of communication (Navetta, 2011). Thus, the world over, a certain trend is emerging with an overriding logic, capable of presenting the social media, not only as the fastest acceptable medium of communication, but as a form of 'digital Darwinism' indicating that the social media constitutes "the survival of the loudest and most opinionated" (McQuail, 2010).

Earnestly, social media and blogs have today become important components of journalism. In fact it is a phenomenon that has assumed the momentum of a revolution in Journalism. They narrow the distance between journalists and the public. They encourage lively, immediate and spirited discussion. They can be vital news-gathering and news-delivery tools. It is assumed that most actors and bloggers are journalists who should uphold the same professional and ethical standards of fairness, accuracy, truthfulness, transparency and independence when using social media (Akasike, 2009). In spite of this representation, we are now ever than before faced with several challenges such as scandal, cybercrime, misrepresentation, and other fraudulent practices. This has made the work of deploying the new media platform for an effective, functional and proactive management and dissemination of information for the wellbeing of the society distorted. In fact, it is unmistaken to state that there is so much information in the cyber space today, such that, our basic challenge now is how to manage it properly for the optimization of society's ends. Interestingly, since the advent of globalization, the Internet and the new media have become vital tools of interaction and networking in private and public organizations (Baran, 2010).

In Nigeria, with the signing into law of the Freedom of Information, Act by Mr. President on 28th May, 2011, we are now faced with the challenge of deploying the new media platform for effective management and dissemination of information. Statistically speaking, social networking now accounts for over 20.5% of all time spent online by citizens in Nigeria, Egypt and South Africa. Also, a total of 123 million people age 13 and older in the Nigeria, Egypt and South Africa use mobile devices (Okunna & Omenugha, 2012). This has nevertheless increased exponentially lately. In the same vein, Twitter is said to have processed more than five hundred million tweets as at December 2014 and averages almost 2 million tweets per day (Okunna & Omenugha, 2012).

The number of social media users age 65 and older grew 88 percent throughout 2014, so that one in four people in that age group are now part of a social networking site. As at September 2014 Facebook has 750 Million users, and whereas the Facebook tops Google for weekly traffic in the U.S and part of Europe, the social media in Africa in general and Nigeria in particular has overtaken pornography as the number one activity carried out on the web (Phillips & Brabham, 2012). Nonetheless, many scandals so far brought to public involve some form of corruption whether it is moral or political. Allegations of corruption become scandals when they are exposed to the public, most often by the media. In contemporary time, various Nigerian governments and government officials (both civil and military) have been subject to different type of allegations of corruption. However, the extent to which the media has been successful in exposing corruption scandals is open to question (Okachie, 2012).

However, the influence of the social media on the society goes far beyond just establishing basic information infrastructure. The availability of social media technology is a foundation for development in the creation, availability and use of network-based services. It offers a number of advantages for the society in general, especially for developing countries such as participation in e-government, e-commerce, e-education, e-health and e-environment with the use of ICT applications (Anyadike, EbezeUche, & Odoemelam, 2014). These variables are seen as enablers for development, as they provide an efficient channel to deliver a wide range of basic services in remote and rural areas. The social media technology has not been captured and factored as a major index in facilitating the achievement of millennium development targets, reducing poverty and improving health and environmental conditions in developing countries. Given the right approach, context, policy framework and implementation processes, investments in social media technology and tools can result in productivity and quality improvements in governance, developmental infrastructure and basic social services (Balkin, 1999).

This study argues that even though social media have the potentials for fighting corruption, bad governance and dysfunctional leadership, there are however certain factors militating against its use in Nigeria. Situated within the framework of social and democratic-participant theory, the paper acknowledges that the conventional mass media, due to their inherent ties with the political as well as the economic forces in the society, are somewhat incapacitated from rising in challenge of corruption in the society. Consequently, the paper presents the social media is as a viable alternative, arguing that social media tools have what it takes through serving as a platform for the citizenry to point out loopholes that may make the system vulnerable to corruption; scrutinise the activities of their leaders and report cases of corruption - all these without fear of victimisation. Nevertheless, given their anonymous nature, social media may have some credibility burden that could hinder its effective use in the anti-corruption fight and could as well pose the risk of malicious slander of character of innocent people.

CONCEPTUAL CLARIFICATION

For adequate understanding and easy clarification of the issues involved in this study, it is necessary to delineate some perceptions which underlie the subject matter. The following concepts therefore will be evaluated to set the ball rolling.

Social Media

Simply put, the social media involves the collection of online platforms that facilitate user-created content and interactive communication between two or more individuals. The defining characteristic of social media is the interactive exchange between users and the availability of communication through the virtual platform (Valkernburg, Peter, & Schouten, 2006). Moreover, social media is defined as "a group of internet-based applications that build on the ideological and technological foundations of Web 2.0 that allow the creation and exchange of user-generated content" (Kaplan & Haenlein, 2010). Recently, social media platforms such as SNS, weblogs, microblogging, and wikis play an increasingly important role in shaping political communication in the US and around the world (Bennett & Serrin, 2005). The potentials of social media appear to be most promising in political context as they can be an enabler for more participation and democracy. 'Social media' refers to "web-based tools and services that allow users to create, share, rate and search for content and information without having to log in to any specific portal site or portal destination. These tools become 'social' in the sense that they are created in ways that enable users to share and communicate with one another" (Bowler & Karp, 2004). This includes social networking sites, blogs, microblogs, video blogs, discussion forums and others.

Social Media and Politics

In many parts of the world today, individuals, groups, organisations and even nations are taking advantage of the opportunities provided by social media and other e-media platforms to mobilise millions of people to support and advance their course. In the political sphere, it has become a veritable tool for interacting and mobilising citizens towards active participation in the political process and democratic projects.

This agrees with the submissions of Okoro and Kenneth (2013) that it is through the media that people are able to participate freely in discussions relevant to public good. Adibe and Orji (2012) also notes that the success of President Obama's Presidential campaigns in 2008 and his eventual emergence as first black president of the United States was largely credited to his active use of Facebook to mobilise millions of volunteers, and voters. Politics has indeed greatly evolved in recent decade with the advent of the new technology. With it, information sharing has greatly improved, allowing citizens to discuss ideas, post news, ask questions and share links.

With social media, politicians reach the masses with the aim of assessing the political atmosphere even before venturing into the campaign. Social media is perhaps the best tool to assess the popularity of a candidate especially by the young people and craft the best language to use as a campaign slogan. Social media also provides a politician with the opportunity to be informally free with the public. This free connection through social media helps politicians to communicate their humour, indicating their approachability and accessibility to the public (Vallor, 2010). Social media grants many people the chance to participate actively and get involved fully in the political discourse by adding their voices on issues posted on the social media sites. Thus, advancing the tenets of participatory democracy that sees media as a debate avenue and aids tremendously in actualising public-sphere journalism. It affords electorates a friendlier avenue of assessing candidates for political offices and promoting transparency in governance.

(Good) Governance

The concept of governance has been variously defined by scholars. Kaufmann (2003) on his part describe governance to mean "the tradition and institutions by which authority in a country is exercised." The Wold Bank also defines governance as "the manner in which power is exercised in the management of a country's economic and social resources for development" (World Bank, 1992). The United Nations Development Programme (UNDP) defines governance as "the exercise of economic, political and administrative authority to manage a country's affairs at all levels. It comprises the mechanisms, processes, and institutions through which citizens and groups articulate their interests, exercise their legal rights, meet their obligations and mediate their differences" (UNDP, 2002).

One of the fundamental principles of good governance is transparency, which ensures that the decision-making and the subsequently due process monitoring and implementation of this information is freely available and directly accessible by all stakeholders. The information provided should be of the highest quality and presented in a way that is easily understood by end users, enabling them to actively participate in the governance process. Transparency must go beyond the mere provision of relevant information (Powell, 2012). State actors must serve as whistle-blowers, and stimulate engagement with all stakeholders (Powell, 2012). Therefore, trust and engagement of citizens is considered a prerequisite to ensure accountability and good governance. Without citizens' participation, democratic governments cannot function properly. Therefore access to information and transparency are considered the backbone for democratic governments as well as important tools for fighting corruption (Boyd & Ellison, 2007).

Political Scandals

Political Scandals have been a part of the political system in many countries especially the advanced democracies since its inception. Political scandals are events that capture a lot of attention and eventually disappear over time and are the source of intense public communication (Waisboard, 2004). A political scandal involves a kind of political corruption that is exposed and becomes a scandal, in which politicians or government officials are accused of engaging in various illegal, corrupt, or unethical practices. The role of the media has subsequently played an important role in both the breaking of these stories and the coverage they receive. In recent decades there have been an increased number of scandals relating to the Internet and social media.

According to John Thompson, a political rhetoric scholar, for an event to be regarded as a scandal rather than simply a piece of news, it must include five specific characteristics. First, the event must involve a "transgression of certain values, norms or moral codes" (Thompson, 2000). Second and third, the incident must include some aspect of secrecy, and there also must be a level of disapproval by nonparticipants surrounding the action. Fourth, there must be "public denouncing" of the actions or events by nonparticipants and finally, that the actions must "damage the reputation of the individuals responsible for them" (Thompson, 2000). Again, it is pertinent to note that because cultural and societal norms vary throughout history and from one society to another, there is a level of scandal sensitivity that must be considered; this presupposes that what constitutes a scandal for some may not really be a scandal for others.

Additionally, Goel (2014) also noted that scandals do not take place in an "historical vacuum," but rather, in all scandal, arise a great deal of meaning as a result of the culture and context in which they occur (Goel, 2014). Nevertheless, perpetrators of a scandal or transgression, as a result of the current political spectrum and increased media attention and scrutiny, can largely be divided into two categories: "Those living a lie and those living out a lifestyle" (Goel, 2014). Politicians largely fall into the first category, feeling that they have something to hide, something that would undermine their public image, and choose instead to "go for the moral high ground," and cling to values that would separate themselves from a given action (Thompson, 2000).

THEORETICAL UNDERPINNINGS

This chapter examines the historical antecedents of social media and the day-to-day condition of political scandal in Nigeria within the periscope of ethical prerequisite. This study employed two theoretical frameworks. The first is image restoration theory which hinges on image repair strategies in the context of crisis communication. The second is social responsibility theory of communication. The image restoration or repair theory was introduced by William Benoit. The theory outlines strategies that can be employed to repair damaged image in an event where reputation has been dented. Image restoration theory can be applied as an approach for understanding personal or organizational crisis situations. The theory builds upon theories of apologia and accounts.

Benoit (1997) claims that the treatments of image restoration focus on identifying options rather than prescribing solutions. He grounds image restoration theory on a comprehensive literature review of apologia and accounts theories. However, specific influences of image restoration theory include Rosenfield's (1968) theory of analog, Ware and Linkugel's (1973) theory of apologia; Kenneth Burke's (1970) theory of goals and purification; Ryan's (1982) kategoria and apologia; Scott and Lyman's (1968) analysis of accounts; Goffman's (1967) remedial moves; and Schlenker's (1980) analysis of impression management and accounts. The theory makes provision for five image repair strategies in a situation of scandal: denial, evasion of responsibility, reducing offensiveness, corrective action, and mortification (Benoit, 1997). Benoit defines denial as, "the accused is denying that the offensive act actually occurred or denies that he or she performed it" and finds that, if the public accepts this denial, he or she should be relieved of any blame for the action (Benoit, 1995).

In evading responsibility, "the actor attempts to suggest that lack of information, volition, or ability means that he or she should not be held fully responsible for the act" (Benoit, 1995). Reducing offensiveness, the most inclusive of Benoit's strategies, occurs when the accused "attempts to reduce the unfavourable feelings toward the actor by increasing the audience's esteem for the actor or by decreasing their negative feelings about the act" (Benoit, 1995). The category includes six different techniques: bolstering, minimization, differentiation, transcendence, attacking one's accuser, and compensation (Benoit, 1995). The fourth strategy, corrective action, may take two forms: "restoring the situation to the state of affairs before the objectionable action and/or promising to 'mend one's ways' and make changes to prevent the recurrence of the undesirable act" (Benoit, 1995). The final strategy, mortification, occurs when the accused "admits responsibility for the wrongful act and asks for forgiveness" (Benoit, 1995). This study therefore uses Benoit's theory as a way of coding each political scandal statement made by Nigerian in response to allegations of misconduct, corruption and many other infractions to determine which methods were used most frequently, and by whom, and in which contexts.

On the other hand, the theory of social responsibility allows for free press without any censorship but at the same time ensures that the content of the press is discussed in public panel and at all media platforms with a caveat to accept any obligation from public interference or professional self-regulations or both (Thompson, 2000). The theory lies between both authoritarian theory and libertarian theory because it gives total media freedom on one hand but on the other hand exerts some external controls. It is on the assumption that the press has a responsibility to society; and therefore should be socially responsible that the social responsibility theory move beyond the simple "objective" reporting, that is, facts reporting to "interpretative" reporting, that is, investigative reporting (Thompson, 2000). In this regard, the theory takes a philosophical analysis of man as a rational being capable of discerning between truth and falsehood and, therefore, can choose between a better and worse alternative. Hence, the total news doled out should be complete facts and truthful even if it is analysed and interpreted. In this circumstance, the theory helped in creating professionalism in media by setting up a high level of accuracy, truth, and information.

THE NATURE AND USAGE PATTERN OF SOCIAL MEDIA IN NIGERIA

The social media practices within Africa have materialized into unprecedented capacities. Consequently, they have led to revolutions such as the Jasmine Revolution Tunisia in North Africa, encouraged protest for change in Egypt against Mubarak, demanded and monitored best practices during elections and transitions in many parts of Africa such as Ghana, Nigeria and South Africa as well as contribute to a larger dynamic of promoting growth on the continent through accountability and dialogue. In fact, social media platforms have become the most visited websites in the Internet across the African continent (Idakwo, 2011).

It is palpable therefore to state that the act of communication is in fact common; but communicating in the context of social media is unique (Holbert & Benoit, 2009). This is so because the social media is a powerful tool that can change the face of any society in the world, Nigeria inclusive. Social media usage varies between adult and youth populations in countries around the world. In general, 81.5% of all

Figure 1. Internet penetration in Africa

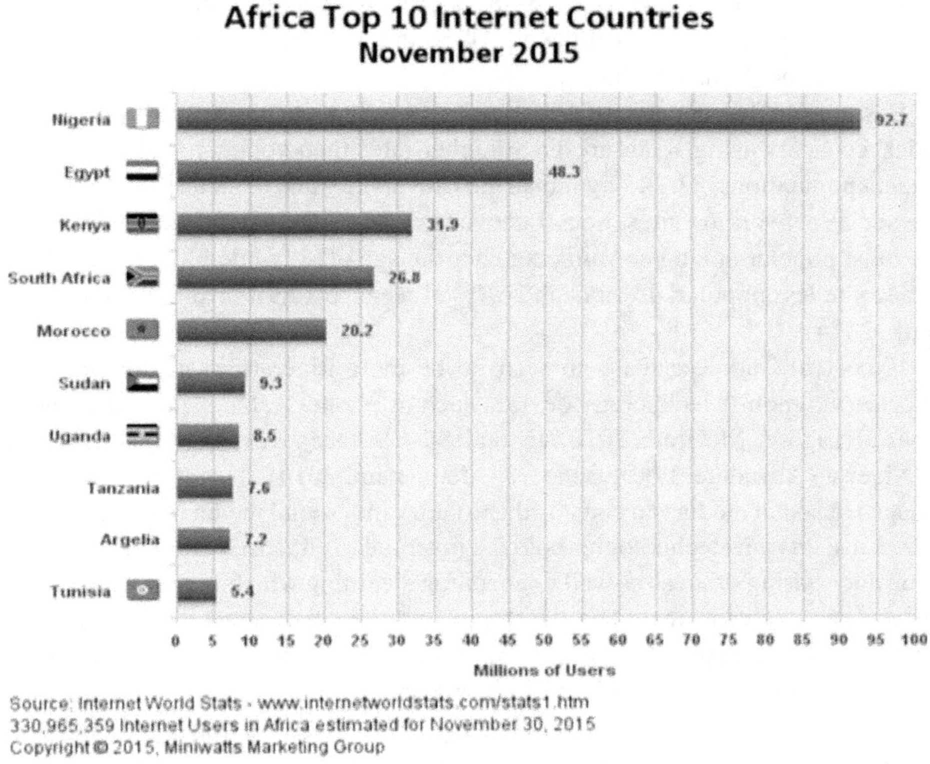

Nigerians from 18 years old and above make use of the Internet occasionally for various activities, with 65.2% of this group going online or engage themselves in online transactions daily (Ibrahim, 2013). There is however, a higher prevalence of adults using social media today than in previous years in Nigeria.

This study found out that 15% of young adults (18 to 30 years old) used the Internet to create and administer a blog and 72% use a social networking site especially the Facebook, while, 14% of adults (aged 28-45 years) run a personal blog to disseminate information of all sort and 42% use social networking sites for divers communication. Furthermore, adults continue to create multiple social networking account profiles with a variety of social network sites, including 14% of adults with social networking accounts having three or more profiles, 33% having two profiles, and 40% having only one profile (Hampton, et al., 2014). In addition, adults are reported to be using Facebook more than other forms of social media (for instance, 73%of adults who use social networking sites have a Facebook account, compared to just 48% for MySpace and 14% for LinkedIn (Hampton, et al., 2014). As of the fall of 2009,overall Internet usage among adults increased with 93% of young adults online between the ages of 18 to 29, 81% of adults between the ages of 30 to 49 online, 70% of adults between the age of 50 to 64 online, and 38% of adults ages 65 older online (Sunstein, 2008).

Besides, adolescents continue to lead in Internet usage across mediums, with older teenagers using social media at higher rates than younger students. Among student populations, 52.7% of youth in the Universities and other tertiary institutions use social networking sites. Social networking sites like Facebook continue to be the most popular among consumers under the age of18, while blogging continues to become less popular, down from 26.4% of teens to 12.9%since 2006 (Hampton, et al., 2014).

Expectedly, adolescents who seem to be more itinerant in nature access the Internet via mobile technology devices such as phones, tablets, and other mobile devices (Light & McGrath, 2010). In total, 90.4% of teenagers are using the Internet in Nigeria (Anyadike, EbezeUche, & Odoemelam, 2014). Therefore, adolescents 'usages of social media warrants further inquiry into social media interactions. This is because this new technologies hold the potential to enhance communication, creation and sharing of ideas as well as encourage learning which is very well required for economic advancement and development (Ajayi & Adesote, 2014). However, it need be mentioned that very many Nigerians especially those living in the rural areas are still not aware of their utilization capacity regarding the social media or competent using its facilities or navigating social media platform particularly for political discussion or exchange of ideas (Ajayi & Adesote, 2014). They may conversely make use of the tool for entertainment and chatting with friends.

In the recent past, the Internet has changed not only Nigerian's relationships by creating new platforms for social engagement, but also their ability to contribute in the development process in the society by creating a space for more diverse political opinions, social and educational viewpoints and a heightened level of audience participation (Idakwo, 2011). The spaces created by the Internet have engendered wide opportunity for engaging the public concerning different issues in Nigeria. That is why these days it has become a common occurrence to see different people contribute in political discourses going on in the country. This was also visible in the way the country officially utilized social media tools for the first time in its political history in the 2011 election, thus, demonstrating the increasing use of the Internet by the Nigerian population (Ibrahim, 2013).

In the election campaign process, it appeared that the different political parties made extensive use of the social media to reach the different segments of the Nigerian populace. In regards to the 2015 elections, the Nigerian Independent National Electoral Commission (INEC) resorted to a wide use of social media: in communicating with the voters; disseminating information about its programmes especially in recruiting members of the public as ad hoc staff for the different polls.

SOCIAL MEDIA AND GOOD GOVERNANCE IN NIGERIA

In Nigeria, understanding the nuances of the social media environment is somewhat complicated. This is because the experience is individualized through one's own choices, as well as through friends in one's network and their proclivities. However, it is true that the social media has changed the way people communicate, the way people have access to electoral information and political parties, but its impact on good governance is yet to be earnestly felt (Helen, Charles, & Jenifer, 2014). In spite of the potentials of the social media used for governance purposes, it is commonly noted that the new media (ICTs) platform favour only those already in power, and the elites. This is so because the reality on ground reveals that until recently, Internet access is still somewhat restricted to the elites, the middleclass as well as the high-income populaces.

Though 70 per cent of the population in Nigeria lives in the rural area; and this people have little/limited or no access to the Internet due to several encumbrances such as power (electricity), Internet access (connectivity), and poverty (affordability), social media especially Facebook is still popular and used through their mobile phones (Helen, Charles, & Jenifer, 2014). This is possible because even without data on your phone, one can still access Facebook free once you are an active subscriber to a particular mobile phone network. Thanks to the new innovation by the Global System of Mobile Communication popularly referred to in Nigeria as (GSM). The Global System of Mobile Communication (GSM) service providers have successfully penetrated the nooks and crannies of Nigeria and can boast of internet connectivity 24/7 at whatever cost to enable them provide effective service to their multitude subscribers. This is pivotal for their business enterprise hence the introduction of this measure as a corporate social responsibility. Therefore, notwithstanding the infrastructural hindrances prevalent in Nigeria, Nigerians are soaring in social networking and the new media.

However, there is no doubt that social media grants many people the chance to participate actively and get involved fully in the political discourse by adding their voices on issues posted on the social media sites. The use of social media tools has high potential for bringing about political and social change, through enhancing opportunities for political participation and opening new spaces for active citizenship (Ibrahim, 2013). This will enable the advancement of the tenets of participatory democracy and good governance. It affords electorates a friendlier avenue of assessing candidates for political offices and promoting transparency in governance.

Table 1. Internet usage and medium in Nigeria

Year	Medium 1	Medium 2	Medium 3	Frequency		
2009	Social Networking sites (SNS)	E-mail	Entertainment	70%	65%	45%
2012	SNS	E-mail	Entertainment	72%	64%	50%
2013	SNS	E-mail	Entertainment	74%	58%	48%
2014	SNS	E-mail	Entertainment	76%	62%	46%
2015	SNS	E-mail	Entertainment	77%	60%	52%

Source: Business Day Research and Intelligence Unit (BRIU) and Terragon Insights

Succinctly identified, the Internet, mobile phones, and other forms of "emancipatory technology" has enable Nigerian citizens to express opinions, mobilise protests, monitor elections, scrutinise government, and deepen participation. In this regard, autocratic governments such as the military are also learning to master these technologies and apply it for educational purposes and career advantage (Idakwo, 2011).

The use of social media in today's political arrangement in Nigeria is not only important but critical. The political campaigns done via these social networks have helped the politicians to connect with their voters. Most of what happens on social media from brands and political campaigns are not conversations, as they are not creating a back-and-forth dialogue with voters, but simply hoping the messaging will get the voters to vote in a certain way (Essoungou, 2011). The social media has grown rapidly in importance as a forum for political activism in its different forms. Social media platforms such as Twitter, Facebook and YouTube provide new ways to stimulate citizen engagement in political life, where elections and electoral campaigns have a central role.

In most cases, this kind of activity is considered luxury to many rural dwellers who struggles on a daily basis for subsistence. However, across most of the states studied in Nigeria (Nigeria has 36 states excluding Abuja, the Federal Capital territory) in particular and Africa in general points to the fact that, Facebook is the most highly accessed social media site. With an estimated population figure of 178.5 million people, Nigeria has been ranked the number one country in the world with over 80% Facebook mobile penetration, according to the latest statistics published by Social Bakers (2016), with 488 million mobile users around the world, Facebook has 50% of its over 900 million monthly active users on mobile phones from Nigeria and its mobile penetration is biggest in Nigeria with 81.2%.

There is however, a strong assumption that Internet access and social media have the capacity to improve transparency, accountability, and good governance in every society, but very little evidence exist on how this is achieved in Nigeria. This is because many governments and government agencies are using e-government strat-

Figure 2. Facebook internet penetration in Nigeria

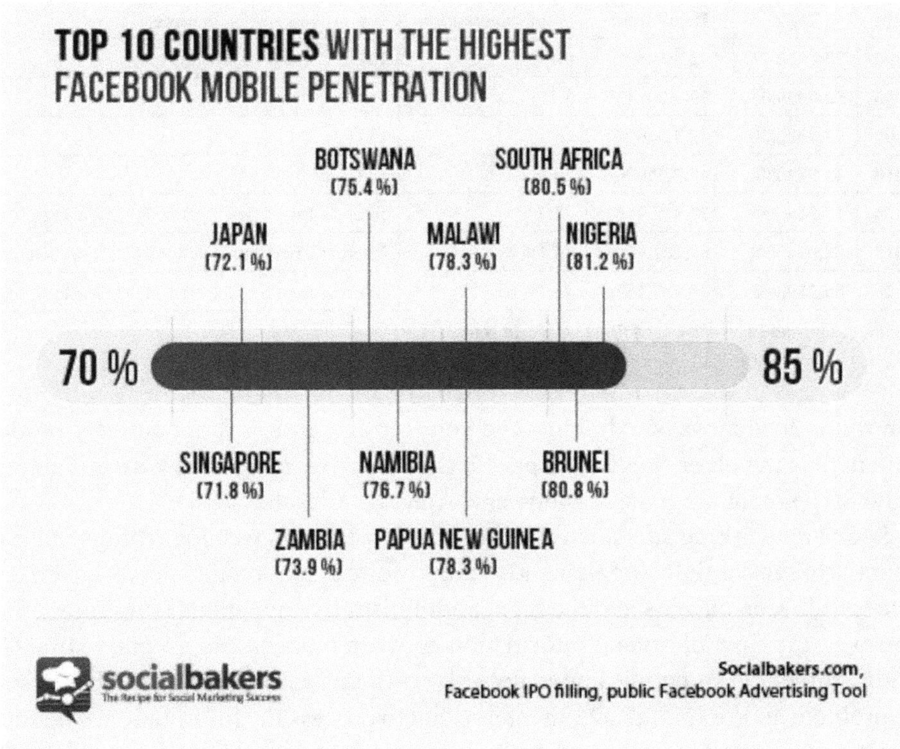

egies and disseminating information through online channels, but not soliciting citizen feedback. Where there are two-way channels of communication, it is very undistinguishable whether citizen feedback is acted upon. In the area of transparency and accountability, there is promising evidence on social media improving transparency of organisations and government ministries, but less evidence on whether this improves accountability (Essoungou, 2011). There are a few discrete examples of e-government working successfully in specific programmes, but the overall evidence base suggests social media is not widely used as a direct route of communication with government.

Realistically, the Internet has become a daily tool for an ever-increasing number of Nigerians. In 2011, for instance, about 89% of Nigerians aged 16 to 74 used the Internet, and three out of four in the same age group used it daily. In the last couple of years, Internet use has grown more common among older members of the population, and even for people aged 65 to 74. There are however some clear differences between age groups: younger people are both more active on the Internet, and use

Table 2. Internet penetration in Nigeria

Year	User	Population	% of Penetration	Source
2000	**200,000**	142,895,600	**0.1%**	**ITU**
2006	**5,000,000**	159, 404, 137	**3.1%**	**ITU**
2009	**23,982,200**	149,229,090	16.1%	**ITU**
2010	**43,982,200**	149,229,090	**28.9%**	**ITU**
2014	**75,746,751**	177,475,986	42.7%	Internet Live Stats, UNDP, ITU, World Bank
2015	**82,094,998**	182,201,960	45.1%	Internet Live Stats, UNDP, ITU, World Bank
2016	**86,219,965**	186,987,563	**46.1%**	Internet Live Stats, UNDP, ITU, World Bank

Source: Internet Live Stats, UNDP, ITU, World Bank

it in more diverse ways. Although the younger age groups more actively produce content than the older ones do, 10 per cent are in active interaction with this content, while 89 per cent are passive followers (Ajayi & Adesote, 2014).

Social networking sites such as Facebook, Twitter and web logs (blogs) have the potential to substantially supplementing the customary communication of governance process between citizens and the higher administrative apparatus (Bar-Tura, 2010). However, the flow of crucial information between citizens and executive branches of government is sometimes interrupted by officials who might be unable to solve the problem and/or might have an interest not to process the information. The social media generally has a potential to function as controlling body such things like corruption, inefficiency, indiscipline and other many infractions.

The use of social media therefore in today's politicking is not only important stride, but it is critical. The political campaigns done via these social networks have helped the politicians to connect with their voters. The social media has grown rapidly in importance as a forum for political activism in its different forms in Nigeria. The various social media platforms especially Facebook and Twitter have provided new ways to stimulate citizen engagement in political life, where elections and electoral campaigns have a central role (Okoro & Kenneth, 2013). They have also aided in no small measure in the fight against corruption and on the pathway for good governance. It is however important to note that although the presence of social media is spreading and media use patterns are changing; online political engagement is largely restricted to people already active in politics and on the Internet. This is very apparent in Nigeria where, the television, print and online newspapers are still the most important sources of political information for millions especially those in the rural areas (Okoro & Kenneth, 2013).

Nevertheless, the roles of the social media in promoting Good Governance are seriously being recognized by the governments and policy-makers in various countries of the world in general and Nigeria in particular. In this respect, there seems to be increasing recognition of the role of social media in governance especially in the development effort in Nigeria. There are also some indicators that social media are being more recognized by the policy-makers as having a central role to play in development. The role of the social media in promoting Good Governance is therefore categorical and accentuated given the Nigerian quest for development (Odoemelam & Adibe, 2012).

SOCIAL MEDIA AND POLITICAL SCANDAL IN NIGERIA

To properly comprehend contemporary politics, scholars must come to grips with the effects of scandal. This is why Thompson (2000) has suggested that charges of corruption though damaging to perpetrators with sombre and injurious effects have remained constant since politics began. Little wonder why contemporary scholarships are embroiled with investigation of the determinants of the destruction of trust in political institutions and its holders in order to establish the reasons behind the plummet in legitimacy, political profile and popularity of political actors (Woessner, 2005). This lends credence to the fact that recent years have seen growing tensions between the ideals and the perceived performance of democratic institutions in Nigeria. For instance, while there is no violent change of government such as military takeover in Burkina Faso, and/or civil revolution and protest in Tunisia and Egypt respectively, many believe that all is not well with the body politic (Okoro & Kenneth, 2013). This is because there are concerns in Nigeria which has focused on widespread cynicism about political institutions and leaders concerning disturbing revelations of corrupt practices resulting into scandals in Nigerian political life which appear unending, thus, fuelling fears about civic disengagement and disenchantment about government and governance (Tumber & Silvio, 2004). The common view however is that the Nigerian public turns off, knows little (do not want to know or deafens up), cares less and stays home (develops apathy) about politics.

Basically though, the dispiritedness experienced among the citizenry stems from the magnitude of corruption with impunity involving political office holders in Nigeria. For instance in the last few years alone, there have been several alarming and scandalous cases of corruption in Nigeria, in which case some of the perpetrators have been charged to court, some cases were never even investigated as many of the cases remain unsolved.

Table 3. High Profile Corruption Scandals Involving Nigerian Politicians/Political Office Holders 1999-2016

S/N	Name	Case Status	Amount Involved	Action Taken on Suspect
1	AlhajiAbdulrasheedMaina	Pension funds scam, arraigned	N195 billion	Not tried, Punishment: None, allowed to flee Nigeria.
2	Mamman Ali, Mahmud Tukur, and other PDP politicians	Fuel Subsidy Scam	$6bn (£4bn)	No convictions, case on-going in court
3	Mr. Stephen Oronsaye, former Head of the Civil Service of the Federation	Treasury Looting	123bn Naira Fraud	Punishment: No action taken
4	Stella Oduah, former Minister of Aviation	Two bulletproof BMW cars purchase scandal	N255m	Punishment: None
5	NNPC	NNPC missing $20billion naira	$20billion naira	Punishment: Only whistle blower was fired
6	Private Jet Arm Scandal	$15 million stuffed in a private Jet belonging to Nigeria seized in South Africa	$15 million	Punishment: government claims involvement in scandal
7	Abba Moro Immigration recruitment scandal	Abba Moro Immigration recruitment scandal	N676 million	No conviction
8	Chief Dan Etete, ex-oil minister	Malabu Oil Scandal	$1.092bn	Punishment: None
9	Crude Oil Theft Scandal	Crude Oil Theft Scandal	£1bn a month	Punishment: None
10	Top generals in the Nigerian army	Arms scandal	$2.6 billion	Punishment: not a publicly acknowledged problem
11	Governor Ayo Fayose of Ekiti and 5 others	Ekiti Gate Election bribery	N4.7b election fund scandal	No punishment
12	Authur Eze and others	$500 Million Dollar defence Contract scandal	$500 Million	No punishment
13	Diepriye Alamieyesegha Ex-convict	Pardon of DiepriyeAlamieyesegha scandal	Stole $700,000 Bayelsa money as governor	Punishment: Presidential Pardon
14	Mohammed Abacha	Mohammed Abacha N446 Billion case scandal	N446 Billion	Punishment: None
15	Farouk Lawan, member House of Representatives	Farouk Lawan $3m bribery scandal	$3m bribery	No punishment

continued on following page

Table 3. Continued

S/N	Name	Case Status	Amount Involved	Action Taken on Suspect
16	Diezanni Allison-Madueke, former Minister of Petrolium	Embezzlement	$20 billion	No punishment
17	Church Leaders N6Billion Bribe scandal	N6Billion Bribe to Christian Religious Leaders by PDP	N6Billion	No punishment
18	BukolaSaraki (President of the Nigerian Senate)	Corruption and false declaration of assets	N10 billion	Arraigned at Code of Conduct Tribunal on a 13-count charge
19	Patricia Etteh (former Speaker Nigeria House of Representative)	Used N71.895 million by the Speaker to furnish her Residence	N71.895 million	Not Charged
20	NNPC	Kerosene subsidy scam	Billions of Naira	Not prosecuted
21	3 members of Nigeria House of Representatives	Prostitution Sex Scandal	Soliciting prostitutes in Cleveland, Ohio	No punishment

Source: Premium Times, Nigeria

Climaxing the concern for institutional decay, Professor Chinua Achebe in his seminal contribution to governance debates in Nigeria in 1983 spilled a lot of ink in his highly esteemed work, entitled "The Trouble with Nigeria" (Achebe, 1983). That was a little beyond three decades ago, but it appears that the rouble with Nigeria is far from ending as the trouble of corruption, which engaged Achebe's studious attention has refused to retreat (Okeke, 2014). Despite the abundance of both human and natural resources that divine benevolent Providence has bestowed on Nigeria, negative indexes characterize its reality as corruption has grown to a level of impunity in the last two decades, such that the country has been variously rated as the most corrupt in the world (Remi & Idike, 2016).

In earnest, "scandal" within the parameter of Nigerian political environment has assumed a dangerous dimension as the Nigerian politicians do not seem to worry about the damage caused by these scandals. In fact, corruption seems to have become legitimized because politicians see their victory as the ticket to loot and amass wealth (Okeke, 2014). However, this explains why there are profusion of allegations, both proved and unproved, that strewn the political landscape, but, in spite of this chaotic and scandalous situation, roughly 75 percent of incumbents politicians who were caught in the web of one scandal or the other returned to office. The culture of corruption through what Nigerians have come to know, as settlement syndrome has become part of the country's political culture (Remi & Idike, 2016). This is simply because all the positive values for development have been ditched and the politicians have no principle to protect as scandals seem to bring them to political limelight.

SOCIAL MEDIA AND STRUGGLE AGAINST POLITICAL CORRUPTION IN NIGERIA

In contemporary Nigeria, social protest which hitherto had been in the domain of activist and union leaders have become an expedient platforms of mass mobilization. The rapid spread and penetration of mobile telephony and Internet seem to be the major driver of social media use in Nigeria. Statistics from International Telecommunication Union (2013) indicate that the mobile telephone penetration in Africa is expanding at an unparalleled level of about 63% as at 2013 with about 16% of the population are using the Internet out of which Nigeria has the highest penetration rate in Africa. The social media, notably Twitter and Facebook, has become the rallying points for Nigerians both at home and in diaspora to give political corruption and other form of maladministration a wide exposure. For instance, the negative post about the ills of Johnathan administration on Facebook in 2012 forced the president to close his own Facebook page. Similarly, Nigerians on social media have unanimously requested that the Nigerian senate president, Mr. Bukola Saraki must resign to face his corruption trial with the Code of Conduct Bureau. Over 3000 Twitter users asked that Mr. Saraki must leave office (his Senate seat) and get prosecuted by the Nigerian Economic and Finance Crime Commission (EFCC) over his false asset declaration. Social media was also employed in Nigeria to prosecute the notorious "occupy Nigeria protest" which began on January, 2012 in response to the removal of fuel subsidy by President Goodluck Jonathan. In that mega protest, most of the country's major cities embarked on mass demonstrations, civil disobedience, general strike and online social activism to express their outrage on the increment of prices of petroleum products. Massive corruption and lack of accountability in the petroleum sector have increased the cost of subsidy to the benefit of few corrupt Nigerians. Politicians and their cronies have grown stupendously rich while majority of the populace continue to wallow in abject poverty (Okachie, 2012). These few incidence mentioned nonetheless have brought to the fore the underlying potential of social media platforms to drive socio-political engagement and social change in Nigeria. In all ramification, the power of the social media network in shaping modern day discourses in Nigeria cannot be under-estimated.

ETHICAL IMPLICATIONS OF SOCIAL MEDIA IN GOVERNANCE

The new media technologies for social networking such as Facebook, Twitter, MySpace, and YouTube in the turn of the 21st century began to transform the social, political and informational spaces and practices of individuals and institutions across the globe, inviting an ethical response from the community of applied ethicists and philosophers (Light & McGrath, 2010). Without mincing words, social media is generally portrayed as a positive thing amongst society but oftentimes, people tend to forget the ethical concerns behind social media especially social networking. What is however more worrying is that young people are probably the most vulnerable when it comes to using social media. While scholarly response continues to be challenged by the rapidly evolving nature of social media technologies, the urgent need for attention to the social media phenomenon is underscored by the fact that it is reshaping how many human beings initiate and/or maintain virtually every type of ethically significant social bond or role (Marturano, 2011). This study therefore presents some serious social media ethical concerns.

Ethics of Politics, Democracy, Freedom and Social Networking Services

Ethical debates about the impact of SNS on civil discourse, freedom and democracy in the public sphere must be seen as extensions of a broader discussion about the political implications of the Internet, one that predates Web 2.0 standards. Much of the literature on this subject focuses on the question of whether the Internet encourages or hampers the free exercise of deliberative public reason, in a manner informed by Jürgen Habermas's (1998) account of discourse in ethics and deliberative democracy in the public sphere (Ess, 2011). There is also the question of the extent to which SNS can facilitate political activism, civil disobedience and popular revolutions resulting in the overthrow of authoritarian regimes. Commonly referenced examples include the 2011 North African revolutions in Egypt and Tunisia, with which Facebook and Twitter were respectively associated (Marturano, 2011; Frick & Oberprantacher, 2011).

When SNS in particular are considered in light of these questions, some distinctive considerations arise. First, sites like Facebook and Twitter (as opposed to narrower SNS utilities such as LinkedIn) facilitate the sharing of, and exposure to, an extremely diverse range of types of discourse. On any given day on Facebook a user may encounter in her Newsfeed a link to an article in a respected political magazine followed by a video of a cat in a silly costume, followed by a link to a new scientific study, followed by a lengthy status update someone has posted about their lunch, followed by a photo of a popular political figure overlaid with a clever and subversive caption. Vacation photos are mixed in with political rants, invitations to cultural events, birthday reminders and data-driven graphs created to undermine common political, moral or economic beliefs (Jimenez, 2004). Thus while a user has a tremendous amount of liberty to choose which forms of discourse to pay closer attention to, and tools with which to hide or prioritize the posts of certain members of her network, she cannot easily shield herself from at least a superficial acquaintance with a diversity of private and public concerns of her fellows. This has the potential to offer at least some measure of protection against the extreme insularity and fragmentation of discourse that is incompatible with the public sphere (Jimenez, 2004).

Secondly, while users can often 'befriend' or systematically hide the posts of those with whom they tend to disagree, the high visibility and perceived value of social connections on these sites makes this option less attractive as a consistent strategy. Philosophers of technology often speak of the affordances or gradients of particular technologies in given contexts (Vallor, 2010) insofar as they make certain patterns of use more attractive or convenient for users (while not rendering alternative patterns impossible). In this respect, social networks like those on Facebook, in which users must take actions somewhat contrary to the site's purpose in order to effectively shield themselves from unwelcome or contrary opinions, may be viewed as having a modestly democratic gradient in comparison to networks deliberately constructed around a particular political cause or identity (Jimenez, 2004). However, this gradient may be undermined by Facebook's own algorithms, which curate users' News Feed in ways that are opaque to them, and which almost certainly prioritize the appeal of the 'user experience' over civic benefit or the integrity of the public sphere.

Thirdly, one must ask whether SNS can skirt the dangers of a plebiscite model of democratic discourse in which minority voices are inevitably dispersed and drowned out by the many. Certainly, compared to the 'one-to-many' channels of communication favoured by traditional media, SNS facilitate a 'many-to-many' model of communication that appears to lower the barriers to participation in civic discourse for everyone, including the marginalized. However, if one's 'Facebook friends' or people you 'follow' are sufficiently numerous, then minority opinions may still be heard as lone voices in the wilderness, perhaps valued for providing some 'spice' and novelty to the broader conversation but failing to receive serious public consideration of their merits. Existing SNS lack the institutional structures necessary to ensure that minority voices enjoy not only free, but qualitatively equal access to the deliberative function of the public sphere.

Fourthly, one must also consider the quality of informational exchanges on SNS and the extent to which they promote a genuinely dialogical public sphere marked by the exercise of critical rationality. While we have noted above that exposure to well-informed opinions and reliable evidential sources are facilitated by many of the most popular SNS, exposure does not guarantee attention or consumption (Light & McGrath, 2010). For example, the number of contacts in the average Facebook user's network is sufficiently large to make it virtually impossible for a typical user to see every relevant post even among those which Facebook's algorithm selects for their News Feed, and only a very small number of those may be closely attended or responded to. Many scholars worry that in SNS environments, substantive contributions to civic discourse increasingly function as flotsam on a virtual sea of trivially amusing or shallow content, weakening the civic habits and practices of critical rationality that we need in order to function as well-informed and responsible democratic citizens (Ess, 2010).

A fifth issue for online democracy relates to the contentious debate emerging on social media platforms about the extent to which controversial or unpopular speech ought to be tolerated or punished by private actors, especially when the consequences manifest in traditional offline contexts and spaces such as the university. For example, the norms of academic freedom in the U.S. have been greatly destabilized by the 'Salaita Affair' and several other cases in which academics were censured or otherwise punished by their institutions as a result of their controversial social media posts. It remains to be seen what equilibrium can be found between civility and free expression in communities increasingly mediated by SNS communications (Light & McGrath, 2010).

There is also the question of whether SNS will necessarily preserve a democratic ethos as they come to reflect increasingly pluralistic and international social networks. The current split between networks such as Facebook and Twitter dominant in Western liberal society and dedicated SNS in countries such as China (RenRen) and Russia (VKontakte) with more communitarian and/or authoritarian regimes may not endure. An even more pressing question is whether civic discourse and activism on SNS will be compromised or manipulated by the commercial interests that currently own and manage the technical infrastructure (Ess, 2010). This concern is driven by the growing economic power and political influence of companies in the technology sector, and the potentially disenfranchising and disempowering effects of an economic model in which users play a fundamentally passive role (Floridi, 2015). Indeed, the relationship between social media users and service providers have become increasingly contentious, as users struggle to demand more privacy, better data security and more effective protections from online harassment in an economic context where they have little or no direct bargaining power. This imbalance was powerfully illustrated by the revelation in 2014 that Facebook researchers had quietly conducted psychological experiments on users without their knowledge, manipulating their moods by altering the balance of positive or negative items in their News Feeds (Goel, 2014). The study adds yet another dimension to growing concerns about the ethics and validity of social science research that relies on SNS-generated data (Buchanan & Zimmer, 2012).

RECOMMENDATIONS

Having dissected the various issues related to the nexus between social media, political scandal, and good governance in Nigeria, the following recommendations could help in mitigating the ethical issues and challenges encountered in the usage of the new media in Nigeria today. Social networks could potentially be used for a broad range of participatory activities, such as demanding for public services like education and water, contacting leaders, political campaigns and discussions, and fighting corruption. They also could play a critical role in citizen engagement and advocacy, which have a major bearing on transparency and accountability in governance and the conduct of public affairs. An effective social media policy should be developed through engagement and dialogue between government, government agencies, social network providers/operators, and the citizenry (users).

Similarly, it will be beneficial for the ethics commission and/or the National Orientation Agency (an agency in-charge of ethical orientation) to work with other agencies across the country to develop an effective social media policy. The Ministry of Communication Technology and Information and Culture in partnership with the Nigeria Communications Commission (NCC) and Nigerian Communications Satellite Ltd (NIGCOMSAT) should sponsor a bill to the National Assembly seeking to amend the Nigerian Freedom of Information Act, as well as the Cybercrimes (Prohibition, Prevention, etc.) Act, 2015, in an attempt to furnish the country with more cyber law and social media provisions. This would help in ensuring that the regulation of content on social media does not infringe on the people's right to freedom of expression.

The Federal Government of Nigeria should in addition train more information security experts to be able to ensure that the country has skilled and competent personnel that can help secure the ICT infrastructure as well as coordinate response to cyber security threats in Nigeria. Finally, in view of the fact that a greater percentage of the population using social media today are the youth, a compulsory course on the proper use of social media should be mounted in our institutions of learning to enlighten the young people on the ethical implications of using social media.

CONCLUSION

This study sought to determine the nexus between social media, political scandal, and good governance in Nigeria. The study found that, what constitutes "scandal politics" or the politics of scandal today remains hotly contested. Much of the recent literature on the rise of scandal politics places prime importance on the move by political parties to move towards the political center, and the corresponding rise of personality politics or identity politics (Amelia, 2008). We surmise that the dramatic growth of media and Internet outlets in the last decade alone in Nigeria, social networks could potentially be used for a broad range of participatory activities, such as demanding for public services like education and water, contacting leaders, political campaigns and discussions, and most importantly fighting corruption. They also could play a critical role in citizen engagement and advocacy, which have a major bearing on transparency and accountability in governance and the conduct of public affairs. Therefore, this calls for an increased focus on communication and higher standards of accountability and ethical considerations.

Though scandal has been a part of the political system in many countries since its inception many years ago, there are numerous contextual factors that make a scandal noteworthy, such as the importance of the people involved, the depth of conspiracy in the scandal, and the cover-up strategies involving policymakers. Political scandals are events that capture a lot of attention and eventually disappear over a period of time and are the source of intense public communication (Bennett & Serrin, 2005). There is a changing nature of political scandals that has resulted from an increased use of social media and the Internet. Politicians are increasingly more vulnerable online as the separation between public and private life has quickly diminished in the increasingly more connected world. Also, political scandals are shifting from illegal or corrupt activities towards personal missteps no longer about illegal or corrupt activities (Bowler & Karp, 2004). Early studies on scandal politics focus primarily on misbehaviour by politicians as the media conveys it to the public. More recent studies, however, focus on how misreporting or intentional creation of scandal in the media by politicians and/or scandals involving misbehaviour by media professionals (Harris, Lang, & Yakes, 2011). In other words, media are no longer simply conveyors of political scandal (if they ever were). Today they are active participants in a scandal politics.

REFERENCES

Achebe, C. (1983). *The Trouble with Nigeria*. Enugu, Nigeria: Fourth Dimension Publishing Company.

Adibe, O., & Orji, L. (2012, November). Social media and political participation in Africa: Issues, problem and prospects. *Paper presented at the ACCE*, FUT Minna.

Ajayi, A. I., & Adesote, S. A. (2014). The New Social Media and consolidation of democracy in Nigeria: Uses, Potentials and Challenges. *Journal of Good Governance and Sustainable Development in Africa*, *2*(4).

Akasike. L. (2009). Corruption in Nigeria: Which Way? *Saturday Champion, 15.*

Amelia, A. (2008). Scandal politics in the new media environment: Analytical note. *Scandal Politics Review*, *9*(1), 75–99.

Anyadike, D. O., EbezeUche V., & Odoemelam C. (2014). Social Media in E-Governance and Political Participation in Enugu State, Nigeria. *The International Journal of Social Sciences and Humanities Invention*, *1*(2), 80–94.

Balkin, J. M. (1999). How Mass Media Simulate Political Transparency. *Cultural Values*, *3*(4), 393–413. doi:10.1080/14797589909367175

Bar-Tura, A. (2010). Wall-to-Wall or Face-to-Face. In D. E. Wittkower (Ed.), *Facebook and Philosophy* (pp. 231–239). Chicago: Open Court.

Baran, S. J. (2010). *Introduction to Mass Communication, Media Literacy and Culture*. McGraw-Hills Companies Inc.

Bennett, W. L., & Serrin, W. (2005). The Watchdog Role. In G. Overholser & K. H. Jamieson (Eds.), *The Press* (pp. 169–188). New York: Oxford University Press.

Benoit, W. L. (1995). *Accounts, Excuses, and Apologies: a Theory of Image Restoration Strategies*. Albany: State University of New York.

Benoit, W. L. (1997). Image Repair Discourse and Crisis Communication. *Public Relations Review*, *23*(2), 177–186. doi:10.1016/S0363-8111(97)90023-0

Bowler, S., & Karp, J. A. (2004). Politicians, Scandals, and Trust in Government. *Political Behavior*, *26*(3), 271–287. doi:10.1023/B:POBE.0000043456.87303.3a

Boyd, D. M., & Ellison, B. N. (2007). Social Networking Sites: Definition of history and Scholarship. *Journal of Computer-Mediated Communication*, *13*(1), 210–230. doi:10.1111/j.1083-6101.2007.00393.x

Buchanan, E. A., & Zimmer, M. (2012). Internet Research Ethics. In Edward N. Zalta (Ed.), *The Stanford Encyclopedia of Philosophy* Retrieved from http://plato.stanford.edu/archives/spr2015/entries/ethics-internet-research/

Ess, C. (2010). The Embodied Self in a Digital Age: Possibilities, Risks and Prospects for a Pluralistic (democratic/liberal) Future? *Nordicom Information*, *32*(2), 105–118.

Ess, C. (2011). Self, Community and Ethics in Digital Mediatized Worlds. In C. Ess & M. Thorseth (Eds.), *Trust and Virtual Worlds: Contemporary Perspectives* (pp. vii–xxix). Oxford: Peter Lang.

Essoungou, A. M. (2011). Nigeria's April elections set new records in use of social media.

Floridi, L. (2011). The Informational Nature of Personal Identity. *Minds and Machines*, *21*(4), 549–566. doi:10.1007/s11023-011-9259-6

Frick, M., & Oberprantacher, A. (2011). Shared is Not Yet Sharing, Or: What Makes Social Networking Services Public? *International Review of Information Ethics*, *15*, 18–23.

Goel, V. (2014). Facebook Tinkers with Users' Emotions in News Feed Experiment, Stirring Outcry. *The New York Times*. Retrieved from http://www.nytimes.com/2014/06/30/technology/facebook-tinkers-with-users-emotions-in-news-feed-experiment-stirring-outcry.html?_r=0

Hampton, K., Rainie, L., Lu, W., Dwyer, M., Shin, I., & Purcell, K. (2014). Social Media and the 'Spiral of Silence'. *Pew Research Center Policy Paper*. Retrieved from http://www.pewinternet.org/2014/08/26/social-media-and-the-spiral-of-silence/

Harris, A. L., Lang, M., Yates, D., & Kruck, S. E. (2011). Incorporating ethics and social responsibility in IS education. *Journal of Information Systems Education*, *22*(3), 183–189.

Helen, N. E., Charles, O.O. & Jenifer. N. O. (2014). The Use of Social Networking Sites among the Undergraduate Students of University of Nigeria, Nsukka. *Library Philosophy and Practice*.

Holbert, R. L., & Benoit, W. L. (2009). A theory of political campaign media connectedness. *Communication Monographs*, *76*(3), 303–332. doi:10.1080/03637750903074693

Ibrahim, O. S. (2013). Deepening Democratic Culture in Nigeria: What Role(S) For New Media? *IOSR Journal of Humanities and Social Science*, *15*(4), 86-91.

Idakwo, L. (2011). The use of social media among Nigerian youths: An exploratory research into the usage habits of social media users in Nigeria. *Political Science Quarterly*, *31*, 182–188.

Jimenez, F. (2004). The Politics of Scandal in Spain: Morality Plays, Social Trust, and the Battle for Public Opinion. *The American Behavioral Scientist*, *47*(8), 1099–1121. doi:10.1177/0002764203262279

Kaplan, A. M., & Haenlein, M. (2010). Users of the world, unite! The challenges and opportunities of social media. *Business Horizons*, *53*(1), 61. doi:10.1016/j.bushor.2009.09.003

Kaufmann, D. (2003). *Rethinking Governance: Empirical Lessons Challenging Orthodoxy*. Washington, D. C: World Bank.

Light, B., & McGrath, K. (2010). Ethics and social networking sites: A disclosive analysis of Facebook. *Information Technology & People*, *23*(4), 290–311. doi:10.1108/09593841011087770

Marturano, A. (2011). The Ethics of Online Social Networks—an Introduction. *International Review of Information Ethics*, *16*, 3–5.

McQuail, D. (2010). *Theories of Mass Communication* (6th ed.). Sage Publications.

Navetta, D. (2011). The Legal Implications of Social Networking: The Basics. Retrieved from http://www.infolawgroup.com/articles/social-networking/the-legal-implications-ofsocial-networking-the-basics-part-one/

Odoemelam, C. C., & Adibe, K. N. (2012). The role of social media in political conflicts and political communication in Africa. In D. Wilson (Ed). The Media, Terrorism & Political Communication in Nigeria. Lagos: African Council for Communication Education (ACCE).

Okachie, L. (2012). The Anti-Corruption Fight. In *Nigeria: How well So Far?* National Mirror.

Okeke, R. C. (2014). Anatomy of the Nigerian elite: Interrogating a blind elite model of the elite theory. *European Scientific Journal*, *10*(4), 320–336.

Okoro, N., & Kenneth, A. N. (2013). Social Media and Political Participation in Nigeria during the 2011 general elections: The lapses and the lessons. *Global Journal of Arts Humanities and Social Sciences*, *1*(3), 29–46.

Okunna, C. S., & Omenugha, K. A. (2012). *Introduction to Mass Communication* (3rd ed.). New Generation Books.

Phillips, L. M. & Brabham, D. C. 2012. How today's digital landscape redefines the notion of power in public relations. *Prism, 9*(2).

Powell, T. (2012). Unleashing the power of social media to improve employee productivity. *CPA Practice Management Forum, 8*(7), 7-12.

Remi, C. O. & Idike, A. N. (2016). The Dialectics of Political Economy and elite Corruption in a Postcolonial State: a Nigerian case study. *Arabian Journal of Business and Management Review, 5*(7).

Social Bakers. (2016). Facebook Statistics. Retrieved from http://www.socialbakers.com/facebook-statistics/

Sunstein, C. (2008). Democracy and the Internet. In J. van den Hoven & J. Weckert (Eds.), *Information Technology and Moral Philosophy* (pp. 93–110). Cambridge, UK: Cambridge University Press.

Thompson, J. B. (2000). *Political Scandal: Power and Visibility in the Media Age.* Cambridge: Polity Press.

Tumber, H., & Silvio, R. (2004). Introduction: Political Scandals and the Media across Democracies: Volume II. *The American Behavioral Scientist, 47*(9), 1143–1152. doi:10.1177/0002764203262340

United Nations Development Programme (UNDP). (2002). *Human Development Report 2002: Deepening Democracy in a Fragmented World.*

Valkernburg, P. M., Peter, J., & Schouten, A. P. (2006). Friend networking sites and their relationship to adolescent wellbeing. *International Journal of Cultural Policy, 16*(2), 200–214.

Vallor, S. (2010). Social networking technology and the virtues. *Ethics and Information Technology, 12*(2), 157–170. doi:10.1007/s10676-009-9202-1

Vallor, S. (2012). Flourishing on Facebook: Virtue Friendship and New Social Media. *Ethics and Information Technology, 14*(3), 185–199. doi:10.1007/s10676-010-9262-2

Waisboard, S. R. (2004). Scandals, Media, and Citizenship in Contemporary Argentina. *The American Behavioral Scientist, 47*(8), 1072–1098. doi:10.1177/0002764203262278

Woessner, M. C. (2005). Scandal, Elites, and Presidential Popularity: Considering the Importance of Cues in Public Support of the President. *Presidential Studies Quarterly, 35*(1), 94–115. doi:10.1111/j.1741-5705.2004.00237.x

World Bank. (1992). *Governance and Development.*

KEY TERMS AND DEFINITIONS

Computer: A computer is a machine that receives or stores or process data quickly according to a stored program.

Good Governance: Good governance is the processes for making and implementing decisions about governance. It is not about making 'correct' decisions, but about the best possible process for making decisions especially good decision-making that should result in good governance.

ICT: Information and Communication Technology.

Media: Is made up of are all those media technologies that are intended to reach a large audience by mass communication. "They include messages communicated through a mass medium to a number of people.

Scandal: Scandal is disgraceful events or an accusation or accusations about people's private lives that receive wide exposure with a negative effect on the credibility of the person or organisation involved. It involves an action, rumour or malicious gossip about scandalous events or actions of an individual or group regarded as morally or legally wrong and causes public outrage.

Social Media: They are forms of electronic communication which facilitate interactive base on certain interests. Social media include web and mobile technology.

Social Networking: The use of internet to make information about yourself available and other people especially people you share an interest with to send messages to them.

Social Networking Sites: A website where people put information about them and can also send information to others.

Tweets: A short message posted on Twitter (a micro blog).

Chapter 8
Government Website, Social Media, and Citizens' Perceptions of Corruption:
Evidence from Chinese Cities

Liang Ma
Renmin University of China, China

ABSTRACT

In this chapter, the author aims to empirically examine the effect of social media use and e-government adoption on citizens' perceived corruption. It is hypothesized that the use of social media by citizens is positively related to their perceptions of corruption, while the use of government websites is negatively related to perceived corruption. The author draws on a recent national telephone survey of citizens in 36 major cities in China to empirically test the above hypotheses. The multilevel model estimates suggest that social media use is insignificantly related to corruption perceptions, but government website use is negatively associated with perceived corruptions. The findings of this study help understand the anti-corruption effects of social media and e-government, and also generate helpful implications for other countries and regions in utilizing digital applications for anti-corruption purposes.

DOI: 10.4018/978-1-5225-2019-1.ch008

INTRODUCTION

Corruption is one of the key challenges to good governance, primarily due to its ubiquitously and chronically negative consequences in various aspects of political operations, economic activities, and social development (Rothstein, 2011). How to fight against corruption and keep the government clean is among the top policy priorities of many countries and regions around the world. The rise and penetration of information and communication technologies (ICTs), particularly the ubiquitous use of Internet and social media applications, is advocated as one effective approach to reduce corruption and retain government integrity (Lee & Lio, 2016). Government transparency can be substantially strengthened through online information disclosure and dissemination, which helps deter and curb corruption (Srivastava, Teo, & Devaraj, 2016). With the help of ICTs, the government can minimize procedural loopholes by digitalizing business processes (Elbahnasawy, 2014). Internet and social media applications equip the ordinary citizens with new means to fight against corruption, since the active online participation of citizens help better monitor and scrutiny government misconducts and embezzlements (Bertot, Jaeger, & Grimes, 2010).

The rise of ICTs also challenges the monopoly of media by the government in many nondemocratic developing countries, e.g., China (Yang, 2009). Given the diversified media channels citizens can access, it is theoretically interesting and practically imperative to examine the differentiating effects of media exposures on citizen attitudes towards corruption. Do citizens relying on social media applications to acquire news and other information perceive a higher level of corruption than those solely consuming government-controlled media? In this chapter, the author aim to empirically examine the effect of social media use on citizens' attitudes towards corruption.

Social media platforms, while not free from state censorship, are often full of rumors and grapevine news with disproportionally negative reports of the government (King, Pan, & Roberts, 2013). Government-controlled media as the mouthpiece of the ruling party, in contrast, are more positive and supportive of the party and the state in eliciting and reporting news (Zhu, Lu, & Shi, 2013). Given the negativity bias embedded in social media applications, citizens who rely on them to acquire information are more likely to perceive the government as corrupted than those who use alternative information sources such as state-owned media. The author hypothesizes that the use of social media by citizens is positively related to their perceptions of government corruption, and the use of mass media attenuates the social media effect on perceived corruption.

The author draws on a recent national survey of citizens in 36 major cities in China to empirically test the above hypotheses. The results partially support the hypotheses, which help understand the effect of social media use on corruption perceptions and anti-corruption effectiveness. The findings from this study also generate helpful implications for other countries and regions in utilizing social media applications for anti-corruption purposes.

The remainder of this chapter is structured as follows. The author first briefly reviews the background and context of this study, particularly government control of media and the recent wave of anticorruption campaigns. In the third section, the author discusses the linkages between social media use and corruption perceptions, and propose the hypotheses to be tested in this study. The author then presents the data and methods used in this study, followed by the key empirical analyses. The author finally discusses the implications and contributions of the research findings reported in this chapter, and conclude with research limitations, policy suggestions, and future research directions.

CONTEXT AND BACKGROUND

Media, Internet, and Corruption in China

China is a unitary polity with one ruling party, the Communist Party of China (CPC). The democratic election is rather symbolic, and the People's Congress as the parliament cannot strongly hold the government accountable. Party and state cadres are appointed by the upper-tier Party committee, and their accountability to the general public is also weak (Ma, 2016). Without strong check and balance, corruption is a natural outcome of this regime (Manion, 2004). Corruption is a severe issue in contemporary China, and the society is plagued by rampant briberies and embezzlements (Wedeman, 2012).

The new Party-state regime installed in late 2012 pledged to crack down corruption, and thousands of senior officials have been condemned to punishments (Manion, 2016). As documented by "Catching Tigers and Flies", an online tool developed by the ChinaFile in January 21, 2016 to visualize China's anti-corruption campaign since Xi Jinping assumed power, totally 1,464 officials, including 146 senior Party and government officials (so-called "tigers"), have been caught by the authorities, with over 6.34 billion RMB (or 963 million USD) embezzled, stolen, or taken by the corrupt officials. The Corruption Perceptions Index developed by the Transparency International acknowledged the progress made in China's anti-corruption campaign, and the latest results suggest that China' rank steadily rise from 100th in 2014 to 83st in 2015. The corruption of the government, however, is still scandalous and chronic.

The CPC as the single ruling party is adept at ideological control and political propaganda. Government-controlled media is employed as the mouthpiece of the CPC, and the space for free media is rather stifling. For instance, traditional mass media (e.g., radios, TVs, newspapers, and magazines) are usually officially owned and run by the government in China, and negative information about the government and officials is often missed from regular news reporting. The attitudes and values of the public are largely shaped by the state media, with few people capable of escaping from their effects. The commercialization of official media has leveraged market-driven values and weakened government control, but still these media are under strict scrutiny by relevant authorities (Stockmann, 2013).

The rise of Internet and other ICTs has substantially transformed the media landscape in China. According to the latest statistics of the China Internet Network Information Center (CNNIC, 2016), there have been 688 million residents in China with Internet access (or 50.3 percent) by December 2015. Approximately 90.1 percent of netizens, or 620 million, access Internet via cell phone. Social media are commonly used among netizens, with 77.0 percent or 530 million in total. The government is active in media control and censorship, but online content is not easy to detect and depress due to its scale and diversity (Ma & Zhang, 2015). The relative free online space enables the public to discuss government corruptions, which may reshape their attitudes to and perceptions of corruption (Yang, 2009). Veteran netizens invent many tactics to bypass government censorship to circulate and discuss online content unwelcomed by the government (King et al., 2013).

The Chinese netizens are keen in exposing and denouncing corrupt officials by social media applications, because of their low cost, high convenience, strong interactivity, and self-protection with anonymity. Many corruption scandals were firstly disclosed by netizens in social media platforms, which then triggered extensive media coverage and followed by government investigation. For instance, Yang Dacai, the former Director of Shaanxi Administration of Work Safety, was accused by netizens for wearing luxurious watches in several occasions in August 2012. He got a nickname of "Watch Uncle", and was later investigated by local Commission for Discipline Inspection for corrupt practices. Without public disclosure, he would otherwise continue his political career as usual. Given the stifling official channels for corruption reporting, political scandals, particularly corruption events, are more likely to be leaked and whistle-blown through social media.

The grassroots campaigns against corruption help challenge the hegemony of the government in cracking down corruption, but online anti-corruption is controversial in leaking personal privacy and wasting government attention. The authorities aim to incorporate and tunnel unorganized online whistle-blowing into institutional and formal anti-corruption approaches, e.g., the 12388 tip-off platform initiated by the Central Commission for Discipline Inspection (CCDI), the 12380 reporting hotline maintained by the Central Department of Organization (CDO), the reporting center of the Supreme People's Procuratorate, the reporting website of the Supreme People's Court, and the reporting mailbox of the Ministry of Land and Resources, among others. Online whistle-blowing through social media platforms, however, is still bourgeoning due to its effectiveness in mobilizing the online community to expose and punish corrupt officials.

Literature Review

There is a growing body of literature dedicated to the study of ICTs, digital government, and (anti)corruption. In this section the author first reviews the literature on citizen perceptions of corruption. The author then reviews the existing studies on the effects of ICTs on corruption perceptions. The author lastly summarizes the key findings of prior studies and highlight the limitations meriting future studies to address.

Corruption perceptions are shaped by multiple factors, including personal experiences, political propensities, and media exposure (Charron, 2015). Apart from personal propensities and actual experiences, media coverage of corruption practices plays a key role in shaping citizens' perceptions of corruption (Zhu et al., 2013). While ICTs are advocated to be powerful in anticorruption, they may also amplify citizens' perceptions of corruption due to wide dissemination and active discussions of corruption-related scandals and topics. Particularly in China and other contexts where news reports were previously monopolized by state-run media acting as national propaganda machinery, the rising use of ICTs may help citizens understand more about and perceive higher level of corrupt practices otherwise being masked by official media. Most existing studies only examine traditional mass media on perceived corruption without taking account the emerging role played by online media. A relevant study of Chinese citizens recently reported shows that citizens with access to grapevine news perceive a higher level of corruption, while consumption of government-controlled media weakens this negative effect (Zhu et al., 2013). The government tightly controls citizen access to foreign media in China, and it is found that citizens with access to foreign media are more likely to challenge the government's political campaigns (Lu, Aldrich, & Shi, 2014). Citizens in China exposed to foreign news are found to less trust in legal authorities (e.g., police and court) than those without access to foreign media (Wu, 2014).

The use of ICTs of the government is found to be an effective instrument to crack down corruption in various countries and regions (Srivastava et al., 2016). Evidence from cross-country studies reveal that the presence of government website is related to lower levels of corruption perceptions (Garcia-Murillo, 2013). Online corruption awareness is found to be negatively related to the perceptions and incidence of corruption, because it can work well as an effective corruption deterrent (Goel, Nelson, & Naretta, 2012). A recent study of Chinese provinces reveals that the relationship between the penetration rate of Internet and cell phone and the amount of corrupt officials documented is inverted U-shaped. The results suggest that ICTs may first help reveal more corruption cases due to the easiness of whistle-blowing, but ICTs then reduce corruptions by deterring government employees from taking bribes and embezzling public money (Lee & Lio, 2016). While these macro-level studies help understand the interaction between ICTs and corruption, the micro-level relationship between ICTs and corruption perceptions is still understudied.

The effect of e-government use on corruption perceptions has been well documented in the literature, but the findings are primarily from the U.S., Hong Kong, and South Korea (Srivastava et al., 2016). Despite lots of studies have examined the effects of e-government adoption and social media use on citizen trust in government (Porumbescu, 2015), their effects on citizen perceptions of corruption have not been fully revealed. In a nutshell, it is helpful to simultaneously examine the effects of citizen exposure to various media channels on perceived corruption.

THEORETICAL HYPOTHESES

Social Media and Corruption Perceptions

Citizens' perceptions of corruption may generate various negative consequences, e.g., lowering citizen satisfaction with and trust in government and eliciting rule-breaking behaviors (Villoria, Van Ryzin, & Lavena, 2013). It is pivotal to understand why citizens perceive higher levels of corruption. Citizens' perceptions of corruption can be shaped by multiple sources of information, including but not limited to personal experiences, words of mouth, news reports, rumors, and grapevines (Zhu et al., 2013). Citizens exposed to only mass media controlled by the government are more likely to perceive lower levels of corruption, since these channels are usually adept at whitewashing government image. The online media, in contrast, are usually full of negative information against the government. Just as one joke said, "China in the CCTV is a paradise, while China in the online space is a hell." The diversification of media channels may help citizens understand the government in a balanced manner and develop independent conscience in filtering government-controlled media.

In the age of digital media, citizens exposed to social media and other online channels are more likely to hold negative attitudes towards the government (Porumbescu, 2013). The information about the government circulated in the social media platform is often at odds with the situations depicted by the mass media controlled by the government. Online platform is usually full of negative sentiments, and real-time and interactive feature of social media further escalates their disparities from those from the mass media. The author thus expects that citizens acquiring government information from social media are more likely to perceive high levels of corruption than those relying on other media channels.

H1: Citizens exposed to social media perceive a higher level of corruption than those do not use social media.

Government Website Use and Corruption Perceptions

Government website is developed and maintained by the government to primarily disclose information, delivery online services, and facilitate online communications with the public (West, 2005). Similar to the mass media controlled by the government, government website is more likely to report good news about the authorities, while negative information is usually hidden or depressed. Government website is more advantageous than traditional approaches (e.g., physical and face-to-face instruments) in delivering public services to the public, with higher levels of efficiency, responsiveness, and effectiveness (Tolbert & Mossberger, 2006). Citizens using e-government features are relatively more likely to perceive a good image of the government, and their perceptions of corruption may be lower (Welch, Hinnant, & Moon, 2005). Government websites themselves are equipped to minimize the opportunities of corruption, which help boosts citizen trust in the government (Srivastava et al., 2016). The author thus predicts that citizens exposed to government site will perceive lower levels of corruption.

H2: Citizens acquiring information from government websites perceive lower levels of corruption than those who do not navigate government websites.

The Interactive Effects of Media Channels

Citizens are usually simultaneously exposed to various media channels, and it is interesting to examine their interactive effects on citizen perceptions of corruption.

The author argues that social media and government website may jointly affect citizens' perceived corruption, and the negative effect of social media consumption on corruption perceptions is mitigated by citizen exposure to government-controlled media, particularly government website. The author can reiterate this argument reversely that the positively effect of government website use on perceived corruption is mitigated by citizen use of social media.

H3: Social media and government website jointly affect citizen perceptions of corruption.

DATA AND METHODS

Sample and Data Sources

The author tests the above hypotheses in the context of China, in which Internet and social media have been dramatically transforming citizens' sources of information and perceptions of corruption. The author draws on a national survey of citizens across 36 major cities, including four province-level municipalities (e.g., Beijing), 27 provincial capital cities (e.g., Guangzhou), and five sub-provincial cities (e.g., Qingdao). These cities are pioneering in adopting ICTs, and they are comparable in terms of administrative autonomy and regional centrality. While it is also interesting to examine cities with small and medium size, the author leaves it for future research. In each city over 700 respondents were randomly recruited and telephone interviewed, and their use of social media and government website and perceptions of corruption were included in the instrument.

Dependent Variables

The author uses one 11-point Likert-like scale item to measure citizen perceptions of government corruption. The respondents were asked about the extent to which they perceive city government employees to be honest and clean. This variable ranges from 0 (strongly disagree) to 10 (strongly agree), and a higher value means a lower level of corruption. To facilitate interpretation of the results, the author reverses the scale with larger values denoting higher levels of corruption. The author expects that citizens exposed to social media are more likely to rate a higher score on this item. While the variable is measured by an ordinal scale, it is usually modeled as an interval variable.

Independent Variables

The author uses a battery of dummy variables to gauge citizen exposure to various media channels. A multiple-choice question is included to ask the channels from which the respondents acquire government information. The respondents are permitted to choose from seven options, including

1. Mass media (e.g., newspaper, TV, and radio),
2. Government website,
3. Business website (e.g., Sohu and Baidu),
4. Social media (e.g., WeChat and Weibo),
5. Short message service (SMS),
6. Oral, and
7. Others.

The author creates dummies for the first six channels, using others as the reference category. Our focus in this study is social media and government website, and the author will specially examine their effects on corruption perceptions.

Control Variables

Citizen perceptions of corruption may be affected by other variables, and it is appropriate to control for them in the model. In line with the existing literature on perceived corruption (Zhu et al., 2013), the author includes the following variables as controls.

The author includes the respondents' gender as a dummy, using female as the reference group. The author measures age as an ordinal variable, ranging from 1 (18-24 years) to 6 (above 59 years).

The author includes a dummy of nationality, using non-Han minorities as the reference group.

The author gauges the respondents' highest education by an ordinal variable, ranging from 1 (primary school and below) to 6 (master's degree and above).

The length of residence in the sampled city ranges from 1 (1-3 years) to 4 (more than 10 years).

The household registration types may affect citizens' perceptions of government corruption, and the author includes three dummies for local urban, local rural, and nonlocal urban residents, using nonlocal rural ones as the reference group.

The respondent's total annual family income is controlled, which ranges from 1 (non-fixed income) to 11 (above 300,000 Yuan).

The author also includes the respondent's occupations, and unemployed respondents are coded 1, otherwise 0.

Citizens' political efficacy may affect their perceptions of government corruption (Zhu et al., 2013), and the author includes an inverse item to gauge its effect. The author asked the respondents the extent to which they as ordinary people can influence government decision-making. This Likert-like scale ranges from 0 (strongly disagree) to 10 (strongly agree), and a higher value corresponds to a lower level of political efficacy. In the same token with the corruption measure, the author reverses this item.

Model Specification

The ordinary least square (OLS) regression assumes the observations are independent, which is not the case of this study. Our respondents are from 36 cities, and they are nested within each sampled city. A pooled OLS may ignore unobserved heterogeneity across cities (clusters), and multilevel model may help address this concern. Given the nested structure of the data (individuals clustered within cities), a multilevel model is estimated to test the hypotheses (Aguinis, Gottfredson, & Culpepper, 2013). In this study, all our variables are measured at the individual-level (Level 1), and the author only controls for city-level variance (Level 2). The author thus uses random-intercept and fixed-slop model to estimate our models.

RESULTS

Descriptive Statistics

The descriptive statistics of key variables included in this study are reported in Table 1. In an 11-point Likert-like scale, the respondent's perceptions of corruption are moderately lower. Part of the reason is that the author uses an inverse item to gauge corruption. Approximately 70 percent of the respondents use mass media as one of their primary sources of government information, followed by business website (40 percent), social media (28 percent), SMS (19 percent), government website (12 percent), and oral (12 percent). The results reveal that the respondents relay more on social media than on government website in eliciting government information.

Table 1. The descriptive statistics of key variables (IGI, 2016)

Variables	*N*	Mean	SD	Min	Max
Corruption	21,804	3.874	2.530	0	10
Mass media	25,370	0.698	0.459	0	1
Government website	25,370	0.123	0.328	0	1
Business website	25,370	0.404	0.491	0	1
Social media	25,370	0.277	0.448	0	1
SMS	25,327	0.192	0.394	0	1
Oral	25,358	0.122	0.328	0	1
Gender	25,370	0.515	0.500	0	1
Age	25,370	3.188	1.669	1	6
Nationality	25,366	0.093	0.290	0	1
Education	22,638	2.782	1.318	1	6
Length of residence	25,370	2.956	1.159	1	4
Local urban	24,197	0.359	0.480	0	1
Local rural	24,197	0.217	0.412	0	1
Nonlocal urban	24,197	0.212	0.409	0	1
Income	21,681	5.656	2.298	1	11
Jobless	23,464	0.065	0.247	0	1
Political efficacy	22,790	3.760	2.517	0	10

Multilevel Model Estimates

The author first estimates the null model without any independent variable to calculate the Intraclass Correlation (ICC). The model estimates show that 0.744 percent of total variance of corruption perceptions can be attributed to city-level variance. Despite a low ICC, the likelihood ratio (LR) test (χ^2=101.25, $p<0.01$) suggests that multilevel model is superior in comparison with pooled OLS model. The author thus uses multilevel model in estimating our hypotheses.

The multilevel model estimates are reported in Table 2. The whole model is statistically different from zero (see Wald χ^2), but its explanatory power is not high, as suggested by the value of R^2. The author finds that among the six media channels (using others as the reference category), two of them are statistically significant related to corruption perceptions (Model 1). Social media use is positively albeit

Table 2. The multilevel model estimates of corruption perceptions (IGI, 2016)

Variables	Model 1		Model 2	
	Coefficient	Standard error	Coefficient	Standard error
Mass media	-0.0570	(0.0558)		
Government website	-0.149**	(0.0588)	-0.0991	(0.0700)
Business website	0.0264	(0.0409)		
Social media	0.0123	(0.0513)	0.0273	(0.0475)
SMS	-0.110*	(0.0644)		
Oral	0.000903	(0.0596)		
Gender (Male=1)	0.271***	(0.0459)	0.273***	(0.0455)
Age	-0.0300	(0.0200)	-0.0295	(0.0198)
Nationality (Han=1)	0.0431	(0.122)	0.0465	(0.121)
Education	0.0582**	(0.0231)	0.0602***	(0.0230)
Length of residence	0.0741***	(0.0202)	0.0721***	(0.0202)
Local urban	0.109	(0.0911)	0.102	(0.0914)
Local rural	0.0849	(0.0780)	0.0804	(0.0783)
Nonlocal urban	0.00574	(0.0780)	-0.00297	(0.0765)
Income	-0.00987	(0.0126)	-0.00972	(0.0126)
Jobless	0.186**	(0.0896)	0.190**	(0.0898)
Political efficacy	0.0883***	(0.0128)	0.0886***	(0.0127)
Interaction term			-0.135	(0.141)
Constant	3.242***	(0.161)	3.188***	(0.145)
Variance (Constant)	0.0515***	(0.0178)	0.0529***	(0.0185)
Variance (Residual)	6.403***	(0.0865)	6.406***	(0.0862)
Log likelihood	-32692.4		-32773.6	
Wald χ^2	125.6***		126.0***	
Snijders/Bosker R^2 Level 1	0.0157		0.0153	
Snijders/Bosker R^2 Level 2	0.0944		0.0792	
Number of cities	36		36	
N	13917		13950	

Note: Robust standard errors adjusted for 36 clusters are reported in parentheses. * $p<0.10$, ** $p<0.05$, *** $p<0.01$. The author drops other media channels in Model 2 due to multicollinearity concerns.

insignificantly related to corruption perceptions, and H1 is not supported. The respondents using government website to acquire government information perceive significantly lower levels of corruption than those using other channels. H2 is supported by the evidence.

The author also finds that the respondents using SMS for government information also perceive lower levels of corruption, although the coefficient is only statistically significant at the 0.10 level. While mass media elicit the respondents to perceive lower levels of corruption, the effect is not statistically significant. Business websites which are commercialized albeit scrutinized by the government have insignificant and positive effect on corruption perceptions. The magnitude of the effect of oral communication is negligible, although it is positively related to corruption perceptions.

The author enters the interaction term of government website and social media, and the results are reported in Model 2. It suggests that the moderating effect of social media use on the relationship between government website and corruption perceptions is not statistically significant. The negative sign of the regression coefficient suggests that social media use may dilute the negative effect of government website use on corruption perceptions, although it is statistically insignificant. In other words, our H3 is not supported.

In terms of our control variables, the author finds that male respondents perceive higher levels of corruption than females. Elder respondents perceive lower levels of corruption, but the coefficient is insignificant. Han respondents perceive higher levels of corruption than minorities, but the coefficient is also insignificant. The author finds that higher-educated respondents are more likely to perceive high levels of corruption, suggesting they are relatively critical of government integrity. The respondents residing longer in the sampled cities perceive higher levels of corruption, partially because they are more informed about and familiar with local corruptions. The differences of corruption perceptions across household registration types and income groups are not significant. Unemployed respondents perceive higher levels of corruption. The respondents perceive higher levels of social deprivation are more likely to attribute their discontent to the underperformance of the government, particularly government corruption. Finally, the author finds that political efficacy is positively and significantly related to corruption perceptions, and it may because people with higher levels of political efficacy are more concerned about political scandals, particularly government corruptions.

DISCUSSIONS

Implications and Contributions

In this chapter the author theoretically develops and empirically tests the effects of media exposure on citizen perceptions of corruption, using a large-scale survey data from Chinese cities. The author expects that social media and government website may have opposite effects on citizens' perceived corruption. Government website use may lower citizen perceptions of corruption, while social media use may increase corruption perceptions. The author also predicts that the two media channels may interactively affect citizen perceptions of corruption. The empirical analyses using multilevel model suggest that only government website use is negatively related to citizen perceptions of corruption, while the direct and interaction effects of social media use are not supported by the results.

The author contributes to the existing literature on social media, e-government, and corruption by adding new evidence on the linkage between government website use and corruption perceptions. The effect of e-government adoption on citizen trust and other political attitudes (e.g., confidence) have been well documented in prior studies, but its effect on corruption perceptions has not yet been fully examined. Our results show that citizens using government websites perceive lower levels of corruption, which provides micro-level evidence on the anticorruption contributions of e-government development.

The author does not find significant effect of social media use on citizen perceptions of corruption, which suggests that our H1 is not supported. This insignificant effect may be attributed to the following reasons. Firstly, during the time of the survey (2014) even official media controlled by the government had been actively revealing corruption scandals, thanks to the anticorruption campaign initiated by President Xi Jinping, which may dilute the negative effect of social media use on corruption perceptions. Secondly, social media have been increasingly censored by the government, and politically sensitive information is usually quickly detected and removed. While the authorities did permit (instead of encouraging) netizens to post and circulate corruption scandals through social media, their impacts are largely under control. Thirdly, social media in China are primarily used for entertainments instead of political participation, which may by and large mitigate their roles in raising citizen awareness of corruption. Corruption scandals are usually disseminated across the public predominantly as political jokes instead of serious thoughts on democratic rights, which significantly mitigates their priming effects on citizen perceptions of corruption.

The author finds that citizens using SMS to acquire government information also perceive a lower levels of corruption. Part of the reasons may be that SMS is also controlled by the government, and its content may help the government achieve its political propaganda and ideological purposes. The author also finds that male, higher-educated, longer-residing, jobless respondents with a higher level of political efficacy perceive relatively higher levels of corruption. These groups of citizens, either because of critical thought or social deprivation, are less satisfied with government integrity.

Our findings suggest that government websites help increase citizen satisfaction with government integrity and honesty, and it is beneficial to develop e-government features to fight against corruption and retain citizen trust. Citizens using government websites perceive lower levels of corruption, suggesting e-government features are effective in reducing corruptions and improving government legitimacy. The government may consider further invest in, improve, and develop e-government features for anticorruption and legitimacy purposes.

Despite social media use does not significantly affect citizen perceptions of corruption in study, it does not mean that public attitudes towards corruption are insulated from the impacts of social media. Given the increasingly penetrative use of social media among the public, the government should also leverage social media platforms to reshape citizen perceptions of corruption (Ma, 2013). For instance, the government could run its own social media accounts as its official portals, which are more live and interactive in attracting user attentions and exerting effects (Ma, 2014).

Limitations and Future Research Directions

The study is limited in the following aspects, which suggest future research directions. Firstly, the data used in this study are cross-sectional, and the relationship between government website and corruption perceptions cannot be used for causal inference. Future studies may collect longitudinal data and experimental design to identify the causal relationships among these variables. Sentiment analysis, opinion mining, and other approaches could be used to glean more objective information about citizen perceptions of and attitudes towards corruption and to identify explore more source-centered and receiver-centered perceptions.

Secondly, our measurement of media use is primarily dichotomy, and the nuanced differences among difference media channels cannot be detected. It helps to include the relative time and weight devoted to each media channel, and ordered or even interval variables may be used to differentiate their varying effects on corruption perceptions. Future studies can incorporate more fine-tuned indicators to measure media use, which may deepen our understanding of media effect on corruption perceptions. It is also meaningful to include measures on government use of social media, which may help understand the competing effects of government social media, government websites, and other media channels.

Thirdly, the linkages between media use and corruption perceptions may be mediated by other variables, and it is interesting to identify the underpinning mechanisms bridging the two variables in future studies. For instance, government websites may increase citizens' perceived government transparency and responsiveness, which in turn affect corruption perceptions. It also helps to look into different types of corruption-related rhetoric and how government machinery plays a critical role in fighting corruptions and shaping public attitudes. Instead of fully relying on quantitative analysis, a qualitative approach (e.g., case study and in-depth interview) helps contribute more valuable insights on the linkage between ICT use and corruption perceptions.

Finally, the findings from China may not be overgeneralized to other countries and regions due to rather differentiating media environments, political regimes, and cultural circumstances. It is meaningful to replicate and extend this study in other contexts, and comparative studies covering multiple countries and regions may also contribute to our understanding of media effects on corruptions.

CONCLUSION

The rise of Internet and social media has remarkably transformed citizens' media environment, which may affect their perceptions of corruption. In this study the author empirically examines the impacts of various media channels on citizen perception of corruption using survey data in Chinese cities. The effect of social media use on citizen perceptions of corruption is not supported by the evidence, but the author does find government website use is negatively related to citizens' perceived corruption. Social media applications challenge government monopoly of mass media and enable citizens to effectively scrutiny corruption, but their effects on citizen perceptions of corruption are not confirmed in this study. The findings suggest that e-government plays a key role in anticorruption, and it is still valuable to invest in e-government features.

REFERENCES

Aguinis, H., Gottfredson, R. K., & Culpepper, S. A. (2013). Best-practice recommendations for estimating cross-level interaction effects using multilevel modeling. *Journal of Management*, *39*(6), 1490–1528. doi:10.1177/0149206313478188

Anti-Corruption. (2016). Catching Tigers and Flies. Retrieved from: http://anticorruption.chinafile.com/

Bertot, J. C., Jaeger, P. T., & Grimes, J. M. (2010). Using ICTs to create a culture of transparency: E-government and social media as openness and anti-corruption tools for societies. *Government Information Quarterly*, *27*(3), 264–271. doi:10.1016/j.giq.2010.03.001

Charron, N. (2015). Do corruption measures have a perception problem? Assessing the relationship between experiences and perceptions of corruption among citizens and experts. *European Political Science Review*, *8*(1), 147–171. doi:10.1017/S1755773914000447

CNNIC. (2016). *The 37th statistical report on internet development in China*. Beijing: China Internet Network Information Center.

Corruption Perceptions Index – Transparencey International. (2015). Retrieved from: http://www.transparency.org/cpi2015

Elbahnasawy, N. G. (2014). E-government, internet adoption, and corruption: An empirical investigation. *World Development*, *57*, 114–126. doi:10.1016/j.worlddev.2013.12.005

Garcia-Murillo, M. (2013). Does a government web presence reduce perceptions of corruption? *Information Technology for Development*, *19*(2), 151–175. doi:10.1080/02681102.2012.751574

Goel, R. K., Nelson, M. A., & Naretta, M. A. (2012). The internet as an indicator of corruption awareness. *European Journal of Political Economy*, *28*(1), 64–75. doi:10.1016/j.ejpoleco.2011.08.003

King, G., Pan, J., & Roberts, M. E. (2013). How censorship in China allows government criticism but silences collective expression. *The American Political Science Review*, *107*(2), 326–343. doi:10.1017/S0003055413000014

Lee, M.-H., & Lio, M.-C. (2016). The impact of information and communication technology on public governance and corruption in China. *Information Development*, *32*(2), 127–141. doi:10.1177/0266666914529293

Lu, J., Aldrich, J., & Shi, T. (2014). Revisiting media effects in authoritarian societies: Democratic conceptions, collectivistic norms, and media access in urban China. *Politics & Society*, *42*(2), 253–283. doi:10.1177/0032329213519423

Ma, L. (2013). The diffusion of government microblogging: Evidence from Chinese municipal police bureaus. *Public Management Review*, *15*(2), 288–309. doi:10.1080/14719037.2012.691010

Ma, L. (2014). Diffusion and assimilation of government microblogging: Evidence from Chinese cities. *Public Management Review*, *16*(2), 274–295. doi:10.1080/14719037.2012.725763

Ma, L. (2016). Performance feedback, government goal-setting, and aspiration level adaptation: Evidence from Chinese provinces. *Public Administration*, *94*(2), 452–471. doi:10.1111/padm.12225

Ma, L., & Zhang, Z. (2015). Microblogging (weibo) and environmental nonprofit organizations in China: The case of urban air pollution monitoring campaign. In H. Asencio & R. Sun (Eds.), *Cases on strategic social media utilization in the nonprofit sector* (pp. 94–121). Hershey, PA, USA: IGI Global. doi:10.4018/978-1-4666-8188-0.ch004

Manion, M. (2004). *Corruption by design: Building clean government in mainland China and Hong Kong*. Cambridge, MA: Harvard University Press.

Manion, M. (2016). Taking China's anticorruption campaign seriously. *Economic and Political Studies*, *4*(1), 3–18. doi:10.1080/20954816.2016.1152094

Porumbescu, G. A. (2013). Assessing the link between online mass media and trust in government: Evidence from Seoul, South Korea. *Policy & Internet*, *5*(4), 418–443. doi:10.1002/1944-2866.POI346

Porumbescu, G. A. (2015). Using transparency to enhance responsiveness and trust in local government: Can it work? *State & Local Government Review*, *47*(3), 205–213. doi:10.1177/0160323X15599427

Rothstein, B. (2011). *The quality of government: Corruption, social trust, and inequality in international perspective*. Chicago: University Of Chicago Press. doi:10.7208/chicago/9780226729589.001.0001

Srivastava, S. C., Teo, T. S. H., & Devaraj, S. (2016). You can't bribe a computer: Dealing with the societal challenge of corruption through ICT. *Management Information Systems Quarterly*, *40*(2), 511–526.

Stockmann, D. (2013). *Media commercialization and authoritarian rule in China*. New York: Cambridge University Press.

Tolbert, C. J., & Mossberger, K. (2006). The effects of e-government on trust and confidence in government. *Public Administration Review, 66*(3), 354–369. doi:10.1111/j.1540-6210.2006.00594.x

Villoria, M., Van Ryzin, G. G., & Lavena, C. F. (2013). Social and political consequences of administrative corruption: A study of public perceptions in Spain. *Public Administration Review, 73*(1), 85–94. doi:10.1111/j.1540-6210.2012.02613.x

Wedeman, A. (2012). *Double paradox: Rapid growth and rising corruption in China*. Ithaca: Cornell University Press. doi:10.7591/cornell/9780801450464.001.0001

Welch, E. W., Hinnant, C. C., & Moon, M. J. (2005). Linking citizen satisfaction with e-government and trust in government. *Journal of Public Administration: Research and Theory, 15*(3), 371–391. doi:10.1093/jopart/mui021

West, D. M. (2005). *Digital government: Technology and public sector performance*. Princeton, NJ: Princeton University Press.

Wu, Y. (2014). The impact of media on public trust in legal authorities in China and Taiwan. *Asian Journal of Criminology, 9*(2), 85–101. doi:10.1007/s11417-013-9177-z

Yang, G. (2009). *The power of the internet in China: Citizen activism online*. New York, NY: Columbia University Press.

Zhu, J., Lu, J., & Shi, T. (2013). When grapevine news meets mass media: Different information sources and popular perceptions of government corruption in mainland China. *Comparative Political Studies, 46*(8), 920–946. doi:10.1177/0010414012463886

KEY TERMS AND DEFINITIONS

Anti-Corruption Campaign: A short-term movement dedicated to fighting against corruptions. It is usually initiated by the installing of new politicians or triggered by controversial events.

Censorship: The control of media by the government, which is characterized by official depression of contested online content in the digital era. The government censors media content for various purposes, but ideological dominance and social stability are among the pivotal ones.

Corruption: The use of public power for private benefits, particularly misconducts by government officials and civil servants.

Media Monopoly: The tight control of media by the government. Media monopoly can be also achieved by the amalgamation of private media, but it is primarily done by government nationalization of media companies.

Multilevel Model: A statistical modeling of regressions suitable for clustered data, in which one level of observations (e.g., individual) is nested in higher levels (e.g., cities or countries). Multilevel models can be used to simultaneously estimate variances at multiple levels.

Social Media: A category of information technology enables real-time, two-way, and interactive communication of various contents (e.g., text, graphs, and videos). Facebook, Twitter, and YouTube are typical applications of social media. Weibo and WeChat are mainstream social media applications in China.

Whistle-Blowing: Reporting and revealing the misconducts of government officials and civil servants by either insiders or external media, citizens, and businesses. To protect themselves, whistle-blowers usually circulate tip-offs through private and anonymous channels, e.g., phone calls, letters, and E-mails.

Chapter 9
Social Media's Role in Alleviating Political Corruption and Scandals:
The Philippines during and after the Marcos Regime

Cecilia G. Manrique
University of Wisconsin-La Crosse, USA

Gabriel G. Manrique
Winona State University, USA

ABSTRACT

This chapter is an attempt to show how the use of social media in one country, the Republic of the Philippines, has grown and has been used to encourage political awareness and participation among the Filipino masses. The country is ranked among the most technologically savvy in the world but ironically is also considered one of the most corrupt countries as well. The authors believe that, as a result of the showings Filipinos have made when called upon via social media to oust corrupt officials, there is a method whereby such knowledge can be harnessed for the good thus alleviating scandals and ultimately corruption in the country. This research points to the direction the country, and various other countries in the world in similar situations, may take in order to combat corruption through greater citizen participation.

DOI: 10.4018/978-1-5225-2019-1.ch009

INTRODUCTION

Data indicate that the Philippines is among the first countries to have rapidly embraced the use of social media via the Internet and cell phones. It ranks among the top countries when it comes to cell phone, Internet and social media usage. At the same time, the Philippines has been plagued by decades of political corruption and scandals which accelerated during the regime of Ferdinand Marcos and continues to the present. It ranks as one of the most corrupt countries in the world based on its placement in the Corruption Perception Index.

It is also true that historically, the Philippines has been able to effect regime changes in a relatively peaceful and non-violent manner as shown by the overthrow of Ferdinand Marcos in 1986 after more than 20 years of his "benevolent dictatorship" via the Epifanio de los Santos Avenue (EDSA) People Power Revolution/Movement from February 22-25, 1986. This led to the eventual installation of Corazon (Cory) Aquino as the legitimate president of the country after a much contested election. People Power 2 or the second EDSA revolution also known as EDSA II (or EDSA 2) led to the ouster of Joseph "Erap" Estrada, the corrupt president who succeeded Fidel Ramos, the successor to Aquino. Gloria Macapagal-Arroyo (GMA), who succeeded Estrada and is rumored to have exceeded Estrada's corruption, was herself driven from office by widespread unrest and protests.

A case may be made that the quick and widespread use of social media in the Philippines and the success of Filipinos in getting rid of corrupt regimes are related phenomena. Political mobilization is made possible by social media, along with the spread of relatively cheap communications like texting. Aside from facilitating the flow of information among the population, the logistics of deploying the masses once the movement for the overthrow of regimes begins is made easier by social media.

However, it is ironic and even tragic that the forces of social media that contribute to the overthrow of corrupt regimes have not yet been able to alleviate the high level of corruption that continues to plague the Philippines. The chapter proposes to examine the extent of the relationship between social media and corrupt regime change in the Philippines during the last three decades. This chapter also proposes to explore the possible ways that social media can alleviate corruption in a country, and the reason why these have not been effective in the Philippines. It is hoped that through the examples and suggestions proposed herein some semblance of domestic policy and even international policy can be effected that can help transform the politics of individual nations and maybe even the international system.

A note of optimism surrounds our initial assessment of the Philippines. Even with such a poor record of corruption, the authors consider the Philippines as a case of a Third World country that, partly through the spread and increasing sophistication of social media, is starting to be transformed during the past 30 years from a highly corrupt country into one that is making great political and economic strides that could still erase its reputation for corruption and economic malaise. In the recent past, it has performed among the best in Asia in two measures – economic growth and stock market returns. Authors thus consider what factors may be responsible for its continuing transformation.

BACKGROUND

The Republic of the Philippines has been called the "promise of Asia" and the "sick man of Asia" alternately ever since its search for stability, prosperity and development began in the 1940s. After centuries of Spanish rule and half a century under American tutelage, the Philippines has struggled with its attempts at political and economic development since 1946. Right after the Second World War and independence from the United States, it was thought that the democratic institutions that had been installed during American colonization would lead the country to the road to economic prosperity as well. And by the 1960s, it seemed that she would be on the right path because at that time the country was considered one of the fastest growing economies in Asia.

However, the ambition of one man, Ferdinand Marcos, aided and abetted by his cronies would lead to a pernicious though seemingly benevolent authoritarianism that would impede political and economic development and would setback the country for decades. A culture of governing primarily for one's personal gain festered and spread leading to the characterization of the Marcos regime as a "Kleptocracy" – a government that exists primarily to plunder a country. It would not be until the Marcos dictatorship was dismantled that the institutions required to rebuild the nation would be re-instituted. By then, so much had already been done to institutionalize corruption which in turn stymied economic development and legitimate business transactions. And as the authors have previously indicated in a paper on the "Digital Divide," there are times when development requires a stimulus for a nation to take off (Manrique & Manrique, 2009). In the case of countries like Singapore, South Korea and Taiwan, it was sparked by the infusion of information technology within the economy in the latter part of the 20th century that spurred economic growth and which continues until today. In the Philippine case, it should have been the massive infusion of foreign direct investment (FDI) that would act as the catalyst for take-off. But such investment would be squandered by Marcos cronies and its promised path to economic growth would not come to fruition. This time as it plays catch up in the early 21st century, the Philippines, like its Asian neighbors, may have to rely on innovations in information technology to sustain its take off but only if accompanied by an improved business climate.

DIGITAL PHILIPPINES

Current data and information about the state of social media worldwide puts the Philippines at the very top of every list. As of January 2015, it was estimated that there were 44.2 million active Filipino Internet users (out of a total population of 101M as of July 2015) 90% of whom have active social media accounts. Since 2010, the Philippines has ranked as the fastest growing country when it comes to Internet access. In fact when it comes to social media visits by country the Philippines ranks first on Facebook (FB) and in the top five on YouTube, Twitter and Google+ (Chaffey, 2016).

Filipinos spend a lot of time on the Internet through their laptop and desktop but more so in terms of their mobile device (cell phone) usage, averaging 6.3 hours per day on the laptop and 3.3 hours on their mobile devices (Revesencio, 2015). Over 40% of Filipinos also own active social media accounts surpassing the South Koreans and Japanese in that respect. It was likewise named the "Selfie Capital of the World" by Time Magazine in 2014.

Much of the growth of social media penetration in the Philippines has been attributed to several factors. Foremost among them is the influx of low-priced mobile devices such as smart phones that has encouraged even the poorest of the poor to be in possession of these devices. Social media penetration has also been spurred by the economic growth that has been experienced by the country over the past few years and the stability brought about by peaceful political transition from one leader to another since Corazon Aquino came into power. It also helps that the Philippines is one of the countries that has encouraged the use of the Internet and social media without blocking content or engaging in censorship unlike a country like China (Barone, 2015). More importantly, the digital lifestyle that Filipinos now adopt in terms of a reality which is "powered by apps, sites and gadgets" is clearly supported by a young, dynamic population (Revesencio, 2015).

RELEVANT LITERATURE

A good summary of what is taking place in the Philippines today can be obtained from the work of Bertelsmann Stiftung which provides an update as to where the

Philippines is in terms of political and economic development (Bertelsman, 2016). Its value lies in tracing not only the economic indicators that have accounted for the optimism about the economy over the past few years but also the focus on the political characteristics of the transformation that is taking place in the democratic institutions of the country starting from the peaceful uprising that ousted Ferdinand Marcos and installed Corazon Aquino as president after 21 years of dictatorial rule to the current peaceful transition from the Presidency of Noynoy Aquino to that of Rodrigo Duterte.

It is widely recognized that despite economic successes such cannot be sustained unless the weak and ineffective political leadership and institutions are converted into efficient and effective ones. Gridlock between the legislative and executive branches of government will need to be alleviated. Much of the country's problems stems from the inability to formulate reasonable and attainable long term policies instead choosing expedient solutions to short term problems. Expediency coupled with a large bureaucracy leads to systemic problems such as red tape, corruption and low quality service.

Political scientists in the realm of political communication literature continue to delve in debates regarding the Internet and social media in regards to the extent to which they can open up communication lines; foster grassroots mobilization and greater political activism and participation; give voice to the voiceless by providing access to political communication channels; and maybe even eventually modify, disrupt or replace the dominance of the politically advantaged in a country (Margolis, Resnick, & Wolfe, 1999; Bimber, 2003; Chadwick, 2006; Hindman, 2009). Some political scientists fall on the side of supporting the notion that the Internet does not do more than just reinforce the already existing political communication power structures (e.g. Margolis, Resnick, & Wolfe, 1999; Hindman, 2009). However, there are those of the belief that "some of the most important examples of how information technology affects politics involve marginalized groups overcoming resource limitations and other more serious barriers to gain political power" (Bimber, 2003, p. 235). This is where a discussion of the Philippine people power movement with the help of social media comes into play.

The literature seems to indicate that with the rise in the use of Facebook, Twitter and blogging sites people anywhere and everywhere are able to continually replay, analyze and discuss issues ad nauseam. The Internet has created an atmosphere where it seems that everything is publicly displayed and no issue can be hidden from the people's eyes. Thus the behavior of government officials, political figures or individuals in positions of power which causes shock and gets people upset because the action is morally or legally wrong is the classic definition of a scandal. Some scandals can be sexual in nature. Some can be illegal in nature such as the workings of a kleptocracy in which leaders steal from their constituents once they assume power. Some can be abuse of power such as the corrupting influence of those who maintain dictatorships so that they can do all of the above as in the case of the Philippines (Fitz, 2014).

Scholars who have researched the new technology within the context of Philippine democracy seem to be divided regarding the role that social media plays in political mobilization, participation and activism. Some like Brisbin, Rafael and Rheingold are of the view that the ouster of Ferdinand Marcos during the first EDSA revolution constituted the first successful revolution facilitated by the electronic media. Likewise, the use of texting to get protestors out into the streets during EDSA 2 re-enforced the belief that the new media has taken politics in the Philippines to a new height in fostering political activism and bringing about change (Brisbin, 1988; Rafael, 2003; Rheingold, 2002). There are scholars who are more skeptical of the transformative nature of social media in the Philippines and other settings. They contend that the role of social media in encouraging political action has been exaggerated (Pertierra, et al., 2002). Others indicate that the ability of the new media to bring about political action is still at a very early stage (Aguirre, 2009). Regardless, it seems that the following can be said about the role of the new media in the Philippines: 1) the new media is just another venue used by those who are already politically motivated and active and heavily into social media anyway (Mirandilla, 2009); 2) the new media has the ability to initiate political controversy but then is picked up by the traditional media to make it more accessible; and 3) whether the new media is able to reflect popular discontent or actually fuel it is still unknown with the direction of the correlation still difficult to determine, but regardless the new media is capable of making the discontent towards an issue or its unpopularity better known to the general public. There is no denying that it has some impact on political reporting and maybe even political action, but its long term effect remains to be seen (Pertierra, 2012).

It cannot be denied that the recent history of the Philippines relied strongly upon social media in leading the Filipino towards transformative participation in the ouster and change in political personalities ruling the country. Accounts of how people were brought out to the streets and communicated with each other via text messaging are rampant (EDSA, 2016; Perral, 2016). And there continue to be stories of how social media has led to the unveiling of corruption, the shaming of politicians and their eventual ouster from power.

Because political corruption remains a major issue in the domestic politics of most developing countries in the world including the Philippines, the material from Ahmed rings true when he posits that the media in general act as the indirect deterrent of corruption in his country of study, Bangladesh. Although the focus of attention is traditional media like newspapers and television, the findings could very well apply to today's social media. They try to assert social responsibility and work towards social accountability by keeping an eye on the powerful, guarding the public interest and protecting it from incompetence, corruption, and misinformation. It can be engaged in uncovering misdeeds of political parties and politicians as well as in educating the masses against the adverse impacts of corruption. Moreover, people can realize the pervasiveness of political corruption from the material that is disseminated through social media (Ahmed, 2013).

THE PHILIPPINES: SOCIAL MEDIA AND CORRUPTION

The Philippine notoriety for being a corrupt country is reinforced by the 20 year data shown in Table 1 below which describes the Philippines and its Corruption Perception Index ranking from the years 1995 to 2015. It ranks among the lowest in terms of clean government and being highly corrupt. In fact from 2003 to 2007 data in Table 1 show that it is stuck at a 2.5 value in terms of the index and the next three years after that showed a decline in the index. If the data is not affected by the change in range valuation which took place in 2012, improvement for the Philippines based on the index has only taken place over the last 4 reporting periods (2012-2015).

The perception of the Philippines being a corrupt country based on the evaluations of businesses and visitors to the country is very difficult to overcome. When coupled with stories of politicians, the elite and prominent personalities engaged in scandalous activities one begins to wonder whether there is hope for the country. The scandals are not only sexual and pornographic in nature such as the sordid affair of Ferdinand Marcos with Dovie Beams which was recorded and disseminated using old traditional media since the newer social media were not yet available then. One can argue that it was a precursor of postings that had gone viral then on various media – radio, newspaper, and television. Nor are the scandals limited to the excesses of those in power such as the infamous shoe collection of Imelda Marcos, although it would have been a favorite of today's social media "fashionistas". Such scandals are not the concern of this chapter. The scandals that have provided the greatest amount of the exhibition of people power are those that are economic and political in nature.

Another useful measure of the Philippine environment for business is the "Doing Business Index" (2015) published by the World Bank. The Philippines ranks poorly on many such measures. In 2016, it ranked 103 in doing business (out of 189). This is worse than in 2015 when it was ranked 97. Oftentimes there is a correlation between the low ranking and the level of corruption.

Table 1. Corruption Perception Index Ranking: Philippines

Year	RANK	OUT OF	TI Index*
1995	36	41	2.77
1996	44	54	2.69
1997	40	52	3.05
1998	55	85	3.3
1999	54	99	3.6
2000	69	90	2.8
2001	65	91	2.9
2002	77	102	2.6
2003	92	133	2.5
2004	102	146	2.5
2005	117	159	2.5
2006	121	160	2.5
2007	131	179	2.5
2008	141	180	2.3
2009	130	180	2.4
2010	134	178	2.4
2011	129	178	2.6
2012	105	176	34**
2013	94	177	36
2014	85	175	38
2015	95	168	35

*0-10 range with 0 as highly corrupt and 10 as very clean

**In 2012 the index was changed to a 0-100 range with 0 as highly corrupt and 100 as very clean

Source: The Corruption Perception Index Retrieved June 13, 2016 from http://www.transparency.org/research/cpi/overview

By documenting processes associated with business practices in various countries, Doing Business rankings are broken down into different categories and these help to illustrate the opportunities for corruption and areas for improvement in a country. For example, the Philippines ranks 165th in the category "Starting a Business" which attests to the difficulties encountered by companies that wish to make inroads in business in the Philippines. It takes more than 3 times as long to start a business compared to advanced countries and relative to a country's income, it is 5 times more expensive to start a business. Likewise, it takes so many days to register property (2016 rank – 112) because of the inordinate number of steps and paper work involved. The point is that long, often unnecessary and duplicate steps in any of the doing business categories give rise to opportunities for corruption to hasten the startup process. It is not uncommon for businesses, both domestic and international, to simply give up on starting businesses because of the unneeded complexity and delay and because many simply refuse to take part in the bribery and corruption that is so prevalent. The authors strongly suggest that the monitoring and reporting of such bottlenecks and corruption traps can improve business conditions.

The judicial system can also be improved by social media monitoring. In the latest Doing Business rankings, the Philippines is 140th in the enforcement of contracts. The difficulty of enforcing contracts entered also serves as a powerful deterrent for doing business. It has been reported repeatedly that some members of the judiciary and the bureaucrats that work in the judiciary have been corrupted. For this reason, the enforcement of contracts suffers from delay or worse it leads to the dependence of ultimate outcomes on the willingness and ability to give bribes and find the right connections. The posting of actual problems with the judiciary on social media and even calling attention to specific locations and personnel via social media can result in a more impartial judiciary and a fairer enforcement of contracts (Doingbusiness.org, 2016).

It should come as no surprise that in the Doing Business ranking for "Trading across Borders," the Philippines ranks 95th and even more telling is that in the Philippines, it costs 4 times as much as in high income Organization for Economic Co-operation and Development (OECD) countries to pass import border compliance procedures. The cost ratio for export border compliance is only slightly lower. That is because the Bureau of Customs (BOC) is considered to be among the most corrupt offices in the Philippines rivaled only by the Bureau of Internal Revenue (BIR) (Gonzales, 2010). It follows that it imposes additional costs to cross-border trade, further retarding an economy that is heavily dependent on international trade. Numerous well-meaning non-political appointees have tried to break through the wall of corruption of this agency to no avail. Perhaps the ubiquitous presence of social media can break through the infested labyrinth that is the Philippine BOC.

The specific listing of some of the political scandals that have plagued the country from the 1990s to the present can be found in Table 2.

Based on the Table 2, corruption and scandals are not only on the national scale but also in the provincial and local level as evidenced by mayoral and gubernatorial cases. The case of Mayor Antonio Sanchez of the city of Calauan in the province of Laguna is an example of the abuse of power of a local official. President Joseph Estrada's nefarious activities have impacted current and former governors such as Richard Gordon and Chavit Singson. Philippine Generals and national artists have had their own share of scandals. And the role of a businesswoman, Janet Napoles

Table 2. Philippine Scandals

YEAR	INVOLVED	BRIEF DESCRIPTION
1993	Mayor Antonio Sanchez	Rape of a student and murder of her boyfriend
1998	Subic Bay Leadership	President Joseph Estrada removes Richard Gordon as chair of the Subic Bay Metropolitan Authority
	President Joseph Estrada	Nepotism exhibited by appointing relatives to government positions
	President Joseph Estrada	Assigned vehicles seized by the Bureau of Customs to Cabinet secretaries and favored political allies
2000	President Joseph Estrada	Profited from stock manipulation scheme
	President Joseph Estrada	Engaged in drinking and gambling sessions in Malacanang Palace
	President Joseph Estrada	Receivedjueteng (Philippine illegal numbers game) payoffs and bribes
2004	President Gloria Macapagal-Arroyo (GMA)	Involved in electoral fraud during 2004 elections
	Jocelyn Bolante	Undersecretary of Agriculture who diverted fertilizer funds to 2004 election campaign of GMA
2008		Government Service Insurance System (GSIS)-Meralco bribery case
		NBN/ZTE deal(or NBN/ZTE mess) involved allegations of corruption in the awarding of a US$329 million construction contract to Chinese telecommunications firm ZTE for the proposed government-managed National Broadband Network (NBN)
	Philippine Generals	Involved Eliseo de la Paz and several Philippine National Police officials who went to Russia on October 2008 to attend the Interpol conference. De la Paz was detained for carrying a large sum of undeclared money.
2009		GMA used presidential prerogative to proclaim four individuals as National Artists without prior nomination by a selection committee
2013	Janet Lim-Napoles	A businesswoman who is allegedly the mastermind of a controversial pork barrel scam involving the misuse of Priority Development Assistance Funds (PDAF)

Source: Wikipedia, 2016

in the PDAF pork barrel scam was covered in Facebook and the Twitterverse. There have also been instances of Twitter wars involving the children of former President, now Manila Mayor Estrada.

The Philippines became the texting (SMS) capital of the world with the encouragement of the proliferation of social media devices under the Fidel Ramos and Joseph Estrada administrations. This was before Facebook and Twitter would take to the airwaves when Filipinos found the use of texting as the most effective way of mobilizing their friends and neighbors. This practice played an important role in the ouster of President Estrada in 2001. When the Senate impeachment trial was suddenly adjourned without verdict, the text message went around to "meet at EDSA (Epifanio de los Santos Avenue)" the same venue which led to the ouster of Ferdinand Marcos. Thus this would be dubbed as People Power II or EDSA 2. Crowds gathered in the middle of the night and refused to leave the main Manila thoroughfare until "Erap," (Estrada's nickname) left the presidential palace.

Today Facebook is being used by more than 25 percent of the Philippine population, sometimes ranking the country 8th in the world in FB use and sometimes even #1. Other social media networks (such as Twitter) are rapidly growing in popularity. In September 2011, the Philippine Trust Index, commissioned by EON The Stakeholder Firm, was released. The study revealed that 68 percent of the respondents view online news sites as the most trusted sources of news and information while 49 percent trust social networking sites.

During the 2011 Philippine State of the Nation Address, some attendees initiated the use of the hashtag #WeWantPnoyTo, a call to make President Benigno (NoyNoy) Aquino aware of the different concerns of advocates. This spread among Expanded Digital Activism participants, as well as among members of their organizations. It became one of the 10 most trending hashtags in the Philippines during that week. We can take this as evidence that there is a hunger for change that can perhaps be harnessed into social pressure to end corruption.

Clearly, development workers saw this avenue as an inexpensive yet effective way to instill advocacy into the stream of public consciousness. The civil society organizations that were trained knew that social media is most effective when it supplements the traditional mode of campaigning to encourage collective action against human rights abuses. As mobile phones reach even the most remote citizens and as Internet penetration – and along with it social media usage – widens its reach in the Philippines, these tools will become potentially more valuable to civil society, citizens, and officials in their advocacy efforts. As skills in these tools are acquired and greater education about the potential of these tools are disseminated, careful attention needs to be paid to how much impact social media is making on the daunting development challenges facing the country (Tapnio & Rood, 2011).

ANALYSIS

Even though the Philippines has been dubbed a major social media country in the world as exhibited by the number of Filipinos who own cell phones; are part of Facebook, Twitter and Instagram; and who engage in blogging the examples of the past few years may not be enough to definitively conclude that social media can be the answer to alleviating corruption in the Philippines. Analysts have gone on both sides of the argument with those who have seen in EDSA 2 and the reporting on the abuses of Gloria Macapagal-Arroyo that mobilizing using the new media has worked and led to greater political awareness, involvement and participation by the Filipino people. On the other side are those who are skeptical about the role of social media in a struggling economic system. The new media is seen as still an instrument of the educated political and economic elite whose role is to reinforce what the traditional media has already uncovered. Thus, the new media is viewed as just another venue to vent discontent but it will still require the support of the traditional media, newspapers, radio and television, to move the rest of the population along.

SOLUTIONS AND RECOMMENDATIONS

The point is that entrenched corrupt ways of doing things can be brought to light much easier with the use of social media. Of course the use of social media to monitor corruption can lead to abuse as well. It may lead to the posting of false accusations, cyber bullying by advocacy groups, and extortion as well. That is the reason why the researchers suggest that countries intent on eradicating a culture of corruption can learn some lessons from sites that have a well-developed verification system and broad participation. Tripadvisor.com and yelp.com are useful examples of such sites. These popular sources of reviews of establishments, services, etc. can provide countries with lessons on how to balance the free flow of information on social media with the need for verification and veracity. It would put the onus on citizens to inform their fellow countrymen of the existence of both good and bad government agencies thereby challenging the "old" ways of doing business.

But for such social media sites to work, certain conditions must be present. It would first need the broad participation of a citizenry committed to improving government who are willing to share personal experiences for the purpose of improving government. Second, it would need an independent overseer to monitor and filter social media postings for their veracity because it is easy to flood such sites with "fake" reviews, both favorable and unfavorable which in turn creates social media noise that negates the usefulness of these sites. Third, there should be some assurance of freedom from retaliation and retribution among those who responsibly participate and publish reviews.

A fourth condition necessary for social media sites to succeed in helping to transform a corrupt society concerns sanctions. Sites such as yelp.com rely on the sanctions and rewards of the marketplace. Consistently poor reviews beget fewer sales. Consistently good reviews can beget greater sales and profits. Unlike such market-driven sites, government-agency monitoring sites (which can be called transparency sites) must be accompanied by a system of sanctions and rewards imposed by the responsible authorities. Here again, it would require further social media pressure to ensure that such proper sanctions and rewards are meted out.

We should also point out that whatever uses of social media develop for transparent government, the traditional media must retain its role as a watchdog and an unbiased source of information. The different media complement each other in any effort to improve governance and to reduce corruption.

Given such scenarios, it should be clear that the Philippines is ripe for people taking politics in their hands. Digital Activism which is the harnessing of the power of online social media for human rights advocacy can also be used for all types of political activism and advocacy. The following specific examples of the use of texting, Facebook and Twitter should provide the reader with a fairly good idea of the shape and importance of their role in Philippine politics today.

FUTURE RESEARCH DIRECTIONS

On May 6, 2016, the Philippines elected a new president for a 6-year term beginning on June 30, 2016 when Rodrigo Duterte was inaugurated. As in the past, the election of a new president brings high hopes that the new regime will be able to tame the corruption that has plagued the Philippines. The new president's approach to improve government and society has admittedly been on the unconventional side, relying on very heavy-handed applications of the law. It is too early to say where such governing tactics will lead or how long it will be effective and be accepted by the people and tolerated by the international community.

While social media has been able to help topple regimes, the more salient question about social media is how it can be effectively used to battle corruption at the retail level. For example, if the driver's license agency extracts bribes before it issues licenses, social media can be used to inundate the agency with protestors as well as a social media campaign can be launched to "shame" the agency. Such timely mobilization can be effective especially if the new president and his lieutenants react as they promised. How the people and government officials react under a new regime will be an interesting follow up to this study.

Aside from Twitter, Facebook and texting, Filipinos in the past have been known to populate other social networks such as Flickr and MySpace. It would be an interesting comparative study to see the role played by such networks which are less popular in other countries because of the different demographic profiles of those who tend to use such social media.

And of course, this study would be enhanced by the more detailed investigation of individual sites like Facebook and Twitter for more specific material on the use of that medium for political activism/participation in the Philippines. Going into specific Philippines sites on FB and using Twitter hashtags relevant to Philippine politicians, events and activities could reveal useful insight into the viability of Filipinos to use "trip-advisor-like" or "yelp-like" sites to encourage political awareness and eventual greater political participation.

CONCLUSION

There are clearly instances when social media has spurred political participation and political change in the Philippines as evidenced by the examples of the ouster of President Joseph Estrada and the million people protest. The big question is can it alleviate political corruption? When politicians know that the people have some semblance of power through social media they may be more reluctant to engage in obvious activities that will get the people out into the street to protest their nefarious activities.

But more importantly the authors suggest that the use of social media has a huge monitoring potential. By setting up systems where people can provide input on people, places and events that border on scandals and corruption and reporting such as those found in, and obtained from, a site like, TripAdvisor.com and Yelp.com greater awareness ensues. People become part of the process and are able to feel that they have an input on the system. In some small ways, they are able to have an impact on alleviating the corruption that may exist in the country. Such can apply not only to the Philippines but all countries that experience the political and economic impact of being in the lowest ranking of the Corruption Perception Index and which are tagged as countries difficult to do business in.

Another issue that seems to come up as in the case of the Philippines is whether such political participation through social media can be sustained? Filipinos have a tendency to be faddish and may not give social media transparency efforts the long-term seriousness it deserves. However, the examples and the data from 1993 to 2013 show the public has staying power and that vigilance on the part of the people in reporting scandals can lead to change. So long as mobile devices remain cheap and accessible especially to the masses, so long as the people feel that such devices help them provide input to the system, and so long as concrete results emanate from such digital activities, political participation using social media can be deemed to be sustainable. Finally, the authors recognize that the powerful and ruling class can co-opt social media and use it to their advantage. After all, ownership of the communication infrastructure lies with oligarchic powers in the Philippines who may choose to use the power of social media to protect the power of their cronies and themselves.

REFERENCES

Aguirre, A. (2009). *ICT and Social Movements in the Philippines: From Estrada to Arroyo*. Philict Research Group.

Ahmed, F. (2013). Role of Media in Uncovering Political Corruption in South Asian Perspective. *Asian Journal of Public Affairs*, *5*(1), 20–37.

Barone, E. (2015, November 23). Which countries censor the Internet? *TIME*.

Bertelsman. (2016). *Shaping Change – Strategies of Development and Transformation: Philippines*. Retrieved from http://bti2006.bertelsmann-transformation-index.de/122.0.html?L=1

Bimber, B. (2003). *Information and American Democracy: Technology in the Evolution of Political Power*. New York, NY: Cambridge University Press. doi:10.1017/CBO9780511615573

Brisbin, D. (1988). Electronic Revolution in the Philippines. *Journal of Popular Culture*, *22*(3), 49–63. doi:10.1111/j.0022-3840.1988.2203_49.x

Chadwick, A. (2006). *Internet Politics: States, Citizens, and New Communication Technologies*. New York, NY: Oxford University Press.

Chaffey, D. (2016). Global social media research summary 2016. *Smartinsights.com*. Retrieved from http://www.smartinsights.com/social-media-marketing/social-media-strategy/new-global-social-media-research/

Doing Business. (2015, October 27). Index. Retrieved from http://www.doingbusiness.org/reports/global-reports/doing-business-2016

EDSA People Power Revolution (2016, January 10). Philippine History. Retrieved from http://www.philippine-history.org/edsa-people-power-revolution.htm

Fitz, P. (2014, February 21). Social media and political scandals. *Miami.edu*. Retrieved from http://students.com.miami.edu/reporting/social-media-and-political-scandals/

Global Voices. (2013, August 27). *Million People March Against Corruption in the Philippines*. Retrieved from https://globalvoices.org/2013/08/27/million-people-march-against-corruption-in-the-philippines/

Gonzales, I. C. (2010, October 6). *Philippine Public Transparency Reporting Project Too Corrupt to Change? The Battle to Reform the Bureau of Customs*. Retrieved from http://peranatinito.net/index.php?option=com_content&view=article&id=135:too-corrupt-to-change-the-battle-to-reform-the-bureau-of-customs&catid=44:stories&Itemid=94

Hindman, M. (2009). *The Myth of Digital Democracy*. Princeton, NJ: Princeton University Press.

Manrique, C. G., & Manrique, G. G. (2009). The Global Digital Divide: What the Indices Reveal. *Paper presented at theAmerican Political Science Association Meeting*, Toronto, Canada.

Margolis, M., Resnick, D., & Wolfe, J. (1999). Party Competition on the Internet in the United States and Britain. *The International Journal of Press/Politics*, *4*(4), 24–47. doi:10.1177/1081180X9900400403

Mirandilla, M. P. (2009). *Cyber campaigning for 2010: The Use and Effectiveness of Websites and Social Networking Sites as Campaign Platforms for the 2010Presidential Election in the Philippines*. Canada: IDRC.

Perral, D. (2016). *EDSA 2*. Retrieved from https://www.scribd.com/doc/61265052/edsa-2

Pertierra, R. (2012). *The New Media, Society & Politics in the Philippines*. Berlin: Fesmedia Asia.

Pertierra, R., Ugarte, E., Pingol, A., Hernandez, J., & Dacanay, N. (2002). *Texting Selves: Cellphones & Philippine Modernity*. Manila: De La Salle University Press.

Rafael, V. L. (2003). The Cell Phone and the Crowd: Messianic Politics in the Contemporary Philippines. *Public Culture*, *15*(3), 399–425. doi:10.1215/08992363-15-3-399

Revesencio, J. (2015). *Philippines: A Digital Lifestyle Capital in the Making?* Retrieved from http://www.huffingtonpost.com/jonha-revesencio/philippines-a-digital-lif_1_b_7199924.html

Rheingold, H. (2002). *Smart Mobs: The Next Social Revolution*. Cambridge: Perseus.

Tapnio, E., & Rood, S. (2011, October). Social Media in the Philippines is Widespread, but what is its Impact? *Asia Foundation*. Retrieved from http://asiafoundation.org/2011/10/12/social-media-in-the-philippines-is-widespread-but-what-is-its-impact/

Transparency.org. (2016). The Corruption Perception Index. Retrieved from http://www.transparency.org/research/cpi/overview

Wikipedia. (2016). List of Political Scandals in the Philippines Retrieved from https://en.wikipedia.org/wiki/List_of_political_scandals_in_the_Philippines

Wilson, C. (2014, March). The Selfiest Cities in the World: TIME's Definitive Ranking. *Time*. Retrieved from http://time.com/selfies-cities-world-rankings/

KEY TERMS AND DEFINITIONS

Corruption Perception Index (CPI): The index measures the perception of the corruption exhibited by politicians and the bureaucracy in a particular country. It is an annual ranking produced by Transparency International.

Digital Activism: Commonly used to refer to the use of digital technology in order to being about political, economic and social change.

Digital Divide: Is a measure of the inequalities that exist between those who have and do not have access to technology and its commensurate peripherals such as computer hardware and software, Internet access, social media connectivity, etc. Such divide is said to exist between developed and developing countries.

Doing Business Index: A World Bank ranking that takes a look at the ease of doing business in various countries of the world including such factors as the ease of obtaining permits, getting credit, getting electricity, paying taxes among others.

EDSA Revolution: Epifanio de los Santos Avenue is the main thoroughfare used by the hundreds of thousands of Filipinos who gathered together in popular demonstrations against the Marcos regime and eventually ousted him.

Kleptocracy: A political system that is ruled by individuals who literally rob their constituents of government funds.

People Power Movement: Also known as the EDSA Revolution. This is a grassroots movement which overthrew Ferdinand Marcos from political power in the Philippines in 1986 and installed Corazon Aquino to the Presidency.

Selfie Capital: TIME Magazine's designation of a city that has the most people taking and posting pictures of themselves using their mobile device specifically their phones (selfies). Makati, a city in the Philippines, has been ranked #1 as such.

TripAdvisor: This is the world's largest website that caters to individual's travel needs including flights, hotels and eating places. Reviews are entered by those who have had experiences with these businesses.

Yelp: A website that helps people find the best businesses in a specific location especially geared towards restaurants and places to dine.

Chapter 10
Participation, Civil Society and the Facebook Use of NGOs in Turkey

Kamil Demirhan
Bülent Ecevit University, Turkey

ABSTRACT

This study finds out the use of Facebook by non-governmental organizations (NGOs) in Turkey to engage the social and political events of the country. NGOs are civil society organizations aiming at promoting participation of citizens in social and political issues. They are a part of democratic system and they have important role to struggle with corruptions and improve the legitimacy of political-legal organization in political system. NGOs work using social networks and promoting civic culture. Therefore, the use of new communication and interaction channels is necessary for NGOs to develop social networks and civic participation. Social media can be a new channel to promote social and political life. This study focuses on Facebook activities of 40 NGOs selected from eight different activity fields: politics, environment, woman rights, economy, emergency, education, human rights, and democracy. It uses content analysis method to understand the NGOs' activities in Facebook, in terms of social and political issues realized in the year of 2012.

DOI: 10.4018/978-1-5225-2019-1.ch010

INTRODUCTION

The use of Internet in political and social issues takes a growing attendance. The use of Internet and social media can be useful for political and social institutions. Civil society organizations can use these new information and communication technologies (ICTs) to improve their activities. This study aims at finding out the Facebook activities of NGOs in Turkey in political and social events. NGOs are the main actors of public sphere in democratic countries. NGOs organize society about public issues and mobilize people around specific political and social problems. NGOs are standing on the heart of political participation of citizens and they promote the accountability of public institutions. NGOs are specialized organizations and they are collaborating with each other in their global network. They operate both in national and international level. NGOs need to channels to set communication with people, to strengthen their social networks and to interact with other organizations for realizing their objectives. One of the NGOs' tactics to reach their goals and find supporters organization is using media to contact with the public (Castells, 2008). Today, media is highly monopolized and it is not inclusionary channel. However, there are new communication channels in the age of social media. Social media has useful functions for communication, information delivery and interaction among people. It is seen as significant to develop citizens' active participation. The use of social media by NGOs is seen as a way to increase the political participation level of citizens and promote accountability. It is a way to increase transparency by the way of citizen's active participation. This study focuses on the Facebook pages of 40 NGOs using content analysis. These NGOs are selected from eight different activity fields that are determined as politics, environment, woman rights, economy, emergency, education, human rights, and democracy. These NGOs are publicly known and popular organizations in Turkey. NGOs' Facebook pages are studied according to specific issues, occurred in the specific time periods, related to NGOs' activity fields. Indicators used in this study are determined with regard to the functions of social media in the processes of communication, interaction, participation, organization and mobilization. Findings present the Facebook use of NGOs during political and social events of Turkey.

PARTICIPATION, CIVIL SOCIETY AND ICTS

In 1990s, after the new liberalization wave in the world and the crisis of representative democracy, democracy has been associated with the concept of open society, transparent government, accountability of institutions, and the participation of various actors such as sub-national and supra-national institutions, social groups, or citizens in politics (Held et al., 1999, p. 187; Wijkman, 1998; Şaylan, 2008). Recently, politics is seen as more related to social area and it is a spontaneous process rather than hierarchical one (Çakır & Demirhan, 2011). Multiple-actors' participation in political issues, has been characterized as the main requirement in order to provide a heterogenic, flexible and strong democracy. These changes caused to the development of new democracy models like deliberative and radical democracy (Habermas, 2006; Mouffe, 2005). New democracy models consist of the political participation of different interest groups, NGOs, and other actors in politics. Political participation of these actors insists on the importance of democratization and the bottom-up model of participation instead of top-down model (Pratt, 2004, p. 319; Falk, 1999). It consists of a socialized public sphere more than constitutional process like periodical elections (Falk, 1999). Political participation of different social and political actors based on their communication. Either this communication would be resulted in an agreement among various groups who have different interests and opinions or it would prepare the conditions for pluralistic democracy for the political competition and conflict among these groups (Habermas, 2006; Benhabib, 2006; Mouffe, 2005).

NGOs are the other component of political participation and democracy. They are emphasized as actors aiming at promoting civil skills for citizens required for active political participation (Verba, 1995). NGOs are independent institutions from governments. NGOs operate as local, national, regional and international level in the fields of woman rights, environment, democracy, human rights, AIDS, security, economic development (Wapner, 2004, p. 377; Boli & Thomas, 2004, p. 264; Falk, 1999). The functions of NGOs are mediating between citizens and government, check and control the use of political authority, supporting citizens' networks, motivating citizens for mobilization, forming public opinion, promoting plurality, reinforcing relations and trust among the members of society, and supporting social and economic development of society (Edwards, 2009).

New innovations in information and communication technologies (ICTs) bring new opportunities for politics. Internet has important functions to increase political participation and to realize the requirements of the new model of democracy and politics (Vaccari, 2011). Internet is thought as a tool to reduce the communication costs, enhance flexibility in the communication process with overcoming the territorial restrictions, and provide platforms to increase interaction between different actors. It is insisted that ICTs provide interaction, communication and participation channels among different actors. These functions lead to better conditions for democracy such as strengthening pluralism and increasing deliberation (Hauben & Hauben, 1997; Dyson, 1997; Tsagarousianou, 1999; Ferdinand, 2000; Krueger, 2002; Macintosh, 2004, p. 3; Chadwick, 2006; Brundidge and Rice, 2009; UN, 2010, p. 84).

Although ICTs have some potentials to provide a more interactive and participative political process, it is important to underline that it needs some requirements for attain these opportunities. Access to digital tools is the most important one of them. Also, socio-economic and cultural conditions like technophobia or inequalities in social and economic opportunities are obstacles for the use of ICTs opportunities in social and political issues. Researches insist the importance of some different factors in relation to the Internet and political participation (Scheufele & Nisbet, 2002). Although structural advantages of Internet is accepted, researches emphasize that the relationship between Internet and political participation is closely related to the individuals' education and income level; and their socio-economic conditions, social relations and social status (Bimber 2003; Price, et al., 2002). Another factor having influence on the relation between Internet and political participation is explained by Weber (2003) as individuals' civic participation tendencies to politics. It stresses that if individuals participate in politics, their political participation via Internet would be more increased. E-voting, e-participation, e-democracy, e-mobilization, and e-activism are indicating the development of Internet use in the field of politics (Chadwick & Howard, 2009; Gibson et. al, 2004; Demirhan & Öktem, 2011). These concepts indicate the functions of Internet in political process such as deliberation, organization, mobilization, participation, and public opinion formation.

There are many recent examples on the use of Internet in politics such as organization of political movements, political campaigns in elections, and consultation to citizens in decision making process, political communication, creating public opinions for political discussions as an alternative channel for communication to classical media (Anduiza, 2009; Römmele, 2003). Social media briefly is a type of interactive media with using of Web 2.0 tools[1]. It means a system open to the social relations and mutual interactions of participants located on the social networks. Social networks in Internet are "web-based services that allow users to build a public or semi-public within a system; articulate a user list with shared relationships; and observe the list of relationships of those persons with other people within the system" (Boyd & Ellison, 2008). Facebook (created in 2005), YouTube (created in 2005) and Twitter (created in 2006) are important social media channels. Although there are many social media channels, Facebook is the most widespread social network site with the most number of users among other social media platforms (Tufekci, 2008). In April 2009, Facebook had 200 million users in worldwide. In 2016, the number of users is 1.090 million (Socialbakers, 2016).

Social media is explained as a channel to transform communication form as dialogic, participative, and democratic with its functions on the political processes (Axford, 2011; Loader, 2011). Some cases presents its growing effects in politics such as WikiLeaks, the election campaigns of Barack Obama, the Arab Springs[2] and social media usage of anti-government groups in the 2009 election in Iran (Krotoski, 2011; Edelman Research, 2009; Ghannam, 2011; Christensen, 2011; Barrons, 2012), and social movements in U.S.A (Gaby & Caren, 2014), Moldova (Mungiu-Pippidi & Munteanu, 2009), Turkey (SMaPP, 2013) and China (Kaiman, 2014). These functions of social media can improve the power of NGOs in society.

ICTs and social media platforms provide opportunities in information, communication and interaction processes for NGOs (Demirhan, 2014). Social media use of NGOs may contribute to develop their organizational networks. It can promote organizational and social relations. Social media can be useful in the process of forming public opinion and enhancing civic relations. Saeed et al, (2009), insist that the connection is an important weakness of civil society organizations working internationally in many activity fields. The use of ICTs is important to realize collaboration among NGOs and connecting with volunteers. The use of ICTs is also functional to find donors and increase financial resources (Saeed et. al., 2008a). ICTs are also useful to realize diversity in operations (Saeed et. al., 2008b). NGOs presence on Internet can improve the era of civil society.

THE POWER OF NGOs AND SOCIAL MEDIA USAGE IN TURKEY

In Turkey, NGOs are not powerful civil organizations. Also citizens do not participate in the political processes actively. Citizens' supports to the political movements or taking role in the election campaigns remains low and limited when compared to the developed countries (Kalaycıoğlu, 2008, pp. 7-9). These limits are explained as "the narrow depth and breadth of civic participation, inadequate skills and resources of NGOs, and undeveloped linkages among NGOs" (TUSEV, 2011, p. 5). However, it is known that there is a tendency to enhance the civil society in Turkey. The first important milestone in the development process of civil society in Turkey was the Habitat Forum, in 1996 (CIVICUS, 2005). After this international meeting, hundreds of NGOs took action. The second important milestone was the Marmara Earthquake in 1999. After this disaster NGOs had an important role in relief and rescue process, and the importance of civil society organizations was remarked by the public. The third important milestone was the acceptance of Copenhagen Criteria, in 2001. It provided legal assurance to citizens for using their freedoms and rights. In addition, in parallel to the liberalization process in Turkey, the distribution of central power, economic liberalization, adoption of the principles of good governance, democratization efforts, and the endeavor of being a part of European Union (EU) were effective in the development of civil society. Civil society organizations contribute to the development of human rights, strength the capacity of emergency assistance, develop political consciousness in society, promote economic and social conditions, organize collective actions, support collaborations, improve dialogue between government and society in decision making process, increase trust among citizens, support to transparency and accountability of government, increase social responsibility (Clarke, 1998; CIVICUS, 2005).

The context of civil society in Turkey can be summarized as the rate of the volunteers who are a member of civil society organization is around the 7 percent of all of the voters (Kalaycıoğlu, 2008). According to the report that is called as "Civil Society in Turkey: A Turning Point" which is prepared by TUSEV and CIVICUS cooperation in 2011, there are 90,578 civil society organizations which are operating in Turkey. The 4,547 of them are foundations and the 86,031 of them are associations. This number will be reached to the 150.000 if unions to be added to this number. The number of NGOs' members, is very low when compared to the population of Turkey. Per 100,000 citizens, only 5790 are registered members of associations. Observations according to this report seem that young people's political participation at the level of the lowest among 55 countries with 8 percent; 11% of young people participate to the sports clubs; 10.4% of women at the level of membership; 18.1% percent of associations in Turkey work for the development of religious services that are mosque associations, of 14.3% are sports clubs, of 13.7% are aid associations, of 9.5% are development and housing associations, of 10% are the professional solidarity organizations. Working areas of the foundations are social assistance (56.1%), education (47.5%) and health (21.84%). According to official records, only 1.28% of foundations are working on democracy, law and the field of human rights. Donation rates are also very low. People's confidence level to civil society is 51% (TUSEV, 2011).

In Turkey, the most popular social media platform for communication is Facebook used by the number of 31 million people in 2011 (Socialbakers, 2012). This number is nearly 41% of all the population of Turkey in 2011. Attention to the social media is ever growing in the public institutions. Especially, the researches in the field of e-government is attracted more attention in terms of the principles of governance such as transparency or accountability (GovCamp, 2011). However; the level of the use of social media by citizens is higher than public organizations. The study on the use of Facebook by policy actors after Van earthquake 2011 in Turkey (Yıldız & Demirhan, 2016) presents that the less number of national and international policy actors utilized the advantages of Facebook in the disaster relief and recovery process in comparison to citizens' usage of Facebook in this process. Digital News Report (2015) explains that people in Turkey use social media as a part of celebrity culture. However, as it is stated about Twitter (Murthy, 2013), social media is event-oriented-media and the use of social media changes according to events breaking out continuously. For example, the use of social media in Turkey during social and politics movements increase dramatically (SMaPP, 2013). Social media use by legal or civic organizations is lower than the use of social media by citizens or social groups. The findings of this study determine whether NGOs realize activity on Facebook after specific social-political issues related to their activity fields. This analyze can indicate the role of social media as a new activity era for NGOs during political events to realize its functions in relation to the development of civil society and democracy.

METHOD

This study focuses on the social media usage capacity of 40 popular NGOs in Turkey. These NGOs are studied by means of indicators to determine their activities on Facebook in specific cases. Studies evaluating the presence of an organization on social media, and aiming at categorizing the contents of communication determine indicators in relation to the context of their researches (Demirhan & Öktem, 2011; Small, 2012; Yıldız & Demirhan, 2016; Demirhan, 2016). This study uses same way like these researches. This study determines the indicators in relation to the aim of research finding out the Facebook activities of NGOs. Therefore, following indicators are determined in terms of the relationship between the functions of social media and its use in socio-political issues. The indicators shown in the Table 1.

Indicators 1 to 4 and 9 to 11 are objective indicators. Measuring these indicators is easier than the indicators 5 to 8. These indicators (5. Informative message; 6. Message to create sensibility; 7. Message for activity; 8. Message for organizing) are determined in relation to the opportunity provided by social media for information sharing, communication, organization, motivation and mobilization during socio-political events. If a message includes any information about the topic under-research, it is defined as an informative message. If a message tries to increase sensibility of the public with some arguments around the issue, it is categorized as a message to create sensibility. If a message including any call for action, it is categorized as a message for activity. And lastly, if a message tries to organize people to do something in direction to a common aim, it is defined as a message for organizing the public.

Table 1. Indicators for Determining NGOs' Activities on Facebook

INDICATORS	
	1. Page in Facebook
	2. The number of likes in the page
	3. Discussion on the specific topic
	4. Number of the message
	5. Informative message
	6. Message to create sensibility
	7. Message for activity
	8. Message for organizing
	9. Sustainability of messages
	10. Link to YouTube
	11. Number of link to YouTube

This study focuses on the Facebook activities of NGOs. These NGOs are researched according to eight different activity fields. These are politics, woman rights, education, emergency aid, human rights, democracy, environment and economy. Five civil society organizations are selected for the each of eight activity fields. It means that forty NGOs are studied in total. These are the influential civil society organizations in Turkey. These organizations are expected to take an action after the political and social cases focused in this research. Selected NGOs are shown in Table 2 and Table 3 with their names, abbreviations of names, and the names of NGOs which are searched in Facebook's search engine. Searching was realized in January and March, 2012 and data of the study collected in this period.

The cases selected for this study are related to the politics, woman rights, education, emergency, human rights, democracy, environment, economy. In total eight different cases are determined for eight different activity fields of NGOs. They are explained below by means of their context in relation to social and political issues. The case for the field of politics is the change of the "Retirement Fund Law" in December, 22, 2011, in order to increase the salaries of deputies who served only two years in parliament (Milliyet, 2011). This law was seen as a fine (like an easy money) for the deputies by the public and it was criticized because of high level of this salary. NGOs' activities were so important to opposition to prevent the enactment of this law or question its different extents, reasons and its legitimacy. In this context, NGOs' pages and their activities in Facebook searched for a week period since this event occurred.

Table 2. Selected NGOs and Activity Fields (First Table)

Fields	The Name of the NGOs	Pages Was Searched in the Facebook As
Politics	Atatürk Thought Association - ATA	Atatürkçü Düşünce Derneği
	Young Civilian - YC	Genç Siviller
	Progressive Journalist Association - PJA	Çağdaş Gazeteciler Derneği
	Turkish Public Union - TPU	Türk Kamu-Sen
	Civil Servants' Union - CSU	Memur-Sen
Human Rights	Human Rights Association - HRA	İnsan Hakları Derneği (Human Rights Association)
	Open Door Association - ODA	Açık Kapı Derneği
	Association to Support A Human Life - ASHL	İnsanca Yaşamı Destekleme Derneği
	Human Rights Foundation of Turkey - HRFT	Türkiye İnsan Hakları Vakfı - Human Rights Foundation of Turkey
	Posivite Living Association - PLA	Pozitif Yaşam Derneği
Democracy	Turkish Democracy Foundation - TDF	Türk Demokrasi Vakfı
	Social Democracy Foundation - SDF	SODEV Sosyal Demokrasi Vakfi (Social Democracy Foundation)
	Association of Liberal Democracy - ALD	Liberal Demokrasi Derneği
	Association of Liberal Thinking - ALT	Liberal Düşünce Topluluğu - Association for Liberal Thinking
	Association of Active Citizenship - AAC	Aktif Vatandaşlık Derneği -AKVATDER
Economy	Turkish Industry and Business Association - TIBA	Türkiye Sanayicileri ve İş Adamları Derneği - TÜSİAD
	Independent Industrialists and Businessmen Association - IIBA	MÜSİAD - Müstakil Sanayici ve İşadamları Derneği
	Association for Consumer Protection - ACP	Tüketici Hakları Koruma Derneği
	Union of Chambers and Commodity Exchanges of Turkey - UCCET	TOBB I Türkiye Odalar ve Borsalar Birliği
	Economic Development Foundation - EDF	İktisadi Kalkınma Vakfı

The case for the field of woman rights is "law draft on prevent to the violence against woman" which was started after the approval of deputies on January, 31, 2012 (CNN Turk, 2012). NGOs' pages and their activities in Facebook searched for a month period since this law draft was declared. The violence against woman is an actual issue in Turkey, because some deaths have been occurred in recent years. Other problem related to violence to young girls that is "child bride". It means young

Table 3. Selected NGOs and Activity Fields (Second Table)

Fields	The Name of the Associations	Pages Was Searched in the Facebook As
Woman Rights	Association for the Support of Woman Candidates – ASWC	Ka.der (Kadın Adayları Destekleme ve Eğitme Derneği)
	Mor Çatı Women's Shelter Foundation - MCWSF	Mor Çatı Kadın Sığınağı Vakfı
	Flying Broom Communication and Research Association - FBCRA	Uçan Süpürge
	Turkish Woman's Union - TWU	Türk Kadınlar Birliği
	Mother Child Education Foundation - MCEF	AÇEV - Anne Çocuk Eğitim Vakfı
Education	Association for the Support of Contemporary Living - ASCL	Çağdaş Yaşamı Destekleme Derneği
	Educational Volunteers Foundation of Turkey - EVFT	Türkiye Eğitim Gönüllüleri Vakfı - TEGV
	Turkish Education Association - TEA	Türk Eğitim Derneği
	Turkish Education Union - TEU	Türk Eğitim-Sen
	Education Association - EA	Eğitim Sen
Emergency	AKUT Search and Rescue Association - AKUT	Akut Arama ve Kurtarma Derneği
	Search and Rescue Association - SRRA	AKA - Arama Kurtarma ve Araştırma Derneği
	ODAK Search and Rescue Association - ODAK	ODAK - Orhangazi Doğa Sporları Arama Kurtarma Derneği
	Turkey Emergency Response, Rescue, Fire and Education Foundation - TERRFEF	Türkiye Acil Yardım, Kurtarma, Yangın ve Eğitim Vakfı
	Earthquake Search and Rescue Association - ESRA	DARK Deprem Arama Kurtarma Derneği
Environment	TEMA The Turkish Foundation for Combating Soil Erosion, For Reforestation and the Protection of Natural Habitats	TEMA VAKFI
	Global Action Group - GAG	Küresel Eylem Grubu
	World Wild Fund for Nature Turkey - WWF TR	WWF Türkiye (Doğal Hayatı Koruma Vakfı)
	Turkey's Nature Conservation Society - TNCS	Türkiye Tabiatını Koruma Derneği
	The Foundation for Environmental Protection and Research - FEPR	ÇEVKOR (Çevre Koruma ve Araştırma Vakfı)

girls' marriage before or in their teenage marriage with an old man. This case is an example of the violence to the woman and also this marriage mostly resulted with violent actions. In addition, honor killing is a different extent of this problem. In this field, NGOs' activities are so important to affect law making process, organizing woman, organizing their demands, and communicating with various public organizations to act together and increasing the public attention on the issue.

The case for the field of education is the scandal of "Transition to Higher Education Exam" in March, 27, 2011 (CNN Turk, 2011). This exam is the only way of students to start their university education. It is carrying out in a central examination system. All students in Turkey engage to this exam. However, in the year of 2011, a scandal released that called as "code scandal". The examination center which was responsible for the implication of the exam was accused by given the codes to some students. The period after the exam was very important. Many students and their parents demanded the cancelation of the exam. In this process, NGOs had a great responsibility to develop public discussion on the different extents of this exam, reliability of the test and on the actions have to be taken urgently. NGOs' pages and their activities in Facebook were searched for a week period since this exam was performed.

The case for the field of emergency aid is Van Earthquake with magnitude 7.2 Richter scale, in October, 23, 2011 and second earthquake with magnitude 5.6 Richter scale in November 9, 2011 (AFAD, 2011). NGOs' pages and their activities in Facebook searched for one month period since this disaster occurred. More than 600 people were killed in both of the earthquakes. More than 2000 people were injured, and more than 4000 building were destroyed (ITU, 2011). NGOs' activities were very important in the process of struggle against the disaster and realizing the process of organization, communication, coordination, recovery, search and rescue processes and taking public attention.

The case for the field of human rights is the issue of conscientious objection, and one week period searched after the expressions of Turkish Prime Minister on the acceptance of "Paid Military Service Act" in November, 16, 2011 (Sabah, 2011b). All Turkish young males have to perform their military duties after 18 years old. Sometimes, government legislate a "Paid Military Service Act" that provides young males right for default. While this act had been discussed in the societal and in the governmental level in terms of amount of this paid and its extent which age would be included. NGOs had an important position both to affect this context of the act and to inform people. Also NGOs are important to discuss demands of the public exactly.

The case for the field of democracy, is selected as the national elections in June, 12, 2011 (YSK, 2011). NGOs are important actors to affect the political processes as well as political parties and they have an important role in political communication. In the process of national elections, they had a potential to affect this election process and campaigns, and it had functions to carry out some important activities such as creating public opinion. In this case, NGOs' pages and their activities in Facebook were searched for a week before and after the elections.

The case for the field of environment is the discussion on the emergence of nuclear energy in Turkey, after the nuclear danger in Japan occurred during the Tsunami disaster in March, 11, 2011 (Deutsche Welle Turkish, 2011). NGOs' Facebook pages and their activities related to the disaster, and the possible negative results of nuclear power station if it would be emerged in Turkey, in the Facebook were searched for one month period after the disaster. Turkey is a growing economy and industry. And it needs more energy, so government support the policies of nuclear energy besides sustainable energy. However, environmental groups point out the possible threats of nuclear energy to the country and environment with regard to the example of Japan. It was an important discussion issue for the public. NGOs are important channels to discuss and affect nuclear policies of government.

The last case for the field of economy is the additional tax hikes on smoking, alcohol drinks, mobile phones and cars in October, 13, 2011 (Sabah, 2011a). NGOs' Facebook pages and activities in Facebook are searched for a week period after the tax hikes. These tax hikes created an extra economic burden for the citizens. It was discussed among people and NGOs also had important function to discuss it with its different extents. They had the role of informing citizens about these changes and act according to the demands of them. The findings of this study presents the selected NGOs' Facebook activities after these cases which are closely linked with socio-political issues related to the activity fields of NGOs.

FINDINGS

The findings about the NGOs Facebook activities are presented in Table 4 and Table 5. Findings clarify that thirty-five NGOs (87.5%) have a page in the Facebook. The number of NGOs page in the Facebook which have at least one discussion or message about the events is nine among the thirty-five NGOs. In other words, at least one message was sent to the Facebook pages of 27.71% of NGOs in the considered time period. The sustainability rate of discussions or messages in NGOs' Facebook pages is 11.42%. It means that only 4 of the NGOs have more than one message about the issue in the page.

Table 4. Action Capacity of NGOs on Facebook - I

FIELDS			WOMAN RIGHTS					EDUCATION					EMERGENCY					ENVIRONMENT				
ASSOCIATIONS			ASWC	MCWSF	FBCRA	TWU	MCEF	ASLC	EVFT	TEA	TEU	EA	AKUT	SRRA	ODAK	TERR-FEF	ESRA	TEMA	GAG	WWF- TR	TNCS	FEPR
INDICATORS	1	Page in Facebook	1	1	1	1	1	1	1	1	1	1	1	1	1	0	1	1	1	1	1	1
	2	The number of likes in the page	221	249	1478	0	11198	12310	41068	85	3893	1727	24511	1987	45	0	96	12710	1852	30.560	772	53
	3	Discussion on the specific topic	1	0	0	0	0	0	0	0	1	0	1	1	0	0	0	1	1	1	0	0
	4	Number of the message	2	0	0	0	0	0	0	0	5	0	130	24	0	0	0	2	71	1	0	0
	5	Informative message	1	0	0	0	0	0	0	0	1	0	1	1	0	0	0	1	1	0	0	0
	6	Message to create sensibility	1	0	0	0	0	0	0	0	0	0	1	1	0	0	0	1	1	1	0	0
	7	Message for activity	0	0	0	0	0	0	0	0	0	0	1	1	0	0	0	0	1	0	0	0
	8	Message for organizing	0	0	0	0	0	0	0	0	0	0	1	0	0	0	0	0	1	0	0	0
	9	Sustainability of the messages	0	0	0	0	0	0	0	0	1	0	1	1	0	0	0	0	1	0	0	0
	10	Link to YouTube	0	0	0	0	0	0	0	0	0	0	0	0	0	0	0	0	0	0	0	0
	11	Number of link to YouTube	0	0	0	0	0	0	0	0	0	0	0	0	0	0	0	0	0	0	0	0

Table 5. Action Capacity of NGOs on Facebook - II

	FIELDS	POLITICS					HUMAN RIGHTS					DEMOCRACY					ECONOMY				
INDICATORS	ASSOCIATIONS	ATA	YC	PJA	TPU	CSU	HRA	ODA	ASHL	HRFT	PLA	TDF	SDF	ALD	ALT	AAC	TIBA	IIBA	ACP	UCCET	EDF
1	Page in Facebook	1	1	1	1	1	1	1	0	1	1	0	1	0	1	1	1	0	1	1	1
2	The number of likes in the page	38777	64319	196	5906	100	7427	42	0	2769	548	0	194	0	988	24	5200	0	1554	93	8
3	Discussion on the specific topic	0	0	0	1	0	0	1	0	0	0	0	0	0	0	0	0	0	0	0	0
4	Number of the message	0	0	0	1	0	0	1	0	0	0	0	0	0	0	0	0	0	0	0	0
5	Informative message	0	0	0	1	0	0	1	0	0	0	0	0	0	0	0	0	0	0	0	0
6	Message to create sensibility	0	0	0	0	0	0	0	0	0	0	0	0	0	0	0	0	0	0	0	0
7	Message for activity	0	0	0	0	0	0	0	0	0	0	0	0	0	0	0	0	0	0	0	0
8	Message for organizing	0	0	0	0	0	0	0	0	0	0	0	0	0	0	0	0	0	0	0	0
9	Sustainability of the messages	0	0	0	0	0	0	0	0	0	0	0	0	0	0	0	0	0	0	0	0
10	Link to YouTube	0	0	0	0	0	0	0	0	0	0	0	0	0	0	0	0	0	0	0	0
11	Number of link to YouTube	0	0	0	0	0	0	0	0	0	0	0	0	0	0	0	0	0	0	0	0

Table 4 indicates that NGOs, which use social media efficiently, operate only in the fields of emergency and environment. In the field of emergency, after Van Earthquake, there are more than one hundred messages in AKUT's Facebook page. Posted messages are related to information sharing, collaboration, communication, organization, and increasing public attention. After the disasters in Van, AKUT had been connected among survivors, relatives of survivors, public institutions, rescue teams and relatives, by means of the Facebook page. Also, visitors are informed about the situation in the place of the event. The number of survivors, the number of victims, and the number of required materials was announced by this page. In this page, citizens informed about earthquake in general and what should be done in the cases of earthquakes. Information is given about the responsibility of public institutions and government. Also, there were discussions about the success of these institutions.

In the field of environment, Global Action Group's (GAG) social media usage presents that this NGO has an effective social media usage level. This Facebook page is located in the second place with 71 messages on the issue related to environment, the usage of nuclear energy in Turkey. Posted messages include indicators related to information sharing, activity organization, mobilization, and increasing public sensibility. The Facebook page of this NGO, gives information about the disaster in Fukushima, possible negative results and risks of the nuclear energy usage for environment and society, Turkish governments' policies about nuclear energy and try to organize social actions using Facebook page. Although AKUT and GAG have an effective usage, the other NGOs like Turkish Educational Union and Open Door Association used social media at the minimum level and not efficiently.

These results of the NGOs' success in the usage of social media in the field of emergency, and environment present evidence for the potential and the power of social media in the process of participation of multiple actors in all fields. These cases are not only related to social and economic processes, they are also political, and include the political participation of citizens because environment has become an issue of the national and international public having importance for all the parts of the society.

Facebook provides social networks for its users to set communication. It is significant to transform the democratic process as a dialogic and participative way. In the design of Facebook, the number of friends gives information about users' social network capacity. In this study, the number of likes is considered as an indicator to evaluate the social network capacity and the number of possible visitors of pages. And this number is compared among NGOs Facebook pages. According to results of this comparison, it is seen that AKUT's Facebook page liked by 25511 users. These visitors were shared information what they have information about the places of the survivors who are debris at the bottom. Global Action Group's (GAG) Facebook page liked by the 1852 users. Despite its low number of visitors relatively to the other NGOs' pages, it is seen that Global Action Group used the social media effectively to share information, organize activity, mobilize people, and create the public sensibility on the issue.

Despite some NGOs have a high number of likes; they did not use social media effectively. For example, Young Civilians (64319), Educational Volunteers Foundation of Turkey (41068), Atatürk Thought Association (38777), World Wild Fund for Nature Turkey (30560), TEMA (12710), Mother Child Education Foundation (11198), Human Rights Association (7427), Turkish Industry and Business Association (5200) are among these NGOs. In addition, it is seen that especially the use of social media by NGOs operating in the fields of woman rights and democracy were so weak. In addition, it is remarkable that Turkish Democracy Foundation does not have any forum. It means that social network capacity is not directly affecting the social media usage capacity of NGOs. NGOs' awareness on these issues and attention to the recent issues in public life are important factors increasing this capacity.

In Turkey, civil society sector is not powerful and it is a developing field. In the last decade, the influence of NGOs in politics and social issues is increased. Habitat Conference in 1996, the successful action of AKUT in relief and rescue process after Marmara Earthquake in 1999, and the acceptance of Copenhagen Criteria are the important millstones in the development process of civil society sector in Turkey. Although the civil society sector is progressed, there are still important problems such as the low level of citizens' participation, the lack of financial resources and limited networks and collaboration among NGOs. NGOs are not developed organizations in Turkey yet. The NGOs researched in this study are powerful organizations in Turkey, and it is clear that some of them like AKUT and GAG used the social media for action in the cases related to their activity fields. This situation presents that apart from the small number of NGOs in Turkey, they do not realize activity on Facebook which can provide new opportunities for NGOs such as increasing the participation of citizens, finding financial resources and setting new networks.

CONCLUSION

This study supports that social media can be a new action area for NGOs to realize their objectives and functions in democracies increasing public awareness about public issues, and mobilizing people around democratic principles to promote accountability, public sensibility and civic culture. An organized civil society will promote democracy and the use of new communication technologies can help NGOs in this process. The development of civil society is closely related to the NGOs success and reliability. The innovations in information and communication technologies are seen as opportunities to develop NGOs' activities. Social media has a potential to provide communication and interaction opportunities for activities in the era of civil society. New channels for communication and interaction can help NGOs and it can contribute to the power of civil society organizations in public life. Political participation and accountability can be provided if new innovations would be used efficiently by NGOs.

In this study, NGOs' activities on Facebook during the political events related to the socio-political life in Turkey is founded as weak. This study presents that the low level of social media usage is seen especially in the fields of democracy, woman rights and human rights though these fields including the most important political issues in contemporary democracies. Social media can help NGOs to find new resources, to expand their networks and to collaborate with other actors. Therefore, NGOs should be more active in events related to the citizens' life and political issues having direct influence on citizens. NGOs should be interested in political and social events in their activity fields and consider the use of social media for a strategy to action in order to be more powerful in public sphere. Social media has an event-oriented nature and organizations should follow the social reactions. Social media has the potential to develop civic culture in a society. However, NGOs need strategies, attention and sincerity about the use of social media for contributing civic culture and democracy.

REFERENCES

AFAD. (2011). The Report of Van Earthquake (Van Depremi Faaliyet Raporu). Retrieved from http://www.afad.gov.tr/

Anduiza, E., Cantijoch, M., & Gallego, A. (2009). Political Participation and the Internet. *Information Communication and Society*, *12*(6), 860–878. doi:10.1080/13691180802282720

Axford, B. (2011). Talk About a Revolution: Social Media and the MENA Uprisings. *Globalizations*, *8*(5), 681–686. doi:10.1080/14747731.2011.621281

Barrons, G. (2012). Suleiman: Mubarak decided to step down #egypt #jan25 OH MY GOD: examining the use of social media in the 2011 Egyptian revolution. *Contemporary Arab Affairs*, *5*(1), 54–67. doi:10.1080/17550912.2012.645669

Benhabib, S. (2006). Introduction: The Democratic Moment and the Problem of Difference. In S. Benhabib (Ed.), *Democracy and Difference: Contesting the Boundaries of the Political*. US: Princeton University.

Bimber, B., & Davis, R. (2003). *Campaigning Online: the internet in US elections*. New York: Oxford University Press.

Boli, J., & Thomas, G. M. (2004). World Culture in the World Polity: A Century of International Non-Governmental Organization. In F.J. Lechner and J. Boli (Eds.), The Globalization Reader (pp. 258-264). USA: Blackwell.

Boyd, D. M., & Ellison, N. B. (2007). Social network sites: Definition, history, and scholarship. *Journal of Computer-Mediated Communication*, *13*(1), 210–230. doi:10.1111/j.1083-6101.2007.00393.x

Brundidge, J., & Rice, R. E. (2009). Political Engagement Online - Do The Information Rich Get Richer And The Like-Minded More Similar? In A. Chadwick & P. N. Howard (Eds.), *Routledge Handbook of Internet Politics*. USA: Routledge.

Çakır, D., & Demirhan, K. (2011). Political Character of the Social Actions in the Process of Globalization: A Case Study. *International Journal of Social Sciences and Humanity Studies*, *3*(2), 159–168.

Castells, M. (2008). The New Public Sphere: Global Civil Society, Communication Networks, and Global Governance. *ANNALS, AAPSS*, *616*(1), 78–92. doi:10.1177/0002716207311877

Chadwick, A. (2006). *Internet Politics*. New York: Oxford University Press.

Chadwick, A., & Howard, P. N. (2009). New directions in internet politics research. In A. Chadwick & P. N. Howard (Eds.), *Routledge Handbook of Internet Politics*. USA: Routledge.

Christensen, C. (2011). Twitter Revolutions? Addressing Social Media and Dissent. *Communication Review, 14*(3), 155–157. doi:10.1080/10714421.2011.597235

CIVICUS (2005). Civil Society Index Report for Turkey. Civil Society in Turkey: An Era of Transition.

Clarke, G. (1998). Non-Governmental Organizations (NGOs) and Politics in the Developing World. *Political Studies, XLVI*(1), 36–52. doi:10.1111/1467-9248.00128

Demirhan, K. (2014). Civil Society and NGOs on Digital Era in Turkey. *Humanities and Social Sciences Review, 3*(1), 265–274.

Demirhan, K. (2016). Relationship between Social Media and Political Parties: The Case of Turkey. In A. M. G. Solo (Ed.), Social Media and Networking: Concepts, Methodologies, Tools, and Applications (Vols. 1–4). pp. 1196–1225). Hershey, PA, USA: IGI Global. doi:10.4018/978-1-4666-8614-4.ch055

Demirhan, K., & Öktem, M. K. (2011). Electronic Participation in the Policy Making Process: A Case Study. *International Journal of eBusiness and eGovernment Studies, 3*(1), 59-78.

Deutsche Welle Turkish. (2011, March, 15). About Nuclear Energy (Haber: Başak Özay, Türkiye'nin nükleer enerji açmazı) Retrieved From http://www.dw.de/dw/article/0,-14911742,00.html

Digital News Report. (2015). How Turkey uses social media. Retrieved from http://www.digitalnewsreport.org/-essays/2015/how-turkey-uses-social-media/

Dyson, E. (1997). Release 2.0: A Design for Living in the Digital Age. New York: Broadway.

Edelman Research. (2009). *The Social Pulpit - Barack Obama's Social Media Toolkit. (Principal Author: Monte Lutz)*. SVP-Digital Public Affairs, Edelman.

Edwards, M. (2009). *Civil Society*. Cambridge: Polity Press.

Falk, R. (1999). *Predatory Globalization: A Critique*. UK: Polity.

Ferdinand, P. (2000). *The Internet, Democracy and Democratization*. London: Frank Cass Publishers.

Gaby, S., & Caren, N. (2012). Occupy Online: How cute old men and Malcolm X Recruited 400,000 U.S. Users to OWS on Facebook. *Social Movement Studies*, *11*(3-4), 367–374. doi:10.1080/14742837.2012.708858

Ghannam, J. (2041). Social Media in the Arab World: Leading up to the Uprisings of 2011, February 3.

Gibson, R. K., Lusoli, W., Römmele, A., & Ward, S. J. (2004). Representative democracy and the Internet. In R. K. Gibson, W. Lusoli, A. Römmele, & S. J. Ward (Eds.), *Electronic Democracy: Mobilisation, Organisation and Participation via New ICTs*. London: Routledge.

Habermas, J. (2006). Three Normative Models of Democracy. In S. Benhabib (Ed.), *Democracy and Difference: Contesting the Boundaries of the Political*. US: Princeton University.

Hauben, M., & Hauben, R. (1997). *Netizens*. London: Wiley / IEEE Computer Society Press.

Held, D., McGrew, A., Goldblatt, D., & Perraton, J. (1999). *Global Transformations*. US: Standford University.

Issa, B. A. (2009). eParticipation. eTransformation in Public Administration: From eGovernment to eGovernance. In T.K. Bensghir (Ed.) *The Proceedings of International Conference on eGovernment Sharing Experiences,* Ankara: TODAİE.

ITU. (2011). Van Eartquake. Retrieved from http://web.itu.edu.tr/~eedmi/Van2011Eq/

Kaiman, J. (2014). Hong Kong's umbrella revolution. *The Guardian*. Retrieved from http://www.theguardian.com/world/2014/sep/30/-sp-hong-kong-umbrella-revolution-pro-democracy-protests

Kalaycıoğlu, E. (2008). *The Reinforcement of Democracy in Turkey (in Turkish, Türkiye'de Demokrasi'nin Pekişmesi: Bir Siyasal Kültür Sorunu - Ergun Özbudun'a Armağan)*. Yetkin Yayınevi.

Kamukampi. (2011). Government Camp 2.0 Turkey. Retrieved from http://www.kamukampi.com/en

Krotoski, A. (2011). WikiLeaks and the New, Transparent World Order. *The Political Quarterly*, *84*(4).

Krueger, B. S. (2002). Assessing the Potential of Internet Political Participation in the United States: A Resource. *American Politics Research*, *30*(5), 476–498. doi:10.1177/1532673X02030005002

Loader, B. D., & Mercea, D. (2011). Networking Democracy? *Information Communication and Society*, *14*(6), 757–769. doi:10.1080/1369118X.2011.592648

Macintosh, A. (2004). Characterizing E-Participation in Policy-Making. *Proceedings of the 37th Hawaii International Conference on System Sciences.*

Milliyet (2011, December, 24). About the "Retirement Fund Law" [Bir gecede iki zam = 20 bin TL]. Retrieved from http://siyaset.milliyet.com.tr/bir-gecede-iki-zam-20-bin-tl/siyaset/siyasetdetay/24.12.2011/1479653/default.htm

Mouffe, C. (2005). *On the Political*. USA: Routledge.

Mungiu-Pippidi, A., & Munteanu, I. (2009). Moldova's "twitter revolution". *Journal of Democracy*, *20*(3).

Murthy, D. (2013). *Twitter: Social Communication in the Twitter Age*. UK: Polity.

Pratt, N. (2004). Bringing Politics Back in: Examining the Link between Globalization and Democratization. *Review of International Political Economy*, *11*(2), 311–336. doi:10.1080/0969229042000249831

Price, V., & Cappella, J. N. (2002). Online deliberation and its influence: The electronic dialogue project in campaign 2000. *IT and Society*, *1*(1), 303–329.

Römmele, A. (2003). *Political Parties, Party Communication and New Information and Communication Technologies. Party Politics*, *9*(1), 7–20.

Sabah.com. (2011a, October, 13). About the additional tax hikes. [Dört Üründe ÖTV Arttı]. Retrieved from http://www.sabah.com.tr/Ekonomi/2011/10/13/otv-artti#

Sabah.com. (2011b, November, 30). About Paid Military Service Act. Retrieved from http://www.sabah.com.tr/gundem/2011/11/30/bedelli-askerlik-tasarisi-yasalasti

Saeed, S., Reichling, T., & Wulf, V. (2008a, April). Applying Knowledge Management to Support Networking among NGOs and Donors. Proceedings of the IADIS international conference on E-Society (pp. 626-628).

Saeed, S., Rohde, M., & Wulf, V. (2008b). A framework towards IT appropriation in voluntary organisations. *International Journal of Knowledge and Learning*, *4*(5), 438–451. doi:10.1504/IJKL.2008.022062

Saeed, S., Rohde, M., & Wulf, V. (2009, June). Technologies within transnational social activist communities: an ethnographic study of the European social forum. *Proceedings of the fourth international conference on Communities and technologies* (pp. 85-94). ACM. doi:10.1145/1556460.1556474

Şaylan, G. (2008). Unavoidable Crisis of Representative Democracy. In *Turkish: Temsili Demokrasinin Önlenemez Krizi*. Ankara: İmge Kitabevi.

Scheufele, D. A., & Nisbet, M. C. (2002). Being a citizen online: New opportunities and dead ends. *The Harvard International Journal of Press/Politics*, *7*(3), 55–75. doi:10.1177/1081180X0200700304

Small, T.A. (2012). What the Hashtag? A Content Analysis of Canadian Politics on Twitter. In B. D. Loader & D. Mercea (Eds.), *Social Media and Democracy* (pp. 109–128). New York: Routledge.

SMaPP. (2013). SMaPP Data Reports, A Breakout Role for Twitter? The Role of Social Media in the Turkish Protests. Retrieved from https://wp.nyu.edu/smapp/papers-and-publications/smapp-data-reports/

Socialbakers (2012). Turkey Facebook Statistics. Retrieved from http://www.socialbakers.com/Facebook-statistics/turkey

Socialbakers, (2016). Turkey Facebook Statistics. Retrieved from https://www.socialbakers.com/statistics/facebook/

Tsagarousianou, R. (1999). Electronic Democracy: Rhetoric and Reality. *Communications*, *24*(2), 189–208. doi:10.1515/comm.1999.24.2.189

Tufekci, Z. (2008). Grooming, Gossip, Facebook and Myspace. *Information Communication and Society*, *11*(4), 544–564. doi:10.1080/13691180801999050

Turk, C. N. N. (2011, April, 2). About the Code Scandal [YGS'de şifre iddiasına açıklama]. Retrieved from http://www.cnnturk.com/2011/turkiye/04/02/ygsde.sifre.iddiasina.aciklama-/611932.0/index.html

Turk, C. N. N. (2012, February, 24). About the "Law draft on prevent to the violence against woman" [Kadına karşı şiddet tasarısı Meclis'te]. Retrieved from http://www.cnnturk.com/2012/turkiye/02/24/kadina.karsi.siddet.tasarisi.mecliste/650604.0/index.html

TUSEV. (2011). The Report for Civil Society in Turkey [Türkiye'de Sivil Toplum: Bir Dönüm Noktası CIVICUS Uluslararası Sivil Toplum Endeksi Projesi (STEP) Türkiye Ülke Raporu II. TÜSEV Yayınları].

United Nations. (2008). *United Nations e-Government Survey 2008*. New York: United Nations.

United Nations. (2010). *United Nations E-Government Survey 2010*. New York: United Nations.

Vaccari, C. (2011). The News Media as Networked Political Actors. *Information Communication and Society*, *14*(7), 981–997. doi:10.1080/1369118X.2011.572984

Verba, S., Schlozman, K. L., & Brady, H. E. (1995). *Voice and Equality: Civic Voluntarism in American Politics*. Cambridge: Harvard University Press.

Wapner, P. (2004). Greenpeace and Political Globalism. In F. J. Lechner & J. Boli (Eds.), *The Globalization Reader* (pp. 377–383). USA: Blackwell.

Weber, L., Loumake, A., & Bergman, J. (2003). Who Participates and Why? An Analysis of Citizens on the Internet and the Mass Public. *Social Science Computer Review*, *21*(1), 26–42. doi:10.1177/0894439302238969

Wijkman, A. (1998). Does Sustainable Development Require Good Governance? *UN Chronicles, 35*(3).

Yıldız, M., & Demirhan, K. (2016). Analysis and Comparison of the Role of Local Governments with Other Policy Actors in Disaster Relief via Social Media: The Case of Turkey. In U. Sadioğlu & K. Dede (Eds.) Theoretical Foundations and Discussions on the Reformation Process in Local Governments (pp. 463-484). Hershey, PA, USA: IGI Global.

YSK. (2011). Yüksek Seçim Kurulu. Information about General Election in 2011 [12 Haziran 2011 XXIV. Dönem Milletvekili Genel Seçimi]. Retrieved from http://www.ysk.gov.tr/ysk/GenelSecimler.html

KEY TERMS AND DEFINITIONS

Accountability: Accountability indicates the responsibility of government for giving account to the public. It is closely related to the transparency of government agents.

Deliberative Democracy: A new model of democracy aims at improving citizens' political participation to political processes. This model consists of consensus in decision making process through critical public discussions. Therefore, the organization of civil society around public issues is an important part of deliberation.

Facebook: Facebook is a social media platform, users develop their social networks and they use it for communication, information sharing and interaction. Institutions, organizations, political parties, citizens, social groups use Facebook and it provides an area for social, political and economic activities for various users.

ICTs: Information and communication technologies providing communication among users. ICTs bring new opportunities for politics.

NGOs: Non-Governmental Organizations, become the important actors of political and social life in the process of globalization. NGOs have responsibility to develop public life. NGOs contribute to civic life and improve democracy promoting participation, accountability and transparency.

Public Opinion: The view of the public about the issues influencing all the society. Political and social agents try to influence the public opinion and manipulate it. Public opinion transforms to politics by the way of social movements, elections or civil society activities.

Social Media: All social networking platforms providing information and communication spaces. Wikis, chat rooms, discussion forums, postcards, blogs or video sharing platforms.

ENDNOTES

1. Wikis, chat rooms, discussion forums, postcards, blogs or video sharing platforms (Chadwick & Howard, 2009; Issa, 2009, pp, 249-250; UN, 2008, p. 62; UN, 2010, p. 88)
2. "About 17 million people in the Arab region are using Facebook, available in Arabic, with 5 million in Egypt alone, and demand is expected to grow on micro-blogging sites. Twitter announced it will launch its Arabic interface in 2011" (Ghannam, 2011).

Compilation of References

Acharya, A., Lavalle, A. G., & Houtzager, P. (2004). Civil Society Representation in the Participatory Budget and Deliberative Councils of São Paulo, Brazil. IDS Bulletin, 35(2), 40-48.

Achebe, C. (1983). *The Trouble with Nigeria*. Enugu, Nigeria: Fourth Dimension Publishing Company.

Ades, A., & Di Tella, R. (1999). Rents, Competition, and Corruption. *The American Economic Review*, *89*(4), 982–993. doi:10.1257/aer.89.4.982

Adibe, O., & Orji, L. (2012, November). Social media and political participation in Africa: Issues, problem and prospects. *Paper presented at the ACCE*, FUT Minna.

AFAD. (2011). The Report of Van Earthquake (Van Depremi Faaliyet Raporu). Retrieved from http://www.afad.gov.tr/

Aguinis, H., Gottfredson, R. K., & Culpepper, S. A. (2013). Best-practice recommendations for estimating cross-level interaction effects using multilevel modeling. *Journal of Management*, *39*(6), 1490–1528. doi:10.1177/0149206313478188

Aguirre, A. (2009). *ICT and Social Movements in the Philippines: From Estrada to Arroyo*. Philict Research Group.

Ahmed, F. (2013). Role of Media in Uncovering Political Corruption in South Asian Perspective. *Asian Journal of Public Affairs*, *5*(1), 20–37.

Ajayi, A. I., & Adesote, S. A. (2014). The New Social Media and consolidation of democracy in Nigeria: Uses, Potentials and Challenges. *Journal of Good Governance and Sustainable Development in Africa*, *2*(4).

Akasike. L. (2009). Corruption in Nigeria: Which Way? *Saturday Champion, 15*.

Akçay, S. (2006). Corruption and Human Development. *The Cato Journal*, *26*(1), 29–48.

Alam, M. S. (1995). A Theory of Limits on Corruption and some Applications. *Kyklos*, *48*(3), 419–435. doi:10.1111/j.1467-6435.1995.tb02323.x

Aljazeera (2016). Palestine papers. Retrieved from http://www.aljazeera.com/palestinepapers/

Allern, S., Kantola, A., Pollack, E., & Blach-Ørsten, M. (2012). Increased Scandalization. Nordic Political Scandals 1980–2010. In S. Allern & E. Pollack (Eds.), *Scandalous! The Mediated Construction of Political Scandals in Four Nordic Countries* (pp. 29–50). Gothenburg: Nordicom.

Allern, S., & Pollack, E. (2012). Mediated Scandals. In S. Allern & E. Pollack (Eds.), *Scandalous! The Mediated Construction of Political Scandals in Four Nordic Countries* (pp. 9–28). Gothenburg: Nordicom.

Allern, S., & Pollack, E. (2016). Nordic political scandals – Frequency, type and consequences. In M. Ludwig, T. Schierl, & C. Von Sikorski (Eds.), *Mediated Scandals* (pp. 146–163). Köln: Halem.

Althusser, L. (2006). *Lenin and Philosophy and Other Essays*. New Delhi: Aakar.

Amelia, A. (2008). Scandal politics in the new media environment: Analytical note. *Scandal Politics Review*, *9*(1), 75–99.

Andersen, K. N., Henriksen, H. Z., Medaglia, R., Danziger, J. N., Sannarnes, M. K., & Enemærke, M. (2010). Fads and facts of E-government: A review of impacts of E-government (2003–2009). *International Journal of Public Administration*, *33*(11), 564–579. doi:10.1080/01900692.2010.517724

Andersen, T. B. (2009). E-government as an anti-corruption strategy. *Information Economics and Policy*, *21*(3), 201–210. doi:10.1016/j.infoecopol.2008.11.003

Andersen, T. B., Bentzen, J., Dalgaard, C. J., & Selaya, P. (2011). Does the Internet Reduce Corruption? Evidence from US States and across Countries. *The World Bank Economic Review*, *25*(3), 387–417. doi:10.1093/wber/lhr025

Anduiza, E., Cantijoch, M., & Gallego, A. (2009). Political Participation and the Internet. *Information Communication and Society*, *12*(6), 860–878. doi:10.1080/13691180802282720

Andvig, J. C., Fjelstad, O., Amundsen, I., & Soreide, T. (2000). *Research on Corruption: A policy oriented survey*. Norwegian Agency for Development Co-operation.

Anti-Corruption. (2016). Catching Tigers and Flies. Retrieved from: http://anticorruption.chinafile.com/

Anyadike, D. O., EbezeUche V., & Odoemelam C. (2014). Social Media in E-Governance and Political Participation in Enugu State, Nigeria. *The International Journal of Social Sciences and Humanities Invention*, *1*(2), 80–94.

Arter, D. (2012). Big Bang Elections and Party System Change in Scandinavia: Farewell to the Enduring Party System? *Parliamentary Affairs*, *65*(4), 822–844. doi:10.1093/pa/gsr050

Asiimwe, E. N., Ake, G., & Wakabi, W. (2013). Using Technology for Enhancing Transparency and Accountability in Low Resource Communities: Experiences from Uganda. In K. Sarajeva (Ed.), *ICT for Anti-Corruption, Democracy and Education in East Africa*. Stockholm: Spider.

Assange, J., Appelbaum, J., & Muller-Maguhn, A. (2012). *Cypherpunks: Freedom and the Future of the Internet*. USA: OR Books.

Astone, N. M., Nathanson, C., Schoen, R., & Kim, Y. (1999). Family Demography, Social Theory, and Investment in Social Capital. *Population and Development Review*, *25*(1), 1–31. doi:10.1111/j.1728-4457.1999.00001.x

Ata, A. Y., & Arvas, M. A. (2011). Determinants of Economic Corruption: A Cross-Country Data Analysis. *International Journal of Business and Social Science*, *2*(13), 161–169.

Avila, R., Feigenblatt, H., Heacock, R., & Heller, N. (2010). *Global mapping of technology for transparency and accountability: New Technologies*. London: Open Society Foundation.

Axford, B. (2011). Talk About a Revolution: Social Media and the MENA Uprisings. *Globalizations*, *8*(5), 681–686. doi:10.1080/14747731.2011.621281

Ayliffe, B. (2013, September 23). *10 reasons to take action to stop Gazprom's Prirazlomnaya oil platform.* Retrieved from http://www.greenpeace.org/international/en/news/Blogs/makingwaves/10-reasons-to-take-action-to-stop-gazproms-pr/blog/46766/?expandid=b99864&entryid=46766

Bachrach, J. (2011). WikiHistory: Did the Leaks Inspire the Arab Spring? *World Affairs Journal*. Retrieved from http://www.worldaffairsjournal.org/article/wikihistory-did-leaks-inspire-arab-spring

Backus, M. (2001). E-governance and developing countries: Introduction and examples. International Institute for Communication and Development.

Badiou, P., Baldwin, R., Carlson, M., Darveau, M., Drapeau, P., Gaston, K., … Wells, J. (2014). Best Buy's Role in the Degradation of the Boreal Forest. *Borealscience.org*. Retrieved from http://borealscience.org/wp-content/uploads/2013/07/conserving-last-great-forests1.pdf

Balkin, J. M. (1999). How Mass Media Simulate Political Transparency. *Cultural Values*, *3*(4), 393–413. doi:10.1080/14797589909367175

Banerjee, A., Duflo, E., Imbert, C., Mathew, S., & Pande, R. (2014). Can E-Governance Reduce Capture of Public Programs? *Poverty Action Lab*. Retrieved from https://www.povertyactionlab.org/evaluation/enhancing-local-public-service-delivery-through-financial-reform-india%E2%80%99s-employment

Baran, S. J. (2010). *Introduction to Mass Communication, Media Literacy and Culture*. McGraw-Hills Companies Inc.

Barassi, V. (2015). *Activism on the Web: Everyday Struggle against Digital Capitalism*. New York, NY: Routledge.

Barone, E. (2015, November 23). Which countries censor the Internet? *TIME*.

Barrons, G. (2012). Suleiman: Mubarak decided to step down #egypt #jan25 OH MY GOD: examining the use of social media in the 2011 Egyptian revolution. *Contemporary Arab Affairs*, *5*(1), 54–67. doi:10.1080/17550912.2012.645669

Barry, G. (2014, August 29). *Democracy and India Protect Mahan Forest and Global Climate from Coal.* Retrieved from www.ecointernet.org

Bar-Tura, A. (2010). Wall-to-Wall or Face-to-Face. In D. E. Wittkower (Ed.), *Facebook and Philosophy* (pp. 231–239). Chicago: Open Court.

Bastos, M. T., Raimundo, R. L. G., & Travitzki, R. (2013). Gatekeeping Twitter: Message Diffusion in Political Hashtags. *Media Culture & Society*, *35*(2), 260–270. doi:10.1177/0163443712467594

Baudrillard, J. (1998). *The Consumer Society: Myths and Structures*. London: Sage.

BBOG Nigeria [BBOGNigeria] (2015, April 14). @BBOG_Nigeria#ChibokGirlsAmbassadors#365DaysOn#NeverToBeForgotten All they want is for the world to unite to #BringBackOurGirls [Tweet]. Retrieved from https://twitter.com/BBOG_Nigeria/status/587927237355302912

Bekri, D., Dunn, B., Oguzertem, I., Su, Y., & Upreti, S. (2011). *Harnessing Social Media Tools to Fight Corruption*. London.

Benhabib, S. (2006). Introduction: The Democratic Moment and the Problem of Difference. In S. Benhabib (Ed.), *Democracy and Difference: Contesting the Boundaries of the Political*. US: Princeton University.

Benkler, Y. (2013). Following the Money: WikiLeaks and the Political Economy of Disclosure. In B. Brevini, A. Hintz, & P. McCurdy (Eds.), *Beyond WikiLeaks: Implications for the Future of Communications, Journalism and Society* (pp. 11–34). UK: Palgrave Macmillan. doi:10.1057/9781137275745_2

Bennett, W. L., & Entman, R. M. (2001). Mediated Politics: An Introduction. In W. L. Bennett & R. M. Entman (Eds.), *Mediated Politics* (pp. 1–33). New York: Cambridge University Press.

Bennett, W. L., & Serrin, W. (2005). The Watchdog Role. In G. Overholser & K. H. Jamieson (Eds.), *The Press* (pp. 169–188). New York: Oxford University Press.

Benoit, W. L. (1995). *Accounts, Excuses, and Apologies: a Theory of Image Restoration Strategies*. Albany: State University of New York.

Benoit, W. L. (1997). Image Repair Discourse and Crisis Communication. *Public Relations Review*, *23*(2), 177–186. doi:10.1016/S0363-8111(97)90023-0

Bernays, E. L. (2004). *Propaganda*. Brooklyn: IG Publishing.

Bertelsman. (2016). *Shaping Change – Strategies of Development and Transformation: Philippines*. Retrieved from http://bti2006.bertelsmann-transformation-index.de/122.0.html?L=1

Bertot, J. C., Jaeger, P. T., & Grimes, J. M. (2010). Using ICTs to Create a Culture of Transparency: E-government and Social Media as Openness and Anti-corruption Tools for Societies. *Government Information Quarterly*, *27*(3), 264–271. doi:10.1016/j.giq.2010.03.001

Bertot, J. C., Jaeger, P. T., & Grimes, J. M. (2012). Promoting transparency and accountability through ICTs, social media, and collaborative e-government. *Transforming Government: People. Process and Policy*, *6*(1), 78–91.

Beyer, J. L. (2014). The Emergence of a Freedom of Information Movement: Anonymous, WikiLeaks, the Pirate Party, and Iceland. *Journal of Computer-Mediated Communication*, *19*(2), 141–154. doi:10.1111/jcc4.12050

Bhatnagar, S. (2003). E-government and Access to Information. *Global Corruption Report*, *2003*, 24–32.

Bhatnagar, S. (2003). *E-government and access to information: Global Corruption Report*. Washington, D.C.: Transparency International.

Bimber, B. (2003). *Information and American Democracy: Technology in the Evolution of Political Power*. New York, NY: Cambridge University Press. doi:10.1017/CBO9780511615573

Bimber, B., & Davis, R. (2003). *Campaigning Online: the internet in US elections*. New York: Oxford University Press.

Bjorkman, M., & Madestam, A. (2003). *Public Expenditure Tracking Survey (PETS): Primary School Pilot*. Stockholm: The World Bank.

Blank, G., & Reisdorf, B. C. (2012). The Participatory Web. *Information Communication and Society*, *15*(4), 537–554. doi:10.1080/1369118X.2012.665935

Boli, J., & Thomas, G. M. (2004). World Culture in the World Polity: A Century of International Non-Governmental Organization. In F.J. Lechner and J. Boli (Eds.), The Globalization Reader (pp. 258-264). USA: Blackwell.

Bong, S., Chung, K., Parkinson, K., Peppard, A., Rabbach, J., & Thiher, N. (2012). *Analyzing Social Media Momentum*. Workshop in International Public Affairs.

Bonsón, E., Torres, L., Royo, S., & Flores, F. (2012). Local E-government 2.0: Social Media and Corporate Transparency in Municipalities. *Government Information Quarterly*, *29*(2), 123–132. doi:10.1016/j.giq.2011.10.001

Boomgaarden, H. G., & Vliegenthart, R. (2007). Explaining the rise of anti-immigrant parties: The role of news media content. *Electoral Studies*, *26*(2), 404–417. doi:10.1016/j.electstud.2006.10.018

Borg, S. (2012). Perussuomalaiset. In S. Borg (Ed.), *Muutosvaalit 2011* (pp. 191–210). Helsinki: Oikeusministeriö.

Bos, L., Van Der Brug, W., & De Vreese, C. (2010). Media Coverage of Right-Wing Populist Leaders. *Communications*, *35*(2), 141–163. doi:10.1515/comm.2010.008

Bowen, G. A. (2009). Document Analysis as a Qualitative Research Method. *Qualitative Research Journal, 9*(2), 27–40. doi:10.3316/QRJ0902027

Bowler, S., & Karp, J. A. (2004). Politicians, Scandals, and Trust in Government. *Political Behavior, 26*(3), 271–287. doi:10.1023/B:POBE.0000043456.87303.3a

Bowman, S., & Willis, C. (2003). *We Media: How audiences are shaping the future of news and information.* Reston: The Media Center.

Boyd, D. M., & Ellison, B. N. (2007). Social Networking Sites: Definition of history and Scholarship. *Journal of Computer-Mediated Communication, 13*(1), 210–230. doi:10.1111/j.1083-6101.2007.00393.x

Breindel, Y. (2013). Assessing success in internet campaigning. *Information Communication and Society, 16*(9), 1419–1440. doi:10.1080/1369118X.2012.707673

Brevini, B., Hintz, A., & McCurdy, P. (2013). Introduction. In B. Brevini, A. Hintz, & P. McCurdy (Eds.), *Beyond WikiLeaks: Implications for the Future of Communications, Journalism and Society* (pp. 1–10). UK: Palgrave Macmillan. doi:10.1057/9781137275745_1

Brisbin, D. (1988). Electronic Revolution in the Philippines. *Journal of Popular Culture, 22*(3), 49–63. doi:10.1111/j.0022-3840.1988.2203_49.x

Bruer, A., Landman, T., & Farquhar, D. (2015). Social Media and Protest Mobilization: Evidence from the Tunisian Revolution. *Democratization, 22*(4), 764–792. doi:10.1080/13510347.2014.885505

Brundidge, J., & Rice, R. E. (2009). Political Engagement Online - Do The Information Rich Get Richer And The Like-Minded More Similar? In A. Chadwick & P. N. Howard (Eds.), *Routledge Handbook of Internet Politics.* USA: Routledge.

Brunetti, A., & Weder, B. (2003). A Free Press is Bad News for Corruption. *Journal of Public Economics, 87*(7), 1801–1824. doi:10.1016/S0047-2727(01)00186-4

Buchanan, E. A., & Zimmer, M. (2012). Internet Research Ethics. In Edward N. Zalta (Ed.), *The Stanford Encyclopedia of Philosophy* Retrieved from http://plato.stanford.edu/archives/spr2015/entries/ethics-internet-research/

Cabannes, Y. (2004). Participatory budgeting: A significant contribution to participatory democracy. *Environment and Urbanization, 16*(1), 27–46. doi:10.1177/095624780401600104

Çakır, D., & Demirhan, K. (2011). Political Character of the Social Actions in the Process of Globalization: A Case Study. *International Journal of Social Sciences and Humanity Studies*, *3*(2), 159–168.

Campos, E. J., Lien, D., & Pradhan, S. (1999). The Impact of Corruption on Investment: Predictability Matters. *World Development*, *27*(6), 1059–1067. doi:10.1016/S0305-750X(99)00040-6

Canovan, M. (1999). Trust the People! Populism and the Two Faces of Democracy. *Political Studies*, *XLVII*(1), 2–16. doi:10.1111/1467-9248.00184

Caselli, F., & Coleman, W. J. II. (2001). Cross-Country Technology Diffusion: The Case of Computers. *The American Economic Review*, *91*(2), 328–335. doi:10.1257/aer.91.2.328

Castells, M. (2008). The New Public Sphere: Global Civil Society, Communication Networks, and Global Governance. *ANNALS, AAPSS*, *616*(1), 78–92. doi:10.1177/0002716207311877

Castells, M. (2009). *The Rise of the Network Society, The Information Age: Economy, Society and Culture* (Vol. I). Malden, MA; Oxford, UK: Blackwell. doi:10.1002/9781444319514

Castells, M. (2010). *The Power of Identity* (2nd ed.). Oxford: Wiley Blackwell, Chakravartty, P., & Roy, S. (2015). Mr. Modi goes to Delhi: Mediated Populism and the 2014 Indian Elections. *Television & New Media*, *16*(4), 311–322. doi:10.1177/1527476415573957

Cecchini, S., & Scott, C. (2003). Can information and communications technology applications contribute to poverty reduction? Lessons from rural India. *Information Technology for Development*, *10*(2), 73–84. doi:10.1002/itdj.1590100203

Chadwick, A. (2006). *Internet Politics*. New York: Oxford University Press.

Chadwick, A. (2006). *Internet Politics: States, Citizens, and New Communication Technologies*. New York, NY: Oxford University Press.

Chadwick, A., & Howard, P. N. (2009). New directions in internet politics research. In A. Chadwick & P. N. Howard (Eds.), *Routledge Handbook of Internet Politics*. USA: Routledge.

Chaffey, D. (2016). Global social media research summary 2016. *Smartinsights.com*. Retrieved from http://www.smartinsights.com/social-media-marketing/social-media-strategy/new-global-social-media-research/

Chaiken, M. (2014). Poll: Americans say WikiLeaks harmed public interest; most want Assange arrested. Retrieved from http://www.washingtonpost.com/wp-dyn/content/article/2010/12/14/AR2010121401650.html

Chakrabarty, B., & Hazra, S. (2016). *Winning the Mandate: The Indian Experience*. India: SAGE Publications.

Chamberlain, G. (2014, June 28). Indian forest villagers' rise up to halt UK firm's bid to clear land for mining. *The Guardian*. Retrieved from http://www.theguardian.com/world/2014/jun/28/india-controversial-forest-coalmine-essar-energy

Chandrachud, N. (2014). *We should be Critical, But Not Dismissive of Emma Watson's UN Campaign.* Retrieved from http://www.huffingtonpost.ca/neha-chandrachud/emma-watson-un-campaign_b_5883200.html

Chang.org. (2014). CNN-IBN Citizen Journalist Show, Retrieved from https://www.change.org/en-IN/organisations/ibncj

Charron, N. (2015). Do corruption measures have a perception problem? Assessing the relationship between experiences and perceptions of corruption among citizens and experts. *European Political Science Review*, *8*(1), 147–171. doi:10.1017/S1755773914000447

Cheung, S. N. S. (1982). Will China Go 'Capitalist'? Institute of Economic Affairs.

Cheung, S. N. S. (1983). The Contractual Nature of the Firm. *The Journal of Law & Economics*, *26*(1), 1–21. doi:10.1086/467023

Christensen, C. (2011). Twitter Revolutions? Addressing Social Media and Dissent. *Communication Review*, *14*(3), 155–157. doi:10.1080/10714421.2011.597235

Christensen, C. (2013). Wave-riding and Hashtag-jumping. *Information Communication and Society*, *16*(5), 646–666. doi:10.1080/1369118X.2013.783609

CIVICUS (2005). Civil Society Index Report for Turkey. Civil Society in Turkey: An Era of Transition.

Clarke, G. (1998). Non-Governmental Organizations (NGOs) and Politics in the Developing World. *Political Studies*, *XLVI*(1), 36–52. doi:10.1111/1467-9248.00128

CNNIC. (2016). *The 37th statistical report on internet development in China*. Beijing: China Internet Network Information Center.

Coalpost.in. (2016, May 3). *Essar Mahan plant's 600 MW unit resumes power generation.* Retrieved from http://www.coalpost.in/essar-mahan-plants-600-mw-unit-resumes-power-generation/

Coase, R. H. (1960). The Problem of Social Cost. *The Journal of Law & Economics*, *26*, 1–21. doi:10.1086/466560

Cohen, W. M., Nelson, R. R., & Walsh, J. P. (2002). Links and impacts: The influence of public research on industrial R&D. *Management Science*, *48*(1), 1–23. doi:10.1287/mnsc.48.1.1.14273

Conley, T. L. (2014). From #RenishaMcBride to #RememberRenisha: Locating Our Stories and Finding Justice. *Feminist Media Studies*, *14*(6), 1111–1113. doi:10.1080/14680777.2014.975474

Coolidge, J., & Rose-Ackerman, S. (1999). Kleptocracy and Reform in African Regimes: Theory and Cases. In K. R. Hope (Ed.), *Corruption and Development in Africa: Lessons from Country Case Studies*. London: Macmillan Press.

Corruption Perceptions Index – Transparencey International. (2015). Retrieved from: http://www.transparency.org/cpi2015

Croteu, D., & Hoynes, W. (2003). *Media/Society: Industries, Images and Audiences*. London: Sage.

Dahlberg, L. (2001). The Internet and Democratic Discourse: Exploring the prospects of online deliberative forums extending the public sphere. *Information Communication and Society*, *4*(4), 615–633. doi:10.1080/13691180110097030

Dahlgren, P. (2005). The Internet, Public Spheres, and Political Communication: Dispersion and Deliberation. *Political Communication*, *22*(2), 147–162. doi:10.1080/10584600590933160

Davis, A. (2010). New media and fat democracy: The paradox of online participation. *New Media & Society*, *12*(5), 745–761. doi:10.1177/1461444809341435

Dehn, J., Reinikka, R., & Svensson, J. (2002). *Survey Tools for Assessing Service Delivery*: World Bank/ Development Research Group.

Demirhan, K. (2016). Relationship between Social Media and Political Parties: The Case of Turkey. In A. M. G. Solo (Ed.), Social Media and Networking: Concepts, Methodologies, Tools, and Applications (Vols. 1–4). pp. 1196–1225). Hershey, PA, USA: IGI Global. doi:10.4018/978-1-4666-8614-4.ch055

Demirhan, K., & Öktem, M. K. (2011). Electronic Participation in the Policy Making Process: A Case Study. *International Journal of eBusiness and eGovernment Studies, 3*(1), 59-78.

Demirhan, K. (2014). Civil Society and NGOs on Digital Era in Turkey. *Humanities and Social Sciences Review, 3*(1), 265–274.

Deutsche Welle Turkish. (2011, March, 15). About Nuclear Energy (Haber: Başak Özay, Türkiye'nin nükleer enerji açmazı) Retrieved From http://www.dw.de/dw/article/0,-14911742,00.html

Devanathan, G. (2009). e-Administration an e-Platform for e-Governance to introduce Transparency and Accountability in Governments and Organisations. *Paper presented at the Annual Meeting of the Southern Political Science Association.* Retrieved from http://citation.allacademic.com/meta/p281478_index.html

Diamond, L. (2010). Liberation Technology. *Journal of Democracy, 21*(3), 69–83. doi:10.1353/jod.0.0190

Digital News Report. (2015). How Turkey uses social media. Retrieved from http://www.digitalnewsreport.org/-essays/2015/how-turkey-uses-social-media/

DiRienzo, C. E., Das, J., Cort, K. T., & Burbridge, J. Jr. (2007). Corruption and the Role of Information. *Journal of International Business Studies, 38*(2), 320–332. doi:10.1057/palgrave.jibs.8400262

Doing Business. (2015, October 27). Index. Retrieved from http://www.doingbusiness.org/reports/global-reports/doing-business-2016

Donchev, D., & Ujhelyi, G. (2009). What Do Corruption Indices Measure? *University of Houston Economics Department Working Paper.*

Dunn, H. S. (2013). Something Old, Something New… "WikiLeaks and the Collaborating Newspapers –Exploring the Limits of Conjoint Approaches to Political Exposure. In B. Brevini, A. Hintz, & P. McCurdy (Eds.), *Beyond WikiLeaks: Implications for the Future of Communications, Journalism and Society* (pp. 85–100). UK: Palgrave Macmillan. doi:10.1057/9781137275745_6

Dutta, S., López-Claros, A., & Mia, I. (Eds.). (2015). *The Global Information Technology Report: ICTs for Inclusive Growth.* World Economic Forum.

Dyson, E. (1997). Release 2.0: A Design for Living in the Digital Age. New York: Broadway.

Eagle, R. B. (2015). Loitering, Lingering, Hashtagging: Women Reclaiming Public Space Via #BoardtheBus, #StopStreetHarassment, and the #EverydaySexism Project. *Feminist Media Studies*, *15*(2), 350–353. doi:10.1080/14680777.2015.1008748

Eaton, M. (2010). Manufacturing community in an online activist organization. *Information Communication and Society*, *13*(2), 174–192. doi:10.1080/13691180902890125

Edelman Research. (2009). *The Social Pulpit - Barack Obama's Social Media Toolkit. (Principal Author: Monte Lutz)*. SVP-Digital Public Affairs, Edelman.

EDSA People Power Revolution (2016, January 10). Philippine History. Retrieved from http://www.philippine-history.org/edsa-people-power-revolution.htm

Edwards, M. (2009). *Civil Society*. Cambridge: Polity Press.

Ekström, M., & Johansson, B. (2008). Talk scandals. *Media Culture & Society*, *30*(1), 61–79. doi:10.1177/0163443707084350

Elbahnasawy, N. G. (2014). E-government, Internet Adoption, and Corruption: An Empirical Investigation. *World Development*, *57*, 114–126. doi:10.1016/j.worlddev.2013.12.005

Emma Watson. Gender Equality is your issue too. (2014). Retrieved from http://www.unwomen.org/en/news/stories/2014/9/emma-watson-gender-equality-is-your-issue-too

Engesser, S., & Humprecht, E. (2015). Frequency or Skillfulness. *Journalism Studies*, *16*(4), 513–529. doi:10.1080/1461670X.2014.939849

Enikolopov, R., Petrova, M., & Sonin, K. (2016). Social Media and Corruption. *CEPR Discussion Paper No. DP11263*. Retrieved from http://ssrn.com/abstract=2777570

Enriquedans (2010). WikiLeaks Mass Mirroring. Retrieved from https://www.enriquedans.com/wp-content/uploads/2010/12/WikiLeaks-Mass-Mirroring-our-website.pdf

Entman, R. (2012). *Scandal and Silence: Media Responses to Presidential Misconduct*. Cambridge: Polity Press.

Essar.com. (2012, December 26). Essar Power commissions 600MW Mahan I power project [Press release]. Retrieved from http://www.essar.com/article.aspx?cont_id=ln2dNPT66RM=

Essarenergy.com. (2016). CSR. Retrieved from http://www.essarenergy.com/sustainability/csr.aspx

Ess, C. (2010). The Embodied Self in a Digital Age: Possibilities, Risks and Prospects for a Pluralistic (democratic/liberal) Future? *Nordicom Information*, *32*(2), 105–118.

Ess, C. (2011). Self, Community and Ethics in Digital Mediatized Worlds. In C. Ess & M. Thorseth (Eds.), *Trust and Virtual Worlds: Contemporary Perspectives* (pp. vii–xxix). Oxford: Peter Lang.

Essoungou, A. M. (2011). Nigeria's April elections set new records in use of social media.

Estellés-Arolas, E., & González Ladrón-de-Guevara, F. (2012). Towards an integrated crowdsourcing definition. *Journal of Information Science*, *38*(2), 189–200. doi:10.1177/0165551512437638

Expandedramblings.com. (2014, April 23). YouTube Statistics: 120 Amazing YouTube Statistics. Retrieved from http://expandedramblings.com/index.php/youtube-statistics/

Falk, R. (1999). *Predatory Globalization: A Critique*. UK: Polity.

Ferdinand, P. (2000). *The Internet, Democracy and Democratization*. London: Frank Cass Publishers.

Fiske, J. (2011). Introduction to Communication Studies (3rd ed.). New York, NY: Routledge.

Fitz, P. (2014, February 21). Social media and political scandals. *Miami.edu*. Retrieved from http://students.com.miami.edu/reporting/social-media-and-political-scandals/

Fjeldstad, O. H. (2004). *Trust in Public Finance: Citizens Views on Taxation by Local Authorities in Tanzania. Chr. Michelsen Institute*. CMI.

Floridi, L. (2011). The Informational Nature of Personal Identity. *Minds and Machines*, *21*(4), 549–566. doi:10.1007/s11023-011-9259-6

Foreignpolicy.com. (2010). Internet freedom. Retrieved from http://foreignpolicy.com/2010/01/21/internet-freedom/

Forest Products Association of Canada. (2015). *Environmental Credentials*. Retrieved from http://www.fpac.ca/sustainable-forestry/

Forestier, E., Grace, J., & Kenny, C. (2002). Can information and communication technologies be pro-poor? *Telecommunications Policy*, *26*(11), 623–646. doi:10.1016/S0308-5961(02)00061-7

Fortune (2013). Social media activism. Retrieved from http://fortune.com/2013/09/12/chinas-tragic-crackdown-on-social-media-activism/

Fox, J. (2007). Government transparency and policymaking. *Public Choice*, *131*(1-2), 23–44. doi:10.1007/s11127-006-9103-3

Fraser, N. (1992). Rethinking the Public Sphere: A Contribution to the Critique of Actually Existing Democracy. In G. Calhoun (Ed.), *Habermas and the Public Sphere* (pp. 109–142). Cambridge: The MIT Press.

Freedom House (2009a). Freedom on the Net: A Global Assessment of Internet and Digital Media.

Freedom House (2009b). Freedom of the Press 2009.

Freedom House (2015). Freedom on the Net 2015.

Frick, M., & Oberprantacher, A. (2011). Shared is Not Yet Sharing, Or: What Makes Social Networking Services Public? *International Review of Information Ethics*, *15*, 18–23.

Fung, A., & Wright, E. O. (2003). *Deepening democracy: institutional innovations in empowered participatory governance*. London: Verso.

Gaby, S., & Caren, N. (2012). Occupy Online: How cute old men and Malcolm X Recruited 400,000 U.S. Users to OWS on Facebook. *Social Movement Studies*, *11*(3-4), 367–374. doi:10.1080/14742837.2012.708858

Galtung, F., & Pope, J. (1999). The Global coalition against corruption: evaluating Transparency International. In A. Schedler, L. Diamond, & M. F. Plattner (Eds.), *The Self-Restraining State: Power and Accountability in New Democracies*. Boulder: Lynne Rienner Publishers.

Ganesh, S., & Zoller, H. M. (2012). Dialogue, Activism, and Democratic Social Change. *Communication Theory*, *22*(1), 66–91. doi:10.1111/j.1468-2885.2011.01396.x

Garcia-Murillo, M. (2013). Does a government web presence reduce perceptions of corruption? *Information Technology for Development*, *19*(2), 151–175. doi:10.1080/02681102.2012.751574

Garrard, J. (2006). Scandals: an overview. In J. Garrard & J. L. Newell (Eds.), *Scandals in past and contemporary politics* (pp. 13–29). Manchester: Manchester University Press.

Gascó-Hernández, M., Equiza-López, F., & Acevedo-Ruiz, M. (2007). *Information communication technologies and human development: Opportunities and challenges*. Hershey, PA, USA: IGI Global. doi:10.4018/978-1-59904-057-8

Gaxprom.com. (2008). Sustainability Report 2008-2009. Retrieved from http://www.gazprom.com/f/posts/71/879403/gazprom_sr_2008-2009_eng.pdf

Gazprom.com. (2016). *About Gazprom*. Retrieved from http://www.gazprom.com/about/

GCC. (2016). *The Grand Council of Cree*. Retrieved from http://www.gcc.ca/issues/paixdesbraves.php

Gerbaudo, P. (2012). *Tweets and the Streets: Social Media and Contemporary Activism*. London: Pluto Press.

Ghannam, J. (2041). Social Media in the Arab World: Leading up to the Uprisings of 2011, February 3.

Ghonkrokta, S. S., & Lather, A. S. (2007). Identification of Role of Social Audit by Stakeholders as Accountability Tool in Good Governance. *Journal of Management Research*, *7*(1), 18–26.

Gibson, M. (2014). *Can A Social Media Campaign Really #BringBackOurGirls*. Retrieved from http://time.com/90693/bringbackourgirls-nigeria-boko-haram/

Gibson, R. K., Lusoli, W., Römmele, A., & Ward, S. J. (2004). Representative democracy and the Internet. In R. K. Gibson, W. Lusoli, A. Römmele, & S. J. Ward (Eds.), *Electronic Democracy: Mobilisation, Organisation and Participation via New ICTs*. London: Routledge.

Global Voices. (2013, August 27). *Million People March Against Corruption in the Philippines*. Retrieved from https://globalvoices.org/2013/08/27/million-people-march-against-corruption-in-the-philippines/

Global Youth Anti-Corruption Network (GYAC). (2011). Global Youth Anti-Corruption Network (GYAC). Retrieved from https://www.facebook.com/GYACNetwork/

Goel, V. (2014). Facebook Tinkers with Users' Emotions in News Feed Experiment, Stirring Outcry. *The New York Times*. Retrieved from http://www.nytimes.com/2014/06/30/technology/facebook-tinkers-with-users-emotions-in-news-feed-experiment-stirring-outcry.html?_r=0

Goel, R. K., Nelson, M. A., & Naretta, M. A. (2012). The internet as an indicator of corruption awareness. *European Journal of Political Economy*, *28*(1), 64–75. doi:10.1016/j.ejpoleco.2011.08.003

Gonzales, I. C. (2010, October 6). *Philippine Public Transparency Reporting Project Too Corrupt to Change? The Battle to Reform the Bureau of Customs.* Retrieved from http://peranatinito.net/index.php?option=com_content&view=article&id=135:too-corrupt-to-change-the-battle-to-reform-the-bureau-of-customs&catid=44:stories&Itemid=94

Goodman, A., & Gonzalez, J. (2013, September 26). *Protest or Piracy? Greenpeace Activists remain jailed in Russia after boarding Arctic oil rig*. Retrieved from http://www.alternet.org/activism/protest-or-piracy-greenpeace-activists-remain-jailed-russia-after-boarding-arctic-oil-rig

Gramsci, A. (1992). *Selection from the Prison Notebooks of Antonio Gramsci* (Q. Hoare & G. N. Smith, Eds.). New York, NY: International Publishers.

Granovetter, M. (1973). The Strength of Weak Ties. *American Journal of Sociology*, *78*(6), 1360–1380. doi:10.1086/225469

Green, H. (2011). Breaking Out of Your Internet Filter Bubble. Retrieved from http://www.forbes.com/sites/work-in-progress/2011/08/29/breaking-out-of-your-internet-filter-bubble/#51d199e5e90a

Greenberg, A. (2016). 'Secret conversations:' end-to-end encryption comes to Facebook messenger. *Wired*. Retrieved from https://www.wired.com/2016/07/secret-conversations-end-end-encryption-facebook-messenger-arrived/

Greenpeace Activists and Arctic. (2015). Retrieved from twitter.com

Greenpeace and Mahan Forest. (2015) Retrieved from facebook.com

Greenpeace and Mahan Forest. (2015) Retrieved from flickr.com

Greenpeace and Mahan Forest. (2015) Retrieved from twitter.com

Greenpeace and Mahan Forest. (2015) Retrieved from youtube.com

Greenpeace Free the Artic. (2016). Retrieved from: www.greenpeace.org/freethearctic30/?fbgpi22oct2

Greenpeace international. (2016, August 1). Updates from the Arctic Sunrise activists. Retrieved from http://www.greenpeace.org/international/en/news/features/From-peaceful-action-to-dramatic-seizure-a-timeline-of-events-since-the-Arctic-Sunrise-took-action-September-18-CET/

Greenpeace Mission. (2015) Retrieved from http://www.greenpeace.org/usa/about/

Greenpeace versus Grazprom. (2015). Retrieved from facebook.com

Greenpeace versus Grazprom. (2015). Retrieved from www.flickr.com

Greenpeace versus Grazprom. (2015). Retrieved from www.youtube.com

Greenpeace versus Resolute Forest Products. (2015). Retrieved from www.facebook.com

Greenpeace versus Resolute Forest Products. (2015). Retrieved from www.flickr.com

Greenpeace versus Resolute Forest Products. (2015). Retrieved from www.twitter.com

Greenpeace versus Resolute Forest Products. (2015). Retrieved from www.youtube.com

Greenpeace.org. (2014a, November 26). *Better Buying in the Boreal Forest.* Retrieved from www.greenpeace.org

Greenpeace.org. (2014b, March 24). *The Importance of Intact Forest Areas.* Retrieved from greenpeace.org

Greenpeace.org. (2016). *Resolute Forest Product Can Save Forests and Jobs and Respect Indigenous Rights.* Retrieved February 19, 2016, from greenpeace.org

Greenpeace.org/india (2016b, May 20). Save Mahan, Our Forest, Our Rights. Retrieved from http://www.greenpeace.org/india/en/What-We-Do/Quit-Coal/save-mahan/

Greenpeace.org/india. (2016a, April 28). Greenpeace: Coal Industry Is Deepening Water Crisis in Maharashtra. Retrieved from http://www.greenpeace.org/india/en/Press/Greenpeace-Coal-Industry-Is-Deepening-Water-Crisis-in-Maharashtra/

Gronlund, A., Heacock, R., Sasaki, D., Hellstrom, J., & Al-Saqaf, W. (2010). *Increasing Transparency and Fighting: Corruption through ICT Empowering People and Communities*. Stockholm: Swedish Program for ICT in Developing Regions.

Guilfoyle, D. (2013, June 17). *Political Motivation and Piracy: What History Doesn't Teach Us About Law*. Retrieved from http://www.ejiltalk.org/political-motivation-and-piracy-what-history-doesnt-teach-us-about-law/

Guneluis, S. (2014). *10 Blog Metrics Bloggers Should Track Through Web Analytics Tools*. Retrieved from http://weblogs.about.com/od/addonsandplugins/tp/10-Blog-Metrics-Bloggers-Should-Track-Through-Web-Analytics-Tools.htm

Gupta, S., Davoodi, H., & Alonso-Terme, R. (2002). Does Corruption Affect Income Inequality and Poverty? *Economics of Governance*, *3*(1), 23–45. doi:10.1007/s101010100039

Habermas, J. (1989). *Structural Transformation of the Public Sphere*. Oxford: Polity Press.

Habermas, J. (1991). *The Structural Transformation of the Public Sphere*. USA: MIT Press.

Habermas, J. (1994). *The Theory of Communicative Action*. Boston: Beacon Press.

Habermas, J. (2006). Three Normative Models of Democracy. In S. Benhabib (Ed.), *Democracy and Difference: Contesting the Boundaries of the Political*. US: Princeton University.

Habib, M., & Zurawicki, L. (2002). Corruption Differentials and Foreign Direct Investment. *Journal of International Business Studies*, *33*(2), 291–308. doi:10.1057/palgrave.jibs.8491017

Hale, H. E. (2013). Did the Internet Break the Political Machine? Moldova's 2009 "Twitter Revolution that Wasn't". *Demokratizatsiya (Washington, D.C.)*, *21*(4), 481–505.

Hallin, D., & Mancini, P. (2004). *Comparing Media Systems: Three Models of Media and Politics*. Cambridge: Cambridge University Press. doi:10.1017/CBO9780511790867

Halpern, D., & Gibbs, J. L. (2013). Social media as a catalyst for online deliberation? Exploring the affordances of Facebook and YouTube for political expression. *Computers in Human Behavior*, *29*(3), 1159–1168. doi:10.1016/j.chb.2012.10.008

Hampton, K., Rainie, L., Lu, W., Dwyer, M., Shin, I., & Purcell, K. (2014). Social Media and the 'Spiral of Silence'. *Pew Research Center Policy Paper.* Retrieved from http://www.pewinternet.org/2014/08/26/social-media-and-the-spiral-of-silence/

Hanifan, L. J. (1916). The Rural School Community Center. *The Annals of the American Academy of Political and Social Science*, *67*(1), 130–138. doi:10.1177/000271621606700118

Harris, A. L., Lang, M., Yates, D., & Kruck, S. E. (2011). Incorporating ethics and social responsibility in IS education. *Journal of Information Systems Education*, *22*(3), 183–189.

Hatakka, N. (2016). When logics of party politics and online activism collide: The populist Finns Partys identity under negotiation. *New Media & Society*. doi:10.1177/1461444816660728

Hauben, M., & Hauben, R. (1997). *Netizens*. London: Wiley / IEEE Computer Society Press.

Heeks, R. B. (2001). Building e-Governance for Development. Retrieved from http://www.man.ac.uk/idpm/idpm_dp.htm#ig

Helander, V. (1971). *Vennamolaisuus populistisena joukkoliikkeenä*. Hämeenlinna: Karisto.

Held, D., McGrew, A., Goldblatt, D., & Perraton, J. (1999). *Global Transformations*. US: Standford University.

Helen, N. E., Charles, O.O. & Jenifer. N. O. (2014). The Use of Social Networking Sites among the Undergraduate Students of University of Nigeria, Nsukka. *Library Philosophy and Practice*.

Herkman, J. (2016a, April). *Neo-populist Scandal: The Nordic Case*. Paper presented at the first international conference of scandalogy in Bamberg, Germany.

Herkman, J. (2015). The Life Cycle Model and Press Coverage of Nordic Populist Parties. *Journalism Studies*. doi:10.1080/1461670X.2015.1066231

Herkman, J. (2016b). Populistiskandaalit: Esimerkkeinä Halla-ahon ja Immosen tapaukset. *Sosiologia*, *53*(4), 238-256.

Hindman, M. (2009). *The Myth of Digital Democracy*. Princeton, NJ: Princeton University Press.

Hintz, A. (2013). Dimensions of Modern Freedom of Expression: WikiLeaks, Policy Hacking, and Digital Freedoms. In B. Brevini, A. Hintz, & P. McCurdy (Eds.), *Beyond WikiLeaks: Implications for the Future of Communications, Journalism and Society* (pp. 146–165). UK: Palgrave Macmillan. doi:10.1057/9781137275745_9

Hirschman, A. O. (1967). *Development Economics Observed*. Washington, DC: Brookings Institution.

Hirschman, A. O. (1970). *Exit, Voice and Loyalty: Responses to Decline in Firms, Organizations and States*. Cambridge: Harvard University Press.

Holbert, R. L., & Benoit, W. L. (2009). A theory of political campaign media connectedness. *Communication Monographs*, *76*(3), 303–332. doi:10.1080/03637750903074693

Hong, S. (2013). Who benefits from Twitter? Social media and political competition in the U.S. House of Representatives. *Government Information Quarterly*, *30*(4), 464–472. doi:10.1016/j.giq.2013.05.009

Hoque, S. M. S. (2005). E-governance in Bangladesh: A scrutiny from the citizens' perspective. In R. Ahmad (Ed.), *The role of public administration in building a harmonious society*. Beijing: Asian Development Bank.

Howard, P. N., Duffy, A., Freelon, D., Hussain, M. M., Mari, W., & Maziad, M. (2011). Opening Closed Regimes: What was the Role of Social Media during the Arab Spring? Retrieved from http://ssrn.com/abstract=2595096

Howe, J. (2009). *Crowdsourcing: Why the Power of the Crowd Is Driving the Future of Business*. London: Random House Business.

Hrw.org. (2016). *Thailand: New whitewash of 2010 political violence*. Retrieved from https://www.hrw.org/news/2016/01/07/thailand-new-whitewash-2010-political-violence

Huntington, S. (1968). *Political Order in Changing Societies*. New Haven: Yale University Press.

Husted, B. W. (1999). Wealth, Culture and Corruption. *Journal of International Business Studies*, *30*(2), 339–359. doi:10.1057/palgrave.jibs.8490073

I Paid a Bribe (2016). *I Paid a Bribe*. Retrieved from http://www.ipaidabribe.com/#gsc.tab=0F

Ibrahim, O. S. (2013). Deepening Democratic Culture in Nigeria: What Role(S) For New Media? *IOSR Journal of Humanities and Social Science*, *15*(4), 86-91.

Idakwo, L. (2011). The use of social media among Nigerian youths: An exploratory research into the usage habits of social media users in Nigeria. *Political Science Quarterly*, *31*, 182–188.

ipaidabribe.com. (2016). About I Paid a Bribe. Retrieved from http://www.ipaidabribe.or.ug/about-i-paid-bribe

Issa, B. A. (2009). eParticipation. eTransformation in Public Administration: From eGovernment to eGovernance. In T.K. Bensghir (Ed.) *The Proceedings of International Conference on eGovernment Sharing Experiences,* Ankara: TODAİE.

ITU. (2011). Van Eartquake. Retrieved from http://web.itu.edu.tr/~eedmi/Van2011Eq/

Jaeger, P. T., & Bertot, J. C. (2010). Transparency and technological change: Ensuring equal and sustained public access to government information. *Government Information Quarterly*, *27*(4), 371–376. doi:10.1016/j.giq.2010.05.003

Jenkins, H. (2008). *Convergence Culture: Where the Old and New Media Collide.* New York: New York University Press.

Jenkins, H. (2009). *Confronting the Challenges of Participatory Culture Media Education for the 21st Century*. Cambridge: The MIT Press.

Jenkins, H., Ford, S., & Green, J. (2013). *Spreadable Media: Creating Value and Meaning in a Networked Culture*. New York, NY: New York University Press.

Jenssen, A. T., & Fladmoe, A. (2012). Ten Commandments for the Scandalization of Political Opponents. In S. Allern & E. Pollack (Eds.), *Scandalous! The Mediated Construction of Political Scandals in Four Nordic Countries* (pp. 51–71). Gothenburg: Nordicom.

Jha, C. K. (2014). Can Social Media and Internet Help Reduce Corruption? *Ideas for India.* Retrieved from http://ideasforindia.in/article.aspx?article_id=353

Jha, C. K., & Sarangi, S. (2014). Social Media, Internet and Corruption. Retrieved from http://ssrn.com/abstract=2391904

Jimenez, F. (2004). The Politics of Scandal in Spain: Morality Plays, Social Trust, and the Battle for Public Opinion. *The American Behavioral Scientist*, *47*(8), 1099–1121. doi:10.1177/0002764203262279

John, A. (2014). *What's Wrong With Our Well-Intentioned Boko Haram Coverage.* Retrieved from http://www.thewire.com/politics/2014/05/whats-wrong-with-our-well-intentioned-boko-haram-coverage/361993/

Jorgenson, D. W. (2001). Information Technology and the US Economy. *The American Economic Review*, *91*(1), 1–32. doi:10.1257/aer.91.1.1

Joshi, A., & Houtzager, P. P. (2012). Widgets or watchdogs? Conceptual explorations in social accountability. *Public Management Review*, *14*(2), 145–162. doi:10.1080/14719037.2012.657837

Jungar, A.-C., & Jupskås, A. R. (2014). Populist Radical Right Parties in the Nordic Region: A New and Distinct Party Family? *Scandinavian Political Studies*, *37*(3), 215–238. doi:10.1111/1467-9477.12024

Kaiman, J. (2014). Hong Kong's umbrella revolution. *The Guardian*. Retrieved from http://www.theguardian.com/world/2014/sep/30/-sp-hong-kong-umbrella-revolution-pro-democracy-protests

Kalaycıoğlu, E. (2008). *The Reinforcement of Democracy in Turkey (in Turkish, Türkiye'de Demokrasi'nin Pekişmesi: Bir Siyasal Kültür Sorunu - Ergun Özbudun'a Armağan)*. Yetkin Yayınevi.

Kamukampi. (2011). Government Camp 2.0 Turkey. Retrieved from http://www.kamukampi.com/en

Kaplan, A. M., & Haenlein, M. (2010). Users of the world, unite! The challenges and opportunities of social media. *Business Horizons*, *53*(1), 61. doi:10.1016/j.bushor.2009.09.003

Kaufmann, D., Kraay, A., & Mastruzzi, M. (2010). *The Worldwide Governance Indicators: A Summary of Methodology, Data and Analytical Issues*. World Bank Policy Research Working Paper.

Kaufmann, D. (2003). *Rethinking Governance: Empirical Lessons Challenging Orthodoxy*. Washington, D. C: World Bank.

Keliher, M., & Wu, H. (2015). How to discipline 90 million people. *The Atlantic*. Retrieved from http://www.theatlantic.com/international/archive/2015/04/xi-jinping-china-corruption-political-culture/389787/

Keller, J. M. (2014). Fiercely Real? Tyra Banks and the making of new media celebrity. *Feminist Media Studies*, *14*(1), 147–164. doi:10.1080/14680777.2012.740490

Khaldarova, I., Laaksonen, S.-M., & Matikainen, J. (2012). *The use of social media in the Finnish Parliament Elections 2011*. Helsinki: Communication Research Centre, University of Helsinki.

Khoja-Moolji, S. (2015). Becoming an Intimate Publics: Exploring the Affective Intensities of Hashtag Feminism. *Feminist Media Studies*, *15*(2), 347–350. doi:10.1080/14680777.2015.1008747

Kim, J. N., & Sriramesh, K. (2009). A descriptive model of activism in global public relations research and practice. In K. Sriramesh & D. Vercic (Eds.), *The global public relations Handbook* (Rev. ed., pp. 79–97). New York: Routledge.

Kim, P. S., Halligan, J., Cho, N., Oh, C. H., & Eikenberry, A. M. (2005). Toward Participatory and Transparent Governance: Report on the Sixth Global Forum on Reinventing Government. *Public Administration Review*, *65*(6), 646–654. doi:10.1111/j.1540-6210.2005.00494.x

Kim, T. (2015). Defining the Occupy Movement: Visual Analysis of Facebook Profile Images Posted by Local Occupy Movement Groups. *Visual Communication Quarterly*, *22*(3), 174–186. doi:10.1080/15551393.2015.1069192

King, G., Pan, J., & Roberts, M. E. (2013). How censorship in China allows government criticism but silences collective expression. *The American Political Science Review*, *107*(2), 326–343. doi:10.1017/S0003055413000014

Klitgaard, R. (1988). *Controlling Corruption*. Berkeley: University of California Press.

Knack, S., & Keefer, P. (1995). Institutions and Economic Performance: Cross-Country Tests Using Alternative Institutional Measures. *Economics and Politics*, *7*(3), 207–227. doi:10.1111/j.1468-0343.1995.tb00111.x

Knack, S., & Keefer, P. (1997). Does Social Capital Have an Economic Payoff? A Cross-Country Investigation. *The Quarterly Journal of Economics*, *112*(4), 1251–1288. doi:10.1162/003355300555475

Kohn, A. (2015). Instagram as a naturalized propaganda tool: The Israel Defense Forces Web site and the phenomenon of shared values. *Convergence (London)*, *1*(18), 1–17. doi:10.1177/1354856515592505

Kolstad, I., & Wiig, A. (2009). Is transparency the key to reducing corruption in resource-rich countries? *World Development*, *37*(3), 521–532. doi:10.1016/j.worlddev.2008.07.002

Koopmans, R., & Muis, J. (2009). The Rise of Right-wing Populist Pim Fortuyn in the Netherlands: A Discursive Opportunity Approach. *European Journal of Political Research*, *48*(5), 642–664. doi:10.1111/j.1475-6765.2009.00846.x

Kriewald, L. (2012). *The Power of Social Media*. Retrieved from http://engineering.tamu.edu/research/2012/the-power-of-social-media

Krotoski, A. (2011). WikiLeaks and the New, Transparent World Order. *The Political Quarterly*, *84*(4).

Krueger, B. S. (2002). Assessing the Potential of Internet Political Participation in the United States: A Resource. *American Politics Research*, *30*(5), 476–498. doi:10.1177/1532673X02030005002

Kumari, D. L., & Kumari, K. S. (2016). Public Distribution System in India: An Overview. *Indian Journal of Applied Research*, *5*(5).

Kuriyan, R., Bailur, S., Gigler, S., & Park, K. (2011). *Technologies for transparency and accountability: Implications for ICT policy and implementation*. Washington, DC: World Bank.

Lamont, T. (2016). Life after the Ashley Madison affair. Retrieved from https://www.theguardian.com/technology/2016/feb/28/what-happened-after-ashley-madison-was-hacked

Lau, B. T., & Sim, C. H. (2003). Exploring the extent of ICT adoption among secondary school Teachers in Malaysia. *International Journal of Computing and ICT Research*, *2*(2), 19–36.

Lea, M., O'Shea, T., Fung, P., & Spears, R. (1992). 'Flamig' in computer-mediated communication. In M. Lea (Ed.), *Contexts of Computer-Mediated Communication* (pp. 89–112). New York: Harvester Wheatsheaf.

Lear, J. (1998). *Open Minded*. Cambridge: Harvard University Press.

Lee, F. L. F., & Chan, J. M. (2016). Digital media activities and mode of participation in a protest campaign: A study of the Umbrella Movement. *Information Communication and Society*, *19*(1), 4–22. doi:10.1080/1369118X.2015.1093530

Lee, H., Oh, S., & Shim, Y. (2005). Do we need broadband? Impacts of broadband in Korea. *Info*, *7*(4), 47–56. doi:10.1108/14636690510607295

Lee, M. H., & Lio, M. C. (2016). The impact of information and communication technology on public governance and corruption in China. *Information Development*, *32*(2), 127–141. doi:10.1177/0266666914529293

Leff, N. H. (1964). Economic Development through Bureaucratic Corruption. *The American Behavioral Scientist*, *8*(3), 8–14. doi:10.1177/000276426400800303

Lenhart, A. (2015). *Teens, Social Media & Technology Overview 2015*. Washington, DC: Pew Research Center.

Lietsala, K., & Sirkkunen, E. (2008). Social Media. Introduction to the tools and processes of participatory economy. Tampere: University of Tampere.

Light, B., & McGrath, K. (2010). Ethics and social networking sites: A disclosive analysis of Facebook. *Information Technology & People*, *23*(4), 290–311. doi:10.1108/09593841011087770

Lio, M.-C., Liu, M.-C., & Ou, Y.-P. (2011). Can the Internet Reduce Corruption? A Cross-country Study based on Dynamic Panel Data Models. *Government Information Quarterly*, *28*(1), 47–53. doi:10.1016/j.giq.2010.01.005

Loader, B. D., & Mercea, D. (2011). Networking Democracy? *Information Communication and Society*, *14*(6), 757–769. doi:10.1080/1369118X.2011.592648

Loken, M. (2014). #BringBackOurGirls and the Invisibility of Imperialism. *Feminist Media Studies*, *14*(6), 1100–1101. doi:10.1080/14680777.2014.975442

Lorentzen, P. (2014). China's Strategic Censorship. *American Journal of Political Science*, *58*(2), 402–414. doi:10.1111/ajps.12065

Lowi, T. (1988). Foreword. In A. S. Markovits & M. Silverstein (Eds.), *The Politics of Scandal: Power and Process in Liberal Democracies* (pp. vii–xii). New York: Holmes & Meier.

Lu, J., Aldrich, J., & Shi, T. (2014). Revisiting media effects in authoritarian societies: Democratic conceptions, collectivistic norms, and media access in urban China. *Politics & Society*, *42*(2), 253–283. doi:10.1177/0032329213519423

Lull, J., & Hinerman, S. (1997). *Media Scandals: Morality and Desire in the Popular Culture Marketplace*. Cambridge: Polity Press.

Macintosh, A. (2004). Characterizing E-Participation in Policy-Making.*Proceedings of the 37th Hawaii International Conference on System Sciences*.

Macrae, J. (1982). Underdevelopment and the Economics of Corruption: A Game Theory Approach. *World Development*, *10*(8), 677–687. doi:10.1016/0305-750X(82)90093-6

Madden, M. (2010). *Older Adults and Social Media*. Washington, DC: Pew Research Center.

Mainville, N. (2015, November 15). *Boreal forest: Cree struggle to save the Broadback goes global*. Retrieved from greenpeace.org

Ma, L. (2013). The diffusion of government microblogging: Evidence from Chinese municipal police bureaus. *Public Management Review*, *15*(2), 288–309. doi:10.1080/14719037.2012.691010

Ma, L. (2014). Diffusion and assimilation of government microblogging: Evidence from Chinese cities. *Public Management Review*, *16*(2), 274–295. doi:10.1080/14719037.2012.725763

Ma, L. (2016). Performance feedback, government goal-setting, and aspiration level adaptation: Evidence from Chinese provinces. *Public Administration*, *94*(2), 452–471. doi:10.1111/padm.12225

Ma, L., & Zhang, Z. (2015). Microblogging (weibo) and environmental nonprofit organizations in China: The case of urban air pollution monitoring campaign. In H. Asencio & R. Sun (Eds.), *Cases on strategic social media utilization in the nonprofit sector* (pp. 94–121). Hershey, PA, USA: IGI Global. doi:10.4018/978-1-4666-8188-0.ch004

Malala Fund [MalalFund], (2015, April 13). #LISTEN: Malala Reads Her Letter to the Abducted Chibok Schoolgirls.

Manion, M. (2004). *Corruption by design: Building clean government in mainland China and Hong Kong*. Cambridge, MA: Harvard University Press.

Manion, M. (2016). Taking China's anticorruption campaign seriously. *Economic and Political Studies*, *4*(1), 3–18. doi:10.1080/20954816.2016.1152094

Manrique, C. G., & Manrique, G. G. (2009). The Global Digital Divide: What the Indices Reveal. *Paper presented at theAmerican Political Science Association Meeting*, Toronto, Canada.

Mansfield-Devine, S. (2015, September). The Ashley Madison Affair. *Network Security*, *2015*(9), 8–15. doi:10.1016/S1353-4858(15)30080-5

Margolis, M., Resnick, D., & Wolfe, J. (1999). Party Competition on the Internet in the United States and Britain. *The International Journal of Press/Politics*, *4*(4), 24–47. doi:10.1177/1081180X9900400403

Marturano, A. (2011). The Ethics of Online Social Networks—an Introduction. *International Review of Information Ethics*, *16*, 3–5.

Marwick, A., & Boyd, D. (2011). To see and be seen: Celebrity Practice on Twitter. *Convergence*, *17*(2), 139–158. doi:10.1177/1354856510394539

Mauro, P. (1995). Corruption and Growth. *The Quarterly Journal of Economics, 110*(3), 681–712. doi:10.2307/2946696

Maxfield, M. (2015). History retweeting itself: Imperial feminist appropriations of "Bring Back Our Girls". *Feminist Media Studies*. doi:10.1080/14680777.2015.1116018

Mazzoleni, G. (2008). Populism and the Media. In D. Albertazzi & D. McDonnell (Eds.), Twenty-First Century Populism: The Spectre of Western European Democracy (pp. 49-64). Hamphshire: Palgrave Macmillan. doi:10.1057/9780230592100_4

Mazzoleni, G. (2003). The Media and the Growth of Neo-Populism in Contemporary Democracies. In G. Mazzoleni, J. Stewart, & B. Horsfield (Eds.), *The Media and Neo-Populism: A Contemporary Comparative Analysis* (pp. 1–20). Westport: Praeger.

McCarthy, M. T. (2015). Toward a Free Information Movement. *Sociological Forum, 30*(2), 439–458. doi:10.1111/socf.12170

McGee, R., & Gaventa, J. (2010). *Review of Impact and Effectiveness of Accountability and Transparency Initiatives: Synthesis Report*. London: Department for International Development.

McGrath, B. (2013). 7 Ways to improve your social media engagement. *Social Media Examiner*. Retrieved from http://www.socialmediaexaminer.com/7-ways-to-improve-your-social-media-engagement/

Mcluhan, M. (2001). *Understanding Media*. New York: Routledge.

McMullan, M. (1961). A Theory of Corruption Based on a Consideration of Corruption in the Public Services and Governments of British Colonies and ex-Colonies in West Africa. *The Sociological Review, 9*(2), 181–201. doi:10.1111/j.1467-954X.1961.tb01093.x

McQuail, D. (2010). *Theories of Mass Communication* (6th ed.). Sage Publications.

Mesežnikov, G., Gyárfášova, O., & Smilov, D. (2008). *Populist Politics and Liberal Democracy in Central and Eastern Europe*. Bratislava: Institute for Public Affairs.

Milliyet (2011, December, 24). About the "Retirement Fund Law" [Bir gecede iki zam = 20 bin TL]. Retrieved from http://siyaset.milliyet.com.tr/bir-gecede-iki-zam-20-bin-tl/siyaset/siyasetdetay/24.12.2011/1479653/default.htm

Miltner, K. M., & Baym, N. K. (2015). The Selfie of the Year of the Selfie: Reflections on a Media Scandal. *International Journal of Communication, 9*, 1701–1715.

Mirandilla, M. P. (2009). *Cyber campaigning for 2010: The Use and Effectiveness of Websites and Social Networking Sites as Campaign Platforms for the 2010Presidential Election in the Philippines.* Canada: IDRC.

Morozov, E. (2009). Iran: Downside to the Twitter Revolution. DISSENT Retrieved from http://www.evgenymorozov.com/morozov_twitter_dissent.pdf

Mouffe, C. (2005). *On the Political.* USA: Routledge.

Mudde, C. (2007). *Populist radical right parties in Europe.* Cambridge: Cambridge University Press. doi:10.1017/CBO9780511492037

Mudde, C., & Kaltwasser, C. R. (2012). Populism and (liberal) democracy: a framework for analysis. In C. Mudde & C. R. Kaltwasser (Eds.), *Populism in Europe and the Americas: Threat of Corrective for Democracy?* (pp. 1–26). Cambridge: Cambridge University Press. doi:10.1017/CBO9781139152365.002

Mufson, S. (2015). This documentary went viral in China. Then it was censored. It won't be forgotten. *Washington Post.* Retrieved from https://www.washingtonpost.com/news/energy-environment/wp/2015/03/16/this-documentary-went-viral-in-china-then-it-was-censored-it-wont-be-forgotten/?utm_term=.fdbb8ae67fb4

Mungiu-Pippidi, A., & Munteanu, I. (2009). Moldova's "twitter revolution". *Journal of Democracy, 20*(3).

Murthy, D. (2011). Twitter: Microphone for the Masses. *Media Culture & Society, 33*(5), 779–789. doi:10.1177/0163443711404744

Murthy, D. (2013). *Twitter: Social Communication in the Twitter Age.* UK: Polity.

Myrdal, G. (1970). *The challenge of world poverty: a world anti-poverty program in outline.* New York: Pantheon Books.

Narayan, D., & Pritchett, L. (1999). Cents and Sociability: Household Income and Social Capital in Rural Tanzania. *Economic Development and Cultural Change, 47*(4), 871–897. doi:10.1086/452436

National Geographic (2016). *Caribou.* Retrieved from http://animals.nationalgeographic.com/animals/mammals/caribou/

National Integrity Action. (2013). Building Integrity…A Work in Progress. Retrieved from https://www.niajamaica.org/publications/NIA%202nd%20Year%20Gleaner%20Supplement.pdf

National Wildlife Federation. (2016). *Accounting for the Costs of Coal.* Retrieved from https://www.nwf.org/What-We-Do/Energy-and-Climate/Climate-and-Energy/Reduce-Fossil-Fuel-Reliance/Accounting-for-Coal

Navetta, D. (2011). The Legal Implications of Social Networking: The Basics. Retrieved from http://www.infolawgroup.com/articles/social-networking/the-legal-implications-ofsocial-networking-the-basics-part-one/

Ndou, V. (2004). E-government for developing countries: Opportunities and challenges. *The Electronic Journal of Information Systems in Developing Countries, 18*(1), 1–24.

Neumayer, E. (2003). *The pattern of aid giving: The impact of good governance on development assistance*. London: Routledge. doi:10.4324/9780203986837

Newley. (2011). *Social media and Thailand's red shirt protests.* Retrieved from http://newley.com/2011/01/25/social-media-and-thailand%E2%80%99s-red-shirt-protests/

Niemi, M. K. (2013). The True Finns Identity Politics and Populist Leadership on the Threshold of the Party's Electoral Triumph. *Javnost – The Public, 20*(3), 77–92.

North, D. C. (1990). *Institutions, Institutional Change, and Economic Performance*. Cambridge: Cambridge University Press. doi:10.1017/CBO9780511808678

North, D. C. (2005). *Understanding the Process of Economic Change*. Princeton: Princeton University Press. doi:10.1515/9781400829484

Nye, J. S. (1967). Corruption and Political Development: A Cost-Benefit Analysis. *The American Political Science Review, 61*(2), 417–427. doi:10.2307/1953254

Odoemelam, C. C., & Adibe, K. N. (2012). The role of social media in political conflicts and political communication in Africa. In D. Wilson (Ed). The Media, Terrorism & Political Communication in Nigeria. Lagos: African Council for Communication Education (ACCE).

Ogunlesi, T. (2014). *Hijacking Nigeria's #BringBackOurGirls campaign: Why does the West assume a tweet can fix Africa's problems.* Retrieved from http://www.aljazeera.com/indepth/opinion/2014/10/hijacking-nigeria-bringback-our-201410221354914 8465.html

Okachie, L. (2012). The Anti-Corruption Fight. In *Nigeria: How well So Far?* National Mirror.

Okeke, R. C. (2014). Anatomy of the Nigerian elite: Interrogating a blind elite model of the elite theory. *European Scientific Journal*, *10*(4), 320–336.

Okoro, N., & Kenneth, A. N. (2013). Social Media and Political Participation in Nigeria during the 2011 general elections: The lapses and the lessons. *Global Journal of Arts Humanities and Social Sciences*, *1*(3), 29–46.

Okunna, C. S., & Omenugha, K. A. (2012). *Introduction to Mass Communication* (3rd ed.). New Generation Books.

Oliner, S. D., & Sichel, D. E. (2000). The Resurgence of Growth in the Late 1990s: Is Information Technology the Story? *The Journal of Economic Perspectives*, *14*(4), 3–22. doi:10.1257/jep.14.4.3

Olson, C. C. (2016). #BringBackOurGirls: Digital communities supporting real-world change and influencing mainstream media agendas. *Feminist Media Studies*. doi:10.1080/14680777.2016.1154887

Olsson, T. (2008). The Practices of Internet Networking – A Resource for Alternative Political Movements. *Information Communication and Society*, *11*(5), 659–674. doi:10.1080/13691180802126760

Opoku-Mensah, A. (2000). ICTs as tools of democratization: African women speak out. In E. M. Rathgeber & E. O. Adera (Eds.), *Gender and the information revolution in Africa*. Ottawa: International Development Research Centre.

Ormont, L. (1995). A View of the Rise of Modern Group Analysis. *Modern Psychoanalysis*, *21*, 31–42.

Oye, N. D. (2013). Reducing Corruption in African Developing Countries: The Relevance of E-Governance. *Greener Journal of Social Sciences*, *3*(1), 6–13. doi:10.15580/GJSS.2013.1.103112183

Paloheimo, H. (2012). Populismi Puoluejärjestelmän vedenjakajana. In S. Borg (Ed.), *Muutosvaalit 2011* (pp. 324–344). Helsinki: Oikeusministeriö.

Papandrea, M. R. (2007). Citizen Journalism and the Reporter's Privilege. *Minnesota Law Review*, *91*, 515–591.

Pathak, R. D., & Prasad, R. S. (2005). Role of e-governance in tackling corruption: The Indian experience. In R. Ahmad (Ed.), *The role of public administration in building a harmonious society*. Beijing: Asian Development Bank.

Pathak, R. D., Singh, G., Belwal, R., Naz, R., & Smith, R. F. I. (2008). E-governance, corruption and public service delivery: A comparative study of Fiji and Ethiopia. *Journal of Administration & Governance*, *3*(1), 65–79.

Pathak, R. D., Singh, G., Belwal, R., & Smith, R. F. I. (2007). E-governance and corruption-development issues in Ethiopia. *Public Organization Review*, *7*(3), 195–208. doi:10.1007/s11115-007-0031-6

Pelucio, L. (2015). Unfaithful narratives: methodological and affective notes about experiences of masculinity in a dating website for married people. *Cadernos Pagu, 44,* 31-60. doi.10.1590/1809-4449201500440031

Perral, D. (2016). *EDSA 2*. Retrieved from https://www.scribd.com/doc/61265052/edsa-2

Pertierra, R. (2012). *The New Media, Society & Politics in the Philippines*. Berlin: Fesmedia Asia.

Pertierra, R., Ugarte, E., Pingol, A., Hernandez, J., & Dacanay, N. (2002). *Texting Selves: Cellphones & Philippine Modernity*. Manila: De La Salle University Press.

Pew Research. (2014, February 3). Six New Facts about Facebook Retrieved from http://www.pewresearch.org/fact-tank/2014/02/03/6-new-facts-about-facebook/

Pewresearchcenter.org (2013, December 27). Social Networking Fact Sheet. Retrieved from pewresearchcenter.org

Phillips, L. M. & Brabham, D. C. 2012. How today's digital landscape redefines the notion of power in public relations. *Prism, 9*(2).

Platform.reprisk.com. (2013). Special Report: Arctic Drilling. Retrieved from https://platform.reprisk.com/downloads/specialreports/32/Arctic Drilling Special Report.pdf

Porter, J. (2008). *Designing for the Social Web*. New Riders Press.

Porumbescu, G. A. (2013). Assessing the link between online mass media and trust in government: Evidence from Seoul, South Korea. *Policy & Internet*, *5*(4), 418–443. doi:10.1002/1944-2866.POI346

Porumbescu, G. A. (2015). Using transparency to enhance responsiveness and trust in local government: Can it work? *State & Local Government Review*, *47*(3), 205–213. doi:10.1177/0160323X15599427

Powell, T. (2012). Unleashing the power of social media to improve employee productivity. *CPA Practice Management Forum, 8*(7), 7-12.

Pratt, N. (2004). Bringing Politics Back in: Examining the Link between Globalization and Democratization. *Review of International Political Economy, 11*(2), 311–336. doi:10.1080/0969229042000249831

Price, V., & Cappella, J. N. (2002). Online deliberation and its influence: The electronic dialogue project in campaign 2000. *IT and Society, 1*(1), 303–329.

Qin, B., Strömberg, D., & Wu, Y. (2016). The Political Economy of Social Media in China.

Radsch, C. (2013). The Revolutions will be Blogged: Cyberactivism and the 4th Estate in Egypt [Unpublished Doctoral Dissertation]. American University.

Rafael, V. L. (2003). The Cell Phone and the Crowd: Messianic Politics in the Contemporary Philippines. *Public Culture, 15*(3), 399–425. doi:10.1215/08992363-15-3-399

Rahimi, B. (2011). The Agonistic Social Media: Cyberspace in the Formation of Dissent and Consolidation of State Power in Postelection Iran. *Communication Review, 14*(3), 158–178. doi:10.1080/10714421.2011.597240

Rahman, H. (2007). *Information and communication technologies for economic and regional developments*. Hershey, PA, USA: IGI Global. doi:10.4018/978-1-59904-186-5

Rambukkana, N. (2015). *Hashtag Publics: The Power and Politics of Discursive Networks*. New York, NY: Peter Lang. doi:10.3726/978-1-4539-1672-8

Reestorff, C. M. (2014). Mediatised Affective Activism: The Activist Imaginary and the Topless Body in the Femen Movement. *Convergence, 20*(4), 478–495. doi:10.1177/1354856514541358

Relly, J. E., & Sabharwal, M. (2009). Perceptions of transparency of government policymaking: A cross-national study. *Government Information Quarterly, 26*(1), 148–157. doi:10.1016/j.giq.2008.04.002

Remi, C. O. & Idike, A. N. (2016). The Dialectics of Political Economy and elite Corruption in a Postcolonial State: a Nigerian case study. *Arabian Journal of Business and Management Review, 5*(7).

Resolute Forest Products. (2016). Boreal Forest Facts. Retrieved from http://borealforestfacts.com

Revesencio, J. (2015). *Philippines: A Digital Lifestyle Capital in the Making?* Retrieved from http://www.huffingtonpost.com/jonha-revesencio/philippines-a-digital-lif_1_b_7199924.html

Rheingold, H. (2002). *Smart Mobs: The Next Social Revolution*. Cambridge: Perseus.

Rios, J., Rios Insua, D., Fernandez, D., & Rivero, J. A. (2005, March 2-4). Participatory Budget Formation through the Web. In M. Bohlen, Gamper, J., Polasek, W., & Wimmer, M. A. (Ed.), *E-Government: Towards Electronic Democracy: Proceedings of theInternational Conference, TCGOV 2005*, Bolzano, Italy (pp. 268-276). Zurich: Springer.

Rivera-Batiz, F. L. (2002). Democracy, governance, and economic growth: Theory and evidence. *Review ofDevelopment Economics*, *6*(2), 225–247. doi:10.1111/1467-9361.00151

Robinson, M. (2006). *Budget Analysis and Policy Advocacy: The Role of Nongovernmental Public Action* (Working Paper No. IDS Working Paper 279). Brighton: Institute of Development Studies

Rogers, S. (2011). WikiLeaks data journalism. *The Guardian.* Retrieved from http://www.theguardian.com/news/datablog/2011/jan/31/wikileaks-data-journalism

Rogstad, I. (2016). Is Twitter just rehashing? Intermedia agenda setting between Twitter and mainstream media. *Journal of Information Technology & Politics*, *13*(2), 142–158. doi:10.1080/19331681.2016.1160263

Römmele, A. (2003). *Political Parties, Party Communication and New Information and Communication Technologies. Party Politics*, *9*(1), 7–20.

Roodjuin, M. (2014). The Mesmerising Message: The Diffusion of Populism in Public Debates in Western European Media. *Political Studies*, *62*(4), 726–744. doi:10.1111/1467-9248.12074

Rose-Ackerman, S. (1978). *Corruption: a study in political economy.* New York: Academic Press.

Rose-Ackerman, S. (1999). *Corruption and government: causes, consequences, and reform*. New York: Cambridge Press. doi:10.1017/CBO9781139175098

Rose-Ackerman, S. (2008). Corruption and government. *International Peacekeeping*, *15*(3), 328–343. doi:10.1080/13533310802058802

Rothstein, B. (2011). *The quality of government: Corruption, social trust, and inequality in international perspective*. Chicago: University Of Chicago Press. doi:10.7208/chicago/9780226729589.001.0001

Roy, A. (2015, April 24). *Coal Mining in India's Mahan Forest: Campaigners Claim Victory*. Retrieved from www.climatechangenews.com/coal-mining-banned-in-indias-mahan-forest/

Roy, A. (2015, April 4). *Coal Mining Banned in India's Mahan Forest*. Retrieved from www.countercurrents.org/aroy050415.htm

Sabah.com. (2011a, October, 13). About the additional tax hikes. [Dört Üründe ÖTV Arttı]. Retrieved from http://www.sabah.com.tr/Ekonomi/2011/10/13/otv-artti#

Sabah.com. (2011b, November, 30). About Paid Military Service Act. Retrieved from http://www.sabah.com.tr/gundem/2011/11/30/bedelli-askerlik-tasarisi-yasalasti

Saeed, S., Reichling, T., & Wulf, V. (2008a, April). Applying Knowledge Management to Support Networking among NGOs and Donors. Proceedings of the IADIS international conference on E-Society (pp. 626-628).

Saeed, S., Rohde, M., & Wulf, V. (2008b). A framework towards IT appropriation in voluntary organisations. *International Journal of Knowledge and Learning*, *4*(5), 438–451. doi:10.1504/IJKL.2008.022062

Saeed, S., Rohde, M., & Wulf, V. (2009, June). Technologies within transnational social activist communities: an ethnographic study of the European social forum. *Proceedings of the fourth international conference on Communities and technologies* (pp. 85-94). ACM. doi:10.1145/1556460.1556474

Sakki, I., & Pettersson, K. (2015). Discursive Construction of Otherness in Populist Radical Right Political Blogs. *European Journal of Social Psychology*, *46*(2), 156–170. doi:10.1002/ejsp.2142

Salbu, S. R. (2001). Information Technology in the War against International Bribery and Corruption: The Next Frontier of Institutional Reform. *Harvard Journal on Legislation*, *38*(1), 67–102.

Saleh, I. (2013). WikiLeaks and the Arab Spring: The Twists and Turns of Media, Culture, and Power. In B. Brevini, A. Hintz, & P. McCurdy (Eds.), *Beyond WikiLeaks: Implications for the Future of Communications, Journalism and Society* (pp. 166–177). UK: Palgrave Macmillan. doi:10.1057/9781137275745_15

Sam, O. K. (2015). *Abducted Nigerian girls still missing, a distracted world must remember*. Retrieved from http://www.latimes.com/opinion/op-ed/la-oe-sam-bring-back-our-girls-20150108-story.html

Sanford, C., & Rose, J. (2007). Characterizing eParticipation. *International Journal of Information Management*, *27*(6), 406–421. doi:10.1016/j.ijinfomgt.2007.08.002

Santiso, C. (2001). World Bank and good governance: good governance and aid effectiveness: the World Bank and conditionality. *Geo. Public Pol'y Rev.*, *7*, 1-137.

Şaylan, G. (2008). Unavoidable Crisis of Representative Democracy. In *Turkish: Temsili Demokrasinin Önlenemez Krizi*. Ankara: İmge Kitabevi.

Scheufele, D. A., & Nisbet, M. C. (2002). Being a citizen online: New opportunities and dead ends. *The Harvard International Journal of Press/Politics*, *7*(3), 55–75. doi:10.1177/1081180X0200700304

Sedghi, A. (2014). Facebook: 10 years of social networking, in numbers. *The Guardian*. Retrieved from https://www.theguardian.com/news/datablog/2014/feb/04/facebook-in-numbers-statistics

Sen, K. (2014). Governance and Development Outcomes in Asia. *Asian Development Bank Economics Working Paper Series*

Seo, H. (2014). Visual Propaganda in the Age of Social Media: An Empirical Analysis of Twitter Images during the 2012 Israeli–Hamas Conflict. *Visual Communication Quarterly*, *21*(3), 150–161. doi:10.1080/15551393.2014.955501

Shailendra, C., Palvia, J., & Sharma, S. S. (2007). E-Government and E-Governance: Definitions/Domain Framework and Status around the World Retrieved from http://www.iceg.net/2007/books/1/1_369.pdf

Shearlaw, M. (2016). Egypt five years on: was it ever a 'social media revolution'? *The Guardian*. Retrieved from https://www.theguardian.com/world/2016/jan/25/egypt-5-years-on-was-it-ever-a-social-media-revolution

Sheridan, W., & Riley, T. B. (2006). Comparing e-government vs. e-governance. Commonwealth Center for e-Governance. *Commonwealth Center for e-Governance*. Retrieved from http://www.egovmonitor.com/node/655

Shim, D. C., & Eom, T. H. (2008). E-government and anti-corruption: Empirical analysis of International data. *International Journal of Public Administration*, *31*(3), 298–316. doi:10.1080/01900690701590553

Shim, D. C., & Eom, T. H. (2009). Anticorruption effects of information communication and technology (ICT) and social capital. *International Review of Administrative Sciences*, *75*(1), 99–116. doi:10.1177/0020852308099508

Shirk, S. (2011). Changing Media, Changing China. In S. Shirk (Ed.), Changing Media, Changing China, 1–37. New York: Oxford University Press.

Shirky, C. (2011). The Political Power of Social Media: Technology, the Public Sphere, and Political Change. In *Foreign Affairs* (pp. 28–41).

Siapera, E., Hunt, G., & Lynn, T. (2015). #GazaUnderAttack: Twitter, Palestine and Diffused War. *Information Communication and Society*, *18*(11), 1297–1319. doi:10.1080/1369118X.2015.1070188

Small, T. A. (2011). What the Hashtag. *Information Communication and Society*, *14*(6), 872–895. doi:10.1080/1369118X.2011.554572

Small, T.A. (2012). What the Hashtag? A Content Analysis of Canadian Politics on Twitter. In B. D. Loader & D. Mercea (Eds.), *Social Media and Democracy* (pp. 109–128). New York: Routledge.

SMaPP. (2013). SMaPP Data Reports, A Breakout Role for Twitter? The Role of Social Media in the Turkish Protests. Retrieved from https://wp.nyu.edu/smapp/papers-and-publications/smapp-data-reports/

Social Bakers. (2016). Facebook Statistics. Retrieved from http://www.socialbakers.com/facebook-statistics/

Socialbakers (2012). Turkey Facebook Statistics. Retrieved from http://www.socialbakers.com/Facebook-statistics/turkey

Socialbakers, (2016). Turkey Facebook Statistics. Retrieved from https://www.socialbakers.com/statistics/facebook/

Soper, D. S. (2007). ICT Investment Impacts on Future Levels of Democracy, Corruption, and E-Government Acceptance in Emerging Countries. *Paper presented at theAmericas Conference on Information Systems*, Keystone Colorado.

Spotnitz, H. (1952). Group Therapy as a Specialized Psychotherapeutic Technique. In G. Bychovsky, & Despart. J.L. (Ed.), Specialized Techniques in Psychotherapy. New York: Basic Books.

Srivastava, S. C., Teo, T. S. H., & Devaraj, S. (2016). You can't bribe a computer: Dealing with the societal challenge of corruption through ICT. *Management Information Systems Quarterly*, *40*(2), 511–526.

Stache, L. C. (2015). Advocacy and Political Potential at the Convergence of Hashtag Activism and Commerce. *Feminist Media Studies, 15*(1), 162–164. doi:10.1080/14680777.2015.987429

Stake, R. (1995). *The art of case study research.* Thousand Oaks, New Jersey: Sage Publications.

Statista (2016). Number of worldwide social network users. Retrieved from https://www.statista.com/statistics/278414/number-of-worldwide-social-network-users/

Stein, K. (2014, December 16). *7 Tips to Improve Your Social Media Posts.* Retrieved from http://www.socialmediaexaminer.com/improve-your-social-media-posts/

Stewart, J., Mazzoleni, G., & Horsfield, B. (2003). Conclusion: Power to the Media Managers. In G. Mazzoleni, J. Stewart, & B. Horsfield (Eds.), *The Media and Neo-Populism: A Contemporary Comparative Analysis* (pp. 217–236). Westport: Praeger.

Stockmann, D. (2013). *Media commercialization and authoritarian rule in China.* New York: Cambridge University Press.

Strandberg, K. (2008). Public Deliberation Goes On-line? An Analysis of Citizens' Political Discussions on the Internet Prior to the Finnish Parliamentary Elections in 2007. *Javnost – The Public, 15*(1), 71-90.

Sunstein, C. (2008). Democracy and the Internet. In J. van den Hoven & J. Weckert (Eds.), *Information Technology and Moral Philosophy* (pp. 93–110). Cambridge, UK: Cambridge University Press.

Sunstein, C. R. (2009). *Republic.com 2.0.* Princeton University Press.

Sustainability (n. d.). Retrieved from http://www.essar.com/section_level1.aspx?cont_id=cBd pT8Ha/0=

Sustainablebrands.com. (2014, November 27). *New Greenpeace Report Calls Out Best Buy for Destroying Ancient Forest.* Retrieved from sustainablebrands.com

Svensson, J. (2005). Eight Questions about Corruption. *The Journal of Economic Perspectives, 19*(3), 19–42. doi:10.1257/089533005774357860

Taggart, P. (2000). *Populism.* Buckingham: Open University Press.

Tanzi, V. (1998). Corruption Around the World: Causes, Consequences, Scope, and Cures. *IMF Staff Papers, 45*(4), 559–594. doi:10.2307/3867585

Tapnio, E., & Rood, S. (2011, October). Social Media in the Philippines is Widespread, but what is its Impact? *Asia Foundation*. Retrieved from http://asiafoundation.org/2011/10/12/social-media-in-the-philippines-is-widespread-but-what-is-its-impact/

Tepper, M. (2003). The Rise of Social Software. *netWorker*, *7*(3), 18–23. doi:10.1145/940830.940831

The White House, Office of the Press Secretary. (2014). *Weekly Address: The First Lady Marks Mother's Day and Speaks Out on the Tragic Kidnapping in Nigeria* [Press Release]. Retrieved from https://www.whitehouse.gov/the-press-office/2014/05/10/weekly-address-first-lady-marks-mother-s-day-and-speaks-out-tragic-kidnap

Thehindu.com. (2011, November 24). Republic is imaginary, social cause is real. Retrieved from thehindu.com

Thompson, J. B. (2000). *Political Scandal Power and Visibility in the Media Age*. UK: Polity Press.

Thompson, J. B. (2000). *Political Scandal. Power and Visibility in the Media Age*. Cambridge: Polity Press.

Thompson, J. B. (2000). *Political Scandal: Power and Visibility in the Media Age*. Cambridge: Polity Press.

Thorsen, E., Sreedharan, C., & Allan, S. (2013). WikiLeaks and Whistle-blowing: The Framing of Bradley Manning. In B. Brevini, A. Hintz, & P. McCurdy (Eds.), *Beyond WikiLeaks: Implications for the Future of Communications, Journalism and Society* (pp. 101–122). UK: Palgrave Macmillan. doi:10.1057/9781137275745_7

Time (2011). The Top 10 Everything of 2011. Retrieved from http://content.time.com/time/specials/packages/article/0,28804,2101344_2101368_2101650,00.html

Tolbert, C. J., & Mossberger, K. (2006). The effects of e-government on trust and confidence in government. *Public Administration Review*, *66*(3), 354–369. doi:10.1111/j.1540-6210.2006.00594.x

Trac.Fm. (2014). What is Trac FM? Retrieved from http://www.tracfm.org

Transparency.org. (2016). The Corruption Perception Index. Retrieved from http://www.transparency.org/research/cpi/overview

Treisman, D. (2000). The Causes of Corruption: A Cross-National Study. *Journal of Public Economics*, *76*(3), 399–457. doi:10.1016/S0047-2727(99)00092-4

Tsagarousianou, R. (1999). Electronic Democracy: Rhetoric and Reality. *Communications*, *24*(2), 189–208. doi:10.1515/comm.1999.24.2.189

Tufekci, Z. (2008). Grooming, Gossip, Facebook and Myspace. *Information Communication and Society*, *11*(4), 544–564. doi:10.1080/13691180801999050

Tumber, H., & Waisbord, S. R. (2004a). Political Scandals and Media across Democracies (Vol. I). *The American Behavioral Scientist*, *47*(8), 1031–1039. doi:10.1177/0002764203262275

Tumber, H., & Waisbord, S. R. (2004b). Political Scandals and Media across Democracies (Vol. II). *The American Behavioral Scientist*, *47*(9), 1143–1152. doi:10.1177/0002764203262340

Turk, C. N. N. (2011, April, 2). About the Code Scandal [YGS'de şifre iddiasına açıklama]. Retrieved from http://www.cnnturk.com/2011/turkiye/04/02/ygsde.sifre.iddiasina.aciklama-/611932.0/index.html

Turk, C. N. N. (2012, February, 24). About the "Law draft on prevent to the violence against woman" [Kadına karşı şiddet tasarısı Meclis'te]. Retrieved from http://www.cnnturk.com/2012/turkiye/02/24/kadina.karsi.siddet.tasarisi.mecliste/650604.0/index.html

TUSEV. (2011). The Report for Civil Society in Turkey [Türkiye'de Sivil Toplum: Bir Dönüm Noktası CIVICUS Uluslararası Sivil Toplum Endeksi Projesi (STEP) Türkiye Ülke Raporu II. TÜSEV Yayınları].

United Nations Development Programme (UNDP). (2002). *Human Development Report 2002: Deepening Democracy in a Fragmented World.*

United Nations. (2008). *United Nations e-Government Survey 2008.* New York: United Nations.

United Nations. (2010). *United Nations E-Government Survey 2010.* New York: United Nations.

United Nations. (2014). Information and Communications Technologies for Inclusive Social and Economic Development. Geneva: UN.

Ureport. (2014). Uganda Voice Matters. Retrieved from http://ureport.ug/

Uslaner, E. M. (2005). Trust and Corruption. In J. G. Lambsdorff, M. Taube & M. Schramm (Eds.) The New Institutional Economics of Corruption (pp. 76-92). USA: Routledge.

Vaccari, C. (2011). The News Media as Networked Political Actors. *Information Communication and Society*, *14*(7), 981–997. doi:10.1080/1369118X.2011.572984

Vainikka, E., & Huhtamäki, J. (2015). Tviittien politiikkaa – poliittisen viestinnän sisäpiirit Twitterissä. *Media & viestintä, 38*(3), 165-183.

Valkernburg, P. M., Peter, J., & Schouten, A. P. (2006). Friend networking sites and their relationship to adolescent wellbeing. *International Journal of Cultural Policy*, *16*(2), 200–214.

Vallor, S. (2010). Social networking technology and the virtues. *Ethics and Information Technology*, *12*(2), 157–170. doi:10.1007/s10676-009-9202-1

Vallor, S. (2012). Flourishing on Facebook: Virtue Friendship and New Social Media. *Ethics and Information Technology*, *14*(3), 185–199. doi:10.1007/s10676-010-9262-2

van Dijk, J. (2006). *The Network Society: Social Aspects of New Media*. London: Sage.

Vandijk, J. (2012). The Networked Society (3rded.). London: Sage.

Vargas, J.A. (2012). Spring Awakening: How an Egyptian revolution began on Facebook. The New York Times. Retrieved from http://www.nytimes.com/2012/02/19/books/review/how-an-egyptian-revolution-began-on-facebook.html

Varnali, K., & Gorgulu, V. (2015). A social influence perspective on expressive political participation in Twitter: The case of #OccupyGezi. *Information Communication and Society*, *18*(1), 1–16. doi:10.1080/1369118X.2014.923480

Vats, A. (2015). Cooking Up Hashtag Activism: #PaulasBestDishes and Counter narratives of Southern Food. *Communication and Critical. Cultural Studies*, *12*(2), 209–213. doi:10.1080/14791420.2015.1014184

Verba, S., Schlozman, K. L., & Brady, H. E. (1995). *Voice and Equality: Civic Voluntarism in American Politics*. Cambridge: Harvard University Press.

Verweij, P. (2012). Twitter links between politicians and journalists. *Journalism Practice*, *6*(5-6), 680–691. doi:10.1080/17512786.2012.667272

Villi, M., & Matikainen, J. (2015). Mobile UDC: Online media content distribution among Finnish mobile Internet users. *Mobile Media & Communication*, *3*(2), 214–229. doi:10.1177/2050157914552156

Villoria, M., Van Ryzin, G. G., & Lavena, C. F. (2013). Social and political consequences of administrative corruption: A study of public perceptions in Spain. *Public Administration Review*, *73*(1), 85–94. doi:10.1111/j.1540-6210.2012.02613.x

Vinod, H. D. (1999). Statistical analysis of corruption data and using the Internet to reduce corruption. *Journal of Asian Economics*, *10*(4), 591–603. doi:10.1016/S1049-0078(00)00034-8

Waisboard, S. R. (2004). Scandals, Media, and Citizenship in Contemporary Argentina. *The American Behavioral Scientist*, *47*(8), 1072–1098. doi:10.1177/0002764203262278

Wallace, K. (2014). *Teen like and FOMO Anxiety.* Digital Life. Retrieved from http://www.cnn.com/2014/10/16/living/teens-on-social-media-like-and-fomo-anxiety-digital-life/index.html

Waller, L., & Taylor, C. A. (2013). A Case Study of Citizen—to—Government Mobile. In Z. Mahmood (Ed.), *E-Government Implementation and Practice in Developing Countries*. Hershey: IGI Global. doi:10.4018/978-1-4666-4090-0.ch008

Wapner, P. (2004). Greenpeace and Political Globalism. In F. J. Lechner & J. Boli (Eds.), *The Globalization Reader* (pp. 377–383). USA: Blackwell.

Watson, E. [EmmaWatson]. (2014, October 8). Between 20th Sep & 2nd Oct there were 1.1 million #HeForShe tweets from 750K different users, reaching 1.2 BILLION unique Twitter users [Tweet]. Retrieved from https://twitter.com/EmWatson/status/519844138716762113

Weber, L., Loumake, A., & Bergman, J. (2003). Who Participates and Why? An Analysis of Citizens on the Internet and the Mass Public. *Social Science Computer Review*, *21*(1), 26–42. doi:10.1177/0894439302238969

Wedeman, A. (2012). *Double paradox: Rapid growth and rising corruption in China.* Ithaca: Cornell University Press. doi:10.7591/cornell/9780801450464.001.0001

Wei, S. (2000). How Taxing is Corruption on International Investors. *The Review of Economics and Statistics*, *82*(1), 1–11. doi:10.1162/003465300558533

Welch, E. W., Hinnant, C. C., & Moon, M. J. (2005). Linking citizen satisfaction with e-government and trust in government. *Journal of Public Administration: Research and Theory*, *15*(3), 371–391. doi:10.1093/jopart/mui021

West, D. M. (2005). *Digital government: Technology and public sector performance*. Princeton, NJ: Princeton University Press.

WhatsApp. (2016). End-to-end Encryption. Retrieved from: https://www.whatsapp.com/faq/en/general/28030015

Widfeldt, A. (2010). Högerpopulismen: ett växande politiskt fenomen. In J. Ekman & J. Linde (Eds.), *Politik, protest, populism – deltagande på nya villkor* (pp. 158–181). Malmö: Liber.

Wijkman, A. (1998). Does Sustainable Development Require Good Governance? *UN Chronicles, 35*(3).

WikiLeaks. (2016). What is WikiLeaks? Retrieved from https://wikileaks.org/What-is-Wikileaks.html

Wikipedia. (2016). List of Political Scandals in the Philippines Retrieved from https://en.wikipedia.org/wiki/List_of_political_scandals_in_the_Philippines

Williams, B. A., & Delli-Carpini, M. X. (2004). Monica and Bill All the Time and Everywhere: The Collapse of Gatekeeping and Agenda Setting in the New Media Environment. *The American Behavioral Scientist, 47*(9), 1208–1230. doi:10.1177/0002764203262344

Williamson, O. (1975). *Markets and Hierarchies: Analysis and Antitrust Implications*. New York: Free Press.

Williamson, O. (1985). *The Economic Institution of Capitalism: Firms, Markets, Relational Contracting*. London: Collier Macmillan.

Wilson, C. (2014, March). The Selfiest Cities in the World: TIME's Definitive Ranking. *Time*. Retrieved from http://time.com/selfies-cities-world-rankings/

Winseck, D. (2013). Weak Links and WikiLeaks: How Control of Critical Internet Resources and Social Media Companies' Business Models Undermine the Networked free Press. In B. Brevini, A. Hintz, & P. McCurdy (Eds.), *Beyond WikiLeaks: Implications for the Future of Communications, Journalism and Society* (pp. 166–177). UK: Palgrave Macmillan. doi:10.1057/9781137275745_10

Wodak, R. (2015). *The Politics of Fear. What Right-Wing Populist Discourses Mean*. London: Sage. doi:10.4135/9781446270073

Woessner, M. C. (2005). Scandal, Elites, and Presidential Popularity: Considering the Importance of Cues in Public Support of the President. *Presidential Studies Quarterly, 35*(1), 94–115. doi:10.1111/j.1741-5705.2004.00237.x

Woods, N. (2000). The challenge of good governance for the IMF and the World Bank Themselves. *World Development, 28*(5), 823–841. doi:10.1016/S0305-750X(99)00156-4

Woolcook, M., & Deepa, N. (2000). Social Capital: Implications for development theory, research, and policy. *The World Bank Research Observer*, *15*(2), 225–249. doi:10.1093/wbro/15.2.225

World Bank. (1992). *Governance and Development.*

World Development Report: Making Services Work for Poor People. (2004). Washington, DC: The World Bank and Oxford University Press.

Wu, Y. (2014). The impact of media on public trust in legal authorities in China and Taiwan. *Asian Journal of Criminology*, *9*(2), 85–101. doi:10.1007/s11417-013-9177-z

Yang, G. (2009). *The power of the internet in China: Citizen activism online*. New York, NY: Columbia University Press.

Yıldız, M., & Demirhan, K. (2016). Analysis and Comparison of the Role of Local Governments with Other Policy Actors in Disaster Relief via Social Media: The Case of Turkey. In U. Sadioğlu & K. Dede (Eds.) Theoretical Foundations and Discussions on the Reformation Process in Local Governments (pp. 463-484). Hershey, PA, USA: IGI Global.

Yin, Y. (2013). *Case Study Research: Design and Methods*. Thousand Oaks, New Jersey: Sage Publications.

York, J. C. (2013). The Internet and Transparency beyond WikiLeaks. In B. Brevini, A. Hintz, & P. McCurdy (Eds.), *Beyond WikiLeaks: Implications for the Future of Communications, Journalism and Society* (pp. 229–235). UK: Palgrave Macmillan. doi:10.1057/9781137275745_14

YSK. (2011). Yüksek Seçim Kurulu. Information about General Election in 2011 [12 Haziran 2011 XXIV. Dönem Milletvekili Genel Seçimi]. Retrieved from http://www.ysk.gov.tr/ysk/GenelSecimler.html

Zhu, J., Lu, J., & Shi, T. (2013). When grapevine news meets mass media: Different information sources and popular perceptions of government corruption in mainland China. *Comparative Political Studies*, *46*(8), 920–946. doi:10.1177/0010414012463886

Zurcher, A. (2016). US election: Why is Clinton's foundation so controversial? *BBC*. Retrieved from http://www.bbc.com/news/election-us-2016-37168505

About the Contributors

Kamil Demirhan has been working as an Assistant Professor at the Department of Political Science and Public Administration, in Bülent Ecevit University, Zonguldak, Turkey since 2016. He received his PhD in Political Science and Public Administration from Hacettepe University in 2015. His research interests include political theory, social media and politics, and e-government. He has publications on social media and politics, ICTs and political participation, and contemporary political issues. He worked as a visiting scholar at Aarhus University. He took part in several projects on social media and politics, Internet and democracy.

Derya Çakır-Demirhan has been working as a Lecturer at the School of Foreign Languages, Bülent Ecevit University, Turkey. She is a PhD candidate in political science, at Hacettepe University. She received her B.A in American Culture and Literature from Hacettepe University. She received her minor degree and M.A in political science from Hacettepe University. Her research interests are citizenship studies, multiculturalism, immigration, women studies, Turkish politics and American politics.

***

Essien D. Essien received his Ph.D. in Social and Religious Ethics from University of Ibadan, Ibadan, Nigeria in 2010. He is a lecturer and a researcher in the University of Uyo, Uyo, Nigeria, where he currently teaches Social Ethics, Comparative Religious and Christian Ethics in the Department of Religious and Cultural Studies of the University. He writes and presents papers widely on issues of Governance and Ethics, Ethics of Political System, Environmental Ethics, Peace Ethics, Comparative Religious Ethics and Development Studies. He has authored two books, six book chapters, and many journal articles in peer reviewed scholarly journals.

Juha Herkman (PhD) is an Academy Research Fellow in the Department of Social Research at the University of Helsinki, Finland. His current research project explores the relationship between populism and the media in the Nordic countries. Formerly Herkman has worked as a full time lecturer of media studies at the University of Tampere, Finland. His research interests have focused on popular culture, political economy of the media and political communication. Herkman has published several academic textbooks in Finnish, and articles in such journals as *Media, Culture & Society*, *Javnost – the Public*, *Nordicom Review*, *Journalism Studies* and *Convergence: The International Journal of Research into New Media Technologies*.

Chandan Jha is an Assistant Professor of Finance in the Madden School of Business at Le Moyne College. He has received a B.A. in Economics from Magadh University, M.A. in Economics from Gokhale Institute of Politics and Economics, and Ph.D. in Economics from Louisiana State University. His research interests include development economics, finance and development, and political economy, with an emphasis on gender issues and corruption. His articles on gender issues and corruption have appeared in popular press such as the Hindu Business Line, a leading Indian business daily, and Ideas for India, an economics and policy portal.

Liang Ma received his BA, MS, and PhD degrees in Public Administration from Xi'an Jiaotong University. He is an Associate Professor at the School of Public Administration and Policy and a Research Fellow at the National Academy for Development and Strategy, Renmin University of China (RUC). Before joining RUC, he was a Research Fellow (2012-2015) and then a Senior Research Fellow (2015-2016) at the Nanyang Centre for Public Administration, Nanyang Technological University, Singapore. His research interests include public organizational innovation, government performance measurement and management, and digital government. His is the author of Public Service Performance and Political Elite Career Advancement: Evidence from China (LAP, 2012) and many journal articles.

Cecilia G. Manrique is a professor and the former chair of the Political Science/Public Administration Department at the University of Wisconsin-La Crosse. She received her doctorate in Political Science from the University of Notre Dame and has published in the fields of immigration and incorporating technology in the Political Science classroom.

Gabriel Manrique is a professor and chairman of the Department of Economics at Winona State University who has also served as Dean of the College of Business and Director of Outreach and Continuing Education. He received a Ph.D. in Economics from the University of Notre Dame. He has published in the areas of international trade, immigration, and economic development.

Janne Matikainen (PhD) is a Senior Researcher in the Department of Social Research at the University of Helsinki, Finland. His expertise is concentrated on the social aspects of the Internet. His research focuses on interaction in online communication, online participation and content-generation motives in social media. In recent years, he has studied the relationship between traditional and social media, especially from the audience's perspective. Matikainen has published several academic textbooks in Finnish, and articles in such journals as *Media & Communication, Mobile Media & Communication, Participations: Journal of Audience & Reception Studies.*

Gayle Pohl is an Associate Professor at the University of Northern Iowa, teaching public relations on the graduate and undergraduate level. She is an accredited public relations practitioner, specializing in nonprofit, special events, healthcare and entertainment, sports and educational public relations. Her research focuses on social media, autoethnographic study on healthcare and relationship management theory, healthcare and corporate social responsibility, and the use of the persuasive strategies used in broadcast mediums.

Smarak Samarjeet holds an MBA in Marketing and HR from Utkal University, Odisha, India. He also has a Master of Arts degree in Mass Communication. He has a Ph.D. in Mass Communication from Pondicherry University, India. He has taught courses such as Communication Theory, Online Journalism, Principles in Journalism, Advertising, Public Relations, and Development Communications at the Postgraduate level. He specializes in Digital Marketing, Social Media Marketing, Public Relations for Digital Media, Content Writing, Technical Writing, and Public Service Advertising (PSA). His research interests include Political Economy of Media, Rhetoric Studies, Semiotics Studies, Film Studies, Advertising, Feminist Media Studies, Ideological Analysis, Sentiment Analysis etc.

Lloyd Waller is the Head/Chair of the Department of Government at the University of the West Indies (Mona Campus) and a Senior Lecturer in Human, Social, and Political Behaviour. His primary areas of research and expertise are: (1) advanced research methodologies (specializing in quantitative, qualitative, and mixed-methods research); and (2) democratic governance (specializing in youth in governance and development, as well as electronic governance). In the last 10 years, Dr. Waller has worked on several e-government and e-governance related projects. He is also the Chairman of the Board for eGov Jamaica Ltd. an agency of the Government of Jamaica which manages the governments ICT infrastructure.

Index

H

I

K

M

N

P

S

T

W

Y

www.ingramcontent.com/pod-product-compliance
Lightning Source LLC
LaVergne TN
LVHW061541290926
849162LV00004B/866